OT 2:
Operator Theory: Advances and Applications
Vol. 2

Edited by

I. Gohberg

Editorial Office

Department of Mathematics
Tel-Aviv University
Ramat-Aviv (Israel)

Birkhäuser Verlag
Basel · Boston · Stuttgart

Topics in Modern Operator Theory

5th International Conference on Operator Theory, Timişoara and Herculane (Romania), June 2–12, 1980

Volume Editors

C. Apostol
R. G. Douglas
B. Sz.-Nagy
D. Voiculescu

Managing Editor

Gr. Arsene

1981

Birkhäuser Verlag
Basel · Boston · Stuttgart

Volume Editorial Office

Department of Mathematics
INCREST
Bd. Pacii 220
79622 Bucharest (Romania)

CIP-Kurztitelaufnahme der Deutschen Bibliothek

Topics in modern operator theory / 5th Internat. Conference on Operator Theory, Timişoara and Herculane (Romania), June 2–12, 1980. Vol. ed. C. Apostol . . . Co-ed. Gr. Arsene. – Basel ; Boston ; Stuttgart : Birkhäuser, 1981.
(Operator theory ; Vol. 2)
ISBN 3–7643–1244–0
NE: Apostol, Constantin [Hrsg.]; International Conference on Operator Theory ⟨05, 1980, Timişoara; Herculane⟩ ; GT

Printed in Germany
ISBN 3–7643–1244–0

CONTENTS

PREFACE

The first of the annual Operator Theory conferences in Timişoara held four years ago was a meeting of operator theory specialists from the National Institute for Scientific and Technical Creation in Bucharest and from the University of Timişoara. Since then, the participation to these conferences has greatly increased, by being attended first by operator theorists from all over the country and (since 1978) by an increasing number of foreign mathematicians. Thus the 1980 Conference can be regarded as a truly international Operator Theory meeting, fifteen countries being represented at it.

These conferences are conceived as a means to promote the cooperation between specialists in all areas of Operator Theory. Among the main topics in 1980 were: dilation theory, invariant subspaces, connections with the theory of C^*-algebras, subnormal operators, multidimensional functional calculus etc. Though not included in this volume, we would like to mention that in 1980 some special sessions concerning other fields of Functional Analysis were organized at the Operator Theory conference.

The research contracts of the Department of Mathematics of INCREST with the National Council for Sciences and Technology of Romania provided the means for developping the research activity in Functional Analysis; these contracts constitute the generous framework for these meetings.

We want also to acknowledge the support of INCREST and the excelent organizing job done by our host - University of Timişoara -. Professor Dumitru Gaşpar and Professor Mircea Reghiş are among those people in Timişoara who contributed in an essential way to the success of the meeting.

We are indebted to Professor Israel Gohberg for including these Proceedings in the OT Series and for valuable help in the editing process. Birkhäuser Verlag was very cooperative in publishing this volume.

Rodica Gervescu and Camelia Minculescu dealt with the difficult task of typing the whole manuscript; they did an excelent job in a very short time.

Organizing Committee

Head of Math.Department of INCREST,	Organizers,
Zoia Ceauşescu	Constantin Apostol
	Dan Voiculescu

September 1980

LIST OF PARTICIPANTS*)

ALBRECHT, Ernst	University of Saarlandes, West Germany
ALBU, Adrian	University of Timişoara
ANDERSON, Joel	Pennsylvania State University, USA
ANDO, Tsuyoshi	Hokkaido University, Japan
APOSTOL, Constantin	INCREST, Bucharest
ARSENE, Grigore	INCREST, Bucharest
BĂBESCU, Gheorghe	Politechnical Institute, Timişoara
BACALU, Ioan	Politechnical Institute, Bucharest
BALINT, Ştefan	University of Timişoara
BĂNULESCU, Martha	University of Bucharest
BÂNZARU, Titus	Politechnical Institute, Timişoara
BARTLE, Robert	University of Illinois, USA
BERECHET, Oprea	INCREST, Bucharest
BOBOC, Nicu	University of Bucharest
BOCŞA, Minerva	University of Timişoara
BIRĂUŞ, Silviu	University of Timişoara
BOROŞ, Emil	University of Timişoara
BUCUR, Gheorghe	INCREST, Bucharest
BURLACU, Eugen	Politechnical Institute, Timişoara
CALIANU, Rodica	Politechnical Institute, Bucharest
CÂMPU, Eugen	University of Bucharest
CEAUŞESCU, Zoia	INCREST, Bucharest
CEAUŞU, Traian	Politechnical Institute, Timişoara
CHARLES, Bernard	University of Montpellier, France
CHARLES, Josette	University of Montpellier, France
CHEVREAU, Bernard	INCREST, Bucharest
CIORĂNESCU, Ioana	INCREST, Bucharest
COFAN, Nicolae	Politechnical Institute, Timişoara
CONSTANTIN, Gheorghe	University of Timişoara
CONSTANTINESCU, Tiberiu	INCREST, Bucharest
COSTINESCU, Roxana	University of Bucharest
CRAIOVEANU, Mircea	University of Timişoara
CRSTICI, Boris	Politechnical Institute, Timişoara
DĂNEŢ, Nicoale	Politechnical Institute, Bucharest
DELCZEG, Adriana	University of Timişoara
DEUTSCH, Emerich	Politechnical Institute of New York, USA
DINESCU, Gabriela	University of Bucharest
DIŢĂ, Petre	Central Institute of Physics, Bucharest
DOGARU, Octavian	University of Timişoara
DOUGLAS, Ronald G.	State University of New York, USA
DRAGOMIR, Achim	University of Timişoara
DRAGOMIR, Paraschiva	University of Timişoara

*) Romanian participants are listed only with the name of their institution.

DRECIN, Gheorghe	University of Timişoara
DURSZT, Endre	University of Szeged, Hungary
ECKSTEIN, Gheorghe	University of Timişoara
FIALKOW, Larry	Western Michigan University, USA
FILLMORE, Peter A.	Dalhousie University, Canada
FRUNZĂ, Ştefan	University of Iaşi
FUGLEDE, Bent	University of Copenhagen, Denmark
GALETAR, Elisabeta	University of Timişoara
GÂNDAC, Florea	Politechnical Institute, Bucharest
GAŞPAR, Dumitru	University of Timişoara
GĂVRUŢĂ, Paşc	Politechnical Institute, Timişoara
GEORGESCU, Horia	University of Bucharest
GEORGESCU, Vladimir	Central Institute of Physics, Bucharest
GILFEATHER, Frank L.	University of Nebraska, USA
GODINI, Gliceria	INCREST, Bucharest
GOLOGAN, Radu-Nicolae	INCREST, Bucharest
GROSU, Corina	CIMIC, Bucharest
GRZYBOWSKI, Henryk T.	University of Gliwice, Poland
GUSSI, Gheorghe	INCREST, Bucharest
HERRERO, Domingo A.	IVIC, Venezuela
HIRIŞ, Viorel	University of Timişoara
HO SI HAU	University of Hanoi, Vietnam
ISTRĂŢESCU, Ioana	Politechnical Institute, Timişoara
JONES, VAUGHAM R.F.	University of Geneva, Switzerland
KÉRCHY, László	University of Szeged, Hungary
LIPOVAN, Octavian	Politechnical Institute, Timişoara
LU, Shijie	University of Nankin, People's Republic of China
MARTIN, Mircea	INCREST, Bucharest
MĂRUŞTER , Ştefan	University of Timişoara
MEGAN, Mihail	University of Timişoara
MENNICKEN, Reinhard	Regensburg University, West Germany
MIEL, George	University of Nevada, USA
MIHALACHE, Georgeta	INCREST, Bucharest
MIHALACHE, Nicolae	INCREST, Bucharest
MINEA, Gheorghe	INCREST, Bucharest
MOLDOVEANU, Emil	TLHS, Bucharest
NAGY, Béla	Budapest Technological University, Hungary
NEAGU, Mihai	Politechnical Institute, Timişoara
NICULESCU, Constantin	University of Craiova
NIKOLSKII, Nikolai K.	Steklov Institute Leningrad, USSR
OBĂDEANU, Virgil	University of Timişoara
OCNEANU, Adrian	INCREST, Bucharest
OLIN, Robert F.	Virginia State University, USA
PAPUC, Dan	University of Timişoara
PASNICU, Cornel	INCREST, Bucharest
PĂUNESCU, Doru	University of Timişoara
PELIGRAD, Costel	INCREST, Bucharest
PELIGRAD, Magda	Center of Mathematical Statistics, Bucharest
PETZ, Denes	Mathematical Institut, Budapest, Hungary
PIMSNER, Mihai	INCREST, Bucharest
POPA, Constantin	University of Timişoara
POPA, Eugen	University of Iaşi
POPA, Nicolae	INCREST, Bucharest
POPA, Sorin	INCREST, Bucharest

POPESCU, Nicolae	University of Timişoara
POTRA, Florian A.	INCREST, Bucharest
PREDA, Petre	University of Timişoara
PUTINAR, Mihai	INCREST, Bucharest
RADU, Viorel	University of Timişoara
REGHIŞ, Mircea	University of Timişoara
REGHIŞ, Monica	University of Timişoara
ROŞU, Radu	University of Bucharest
ŞABAC, Mihai	University of Bucharest
SCHMÜDGEN, Konrad	Karl Marx University, GDR
SETELECAN, Alexandru	University of Bucharest
SINGER, Ivan	INCREST, Bucharest
STAN, Ilie	Politechnical Institute, Timişoara
STÂNĂŞILĂ, Octavian	Politechnical Institute, Bucharest
STANCU, Dimitrie D.	University of Cluj
STANCU, Felicia	University of Cluj
STEPAN, Aurel	University of Timişoara
STOICA, Lucreţiu	INCREST, Bucharest
STRĂTILĂ, Şerban	INCREST, Bucharest
SUCIU, Ioan	INCREST, Bucharest
SUCIU, Nicolae	University of Timişoara
SZÖKEFALVI-NAGY, Béla	University of Szeged, Hungary
TELEMAN, Silviu	INCREST, Bucharest
TEODORESCU, Radu	University of Braşov
TERESCENCO, Alexandru	Electrotimiş, Timişoara
TIMOTIN, Dan	INCREST, Bucharest
TOPUZU, Elena	Politechnical Institute, Timişoara
TOPUZU, Paul	University of Timişoara
TROIE, Valeriu	Politechnical Institute, Bucharest
TUDOR, Constantin	University of Bucharest
VALUŞESCU, Ilie	INCREST, Bucharest
VASILESCU, Florian H.	INCREST, Bucharest
VOICULESCU, Dan	INCREST, Bucharest
VUZA, Dan	INCREST, Bucharest
WILLIAMS, JAMES P.	University of Indiana, USA
ZOPOTA, Nicolae	Politechnical Institute, Timişoara

PROGRAM OF THE CONFERENCE

MONDAY, June 2

SECTION A

Chairman: S.Teleman

16:30 - 17:00 R.N.GOLOGAN: Akcoglu's ergodic theorem for some nonpositive L^2-contractions.
17:10 - 17:40 C.APOSTOL; M.MARTIN: A C*-algebra approach to a theorem of Cowen-Douglas.
17:50 - 18:20 R.MENNICKEN: Analytic perturbations of semi-Fredholm operators in locally convex spaces.
18:30 - 19:00 F.L.GILFEATHER: Nest subalgebras of von Neumann algebras.

SECTION B

Chairman: Gh. Bucur

16:30 - 17:00 M.PELIGRAD: A tightness criterion for a class of random elements of D[0,1].
17:10 - 17:40 C.TUDOR: Solutions of stochastic integral equations.

TUESDAY, June 3

JOINT SESSION

Chairman: D.Voiculescu

9:30 - 10:15 L.FIALKOW: Generalized derivations.
10:30 - 11:15 D.A.HERRERO: Quasidiagonality, similarity and approximation by nilpotent operators.
11:30 - 12:15 R.G.DOUGLAS: On the smoothness of elements of Ext.

SECTION A

Chairman: P.Fillmore

16:30 - 17:00 M.PIMSNER: Imbedding the irrational rotation C*-algebra into an AF-algebra.
17:10 - 17:40 D.VOICULESCU: Remarks on Hilbert-Schmidt perturbations of almost normal operators.
17:50 - 18:20 S.POPA: Remarks on the Calkin algebra for certain singular extensions.
18:30 - 19:00 D.PETZ: On some subsets of von Neumann algebras.

SECTION B

Chairman: I.Singer

16:30 - 17:00 Ş.BALINT; A.STEPAN: Sur un système d'equations diferentielles intervenant dans un processus de separation.
17:10 - 17:40 E.DEUTSCH: Nested bounds for the Perron root of a nonnegative irreducible matrix.
17:50 - 18:20 F.POTRA: Error analysis for a class of Newton-like methods.

WEDNESDAY, June 4

JOINT SESSION

Chairman: R.G.Douglas

9:30 - 10:15 I.SUCIU: Modelling by L^2-bounded analytic functions.
10:30 - 11:15 B.SZŐKEFALVI-NAGY: The functional model of a contraction and the space L^1.
11:30 - 12:15 N.K.NIKOLSKIĬ: Deux applications des opérateurs de Hankel.

SECTION A

Chairman: N.K.Nikolskii

16:30 - 17:00 B.NAGY: The spectral residuum of closed operators.
17:10 - 17:40 N.SUCIU; I.VALUŞESCU: The maximal function of doubly commuting contractions.
17:50 - 18:20 L.KÉRCHY: p-weak contractions.
18:30 - 19:00 E.DURSZT: Some connections between contractions and power-bounded operators.

SECTION B

Chairman: B.Fuglede

16:30 - 17:00 E.POPA: Morphisms of H-cones.
17:10 - 17:40 N.BOBOC; G.BUCUR: Strong Ray semigroups and standard H-cones.
17:50 - 18:20 L.STOICA: Feller resolvents.

THURSDAY, June 5

JOINT SESSION

Chairman: B.Szökefalvi-Nagy

9:30 - 10:15 V.GEORGESCU: Algebraic scattering theory.
10:30 - 11:15 B.CHEVREAU: On M-spectral sets and rattionally-invariant subspaces.
11:30 - 12:15 C.APOSTOL: The spectral flavour of Scott Brown's technique.

SECTION A

Chairman: D.A.Herrero

16:30 - 17:00 R.F.OLIN: Algebras of subnormal operators.
17:10 - 17:40 I.CIORĂNESCU: On distribution-semigroups of subnormal operators.
17:50 - 18:20 D.TIMOTIN: On Scott Brown's theorem.
18:30 - 19:00 N.PAVEL: Invariant subcones of a linear operator.

SECTION B

Chairman: M.Reghiş

16:30 - 17:00 T.GRZYBOWSKI: General procedure for distorted pattern reconstitution.
17:10 - 17:40 E.CÂMPU: Multi-application associées aux multiequations differentielles à retardement.
17:50 - 18:20 V.TROIE: Characteristic numbers for solutions of linear differential equations at a singular point.
18:30 - 19:00 G.MIEL: Analysis of equations with smooth coefficients.

SATURDAY, June 7

JOINT SESSION

Chairman: J.P.Williams

9:30 - 10:15 S.TELEMAN: Applications of Choquet theory to reduction theory.
10:30 - 11:15 J.ANDERSON: Irreducible representations of $B(H)$.
11:30 - 12:15 P.FILLMORE: Kasparov's stability theorem.

MONDAY, June 9

JOINT SESSION

Chairman: N.Boboc

9:30 - 10:15 V.JONES: Invariants for group actions on algebras.
10:30 - 11:15 A.OCNEANU: Actions of amenable groups on von Neumann algebras.
11:30 - 12:15 B.FUGLEDE: The fine topology in potential theory.

SECTION A

Chairman: D.Gaşpar

16:30 - 17:00 P.GĂVRUŢĂ: On the continuity of averaging type operators on some function spaces.
17:10 - 17:40 G.GODINI: On certain classes of normed vector spaces.
17:50 - 18:20 N.POPA: Complemented sublattices in Lorenz sequence spaces without local-convexity.
18:30 - 19:00 D.VUZA: A theorem of Hahn-Banach type for modules over ordered rings.

TUESDAY, June 10

JOINT SESSION

Chairman: C.Apostol

9:30 - 10:15 N.BOBOC; G.BUCUR: Potentials on standard H-cones.
10:30 - 11:15 T.ANDO: Generators of positivity preserving semigroups.
11:30 - 12:15 F.H.VASILESCU: Anticommuting selfadjoint operators.

SECTION A

Chairman: T.Ando

16:30 - 17:00 G.ECKSTEIN: Exact controllability and spectrum assignement.
17:10 - 17:40 GR.ARSENE; Z.CEAUŞESCU: A functional model for intertwining dilations.
17:50 - 18:20 C.PELIGRAD: Derivations of C*-crossed products.
18:30 - 19:00 N.K.NIKOLSIĬ: Les sous-espaces invariantes et une notion de capacité.

SECTION B

Chairman: D.D.Stancu

16:30 - 17:00 O.STĂNĂŞILĂ; D.STANOMIR: On certain non-linear systems.
17:10 - 17:40 G.MINEA: First integrals for the Euler equation of incompressible fluids.
17:50 - 18:20 O.BERECHET: Parabolic equations with unbounded coefficients.

WEDNESDAY, June 11

JOINT SESSION

Chairman: F.H.Vasilescu

9:30 - 10:15 K.SCHMÜDGEN: On perturbation of spectra of diagonal operators.
10:30 - 11:15 J.P.WILLIAMS: The range of a derivations: Open problems.
11:30 - 12:15 E.ALBRECHT: On closed operator algebras generated by analytic functional calculi.

SECTION A

Chairman: J.Anderson

16:30 - 17:00 M.PUTINAR: Functional calculus with sections of an analytic space.
17:10 - 17:40 G.DINESCU: Some results concerning semi-scalar operators.
17:50 - 18:20 T.CONSTANTINESCU; A.GHEONDEA: Algebraic aspects of the meromorphic functional calculus.
18:30 - 19:00 C.GROSU: Spectra of selfadjoint tensor product operators and related applications.

THURSDAY, June 12

SECTION B

Chairman: I.Suciu

9:30 - 10:00 I.A.RUS: Fixed point theorems for the sum of two maps.

10:10 - 10:40 D.O.RUS: Approximation properties of some classes of linear positive operators of spline type.

10:50 - 11:20 V.HIRIŞ; M.MEGAN: Asymptotic behaviour for linear systems with control.

11:30 - 12:00 P.TOPUZU: On the characteristic function and positive systems in Hilbert spaces.

ON CLOSED OPERATOR ALGEBRAS GENERATED BY ANALYTIC FUNCTIONAL CALCULI

Ernst Albrecht

In this note we investigate closed operator algebras generated by analytic functional calculi for n-tuples of commuting operators which are decomposable or quasi-decomposable. In particular, we obtain semisimplicity criteria which generalize a corresponding result for the closed full algebra generated by a spectral operator resp. by a decomposable operator due to U.Fixman and L.Tzafriri resp. F.-H. Vasilescu.

0. INTRODUCTION

In the following let X be a complex Banach space and denote by L(X) the Banach algebra of all continuous linear operators on X. For $T \in L(X)$, sp(T,X) is the spectrum of T in L(X) and r(T) is the spectral radius of T. The starting point of our investigations is the following result of U. Fixman and L. Tzafriri [5]:

THEOREM. *Let* $T \in L(X)$ *be a spectral operator* (in the sense of N.Dunford [4]) *with resolution of the identity* E(·) *and suppose that*

$$(*) \qquad E(\partial sp(T,X))=0.$$

Then the closed full subalgebra $\mathcal{U}(T)$ *generated by* T *in* L(X) *is semisimple.*

In [11] F.-H. Vasilescu has generalized this result to the case of operators which are decomposable in the sense of C.Foiaş [2,6]. The condition (*) has then to be replaced by "$\mathcal{E}(\partial sp(T,X))=\{0\}$", where $\mathcal{E}$ denotes the spectral capacity for T (cf.[6]). The purpose of this paper is to develop the main idea behind these results and to show how it can be used to extend them into several directions. In particular, we are interested in

i) operators with weaker spectral decomposition properties,

ii) restrictions of decomposable operators to an invariant subspace and similar situations,

iii) n-tuples of commuting operators, and

iv) algebras which are different from $\mathcal{U}(T)$ (larger or smaller).

1. THE MAIN RESULT

First, we shall need some notations. Let $T=(T_1,\ldots,T_n)$ be a n-tuple of commuting operators $T_1,\ldots,T_n \varepsilon L(X)$. The joint spectrum in the sense of J.L. Taylor [9,10] of $T=(T_1,\ldots,T_n)$ with respect to X will again be denoted by sp(T,X). J.L. Taylor has shown in [10] that there exists a unital continuous homomorphism

$$\Phi_T: H(sp(T,X)) \longrightarrow L(X)$$

from the algebra H(sp(T,X)) of all germs of locally holomorphic functions on sp(T,X) to L(X), such that:

(1) $\Phi_T(p)=p(T)$ for all polynomials $p \varepsilon \mathbb{C}[Z_1,\ldots,Z_n]$.

(2) $sp(\Phi_T(f),X)=f(sp(T,X))$ for all $f \varepsilon H(sp(T,X))$. (Notice that the values of f on sp(T,X) are well defined.)

(3) If $S=(S_1,\ldots,S_n)$ is a second n-tuple of commuting operators $S_1,\ldots,S_n \varepsilon L(Y)$ on a Banach space Y and if $A:X \to Y$ is a continuous linear mapping with $AT_j=S_jA$ for $j=1,\ldots,n$, then for all $f \varepsilon H(sp(T,X) \cup sp(S,Y))$ we have $A\Phi_T(f)=\Phi_S(f)A$.

If $\mathcal{F}$ is a subalgebra of H(sp(T,X)) then $\mathcal{U}_u(T,\mathcal{F})$ will be the closure of $\Phi_T(\mathcal{F})$ in L(X) with respect to the operator norm and $\mathcal{U}_q(T,\mathcal{F})$ denotes the quasi-closure of $\Phi_T(\mathcal{F})$ in L(X) with respect to the weak operator topology, i.e. $\mathcal{U}_q(T,\mathcal{F})$ is the linear hull of the closure of the unit ball of $\Phi_T(\mathcal{F})$ in the weak operator topology. Endowed with the operator norm, $\mathcal{U}_u(T,\mathcal{F})$ and $\mathcal{U}_q(T,\mathcal{F})$ are again Banach algebras; $\mathcal{U}_q(T,\mathcal{F})$ is in general strictly larger than $\mathcal{U}_u(T,\mathcal{F})$.

If X is a Hilbert space, then $\mathcal{U}_q(T,\mathcal{F})$ is the closure of $\Phi_T(\mathcal{F})$ in the σ-weak (and hence in the σ-strong) operator topology (see [3], p.38, Th.1).

The following choices for $\mathcal{F}$ will be of particular interest:

(a) $\mathcal{F}=\mathbb{C}[Z_1,\ldots,Z_n]$, the algebra of all polynomials in n variables with complex coefficients. In this case $\mathcal{U}_u(T,\mathcal{F})$ is the closed subalgebra of L(X) generated by $I,T_1,\ldots,T_n$.

(b) $\mathcal{F}=R(sp(T,X))$, the algebra of all rational functions on $\mathbb{C}^n$ with singularities outside of sp(T,X). Then $\mathcal{U}_u(T,\mathcal{F})$ is the closed full subalgebra of L(X) generated by $T_1,\dots,T_n$.

(c) $\mathcal{F}=H(sp(T,X))$.

As we shall see, the description of the algebras $\mathcal{U}_u(T,\mathcal{F})$ and $\mathcal{U}_q(T,\mathcal{F})$ is closely related to a certain part of the topological boundary of sp(T,X), which will now be introduced:

Let K be a compact subset of $\mathbb{C}^n$ and denote by ∂K the topological boundary of K. If f is a continuous complex valued function defined on K, then $||f||_K:=\sup_{z\in K}|f(z)|$. A point $w\in\partial K$ will be called *a point of analytic continuation for a subalgebra* $\mathcal{F}$ *of* H(K), if there exists a compact neighborhood U of w such that for every $f\in\mathcal{F}$ there exists a function f_e which is defined and locally holomorphic in some neighborhood of $K\cup U$ such that the germ of f_e on K coincides with f and such that we have $||f_e||_{K\cup U}=$ $=||f||_K$. The $\mathcal{F}$*-boundary* $\partial_{\mathcal{F}}K$ *of* K is then the set of all $w\in\partial K$ which are not points of analytic continuation for $\mathcal{F}$.

1. REMARKS. (a) If n=1 then $\partial_{H(K)}K=\partial_{R(K)}K=\partial K$ for all compact $K\subset\mathbb{C}$. If $\mathcal{F}$ is the algebra of all (germs on K of) polynomials then (by the maximum principle) $\partial_{\mathcal{F}}K$ is the boundary of the unbounded component of $\mathbb{C}\setminus K$. Thus, $\partial_{\mathcal{F}}K$ may be strictly smaller than the topological boundary of K, even in the case n=1.

(b) For n>1, $\partial_{H(K)}K$ may be strictly smaller than ∂K. For example, if $K:=\{(z,w)\in\mathbb{C}^2 \mid |z|\le|w|\le 1\}$, then by [8], Th. 2.4.6, every function f which is holomorphic in some open neighborhood of K has an extension f_e which is holomorphic in some neighborhood of $U:=\{(z,w)\in\mathbb{C}^2 \mid |z|\le 1 \text{ and } |w|\le 1\}$. By the maximum principle we have $||f_e||_U=||f||_K$. Thus, in this case the H(K)-boundary $\partial_{H(K)}K=\{(z,w) \mid |z|\le|w|=1\}$ is strictly smaller than ∂K.

We give now a representation theorem for elements of $\mathcal{U}_q(T,\mathcal{F})$ on certain closed linear subspaces of X which are invariant for $T_1,\dots,T_n$. This theorem will be our main tool in the next section.

2. THEOREM. *Let* $T=(T_1,\dots,T_n)$ *be a n-tuple of commuting operators in* L(X) *and let* $\mathcal{F}$ *be a subalgebra of* H(sp(T,X)) *and consider a closed set* $V\subset\mathbb{C}^n$ *such that for every* $f\in\mathcal{F}$ *there exists an extension* f_V *which is locally holomorphic in some neighborhood of* $V\cup sp(T,X)$ *such that the germ of* f_V *on* sp(T,X) *coincides with*

f and $||f_V||_{V\cup sp(T,X)} = ||f||_{sp(T,X)}$. *Denote by* U *the interior of* $V\cup sp(T,X)$. *If* $A\in\mathcal{U}_q(T,\mathcal{F})$ *then there exists a bounded function which is locally holomorphic on* U *such that for every closed linear subspace* Y *of* X *which is invariant for* $T_1,\ldots,T_n$ *and satisfies* $sp(T,Y)\subset U$ *we have* $A|Y=\Phi_{T|Y}(f)$. *Hence* (by the spectral mapping theorem (2)), *if* A *is quasinilpotent then* $f|sp(T,Y)=0$.

PROOF. By the definition of $\mathcal{U}_q(T,\mathcal{F})$ there is a net $(f_\alpha)_{\alpha\in I}$ in $\mathcal{F}$ such that $(\Phi_T(f_\alpha))_{\alpha\in I}$ is bounded and $\Phi_T(f_\alpha)\longrightarrow A$ in the weak operator topology. By the spectral mapping theorem we have

$$||f_{\alpha,V}||_{V\cup sp(T,X)} = ||f_\alpha||_{sp(T,X)} = r(\Phi_T(f_\alpha)) \leq ||\Phi_T(f_\alpha)||$$

so that $(f_{\alpha,V})_{\alpha\in I}$ is uniformly bounded on U. By the Montel theorem there exists an adherent point f of $(f_{\alpha,V})_{\alpha\in I}$ in H(U) (the space of all locally holomorphic functions on U, endowed with the topology of uniform convergence on all compact subsets of U). Fix now $\varepsilon>0$ and let W be a compact neighborhood of sp(T,Y) with $W\subset U$. Then there exists a cofinal subnet $(f_{\beta,V})_{\beta\in B}$ of $(f_{\alpha,V})_{\alpha\in I}$ such that

$$\forall\beta\in B: ||f-f_{\beta,V}||_W < \varepsilon/(2C+1),$$

where C is the operator norm of the continuous linear mapping induced by $\Phi_{T|Y}$ on the Banach space of all continuous functions on W which are locally holomorphic in intW. Fix $y\in Y$ and $x^*\in X^*$ with $||y||\leq 1$ and $||x^*||\leq 1$. Then there exists a $\beta\in B$ with

$$|\langle(\Phi_T(f_\beta)-A)y,x^*\rangle| < \varepsilon/2.$$

Using the fact that $\Phi_T(f_\beta)|Y=\Phi_{T|Y}(f_{\beta,V})$ which follows by (3) as the germ of $f_{\beta,V}$ on sp(T,**X**) coincides with f_β , we obtain

$$|\langle(\Phi_{T|Y}(f)-A)y,x^*\rangle| \leq |\langle(\Phi_{T|Y}(f)-\Phi_{T|Y}(f_{\beta,V}))y,x^*\rangle| +$$
$$+|\langle(\Phi_T(f_\beta)-A)y,x^*\rangle| \leq \varepsilon C/(2C+1)+\varepsilon/2 < \varepsilon.$$

Hence,

$$||\Phi_{T|Y}(f)-A|Y|| < \varepsilon,$$

and we obtain even $\Phi_{T|Y}(f)=A|Y$, as $\varepsilon>0$ was arbitrary.

2. APPLICATIONS TO DECOMPOSABLE OPERATORS

Let $T=(T_1,\ldots,T_n)$ be a n-tuple of commuting operators in L(X). T is called *(quasi-) decomposable* if there exists a mapping $\mathcal{E}$ from the family $\mathcal{C}\ell(\mathbb{C}^n)$ of all closed subsets of $\mathbb{C}^n$ into the family Lat(T) of all those closed linear subspaces of X which are invariant for $T_1,\ldots,T_n$ such that the following conditions are satisfied:

(i) $E(\emptyset)=\{0\}$, $E(\mathbb{C}^n)=X$.

(ii) $E(\bigcap_{j=1}^{\infty} F_j)=\bigcap_{j=1}^{\infty} E(F_j)$ for all sequences $(F_j)_{j=1}^{\infty}$ in $C\ell(\mathbb{C}^n)$.

(iii) If $\{U_1,\ldots,U_k\}$ is a finite open covering of $\mathbb{C}^n$ then

$$X=\sum_{j=1}^{k} E(\overline{U}_j) \quad (\text{resp. } X=\overline{\sum_{j=1}^{k} E(\overline{U}_j)}).$$

(iv) $sp(T,E(F))\subset F$ for all $F\in C\ell(\mathbb{C}^n)$.

A mapping $E:C\ell(\mathbb{C}^n)\to \mathrm{Lat}(T)$ with the properties (i)-(iv) will be called a *(quasi-) spectral capacity for* T. For the theory of decomposable n-tuples we refer to [7] and the monograph [13]. Notice, that the example in [1] shows that the class of quasi-decomposable n-tuples is strictly larger than the class of decomposable n-tuples (even in the case n=1).

3. LEMMA. *Let* $T=(T_1,\ldots,T_n)$ *be a* n-*tuple of commuting operators in* L(X). *If* $Y\in \mathrm{Lat}(T)$ *with* $sp(T,Y)\cap sp(T,X)=\emptyset$ *then* $Y=\{0\}$.

PROOF. (cf. the proof of the theorem in [12]). As $sp(T,Y)\cap sp(T,X)=\emptyset$, there exists a function h which is locally analytic in a neighborhood of $sp(T,Y)\cup sp(T,X)$ and satisfies $h\equiv 1$ in a neighborhood of sp(T,Y) and $h\equiv 0$ in a neighborhood of sp(T,X). Let $A:Y\to X$ be the canonical inclusion mapping. Then we may apply (3) and obtain

$$A=A\Phi_{T|Y}(h)=\Phi_T(h)A=0$$

and therefore, $Y=\{0\}$.

4. LEMMA. *Let* $T=(T_1,\ldots,T_n)$ *be a quasi-decomposable* n-*tuple in* L(X) *with a spectral quasi-capacity* $E:C\ell(\mathbb{C}^n)\to \mathrm{Lat}(T)$.

(a) *If* $F\in C\ell(\mathbb{C}^n)$ *with* $F\cap sp(T,X)=\emptyset$, *then* $E(F)=\{0\}$.

(b) *For all closed* $F\subset\mathbb{C}^n$ *we have* $E(F)=E(F\cap sp(T,X))$ *and hence* $sp(T,E(F))\subset F\cap sp(T,X)$.

(c) *Let* $U\subset\mathbb{C}^n$ *be an open set. If* $E(\overline{U})=\{0\}$ *then* $U\cap sp(T,X)=\emptyset$.

(d) $sp(T,X)\cap \mathrm{int}F\subset sp(T,E(F))$ *for all closed* $F\subset\mathbb{C}^n$.

PROOF. (a) is an immediate consequence of the preceeding

lemma and property (iv) of the quasi-spectral capacity for T.

(b) Put $U_k := \{z\in\mathbb{C}^n \mid \operatorname{dist}(z,sp(T,X))<2/k\}$ and $V_k := \{z\in\mathbb{C}^n \mid \operatorname{dist}(z,sp(T,X))>1/k\}$ for $k\in\mathbb{N}$. Then $U_k \cup V_k = \mathbb{C}^n$ and $\overline{V}_k \cap sp(T,X) = \emptyset$. By (a) and property (iii) of E we obtain

$$X=E(\overline{U}_k)+E(\overline{V}_k)=E(\overline{U}_k)$$

and hence, by property (ii) of E,

$$X=\bigcap_{k=1}^{\infty} E(\overline{U}_k)=E(sp(T,X)).$$

Therefore,

$$E(F)=E(F)\cap X=E(F)\cap E(sp(T,X))=E(F\cap sp(T,X)).$$

(c) Assume that $E(\overline{U})=\{0\}$ and that there exists a point $z\in U\cap sp(T,X)$. Then there exists an open polydisc P with $z\in P$ and $\overline{P}\subset U$. We have $U\cup(\mathbb{C}^n\setminus\overline{P})=\mathbb{C}^n$ and therefore,

$$X=E(\overline{U})+E(\overline{\mathbb{C}^n\setminus\overline{P}})=E(\mathbb{C}^n\setminus P) .$$

Hence, $sp(T,X)\subset\mathbb{C}^n\setminus P$ which is a contradiction to $z\in sp(T,X)$.

(d) Assume that there exists a point $z\in sp(T,X)\cap \operatorname{int} F$ with $z\notin sp(T,E(F))$. Then we can find an open neighborhood U of z with $\overline{U}\subset \operatorname{int} F$ and $\overline{U}\cap sp(T,E(F))=\emptyset$. $E(\overline{U})$ is a closed subspace of $E(F)$ (because of $\overline{U}\subset \operatorname{int}F\subset F$ and property (ii) of E) and $sp(T,E(\overline{U}))\cap sp(T,E(F))\subset\overline{U}\cap sp(T,E(F))=\emptyset$ so that $E(\overline{U})=\{0\}$ by the preceeding lemma. Because of (c) this is a contradiction to $z\in sp(T,X)$.

Before we state our semi-simplicity result which generalizes the theorems of Fixman - Tzafriri and Vasilescu we have to introduce a further part of the topological boundary of a compact set. A point z in a compact set $K\subset\mathbb{C}^n$ will be called a *point of uniqueness with respect to* K, if for any function f which is analytic in some open polydisc P with $z\in P$ we have $f\equiv 0$ on U whenever $f\equiv 0$ on $U\cap K$. The set of all points $z\in K$ which are not points of uniqueness with respect to K will be denoted by $\partial^u K$. Of course, $\partial^u K\subset\partial K\setminus\partial(\operatorname{int}K)$ by the identity theorem. In the case n=1, $\partial^u K$ is the set of all isolated points of K. In higher dimensions the situation is more complicated.

5. THEOREM. *Let* $T=(T_1,\ldots,T_n)$ *be a quasi-decomposable* n-*tuple in* L(X) *with a quasi-spectral capacity* $E:C\ell(\mathbb{C}^n)\longrightarrow \operatorname{Lat}(T)$ *and let* F *be a subalgebra of* H(sp(T,X)). *If* $A\in U_q(T,F)$ *is quasinil-*

potent then $R(A)\subset E(\partial^{u}sp(T,X)\cup\partial_{F}sp(T,X))$. *Hence, if* $E(\partial^{u}sp(T,X)\cup\partial_{F}sp(T,X))=\{0\}$, *then every quasinilpotent operator in* $U_q(T,F)$ *is* 0, *i.e.* $U_q(T,F)$ *is semi-simple.*

PROOF. Fix $z\in sp(T,X)$ with $z\notin\overline{\partial^{u}sp(T,X)\cup\partial_{F}sp(T,X)}$. Then there are open polydiscs U,V,W with $z\in U\subset\overline{U}\subset V\subset\overline{V}\subset W$ such that for every $f\in F$ there exists a (germ of a) function $f_W\in H(\overline{W}\cup sp(T,X))$ with the property that the germ of f_W on sp(T,X) coincides with f and $||f_W||_{\overline{W}\cup sp(T,X)}=||f||_{sp(T,X)}$. Notice, that

$$sp(T,E(\overline{V}))\subset\overline{V}\subset int(\overline{W}\cup sp(T,X)).$$

Hence, by Theorem 2, there exists a function f which is locally holomorphic on $int(\overline{W}\cup sp(T,X))$ and has the property that

$$A|E(\overline{V})=\Phi_{T|E(\overline{V})}(f).$$

By the spectral mapping theorem and part (d) of the preceeding lemma we obtain

$$f(V\cap sp(T,X))\subset f(sp(T,E(\overline{V})))=sp(A,E(\overline{V}))=\{0\},$$

as A is quasinilpotent. Now z is a point of uniqueness with respect to sp(T,X) so that we obtain $f\equiv 0$ on W and therefore $A|E(\overline{V})=\Phi_{T|E(\overline{V})}(f)=0$. As $V\cup(\mathbb{C}^n\setminus\overline{U})=\mathbb{C}^n$ we have

$$X=\overline{E(\overline{V})+E(\mathbb{C}^n\setminus U)}.$$

Hence,

(4) $$R(A)=A(X)\subset\overline{A(E(\overline{V}))+A(E(\mathbb{C}^n\setminus U))}=\overline{A(E(\mathbb{C}^n\setminus U))}\ .$$

In our next step we prove

(5) $A(E(F))\subset E(F)$ *for every closed* $F\subset\mathbb{C}^n$.

For decomposable T this follows from the fact that the spaces $E(F)$ are then spectral maximal and hence hyperinvariant for T (see [7] and [12]). To prove (5) for quasi-decomposable n-tuples, notice that because of (3) and $sp(T,E(F))\subset F\cap sp(T,X)\subset sp(T,X)$ we have $\Phi_T(h)(E(F))\subset E(F)$ for all $h\in H(sp(T,X))$. Therefore, if $(f_\alpha)_{\alpha\in I}$ is a net in H(sp(T,X)) such that $\Phi_T(f_\alpha)\to A$ in the weak operator topology, then we have for all $x\in E(F)$ and all $x^*\in E(F)^{\perp}$,

$$<Ax,x^*>=\lim_\alpha<\Phi_T(f_\alpha)x,x^*>=0,$$

and hence, $A(E(F))\subset E(F)$.

From (4) and (5) we conclude that $R(A)\subset\overline{E(\mathbb{C}^n\setminus U)}$. We have proved that for every $z\in sp(T,X)$ with $z\notin K:=\overline{\partial^{u}sp(T,X)\cup\partial_{F}sp(T,X)}$

there exists an open neighborhood $U(z)$ of z such that

$$R(A)\subset E(\mathbb{C}^n\setminus U(z)).$$

From the open covering $\{U(z)\mid z\in sp(T,X)\setminus K\}$ of $sp(T,X)\setminus K$ we may choose a countable subcovering $\{U(z_k)\mid k\in\mathbb{N}\}$ and conclude by means of property (ii) of E that

$$R(A)\subset\bigcap_{k=1}^{\infty}E(\mathbb{C}^n\setminus U(z_k))=E(\bigcap_{k=1}^{\infty}(\mathbb{C}^n\setminus U(z_k))\cap sp(T,X))\subset E(K).$$

The following theorem is a kind of identity theorem for operators in $U_q(T,F)$.

6. THEOREM. *Let* $T=(T_1,\ldots,T_n)$ *be quasi-decomposable in* $L(X)$ *with a quasi-spectral capacity* $E:C\ell(\mathbb{C}^n)\to Lat(T)$ *and suppose that* $G:=\operatorname{int}sp(T,X)$ *is connected and* $\overline{G}=sp(T,X)$. *Let* A *and* B *be two operators in* $U_q(T,F)$. *If there exists a subspace* $Y\in Lat(T)$ *such that*

i) $sp(T,Y)\subset G$,

ii) *if* $f:G\to\mathbb{C}$ *is holomorphic then* $f\equiv 0$ *on* $sp(T,Y)$ *if and only if* $f\equiv 0$ *on* G, *and*

iii) $A|Y=B|Y$,

then, $R(A-B)\subset E(\partial_F sp(T,X))$. *Hence, if* $E(\partial_F sp(T,X))=\{0\}$, *then* $A=B$.

PROOF. Fix $z\in\partial sp(T,X)\setminus\partial_F sp(T,X)$. Then there exists an open polydisc U around z such that for every $f\in H(sp(T,X))$ there is a a $f_U\in H(\overline{U}\cup sp(T,X))$ such that the germ of f_U on $sp(T,X)$ coincides with f and $\|f\|_{\overline{U}\cup sp(T,X)}=\|f\|_{sp(T,X)}$. By Theorem 2 there are functions f,h which are holomorphic on the connected open set $U\cup G$ such that $A|Y=\Phi_{T|Y}(f)$ and $B|Y=\Phi_{T|Y}(h)$. If $A|Y=B|Y$ then, by the spectral mapping theorem (2) we have $f|sp(T,Y)\equiv h|sp(T,Y)$ and therefore $f\equiv h$ on $U\cup G$. Let now F be a closed subset of $U\cup G$. By the proof of Theorem 2 we have with the same functions f and h as before, $A|E(F)=\Phi_{T|E(F)}(f)$ and $B|E(F)=\Phi_{T|E(F)}(h)$, hence $A|E(F)=$ $=B|E(F)$ as $f\equiv g$ in an open neighborhood of $sp(T,E(F))\subset F$. Consider now open sets V_k, W_k $(k\in\mathbb{N})$ with $\overline{V}_k\subset W_k\subset\overline{W}_k\subset U\cup G$ and $\bigcup_{k=1}^{\infty}V_k=U\cup G$. Then, $\mathbb{C}^n=W_k\cup(\mathbb{C}^n\setminus\overline{V}_k)$ and therefore,

$$X=\overline{E(\overline{W}_k)+E(\overline{\mathbb{C}^n\setminus\overline{V}_k})}=\overline{E(\overline{W}_k)+E(\mathbb{C}^n\setminus V_k)}.$$

Hence, $\overline{(A-B)(X)\subset(A-B)(E(\overline{W}_k))+(A-B)(E(\mathbb{C}^n\setminus V_k))}=\overline{(A-B)(E(\mathbb{C}^n\setminus V_k))}$.

As in the proof of (5) we have $(A-B)(E(\mathbb{C}^n\setminus V_k))\subset E(\mathbb{C}^n\setminus V_k)$. We obtain

$$(A-B)(X)\subset\bigcap_{k=1}^{\infty} E(\mathbb{C}^n\setminus V_k)=E(\bigcap_{k=1}^{\infty}(\mathbb{C}^n\setminus V_k)\cap sp(T,X))\subset$$
$$\subset E(\partial sp(T,X)\setminus U).$$

As in the final part of the proof of the preceeding theorem, one now easily shows by means of property (ii) of E that

$$(A-B)(X)\subset E(\partial_F sp(T,X)),$$

and the proof is complete.

7. THEOREM. *Let* X *and* Y *be Banach spaces and suppose that* $T=(T_1,\dots,T_n)$ *is a* n-*tuple of commuting operators in* L(X) *and* $S=(S_1,\dots,S_n)$ *is a decomposable* n-*tuple in* L(Y) *with a spectral capacity* $E:C\ell(\mathbb{C}^n)\to \mathrm{Lat}(S)$ *such that* $sp(S,Y)\subset sp(T,X)$. *If* $J:X\to Y$ *is a continuous linear mapping with* $S_jJ=JT_j$ *for* $j=1,\dots,n$ *and if* $A\in U_u(T,F)$ *is quasinilpotent then*

$$JA(X)\subset E(\partial_F sp(T,X)\cap sp(S,Y)).$$

Hence, if $J^{-1}(E(\partial_F sp(T,X)\cap sp(S,Y)))=\{0\}$, *then* $A=0$.

PROOF. Let $(f_k)_{k=1}^{\infty}$ be a sequence in F with $\Phi_T(f_k)\to A$ in the operator norm for $k\to\infty$. As $sp(A,X)=\{0\}$ we have, by the upper semi--continuity of the spectrum, $r(\Phi_T(f_k))\to 0$ and hence $\|f_k\|_{sp(T,X)}\to 0$ for $k\to\infty$. This argument has also been used in the proofs of [5] and [11]. Fix now an arbitrary $z\in sp(T,X)$ with $z\notin\partial_F sp(T,X)$. Then there exist open polydiscs U,V,W with $z\in U\subset\bar{U}\subset V\subset\bar{V}\subset W$ such that for all $k\in\mathbb{N}$ there exists a $g_k\in H(\bar{W}\cup sp(T,X))$ with $\|g_k\|_{\bar{W}\cup sp(T,X)}=$ $=\|f_k\|_{sp(T,X)}$ such that the germ of g_k on $sp(T,X)$ coincides with f_k. Because of $V\cup(\mathbb{C}^n\setminus\bar{U})=\mathbb{C}^n$ we have $Y=E(\bar{V})+E(\mathbb{C}^n\setminus U)$. Hence, if $x\in X$, then there are $y_1\in E(\bar{V})$ and $y_2\in E(\mathbb{C}^n\setminus U)$ with $Jx=y_1+y_2$. Therefore, by (3),

$$J\Phi_T(f_k)x=\Phi_S(f_k)Jx=\Phi_S(g_k)(y_1+y_2)=$$
$$=\Phi_{S|E(\bar{V})}(g_k)y_1+\Phi_S(g_k)y_2 .$$

As $g_k\to 0$ uniformly in the open neighborhood W of $sp(S,E(\bar{V}))\subset\bar{V}$, we have $\Phi_{S|E(\bar{V})}(g_k)y_1\to 0$ and therefore,

$$JAx=\lim_{k\to\infty}J\Phi_T(f_k)x=\lim_{k\to\infty}\Phi_S(g_k)y_2\in E((\mathbb{C}^n\setminus U)\cap sp(S,Y)).$$

As in the final part of the proof of Theorem 5 we obtain by means of property (ii) of E,

$$JA(X)\subset E(\partial_F sp(T,X)\cap sp(S,Y)),$$

and the theorem is proved.

8. COROLLARY. *Let* $S=(S_1,\ldots,S_n)$ *be a decomposable* n-*tuple on a Banach space* Y *with spectral capacity* $E:C\ell(\mathbb{C}^n)\to \mathrm{Lat}(S)$, *let* Y *be a closed invariant subspace for* $S_1,\ldots,S_n$ *and put* $T:=S|Y:=$ $:=(S_1|Y,\ldots,S_n|Y)$. *Let* F *be a subalgebra of* $H(sp(T,X))$ *and suppose that* $sp(S,Y)\subset sp(T,X)$ *and that* $E(\partial_F sp(T,X)\cap sp(S,Y))=\{0\}$. *Then* $U_u(T,F)$ *is semi-simple.*

PROOF. Take in the preceeding theorem for J the canonical inclusion mapping $J:X\to Y$.

REFERENCES

1. Albrecht, E.: An example of a weakly decomposable operator which is not decomposable, *Rev.Roumaine Math.Pures Appl.* 20 (1975), 855-861.
2. Colojoară, I.; Foiaş, C.: *Theory of generalized spectral operators*, Gordon and Breach, New York, 1968.
3. Dixmier, J.: *Les algèbres d'opérateurs dans l'espace Hilbertien (Algèbres de von Neumann)*, Gauthier-Villars, Paris, 1969.
4. Dunford, N.; Schwartz, J.T.: *Linear operators, Part* III: *Spectral operators*, Wiley-Interscience, New York, 1971.
5. Fixman, U.; Tzafriri, L.: The full algebra generated by a spectral operator, *J.London Math.Soc.* 4 (1971), 39-45.
6. Foiaş, C.: Spectral capacities and decomposable operators, *Rev.Roumaine Math.Pures Appl.* 13 (1968), 1539-1545.
7. Frunză, St.: The Taylor spectrum and spectral decompositions, *J.Functional Analysis* 19 (1975), 390-421.
8. Hörmander, L.: *An introduction to complex analysis in several variables*, Van Nostrand, Princeton, 1966.
9. Taylor, J.L.: A joint spectrum for several commuting operators, *J.Functional Analysis* 6 (1970), 172-191.
10. Taylor, J.L.: The analytic-functional calculus for several commuting operators, *Acta Math.* 125 (1970), 1-38.
11. Vasilescu, F.-H.: Remark on a theorem of semi-simplicity, *Rev.Roumaine Math.Pures Appl.* 17 (1972), 451-452.
12. Vasilescu, F.-H.: An application of Taylor's functional calculus, *Rev.Roumaine Math.Pures Appl.* 19 (1974), 1165-1167.
13. Vasilescu, F.-H.: *Calcul functional analitic multidimensional*, Editura Academiei, Bucureşti, 1979.

Ernst Albrecht, Fachbereich Mathematik, Universität des Saarlandes, D-6600 Saarbrücken, West Germany

A CONJECTURE CONCERNING THE PURE STATES OF B(H) AND A RELATED THEOREM[1)]

Joel Anderson[2)]

INTRODUCTION

The purpose of this note is twofold. First to present a conjecture concerning the form of the pure states on $\mathcal{B}(\mathcal{H})$ and second to prove a theorem related to this conjecture.

Suppose $\mathcal{A}$ is a unital C^*-algebra with state space $\mathcal{S}(\mathcal{A})=\{f\varepsilon\mathcal{A}^*:||f||=f(1)=1\}$ and pure states $\mathcal{P}(\mathcal{A})$. If $\mathcal{A}$ is abelian, then by the Gelfand theory $\mathcal{A}$ is isomorphic to C(X), the continuous complex functions on a compact Hausdorff space X and $\mathcal{P}(\mathcal{A})$ consists of the point evaluations induced by elements in X. If $\mathcal{A}=\mathcal{B}(\mathcal{H}_n)\cong\mathcal{M}_n$, the operators on a complex Hilbert space of dimension n (equivalently, the n by n complex matrices), then $\mathcal{P}(\mathcal{A})$ consists of the vector states induced by unit vectors in $\mathcal{H}_n$. More generally, if $\mathcal{K}=\mathcal{K}(\mathcal{H})$ denotes the compact operators on the Hilbert space $\mathcal{H}$, then $\mathcal{P}(\mathcal{K})$ also consists of the vector states. Beyond these simple cases, however, little is known. In a sense this is not surprising, for one should not expect to obtain such precise information in the general case. Nevertheless it is sometimes possible to get a satisfactory classification for more general C^*-algebras. In particular this is so if $\mathcal{A}$ is a UHF algebra.

1. THE PURE STATES OF A UHF ALGEBRA

The facts that will be used in this section are all familiar and, except for the Powers transitivity theorem, are not deep.

1) This work is an expanded version of a talk given at the Vth Operator Theory conference held June 2-12, 1980, in Timişoara and Herculane, Romania.
2) Research supported in part by a grant from the National Science Foundation.

This in fact is the main point of this section. It is hoped that the simplicity of the arguments and the natural way in which they fit together will support the conjecture presented in the next section.

Recall that A is a UHF algebra if it can be written as the uniform closure of $\bigcup A_n$, where $\{A_n\}$ is an increasing sequence of full matrix algebras. For simplicity, let us assume that A_n is isomorphic to the 2^n by 2^n complex matrices and A_n is embedded into A_{n+1} via the map $a \mapsto a \oplus a$. For each n, let $\mathcal{D}_n$ denote the diagonal matrices in A_n and write $\mathcal{D}$ for the uniform closure of $\bigcup \mathcal{D}_n$. It is clear that $\mathcal{D}$ is abelian and it will be shown shortly that $\mathcal{D}$ is a masa, i.e., a maximal abelian self-adjoint subalgebra of A.

ASSERTION 1. *If* f *is a state on a unital* C^**-algebra* A *and* f *is multiplicative when restricted to a subalgebra* B, *then*

$$f(ab)=f(ba)=f(a)f(b)$$

for all a *in* A, b *in* B.

PROOF. By the Cauchy-Schwartz inequality

$$|f(ab)-f(a)f(b)|^2=|f(a(b-f(b)1))|^2\leq$$
$$\leq f(aa^*)f((b-f(b)1)^*(b-f(b)1))=0.$$

Hence, f is B-multiplicative.

ASSERTION 2. *If* d_1 *and* d_2 *belong to* $\mathcal{D}$ *and* a *belongs to* A, *then*

$$||d_1+[d_2,a]||\geq||d_1||.$$

PROOF. Fix a complex homomorphism h on $\mathcal{D}$ such that $|h(d_1)|=||d_1||$ and extend h to a state f on A. By Assertion 1, $f([d_2,a])=0$. Hence

$$||d_1||=|h(d_1)|=|f(d_1+[d_2,a])|\leq||d_1+[d_2,a]||.$$

ASSERTION 3. *If* $a=(\alpha_{ij})$ *is a matrix in* A_n *with* 0 *diagonal, then*

$$a=[d,b]$$

where $d\in\mathcal{D}_n$ *and* $b\in A_n$. *Therefore* $A_n=\mathcal{D}_n\dot{+}[\mathcal{D}_n,A_n]$ *where the symbol* $\dot{+}$ *denotes the algebraic direct sum.*

PROOF. As every matrix of the form [d,b] with d in $\mathcal{D}_n$ has

0 diagonal and every matrix is the unique sum of a diagonal matrix and a matrix with 0 diagonal, the second assertion follows from the first. Write d for the element of $\mathcal{D}_n$ with diagonal entries $\delta_{ii}=i$, $1\le i\le 2^n$ and define

$$\beta_{ij}=\begin{cases}\alpha_{ij}/(i-j) & \text{if } i\neq j\\ 0 & \text{if } i=j\end{cases}.$$

It is straightforward to check that if $b=(\beta_{ij})$, then $a=[d,b]$.

ASSERTION 4. *There is a unique norm one projection P of A onto $\mathcal{D}$.*

PROOF. By Assertion 3, the map $d_1+[d_2,b]\mapsto d_1$ is well-defined on A_n and by Assertion 2 it is continuous and of norm 1. The map therefore extends uniquely to a norm one projection P of A onto $\mathcal{D}$. As all such projections are 0 on $[\mathcal{D},A]$ (by Tomiyama's theorem), P is unique.

ASSERTION 5. *If J denotes the norm closure of $[\mathcal{D},A]$ then J is a subspace of A and*

$$\mathcal{D}\dot{+}J=A .$$

PROOF. It suffices to show J is the null space of P. By Tomiyama's theorem it is clear that $J\subseteq P^{-1}(0)$. To show the reverse inclusion suppose $P(a)=0$ for some a in A. Select a sequence $\{a_n\}$ with a_n in A_n and $\lim\|a-a_n\|=0$. By Assertion 3 we may write $a_n=d_n+[d_n',b_n]$ with d_n,d_n' in $\mathcal{D}_n$. Hence,

$$\|d_n\|=\|P(a_n)\|=\|P(a-a_n)\|\le\|a-a_n\|$$

so that $\lim\|d_n\|=0$. Therefore $\lim\|a-[d_n',b_n]\|=0$ and $a\in J$.

PROPOSITION. *Fix a complex homomorphism* h *on* $\mathcal{D}$.

i) *The formula* $f=h\circ P$ *defines a pure state on* A.

ii) *The functional* f *is the unique state extension of* h *to* A.

PROOF. By a familiar argument extreme points of $\{g\in S(A):g|_{\mathcal{D}}=h\}$ are pure states. Hence, i) follows from ii). Suppose g is a state on A that agrees with f on $\mathcal{D}$. If $a\in A_n$, then $a=d_1+[d_2,b]$ and so by Assertion 1

$$g(a)=g(d_1)=h(d_1)=f(d_1)=f(a).$$

COROLLARY. $\mathcal{D}$ is a masa in A.

PROOF. If $\mathcal{D}$ were not a masa in A, then by the Stone-Weierstrass theorem some homomorphism h on $\mathcal{D}$ would have many distinct state extensions to A.

THEOREM. *If* f *is a pure state on UHF algebra* A, *then there is a masa* C *in* A, *a unique norm one projection* P_C *of* A *onto* C *and a complex homomorphism* k *on* C *such that*

$$f = k \circ P_C \; .$$

Moreover, C *is isomorphic to the diagonal masa* $\mathcal{D}$.

PROOF. Write $f_h = h \circ P_{\mathcal{D}}$ for the pure state considered in the Proposition. By the Powers transitivity theorem [7, Corollary 3.8] there is a *-automorphism θ of A such that $f = f_h \circ \theta$. Thus,

$$f = h \circ P_{\mathcal{D}} \circ \theta = (h \circ \theta)(\theta^{-1} \circ P_{\mathcal{D}} \circ \theta).$$

Write $C = \theta^{-1}(\mathcal{D})$, $P_C = \theta^{-1} \circ P_{\mathcal{D}} \circ \theta$, and $k = h \circ \theta$. It is clear that C, P_C and k have the required properties.

2. THE CONJECTURE

Throughout H shall denote a complex separable infinite-dimensional Hilbert space and $B(H)$ the bounded linear operators on H.

It has often been observed that $B(H)$, $T(H)$ (the trace class operators) and $K(H)$ are the noncommutative analogues of ℓ^∞, ℓ_1 and c_0. In particular $B(H) \cong T(H)^* \cong K(H)^{**}$. We should therefore expect that $S(B(H))$ and $P(B(H))$ are the "noncommutative" analogues of $S(\ell^\infty)$ and $P(\ell^\infty)$. Now $\ell^\infty \cong C(\beta\mathbb{N})$ where $\beta\mathbb{N}$ denotes the Stone-Čech compactification of the integers. This correspondence arises as follows. If $\mathcal{U}$ is an ultrafilter in $\beta\mathbb{N}$, then the formula

$$h_{\mathcal{U}}(\langle \alpha_n \rangle) = \lim_{\mathcal{U}} \alpha_n$$

defines a complex homomorphism on ℓ^∞. Conversely, it is easy to show that every complex homomorphism is induced by an ultrafilter limit. Homomorphisms on ℓ^∞ divide into two classes. If $\mathcal{U}_k = \{\sigma \subseteq N : k \in \sigma\}$ denotes the principal ultrafilter at k, then $\mathcal{U}_k$ induces the normal state h_k where

$$h_k(<\alpha_n>)=\alpha_k \ .$$

The remaining homomorphisms, those induced by free ultrafilters, annihilate c_0.

In $B(H)$ the vector states are pure and if f is a pure state on $B(H)$, then either f is a vector state or else f annihilates $K(H)$ (in this latter case f is said to be a *singular* pure state). Thus, the normal pure states on $B(H)$ are the vector states and so give the appropriate noncommutative version of the principal ultrafilter states. One might guess that the singular pure states on $B(H)$ have the form

$$f(\cdot)=\lim_{U}\omega_n(\cdot)=\lim_{U}(\cdot\eta_n,\eta_n)$$

where U is a free ultrafilter and $\{\omega_n\}$ is the sequence of vector states induced by the vectors $\{\eta_n\}$. This is indeed the case. Unfortunately, however, this does not settle the question. For Wils [8] showed that every singular state (pure or not) has this form. In fact there is a sequence $\{\eta_n\}$ of unit vectors that converges weakly to 0 and a free ultrafilter U such that the associated state induces a type II_∞ factor representation of $B(H)$. (This follows from [3, Theorem 5] and [2, (6.2)].) On the other hand it is proved in [3, Corollary 3] that if $\{e_n\}$ is an othonormal basis for H and $U\varepsilon\beta\mathbb{N}$, then the state f defined by

(*) $$f(T)=\lim_{U}(Te_n,e_n)$$

is pure. Let us say that states of the form (*) are *diagonalizable*.

CONJECTURE. A state f on $B(H)$ is pure if and only if it is diagonalizable.

The conjecture can be rephrased in terms analogous to those of Section 1 as follows. Fix an orthonormal basis $\{e_n\}$ for H and write D for the operators that are diagonal with respect to this basis. That is, $D\varepsilon\mathcal{D}$ if and only if each e_n is an eigenvector for D. As is well-known, $\mathcal{D}$ is a masa in $B(H)$. Algebras of this form are called *atomic* masas in $B(H)$. There is a unique norm one projection $P_{\mathcal{D}}=P$ of $B(H)$ onto $\mathcal{D}$ given by $P(T)=\Sigma(Te_n,e_n)e_n\otimes e_n$. Clearly $\mathcal{D}$ is isomorphic to ℓ^∞ and its complex homomorphisms are given by ultrafilter limits of the vector states induced by $\{e_n\}$.

Note that a state f is diagonalizable (with respect to the basis $\{e_n\}$) if and only if $f=h\circ\mathcal{P}$ for some homomorphism h on $\mathcal{D}$. Thus, in this context the conjecture may be restated as follows.

CONJECTURE. A state f on $\mathcal{B}(H)$ is pure if and only if there is an atomic masa $\mathcal{D}$ and a complex homomorphism h on $\mathcal{D}$ such that $f=h\circ\mathcal{P}$, where $\mathcal{P}$ is the unique norm one projection of $\mathcal{B}(H)$ onto $\mathcal{D}$.

As noted above, states of the form $h\circ\mathcal{P}$ are pure. The converse is implied by the following statements.

(A) If f is a pure state on $\mathcal{B}(H)$, then there is an atomic masa $\mathcal{D}$ such that f is a homomorphism on $\mathcal{D}$. ($\mathcal{B}(H)$ has the atomic restriction property.)

(B) If $\mathcal{D}$ is an atomic masa in $\mathcal{B}(H)$ with associated projection $\mathcal{P}$ and h is a complex homomorphism on $\mathcal{D}$, then $h\circ\mathcal{P}$ is the unique state extension of h to $\mathcal{B}(H)$. ($\mathcal{D}$ has the *extension property* with respect to $\mathcal{B}(H)$.)

Note that the exact analogues of these statements are true in a UHF algebra. In the UHF setting statement (A) follows from the Powers transitivity theorem. As $\mathcal{B}(H)$ has only inner automorphisms and $\mathcal{P}(\mathcal{B}(H))$ has cardinality 2^c, the pure states on $\mathcal{B}(H)$ are not transitive. It is trivial, however, that the vector states are transitive and the remainder, the singular pure states, are induced by the pure states of the Calkin algebra $\mathcal{Q}(H)=\mathcal{B}(H)/\mathcal{K}(H)$. Thus, it is natural to ask if the pure states of the Calkin algebra are transitive. Note that if this were so, then by a simple cardinality argument, the Calkin algebra would admit outer automorphisms.

The statement (B) is equivalent to an interesting and apparently difficult question in operator theory.

THEOREM. [2, (3.6) and (3.7)]. *Fix an atomic masa $\mathcal{D}$ in $\mathcal{B}(H)$. The following are equivalent.*

i) *$\mathcal{D}$ has the extension property with respect to $\mathcal{B}(H)$.*

ii) *$\mathcal{D}\dotplus[\mathcal{D},\mathcal{B}(H)]^-=\mathcal{B}(H)$, where the bar denotes norm closure.*

iii) *If $T\in\mathcal{B}(H)$ and $\mathcal{P}(T)=0$ (i.e., T has 0 diagonal) then for each $\varepsilon>0$ there are projections $P_1,\ldots,P_n$ in $\mathcal{D}$ such that $P_iP_j=0$ if $i\neq j$, $P_1+\ldots+P_n=1$ and*

$$||P_i T P_i|| < \varepsilon, \quad 1 \le i \le n.$$

If S denotes the unilateral shift, then it is easy to see that S has property iii) above (with respect to the usual orthonormal basis). In fact every element in $C^*(S)$ (in particular, every Toeplitz operator with continuous symbol) with zero diagonal also has property iii). The question of whether every Toeplitz operator with zero diagonal has property iii) is open.

REMARK. $\mathcal{B}(H)$ also contains *continuous* masas. (Recall that a masa M is continuous if it is isomorphic to the algebra of multiplications of $L^2(0,1)$ by elements of $L^\infty(0,1)$.) These masas do not seem to play an important role in the study of $P(\mathcal{B}(H))$. In particular they do not enjoy the extension property with respect to $\mathcal{B}(H)$ [6]. Of course there are pure states on $\mathcal{B}(H)$ that restrict to homomophisms on a continuous masa. The conjecture therefore implies the existence of pure states on $\mathcal{B}(H)$ that simultaneously restrict to homomorphisms on both atomic and continuous masas. It is shown in [3, Corollary 11] that every homomorphism h of a continuous masa has 2^c distinct pure state extensions that restrict to homomorphisms on an atomic masa. Finally it should be noted that results related to these questions have appeared in [4 and 5].

3. AN APPLICATION OF CONVEXITY THEORY

Fix an atomic masa $\mathcal{D}$ in $\mathcal{B}(H)$. Let $\mathcal{B}(H)_s$, $\mathcal{B}(H)_{sk}$ and $\mathcal{D}_s$ denote the real Banach spaces of self-adjoint operators, skew-adjoint operators and self-adjoint operators in $\mathcal{D}$ and write

$$\mathcal{J} = [\mathcal{D}_s, \mathcal{B}(H)_s]^-$$

where the bar denotes norm closure. It will be shown below that $\mathcal{J}$ is an order ideal in $\mathcal{B}(H)_s$ and the quotient

$$A = \mathcal{B}(H)_s / \mathcal{J}$$

is a complete order unit space in a certain ordering. (It will be assumed that the reader is familiar with the theory of compact convex sets as expounded in [1] for example.)

Let υ denote the natural map of $\mathcal{B}(H)_s$ onto A. It follows from the Theorem in Section 2 that $\mathcal{D}$ has the extension property with respect to $\mathcal{B}(H)$ if and only if $\upsilon(\mathcal{D}_s) = A$.

The main theorem of this section yields a corollary that is a partial result in this direction. The following lemma is basic to all of the results in this section.

Let us say that a finite subset $\{P_1,\ldots,P_n\}$ of $\mathcal{D}$ is a *$\mathcal{D}$-partition* (of the identity) if each P_i is a projection, $P_iP_j=0$ if $i\neq j$, and $P_1+\ldots+P_n=1$.

LEMMA 1. *An operator* A *in* $B(H)_s$ *is in* $\mathcal{J}$ *if and only if for every* $\varepsilon>0$ *there is a* $\mathcal{D}$*-partition* $\{P_1,\ldots,P_n\}$ *such that*

$$||P_iAP_i||<\varepsilon\ , \qquad 1\leq i\leq n\ .$$

PROOF. Fix A in $\mathcal{J}$ and $\varepsilon>0$. Select self-adjoint operators D and B with D in $\mathcal{D}$ such that $||A-[D,B]||<\varepsilon$. As D is diagonal, there is a $\mathcal{D}$-partition $\{P_1,\ldots,P_n\}$ and real numbers $\delta_1,\ldots,\delta_n$ such that

$$||DP_i-\delta_iP_i||=||P_iD-\delta_iP_i||<\varepsilon(2||B||)^{-1}\ .$$

If $1\leq i\leq n$, then

$$||P_iAP_i||\leq||P_i[D,B]P_i||+\varepsilon=||P_i[D-\delta_i1,B]P_i||+\varepsilon\leq 2\varepsilon\ ,$$

and A has the desired property.

For the converse, first suppose A is a self-adjoint operator and that $\Sigma P_iAP_i=0$ for some $\mathcal{D}$-partition $\{P_1,\ldots,P_n\}$. If we write $D=\Sigma iP_i$ and $B=\sum_{i\neq j}(i-j)^{-1}P_iAP_j$, then $A=[D,B]$ and $A\in\mathcal{J}$. Now assume A has the property in the statement of the Lemma and fix $\varepsilon>0$. Select a $\mathcal{D}$-partition $\{P_1,\ldots,P_n\}$ with $||\Sigma P_iAP_i||<\varepsilon$ and write $A_\varepsilon=A-\Sigma P_iAP_i$. Since $P_iA_\varepsilon P_i=0$, $A_\varepsilon\in\mathcal{J}$. Moreover,

$$||A-A_\varepsilon||=||\Sigma P_iAP_i||<\varepsilon$$

and therefore $A\in\mathcal{J}$.

Note that the argument in the second paragraph of the proof shows that if $\{P_1,\ldots,P_n\}$ is a $\mathcal{D}$-partition, then $\upsilon(A)=\upsilon(\Sigma P_iAP_i)$ for each A in $B(H)_s$.

COROLLARY 2. *If* $B(H)_s$ *is given its usual order, then* $\mathcal{J}$ *is an order ideal.*

PROOF. To see that $\mathcal{J}$ is a (linear) subspace of $B(H)_s$ fix $[D_1,A_1]$ and $[D_2,A_2]$ in $[\mathcal{D}_s,B(H)_{sk}]$ and $\varepsilon>0$. Select (by Lemma 1) $\mathcal{D}$-partitions $\{P_1,\ldots,P_n\}$ and $\{Q_1,\ldots,Q_m\}$ so that

$$||\Sigma P_i[D_1,A_1]P_i||<\varepsilon \text{ and } ||\Sigma Q_j[D_2,A_2]Q_j||<\varepsilon .$$

If $\{R_1,\ldots,R_{mn}\}$ is the refined $\mathcal{D}$-partition of products of the form P_iQ_j, then for $R_k=P_iQ_j$

$$||R_k([D_1,A_1]+[D_2,A_2])R_k||\leq||P_i\ [D_1,A_1]P_i||+||Q_j[D_2,A_2]Q_j||.$$

As the right hand side is $<2\varepsilon$, by Lemma 1 $[D_1,A_1]+[D_2,A_2]\varepsilon\mathcal{J}$ and $\mathcal{J}$ is a subspace.

Suppose $A\varepsilon\mathcal{B}(\mathcal{H})_s$, $B,C\varepsilon\mathcal{J}$ and $B\leq A\leq C$. If $\varepsilon>0$, then Lemma 1 and a refinement argument similiar to that of the first part of the proof show that there is a $\mathcal{D}$-partition $\{R_1,\ldots,R_n\}$ such that

$$-\varepsilon 1\leq\Sigma R_iBR_i\leq\Sigma R_iAR_i\leq\Sigma R_iCR_i\leq\varepsilon 1.$$

Hence, $||\Sigma R_iAR_i||<\varepsilon$ and by Lemma 1 $A\varepsilon\mathcal{J}$.

There is a natural order $(\leq)$ on $\mathcal{A}$ that arises as follows. Let $\mathcal{A}^+$ denote the set of images of positive elements of $\mathcal{B}(\mathcal{A})_s$. As $\mathcal{J}$ is an order ideal, $\mathcal{A}^+$ is a proper cone in $\mathcal{A}$ [1, Proposition II.1.1] and so determines an order in $\mathcal{A}$ by $a\leq b$ if and only if $b-a\varepsilon\mathcal{A}^+$. Moreover, if we put $e=\upsilon(1)$, then for each A in $\mathcal{B}(\mathcal{H})_s$,

$$-||A||e\leq\upsilon(A)\leq||A||e$$

so that e is an order unit for $(\mathcal{A},\leq)$. Unfortunately it is not clear whether or not $(\mathcal{A},\leq)$ is Archimedian. In fact it will be shown later that this is the case if and only if $\mathcal{A}=\upsilon(\mathcal{D}_s)$. It is therefore necessary to introduce a new order $(\preccurlyeq)$ in which $(\mathcal{A},e)$ is Archimedian. Write

$$\mathcal{C}=\{a\varepsilon\mathcal{A}\text{: for each n there is } A_n \text{ in } \mathcal{B}(\mathcal{H})_s \text{ with } A_n\geq(-1/n)1 \text{ and } \upsilon(A_n)=a\}.$$

PROPOSITION 3. *The set* $\mathcal{C}$ *is a proper cone in* $\mathcal{A}$ *and* $\mathcal{A}^+\subseteq\mathcal{C}$.

PROOF. It is trivial that $\mathcal{A}^+\subseteq\mathcal{C}$ and that $\mathcal{C}$ is a cone in $\mathcal{A}$. Suppose $a\varepsilon\mathcal{C}\cap-\mathcal{C}$. For each n select A_n and B_n in $\mathcal{B}(\mathcal{H})_s$ such that $A_n,B_n\geq-(1/n)1$ and $\upsilon(A_n)=\upsilon(-B_n)=a$. Fix $A\varepsilon\mathcal{B}(\mathcal{H})_s$ with $\upsilon(A)=a$. As $A-A_n\varepsilon\mathcal{J}$ and $A+B_n\varepsilon\mathcal{J}$, there are (by Lemma 1) $\mathcal{D}$-partitions $\{P_1,\ldots,P_n\}$, $\{Q_1,\ldots,Q_m\}$ such that

$$||\Sigma P_i(A-A_n)P_i||\leq 1/n \text{ and } ||\Sigma Q_j(A+B_n)Q_j||\leq 1/n .$$

If $\{R_k\}$ denotes the refinement of these $\mathcal{D}$-partitions, then

$$(-2/n)R_k \le R_k A_n R_k + R_k(A-A_n)R_k = R_k A R_k =$$
$$= R_k(A+B_n)R_k - R_k B_n R_k \le (2/n)R_k$$

so that again by Lemma 1, $A \in \mathcal{J}$.

Let ($\preccurlyeq$) denote the order in $\mathcal{A}$ induced by the proper cone $\mathcal{C}$. Note that if $a \le b$ in $\mathcal{A}$, then since $\mathcal{A}^+ \subseteq \mathcal{C}$, $a \preccurlyeq b$ and therefore e is an order unit for $(\mathcal{A},\preccurlyeq)$. Moreover, it is immediate from the definition of $\mathcal{C}$ that the ordering is Archimedian so that $(\mathcal{A},\preccurlyeq,e)$ is an order unit space.

As $\mathcal{J}$ is uniformly closed $\mathcal{A}$ is complete in its quotient norm $||\cdot||_q$. There are also two other norms on $\mathcal{A}$ that arise from the orders ($\le$) and ($\preccurlyeq$) as follows. For a in $\mathcal{A}$ write

$$||a||_1 = \inf\{\lambda>0 : -\lambda e \le a \le \lambda e\} \quad \text{and}$$
$$||a||_2 = \inf\{\lambda>0 : -\lambda e \preccurlyeq a \preccurlyeq \lambda e\}.$$

Clearly $||a||_2 \le ||a||_1$ for all a in $\mathcal{A}$ and $||\cdot||_1$ and $||\cdot||_2$ are seminorms. Since $(\mathcal{A},\preccurlyeq,e)$ is Archimedian $||\cdot||_2$ is a norm [1, Proposition II.1.2] and since $||\cdot||_2 \le ||\cdot||_1$, $||\cdot||_1$ is also a norm. In fact these three norms are equal. To see this it is convenient to introduce a fourth norm on $\mathcal{A}$. If $a=\upsilon(A)$ is in $\mathcal{A}$, then define

$$||a||_p = \inf\{||\Sigma P_i A P_i|| : \{P_1,\ldots,P_n\} \text{ is a } \mathcal{D}\text{-partition}\}.$$

It is easy to see that the right hand side above defines a seminorm on $\mathcal{B}(\mathcal{H})_s$. Moreover, by Lemma 1 its null space is precisely $\mathcal{J}$ so that $||\cdot||_p$ is a well-defined norm on $\mathcal{A}$.

PROPOSITION 4. *The four norms* $||\cdot||_q$, $||\cdot||_1$, $||\cdot||_2$, $||\cdot||_p$ *are equal.*

PROOF. If $\{P_1,\ldots,P_n\}$ is a $\mathcal{D}$-partition, then as shown in the proof of Lemma 1, $A-\Sigma P_i A P_i \in \mathcal{J}$ for A in $\mathcal{B}(\mathcal{H})_s$. So if $a=\upsilon(A)\in\mathcal{A}$ then

$$\inf\{||A+B|| : B\in\mathcal{J}\} \le \inf\{||A-(A-\Sigma P_i A P_i)||\}$$

were the right hand inf is taken over all $\mathcal{D}$-partitions $\{P_1,\ldots,P_n\}$. Hence, $||\cdot||_q \le ||\cdot||_p$. To show $||\cdot||_p \le ||\cdot||_2$, fix a in $\mathcal{A}$, $\varepsilon>0$ and write $\lambda=||a||_2$. Select A and B in $\mathcal{B}(\mathcal{H})_s$ such that $\upsilon(A)=\upsilon(B)=a$ and $-(\lambda+\varepsilon)1 \le A, B \le (\lambda+\varepsilon)1$. As $A-B\in\mathcal{J}$ there is (by Lemma 1) a $\mathcal{D}$-partition $\{P_1,\ldots,P_n\}$ such that $||\Sigma P_i(A-B)P_i||<\varepsilon$. Hence,

$$-(\lambda+\varepsilon)P_i \leq P_iAP_i \leq P_iBP_i+\varepsilon P_i \leq (\lambda+2\varepsilon)P_i$$

for $1\leq i\leq n$ so that $||\Sigma P_iAP_i||\leq\lambda+2\varepsilon$ and therefore $||a||_p\leq||a||_2$. Since $||\cdot||_2\leq||\cdot||_1$, to complete the proof it only remains to show $||\cdot||_1\leq||\cdot||_q$. Fix a in A and choose A in $B(H)_s$ such that $\upsilon(A)=a$ and $||a||_q+\varepsilon\geq||A||$. Since $-||A||1\leq A\leq||A||1$, $-(||a||_q+\varepsilon)e\preceq$ $\preceq a\preceq(||a||_q+\varepsilon)e$ and $||a||_1\leq||a||_q$.

Let us denote the norm on A by $||\cdot||$. Since J is uniformly closed and $||\cdot||=||\cdot||_q=||\cdot||_1$, $(A,\preceq,e)$ is a complete order unit space. Hence, by Kadison's theorem [1, Theorem II.1.8] A is isometrically and order isomorphic to A(K), the continuous affine functions on the state space K of A. The set K may be identified with the set of states on $B(H)$ that are $\mathcal{D}$-central in the sense that for a state f, f(DT)=f(TD) for all D in $\mathcal{D}$ and all T in $B(H)$. Indeed, if f is a $\mathcal{D}$-central state on $B(H)$, then $f\circ\upsilon^{-1}\varepsilon K$ and if $x\varepsilon K$, then $x\circ\upsilon$ is $\mathcal{D}$-central on $B(H)_s$ and extends to a $\mathcal{D}$-central state on $B(H)$. Note that since $P(J)=0$, P may be viewed as acting on A. Further, P^* maps K into itself by the formula $x\mapsto x\circ P$. The set $F=P^*(K)$ consists of those states on A of the form $f\circ P\circ\upsilon^{-1}$, where f is any state on $B(H)$. The remainder of this section will be devoted to showing that F is a closed split face in K.

If J_1 denotes $\{a\varepsilon A:P(a)=0\}$, then $F=J_1^{\perp}=\{x\varepsilon K:x(a)=0$ for all a in $J_1\}$ and $F^{\perp}=\{a\varepsilon A:x(a)=0$ for all x in $F\}=J_1$. These assertions follow from the facts that x is in F if and only if $x(a-P(a))=0$ for all a in A and if $a\varepsilon F^{\perp}$ then $a=\upsilon(A)$ for some A in $B(H)_s$ with $P(A)=0$.

PROPOSITION 5. *The set* F *is a closed face in* K.

PROOF. As $F=J_1^{\perp}$, it is closed. Fix x in F and suppose that there are x_1 and x_2 in K and $0<t<1$ such that $x=tx_1+(1-t)x_2$. Also fix a in I_1 and $\varepsilon>0$. Since $a=\upsilon(A)$ for some A in $B(H)_s$ with $P(A)=0$ it follows from [3, Proposition 4] that there is an element b in A such that $b\succeq 0$, $-b\preceq a\preceq b$ and $x(b)<\varepsilon$. Since $x_i(b)\geq 0$ and $0\leq tx_1(b)+$ $+(1-t)x_2(b)=x(b)<\varepsilon$, $x_i(b)<\varepsilon$, $i=1,2$. Similarly since $b-a\succeq 0$ and $a+b\succeq 0$, $x_i(a)\leq x_i(b)$ and $-x_i(b)\leq x_i(a)$ and therefore $|x_i(a)|<\varepsilon$. As ε was arbitrary $x_i(a)=0$ and $x_1,x_2\varepsilon F$.

The following facts are easy to establish and their proofs

will be omitted.

1) The formula $\upsilon(D)\upsilon(A)=\upsilon(\frac{1}{2}(AD+DA))=\upsilon(A)\upsilon(D)$ with D in $\mathcal{D}_s$ and A in $\mathcal{B}(H)_s$ defines an abelian multiplication of A by $\upsilon(\mathcal{D})$. This multiplication is well-defined because $\mathcal{D}J=J\mathcal{D}=J$. Note that states on A are $\upsilon(\mathcal{D})$-central.

2) Let $H(\mathcal{D})$ denote the complex homomorphisms of $\mathcal{D}$. There is a bijection between $H(\mathcal{D})$ and the extreme points of F given by the formula

$$h \mapsto h\circ P\circ \upsilon^{-1}=x_h.$$

3) There is a bijection between the projections P in $\mathcal{D}$ and the subsets σ of $\mathbb{N}$ given by

$$P \mapsto \{n: Pe_n=e_n\}=\sigma.$$

The projection in $\mathcal{D}$ corresponding to the subset σ of $\mathbb{N}$ shall be denoted by P_σ and its image in A by p_σ.

For $\sigma\subseteq\mathbb{N}$ write

$$K_\sigma=\{x\varepsilon K: x(p_\sigma)=1\}$$

and for h in $H(\mathcal{D})$ write

$$K_h=\bigcap\{K_\sigma: x_h(p_\sigma)=1\}.$$

Note that by Assertion 1 of Section 2 if $x\varepsilon K_\sigma$ then $x(p_\sigma a)=x(a)$ $=x(ap_\sigma)$ for all a in A.

Recall that if K_0 is a face in K, then its complementary set K_0' is the union of all faces disjoint from K_o and that K_o is a split face if K_0' is convex (i.e., a face) and every point in K can be written uniquely as a convex combination of points from K_0 and K_0'.

PROPOSITION 6. *If* $\sigma\subseteq\mathbb{N}$, *then* K_σ *is a closed split face of* K. *If* $h\varepsilon H(\mathcal{D})$, *then* K_h *is a closed split face of* K.

PROOF. It is straightforward that K_σ is a closed face of K. To see that K_σ is split let us begin by showing $K_\sigma'=K_{\mathbb{N}\setminus\sigma}$. It is clear that the face $K_{\mathbb{N}\setminus\sigma}$ is disjoint from K_σ and so $K_{\mathbb{N}\setminus\sigma}\subseteq K_\sigma'$. For the reverse inclusion suppose $x\varepsilon K_\sigma'$ and write $t=x(p_\sigma)$. As $x\varepsilon K_\sigma'$, $t<1$. If $t>0$, define x_1 and x_2 on A by

$$x_1(a)=t^{-1}x(p_\sigma a) \text{ and } x_2(a)=(1-t)^{-1}x((e-p_\sigma)a).$$

As $0<t<1$ and states on A are $\upsilon(\mathcal{D})$-central, x_1 and x_2 are well-defined and belong to K. Further, $x=tx_1+(1-t)x_2$ so that $x_1\varepsilon$ face$(x)\subseteq K_\sigma'$. On the other hand $x_1\varepsilon K_\sigma$ which is impossible. Hence,

$t=0$ and $x \varepsilon K_{\mathbb{N}\setminus\sigma}$. To show K is the direct convex sum of K_σ and $K_{\mathbb{N}\setminus\sigma}$ it suffices to show that the linear spaces $\langle K_\sigma \rangle$ and $\langle K_{\mathbb{N}\setminus\sigma} \rangle$ generated by K_σ and $K_{\mathbb{N}\setminus\sigma}$ respectively have 0 intersection [1, Proposition II.6.1]. If $f \varepsilon \langle K_\sigma \rangle \cap \langle K_{\mathbb{N}\setminus\sigma} \rangle$, then $f(a)=f(p_\sigma a)=f((e-p_\sigma)p_\sigma a)=0$ for all a in A and so $f=0$. Thus, each K_σ is a closed split face in K. As arbitrary intersections of closed split faces are split [1, Proposition II.6.20], K_h is also split.

The following fact will be needed in the sequel. No doubt it has been observed before.

PROPOSITION 7. *If* X *is a compact convex subset of a locally convex space and* x *is an extreme point of* X, *then each* y *in* X *may be written uniquely as* $tx+(1-t)z$ *with* $0 \le t \le 1$ *and* $z \varepsilon \{x\}'$.

PROOF. Since $\{x\}$ is a closed face, by [1, Proposition II.6.5] there is a representation $y=tx+(1-t)z$ as above. Suppose $y=sx+$ $+(1-s)w$ with $0 \le s \le 1$ and $w \varepsilon \{x\}'$, and assume $s \le t$. As $w \varepsilon \{x\}'$, there is a sequence a_n in $A(X)$ such that $a_n \ge 0$, $x(a_n) \ge 1$ and $w(a_n) \to 0$ as $n \to \infty$ [1, Proposition II.6.5]. Now $t-s \ge 0$. On the other hand, since $(t-s)x=(1-s)w-(1-t)z$

$$0 \ge \limsup\{(1-s)w(a_n)-(1-t)z(a_n)\} \ge \liminf (t-s)x(a_n) \ge t-s$$

so that $t=s$ and $w=z$.

The proof that F is a closed split face rests on the fact that each $\{x_h\}$ is a closed split face. This in turn follows from the fact that $\{x_h\}$ is split in K_h. The heart of the proof of this latter fact is the content of the next Proposition.

PROPOSITION 8. *Fix* h *in* $H(\mathcal{D})$ *and suppose* $x \varepsilon K_h \cap \{x_h\}'$. *If* f *and* f_h *denote the states on* $B(H)$ *induced by* x *and* x_h *respectively, then* f *and* f_h *are disjoint.*

PROOF. Let $\{\pi, H_\pi, \xi\}$ denote the representation of $B(H)$ induced by f, where ξ represents the cannonical cyclic vector. It must be shown there is no unit vector η in H_π such that $f_h = \pi \circ \omega_\eta$ where ω_η denotes the vector state induced by η. Assume such a vector η exists and write H_h for the closure of $\{\pi(T)\eta : T \varepsilon B(H)\}$. Note that the restriction of π to H_h is equivalent to the representation induced by f_h. If $\eta_1 \varepsilon H_h \cap \{\eta\}^\perp$, then by [3, proof of

Corollary 3] there is a sequence $\{P_n\}$ of projections in $\mathcal{D}$ such that $\pi(P_n)\eta=\eta$ and $||\pi(P_n)\eta_1|| \to 0$ as $n \to \infty$. As $x\varepsilon K_h$, $f(P_n)=h(P_n)=$ $=f_h(P_n)=1$ and so (by Cauchy-Schwarz) $\pi(P_n)\xi=\xi$. Hence, $(\xi, \eta_1)=$ $\lim(\pi(P_n)\xi,\eta_1)=\lim(\xi,\pi(P_n)\eta_1)=0$ and therefore $\xi=\alpha\eta+\xi'$, for some vector ξ' in $H_h^{\perp}$ and some complex number α. Since H_h is reducing for $\pi(B(H))$, $f=|\alpha|^2 f_h+(1-|\alpha|^2)g$, where g is the composition of π with the vector state induced by the appropriate multiple of ξ'. Since g is $\mathcal{D}$-central and $x\varepsilon\{x_h\}'$ $\alpha=0$. Hence $\xi\perp H_h$. As ξ is cyclic, this is impossible so no such η can exist.

THEOREM 9. *If* $h\varepsilon H(\mathcal{D})$, *then* $\{x_h\}$ *is a closed split face in* K.

PROOF. As F is a face x_h is an extreme point of K and so in view of Proposition 7 it suffices to show $\{x_h\}'$ is convex. This will be accomplished in two steps. Let us first show $K_h\cap\{x_h\}'$ is convex. Suppose $x=tx_1+(1-t)x_2$ is a convex combination of elements of $K_h\cap\{x_h\}'$. Let f, f_1, and f_2 denote the states on $B(H)$ arising from x, x_1, and x_2 and let $\{\pi,H_\pi,\xi\}$, $\{\pi_1,H_1,\xi_1\}$ and $\{\pi_2,H_2,\xi_2\}$ denote the representations induced by f, f_1, f_2. Note that π is equivalent to a subrepresentation of $\pi_1\oplus\pi_2$. In fact it may be assumed that $\xi=(t)^{\frac{1}{2}}\xi_1+(1-t)^{\frac{1}{2}}\xi_2$. As K_h is a face $x\varepsilon K_h$. If $x\notin\{x_h\}'$, then $x=sx_h+(1-s)y$ with $0<s\leq 1$ and $y\varepsilon\{x_h\}'$. It follows that there is a unit vector η in the closure of $\{\pi(T)\xi:T\varepsilon B(H)\}$ such that $f_h=\pi\circ\omega_\eta$. Now by Proposition 8, f_h is disjoint from f_1 and f_2 and so $\eta\perp\{\pi(B(H))\xi_1\}+\{\pi(B(H))\xi_2\}$. Hence no such η exists and $x\varepsilon\{x_h\}'$. Thus $K_h\cap\{x_h\}'$ is convex and so by Proposition 7 $\{x_h\}$ is a closed split face in K_h. To complete the proof it is enough to show that $\{x_h\}'$ is the convex hull of K_h' and $K_h\cap\{x_h\}'$. Fix x in $\{x_h\}'$. As K_h is split, x has a unique representation $x=ty+(1-t)z$, where $y\varepsilon K_h$ and $z\varepsilon K_h'$. Since $\{x_h\}$ is split in K_h , y has a unique representation $y=sx_h+(1-s)z_1$, where $z_1\varepsilon K_h\cap\{x_h\}'$. Thus, $x=stx_h+(1-st)w$, where w is convex combination of z and z_1. Since $x\varepsilon\{x_h\}'$, st=0 and x=w so that x belongs to the convex hull of K_h' and $K_h\cap\{x_h\}'$. For the reverse inclusion suppose $x\varepsilon K_h'$, $y\varepsilon K_h\cap\{x_h\}'$ and $tx+(1-t)y=$ $=sx_h+(1-s)z$ for some $0\leq t\leq 1$, $0\leq s\leq 1$ and $z\varepsilon\{x_h\}'$. As K_h is split, $z=rz_1+(1-r)z_2$ with $z_1\varepsilon K_h$, $z_2\varepsilon K_h'$, and $0\leq r\leq 1$. Since the decomposition $tx+(1-t)y$ is unique with respect to K_h and K_h' , $(1-t)y=$ $=sx_h+(1-s)rz_1$. But

$y\varepsilon\{x_h\}'$ so $s=0$ and $tx+(1-t)y\varepsilon\{x_h\}'$.

THEOREM 10. *F is a closed split face in* K.

PROOF. By [1, Theorem II.6.18] it suffices to show that if b is a real-valued function on K such that its restriction to F belongs to $A(F)^+$ and its restriction to $K\setminus F$ is 0, then $\hat{b}$ is affine. (Recall that $\hat{b}(x)=\inf\{a(x):a\varepsilon A(K),\ a\geq b\}$.) Let b denote such a function and fix $x,y\varepsilon K$ and $0<t<1$. It is immediate from its definition that $\hat{b}(tx+(1-t)y)\geq t\hat{b}(x)+(1-t)\hat{b}(y)$. To establish the reverse inequality it will be shown that $\{a\varepsilon A(K):a\geq b\}$ is "almost downward directed". Fix $\varepsilon>0$ and select a_1,a_2 in $A(K)$ such that $a_i\geq b, i=1,2$ and $\varepsilon+b(x)>a_1(x)$, $\varepsilon+b(y)>a_2(y)$. Note that the restriction of $\upsilon(\mathcal{D}_s)$ to F is A(F) so that there is $d=\upsilon(D)$ with D in $\mathcal{D}$ such that d agrees with b on F. (Throughout the proof no distinction will be made between A and A(K).) Select a $\mathcal{D}$-partition $\{P_1,\ldots,P_n\}$ and non-negative real numbers δ_i so that $||D-\Sigma\delta_iP_i||<\varepsilon$. If $h\varepsilon H(\mathcal{D})$ then

$$a_1(x_h)\geq b(x_h)=d(x_h)=h(D)>h(\Sigma\delta_iP_i)-\varepsilon=\delta_j-\varepsilon.$$

Similarly, $a_2(x_h)>\delta_j-\varepsilon$. (Here j is the unique index such that $h(P_j)=1$.) Since $\{x_h\}$ is split, by [1, Theorem II.6.15] there is a_h in A(K) such that $a_i\succcurlyeq a_h\succcurlyeq -\varepsilon e$, $i=1,2$ and $a_h(x_h)=d(x_h)>\delta_j-\varepsilon$. For each h, let j denote the index such that $h(P_j)=1$ and choose a projection Q_h in $\mathcal{D}$ such that $Q_h\leq P_j$, $h(Q_h)=1$, and if $k\varepsilon H(\mathcal{D})$ with $k(Q_h)=1$, then $a_h(x_k)>\delta_j-2\varepsilon$. (The projection Q_h exists because $H(\mathcal{D})$ is hyperstonean and $\mathcal{D}\cong C(H(\mathcal{D}))\cong A(F)$.) The family $\{Q_h:h\varepsilon H(\mathcal{D})\}$ determines an open cover of $H(\mathcal{D})$. Let $\{Q_1,\ldots,Q_m\}$ denote a subset of this family corresponding to a finite subcover. By refining the subset if necessary, it may be assumed that $\{Q_1,\ldots,Q_m\}$ is a $\mathcal{D}$-partition. In addition this set enjoys the following properties. If $1\leq i\leq m$, there is a P_j such that $Q_i\leq P_j$ and there is a self-adjoint operator A_i such that if k is in $H(\mathcal{D})$ with $k(Q_i)=1$, then $\upsilon(A_i)(x_k)>\delta_j-2\varepsilon$ and $-\varepsilon e\preccurlyeq\upsilon(A_i)\preccurlyeq a_1,a_2$. Thus, if we write $a=\upsilon(\Sigma Q_iA_iQ_i)$, then $a\succcurlyeq-\varepsilon e$, $a\preccurlyeq a_1,a_2$ and if $h\varepsilon H(\mathcal{D})$ with $h(P_j)=1$, then $a(x_h)>\delta_j-2\varepsilon>b(x_h)-3\varepsilon$. Since $\{x_h:h\varepsilon H(\mathcal{D})\}$ are the extreme points of F, $a+3\varepsilon e$ is greater than b on F. Since $a+3\varepsilon e\succcurlyeq 0$, $a+3\varepsilon e$ is greater than b on $K\setminus F$ and so $a+3\varepsilon e\geq b$. Hence,

$$4\varepsilon+t\hat{b}(x)+(1-t)\hat{b}(y)\geq 3\varepsilon+ta_1(x)+(1-t)a_2(y)\geq 3\varepsilon+a(tx+(1-t)y)\geq \geq\hat{b}(tx+(1-t)y).$$

COROLLARY 11. *If* A *is a self-adjoint operator with* $P(A)=0$, *and* $\varepsilon>0$, *then there are self-adjoint operators* A_1 *and* A_2 *such that*

i) $P(A_1)=P(A_2)=0$

ii) $A=A_1-A_2$

iii) $||A_i||\leq A+\varepsilon$, $i=1,2$

iv) *For each* $\delta>0$ *there is a* $\mathcal{D}$*-partition* $\{P_1,\ldots,P_n\}$ *such that* $\Sigma P_i A_j P_i\geq -\delta 1$, $j=1,2$.

PROOF. This follows immediately from the Theorem and [1, Corollary II.6.16].

REMARKS. 1) Note that $\mathcal{D}$ has the extension property with respect to $\mathcal{B}(H)$ if and only if every extreme point of the $\mathcal{D}$-central states has the form $h\circ P$ for some h in $H(\mathcal{D})$ and this occurs if and only if F=K. As F is a Bauer simplex it is natural to ask if K is a (Bauer) simplex.

2) Suppose $A^+=C$; that is, suppose the orders ($\prec$) and ($\leq$) coincide. If $A\in\mathcal{B}(H)_s$ and $P(A)=0$, then $\upsilon(A)$ is 0 on F and since F is split in K there are a^+ and a^- in A such that $\upsilon(A)=a^+-a^-$, a^+ and a^- are 0 on F and $a^+,a^-\geq 0$. It follows that there are positive operators A^+ and A^- and B in $\mathcal{J}$ such that $A=A^+-A^-+B$ and $P(A^+)=P(A^-)=0$. But P is faithful on $\mathcal{B}(H)$ so $A^+=A^-=0$ and $A\in\mathcal{J}$. Thus, if $A^+=C$ then $\upsilon(\mathcal{D}_s)=A$ and $\mathcal{D}$ has the extension property with respect $\mathcal{B}(H)$.

REFERENCES

1. Alfsen, E.M.: *Compact convex sets and boundary integrals*, Springer-Verlag, New York/Heidelberg/Berlin, 1971.
2. Anderson, J.: Extensions, restrictions and representations of states on C*-algebras, *Trans.Amer.Math.Soc.* 249 (1979), 303-329.
3. Anderson, J.: Extreme points in sets of positive linear maps on B(H), *J.Functional Analysis* 31 (1979), 195-217.
4. Anderson, J.: A maximal abelian subalgebra with the extention property, *Math.Scand.* 42 (1978), 010-110.
5. Anderson, J.: Pathology in the Calkin algebra, *J.Operator Theory* 2 (1979), 159-167.

6. Kadison, R.V.; Singer, I.M.: Extensions of pure states, *Amer.J.Math.* 81 (1959), 383-400.

7. Powers, R.T.: Representations of uniformly hyperfinite algebras and their associated von Neumann rings, *Ann.Math.* 86 (1967), 138-171.

8. Wils, I.M.: Stone-Čech compactifications and representations of operator algebras, *Ph.D. thesis*, Catholic University of Nijmegen, 1968.

Joel Anderson
Department of Mathematics,
Pennsylvania State University,
University Park, PA 16802,
U.S.A.

A C^*-ALGEBRA APPROACH TO THE COWEN-DOUGLAS THEORY

C.Apostol and M.Martin

Let $\mathcal{H}$ be a separable infinite-dimensional Hilbert space over the complex field C and let $\mathcal{L}(\mathcal{H})$ denote the algebra of all bounded linear operators on $\mathcal{H}$.

For any open connected subset Ω of C and for any positive integer n, let $\mathcal{B}_n(\Omega)$ denote the operators S in $\mathcal{L}(\mathcal{H})$ which satisfy:

(i) $(\omega-S)(\mathcal{H})=\mathcal{H}, \quad \omega\in\Omega$

(ii) $\bigvee_{\omega\in\Omega} \ker(\omega-S)=\mathcal{H}$

(iii) $\dim\ker(\omega-S)=n, \quad \omega\in\Omega.$

M.J.Cowen and R.G.Douglas [2] initiated a systematic study of the unitary orbit associated with an element of $\mathcal{B}_n(\Omega)$ by means of complex Hermitian geometry techniques. To be more specific, they proved that $\tilde{T}\in\mathcal{B}_n(\Omega)$ is unitarily equivalent with $T\in\mathcal{B}_n(\Omega)$ if and only if $\tilde{T}|\ker(\omega-\tilde{T})^{n+1}$ is unitarily equivalent with $T|\ker(\omega-T)^{n+1}$ for any $\omega\in\Omega$ (the corresponding unitary operators depend on ω).

Let $\mathcal{S}$ be a subset in $\mathcal{L}(\mathcal{H})$ containing the identity operator I and an operator $T\in\mathcal{B}_n(\Omega)$ and let $\varphi:\mathcal{S}\to\mathcal{L}(\mathcal{H})$ be a map such that $\varphi(I)=I$ and $\varphi(T)\in\mathcal{B}_n(\Omega)$. The assumption $I\in\mathcal{S}$ is not essential in the sequel, but we use it to shorten some proofs.

Suppose $\mathcal{S}$ is included in $\{T\}'$, the commutant of T and $\varphi(\mathcal{S})\subset\varphi(T)\}'$; in Theorem C below we show that φ is the restriction to $\mathcal{S}$ of an inner automorphism in $\mathcal{L}(\mathcal{H})$ if and only if $\varphi(X)|\ker(\omega-\varphi(T))^{n+1}$ is unitarily equivalent with $X|\ker(\omega-T)^{n+1}$ for any $X\in\mathcal{S}$, $\omega\in\Omega$ (the corresponding unitary operators depend on ω only). If $\mathcal{S}=\{T,I\}$ we recapture the result of Cowen and Douglas.

In fact we shall give a local description of the restrictions to $\mathcal{S}$ of inner automorphisms in $\mathcal{L}(\mathcal{H})$, without the assumption $\mathcal{S}\subset\{T\}'$ (see Theorem B).

The above results are consequences of our main Theorem A on

some C^∞-fields of finite-dimensional C^*-algebras.

Throughout the paper $\mathcal{S}$ will denote a subset in $\mathcal{L}(\mathcal{H})$ containing I and $T\varepsilon\mathcal{B}_n(\Omega)$, where Ω is an open subset in C.

For any $\omega\varepsilon\Omega$, the operators R_ω, P_ω will be defined by the equations:

$$R_\omega=(\omega-T)^*[(\omega-T)(\omega-T)^*]^{-1}$$
$$P_\omega=I-R_\omega(\omega-T).$$

It is plain that P_ω is the orthogonal projection of $\mathcal{H}$ onto $\ker(\omega-T)$.

For each $\omega\varepsilon\Omega$ and each non-negative integer k put

$$\mathcal{A}^k_\omega=\{P_\omega R_\omega^{*p}Y^*XR_\omega^qP_\omega : 0\le p,q\le k,\quad X,Y\varepsilon\mathcal{S}\}$$

$$\mathcal{B}^k_\omega=\{P_\omega R_\omega^{*p}Y^*XR_\omega^qP_\omega : \max(p,q)=k+1, \min(p,q)\le k,\ X,Y\varepsilon\mathcal{S}\}$$

and denote by $\mathcal{C}^k_\omega$, $\mathcal{D}^k_\omega$ the C^*-algebras generated in $\mathcal{L}(\mathcal{H})$ by $\mathcal{A}^k_\omega$, resp. $\mathcal{A}^k_\omega\cup\mathcal{B}^k_\omega$.

The union $\bigcup_{k\ge0}\mathcal{C}^k_\omega$ is obviously a C^*-algebra which we shall denote by $\mathcal{C}^\infty_\omega$.

Let $C^\infty(\Omega,\mathcal{L}(\mathcal{H}))$ denote the *-algebra of all $\mathcal{L}(\mathcal{H})$-valued infinitely differentiable functions defined in Ω, with the involution defined by the equation

$$A^*(\omega)=A(\omega)^*,\qquad A\varepsilon C^\infty(\Omega,\mathcal{L}(\mathcal{H}))$$

and let $C^\infty(\Omega)$ denote all C-valued infinitely differentiable functions defined in Ω.

We shall denote by $\Gamma(\Omega,\mathcal{C}^k)$, $\Gamma(\Omega,\mathcal{D}^k)$, $\Gamma(\Omega,\mathcal{C}^\infty)$ the *-subalgebras in $C^\infty(\Omega,\mathcal{L}(\mathcal{H}))$ determined by the conditions:

$$\Gamma(\Omega,\mathcal{C}^k)=\{A\varepsilon C^\infty(\Omega,\mathcal{L}(\mathcal{H})) : A(\omega)\varepsilon\mathcal{C}^k_\omega\}$$

$$\Gamma(\Omega,\mathcal{D}^k)=\{A\varepsilon C^\infty(\Omega,\mathcal{L}(\mathcal{H})) : A(\omega)\varepsilon\mathcal{D}^k_\omega\}$$

$$\Gamma(\Omega,\mathcal{C}^\infty)=\{A\varepsilon C^\infty(\Omega,\mathcal{L}(\mathcal{H})) : A(\omega)\varepsilon\mathcal{C}^\infty_\omega\}.$$

We have $P\varepsilon\Gamma(\Omega,\mathcal{C}^0)$, $R\varepsilon C^\infty(\Omega,\mathcal{L}(\mathcal{H}))$ where P and R are defined by the equations

$$P(\omega)=P_\omega,\quad R(\omega)=R_\omega.$$

Finally observe that the usual $\frac{\partial}{\partial\omega}$ and $\frac{\partial}{\partial\bar{\omega}}$ derivatives determine two linear maps in $C^\infty(\Omega,L(H))$. We shall denote this maps by D resp. $\bar{D}$. It is plain that we have

$$(DA)^* = \bar{D}A^*, \quad A\in C^\infty(\Omega,L(H)).$$

THEOREM A. *There exist an open nonempty subset* $\Omega_o\subset\Omega$ *and* $1\le k\le n$ *with the properties:*

(i) $\Gamma(\Omega_o,C^k)=\Gamma(\Omega_o,C^\infty)$

(ii) *if* $\psi:\Gamma(\Omega_o,C^\infty)\to C^\infty(\Omega_o,L(H))$ *is an algebraic homomorphism such that*

$$\psi(P(D^p\bar{D}^qA)P)=\psi(P)(D^p\bar{D}^q\psi(A))\psi(P), \quad 0\le p,q\le 1, \quad A\in\Gamma(\Omega_o,C^{k-1})$$

then

$$\psi(P(D^p\bar{D}^qA)P)=\psi(P)(D^p\bar{D}^q\psi(A))\psi(P), \quad 0\le p,q, \quad A\in\Gamma(\Omega_o,C^\infty).$$

The proof of this theorem will be given after some preliminary lemmas.

1. LEMMA. *For any* ω *in* Ω *we have:*

(i) $(\omega-T)R_\omega = I$ *and* $P_\omega R_\omega=0$

(ii) $\ker(\omega-T)^{k+1}=\bigvee_{j=0}^{k} R_\omega^j P_\omega(H)$ *for each* $0\le k$

(iii) $H=\bigvee_{j\ge 0} R_\omega^j P_\omega(H)$.

PROOF. The relations (i) are obvious. Clearly, (ii) will easily follow if we prove that

$$\ker(\omega-T)^{k+1}=P_\omega(H)\oplus R_\omega(\ker(\omega-T)^k).$$

Since $(\omega-T)(\ker(\omega-T)^{k+1})\subset\ker(\omega-T)^k$ and $R_\omega(\omega-T)=I-P_\omega$ we have $\ker(\omega-T)^{k+1}\ominus P_\omega(H)\subset R_\omega(\ker(\omega-T)^k)$ hence

$$\ker(\omega-T)^{k+1}\subset P_\omega(H)\oplus R_\omega(\ker(\omega-T)^k)$$

and the reverse inclusion is obvious.

Using [1], Lemma 1.7 we know that we have

$$H=\bigvee_{\lambda\in\Omega}\ker(\lambda-T)=\bigvee_{k\ge 0}\ker(\omega-T)^k$$

thus (iii) becomes a consequence of (ii).

2. LEMMA. *The following relations hold:*

$$DR=-R^2,\ DR^*=R^*RP \text{ and } DP=-RP.$$

The proof is obvious, therefore we omit it.

As easy corollary of Lemma 2 is the following

3. LEMMA. *If* $PD\Gamma(\Omega_o,C^k)\subset\Gamma(\Omega_o,C^k)$ *for some open nonempty subset* $\Omega_o\subseteq\Omega$ *and* $1\leq k$, *then*

$$\Gamma(\Omega_o,C^k)=\Gamma(\Omega_o,C^\infty).$$

4. LEMMA. *Let* $V,W\in C^\infty(\Omega,L(H))$ *be given such that* $VWV=V$. *Then we have:*

$$DV=V(DF)+(DE)V-V(DW)V$$
$$\bar{D}V=V(\bar{D}F)+(\bar{D}E)V-V(\bar{D}W)V$$

where $F=WV$, $E=VW$.

PROOF. Since $VF=EV=V$ it follows that

$$V(DF)+(DE)V=V(DW)V+VW(DV)+(DE)V=$$
$$=V(DW)V+E(DV)+(DE)V=V(DW)V+D(EV)=V(DW)V+DV.$$

The rest of the proof is similar.

5. LEMMA. *Let* $E\in\Gamma(\Omega,C^\infty)$ *be a selfadjoint projection such that* $P(DE)=0$ *and* $E\Gamma(\Omega,C^1)(P-E)=\{0\}$. *Then we have* $E\Gamma(\Omega,C^\infty)(P-E)=\{0\}$.

PROOF. Let $A\in\Gamma(\Omega,C^\infty)$ be such that $EA(P-E)=0$. Since we have $0=D(EA(P-E))=(DE)A(P-E)+E(DA)(P-E)+EA(D(P-E))$ and by our assumption and Lemma 2 $E(DE)=P(D(P-E))=0$, it follows $E(DA)(P-E)=0$ and analogously $E(\bar{D}A)(P-E)=0$. Because $E(\omega)A^1_\omega(P_\omega-E(\omega))=\{0\}$ applying again Lemma 2 we derive easily $E\Gamma(\Omega,C^\infty)(P-E)=\{0\}$.

Our next lemma is a restatement of [2], Lemma 3.4.

6. LEMMA. *Let* $A\in C^\infty(\Omega,L(H))$ *be such that* $A=A^*=PA$. *Then there exist an open nonempty subset* $\Omega_o\subseteq\Omega$, *and two collections* $\{P_\alpha:1\leq\alpha\leq m\}\subset C^\infty(\Omega_o,L(H))$, $\{\mu_\alpha:1\leq\alpha\leq m\}\subset C^\infty(\Omega_o)$ *with the properties:*

(i) $\{P_\alpha(\omega):1\leq\alpha\leq m\}$ *are selfadjoint pairwise orthogonal projections in the* C^**-algebra generated in* $L(H)$ *by* $\{P_\omega,A(\omega)\}$.

(ii) $P=\sum_\alpha P_\alpha$ *and* $A=\sum_\alpha \mu_\alpha P_\alpha$ *in* $C^\infty(\Omega_o,L(H))$.

THE PROOF OF THEOREM A. By a repeated use of Lemma 6 we can find an open connected nonempty subset $\Omega_o\subset\Omega$, an integer $\min(2,n)\leq$ $\leq k\leq n$ and a pairwise orthogonal decomposition of P:

$$\{P_\alpha : 1\leq\alpha\leq m\}\subset\Gamma(\Omega_o,\mathcal{C}^{k-1})$$

where $P_\alpha(\omega)$ is a selfadjoint projection which is minimal in $\mathcal{C}^k_\omega$, $\omega\varepsilon\Omega_o$. Moreover, arguing as in [4], Ch.I, §11, we may assume that

$$P_\alpha\Gamma(\Omega_o,\mathcal{D}^{k-1})P_\beta=C^\infty(\Omega_o)U_{\alpha\beta}$$

where $U_{\alpha\beta}$ enjoy the properties:

$$U_{\alpha\alpha}=P_\alpha \ ,U^*_{\alpha\beta}=U_{\beta\alpha}=P_\beta U_{\beta\alpha} \ ,(U_{\alpha\beta}U^*_{\alpha\beta})^2=U_{\alpha\beta}U^*_{\alpha\beta}.$$

It is clear that either $U_{\alpha\beta}=0$ or $U_{\alpha\beta}U^*_{\alpha\beta}=P_\alpha$, $U^*_{\alpha\beta}U_{\alpha\beta}=P_\beta$.

Let $1\leq\alpha,\beta\leq m$ be given and suppose $U_{\alpha\beta}=0$. Denote by E the sum of all P_γ such that $U_{\alpha\gamma}\neq 0$. Since obviously E is a central projection in $\Gamma(\Omega_o, \mathcal{D}^{k-1})$ and under our assumption we have $k\geq 2$, therefore $\Gamma(\Omega_o,\mathcal{D}^{k-1})\supset\Gamma(\Omega_o,\mathcal{C}^1)$, and consequently

$$E\Gamma(\Omega_o,\mathcal{C}^1)(P-E)=\{0\}.$$

But we also have

$$E(DE)=E(DE)E=0, \quad (P-E)(D(P-E))=(P-E)(D(P-E))(P-E)=0$$

whence it follows $P(DE)=0$. Now applying Lemma 5 we derive $P_\alpha\Gamma(\Omega_o,\mathcal{C}^\infty)P_\beta=\{0\}$ and in particular

$$P_\alpha\Gamma(\Omega_o,\mathcal{C}^k)P_\beta=C^\infty(\Omega_o)U_{\alpha\beta}.$$

Remark that if $U_{\alpha\beta}\neq 0$, the last relation holds valid in view of the minimality of $P_\alpha(\omega)$ and $P_\beta(\omega)$ in $\mathcal{C}^k_\omega$, $\omega\varepsilon\Omega_o$. Because we have $\Gamma(\Omega_o,\mathcal{C}^k)=\sum_{\alpha,\beta=1}^{m} P_\alpha\Gamma(\Omega_o,\mathcal{C}^k)P_\beta$ we deduce

$$(*) \qquad \Gamma(\Omega_o,\mathcal{C}^k)=\sum_{\alpha,\beta=1}^{m} C^\infty(\Omega_o)U_{\alpha\beta}.$$

To conclude the proof it sufficies to prove that we have

(1) $\quad P(DU_{\alpha\beta})\varepsilon\Gamma(\Omega_o,\mathcal{C}^k)$

(2) $\quad \begin{cases}\psi(P(DU_{\alpha\beta}))=\psi(P)(D(\psi(U_{\alpha\beta})))\\ \psi((\bar{D}U_{\alpha\beta})P)=(\bar{D}(\psi(U_{\alpha\beta})))\psi(P), \qquad 1\leq\alpha,\beta\leq m.\end{cases}$

Indeed (i) of our theorem will follow by Lemma 3, from (1) and (*), whence (ii) will be a consequence of (2) and (*).

Let us put $G=\{P_\alpha A(D^p\bar{D}^qB)CP_\beta : 0\leq p+q\leq 1, A,B,C\varepsilon\Gamma(\Omega_o,\mathcal{C}^{k-1})\}$. We leave to the reader as an exercise to show that, eventually decreasing Ω_o, we may suppose that any $U_{\alpha\beta}\neq 0$ is a finite product of $U_{\alpha',\beta'}$'s belonging to G. A hint for this exercise is that if

$\omega_o \varepsilon \Omega_o$ is given then $U_{\alpha\beta}(\omega_o)$ is a finite product of elements belonging to G, evaluated at ω_o. Thus we are allowed to prove (1) and (2) assuming $U_{\alpha\beta} \varepsilon G$.

Let $U_{\alpha\beta}=P_\alpha A(DB)CP_\beta$ be given. We derive easily that

$$(\bar{D}U_{\alpha\beta})P,\ P(DU^*_{\alpha\beta})\varepsilon\Gamma(\Omega_o,C^k)$$

and

$$\psi((\bar{D}U_{\alpha\beta})P)=(\bar{D}(\psi(U_{\alpha\beta})))\psi(P)$$
$$\psi(P(DU^*_{\alpha\beta}))=\psi(P)(D(\psi(U^*_{\alpha\beta}))).$$

Putting in Lemma 4 $V=U_{\alpha\beta}$, $W=U^*_{\alpha\beta}$ and $E=P_\alpha$, $F=P_\beta$ we have

$P(DU_{\alpha\beta})=U_{\alpha\beta}(DP_\beta)+P(DP_\alpha)U_{\alpha\beta}-U_{\alpha\beta}(DU^*_{\alpha\beta})U_{\alpha\beta}\varepsilon\Gamma(\Omega_o,C^k)$.

If we put in Lemma 4 $V=\psi(U_{\alpha\beta})$, $W=\psi(U^*_{\alpha\beta})$ and $E=\psi(P_\alpha)$, $F=\psi(P_\beta)$ then, under our assumptions, we obtain

$\psi(P)(D(\psi(U_{\alpha\beta})))=\psi(U_{\alpha\beta})\psi(DP_\beta)+\psi(P)\psi(DP_\beta)\psi(U_{\alpha\beta})-\psi(U_{\alpha\beta})\psi(DU^*_{\alpha\beta})\psi(U_{\alpha\beta})=$ $=\psi(P(DU_{\alpha\beta}))$ and (1) and (2) are proved. We proceed analogously if $U_{\alpha\beta}=P_\alpha A(\bar{D}B)CP_\beta$.

THEOREM B. *Let $\varphi:S\to L(H)$ be a map such that $\varphi(I)=I$, $\tilde{T}=$ $=\varphi(T)\varepsilon B_n(\Omega)$. The following conditions are equivalent:*

(i) *φ is the restriction to S of an inner automorphism in $L(H)$*

(ii) *there exists a partial isometry U_ω such that*

$$U^*_\omega U_\omega=P_\omega,\quad U_\omega U^*_\omega=\tilde{P}_\omega$$

and

$$\tilde{P}_\omega\tilde{R}^{*p}_\omega\varphi(Y)^*\varphi(X)\tilde{R}^q_\omega\tilde{P}_\omega=U_\omega R^{*p}_\omega Y^*XR^q_\omega U^*_\omega$$

for any $\omega\varepsilon\Omega$, $0\le p,q\le n$, $X,Y\varepsilon S$, where ~-symbols are associated with $\tilde{T}$.

PROOF. It is clear that (i) implies (ii). Let $\Omega_o\subset\Omega$, $1\le k\le n$ be produced by Theorem A. If we define ψ by the equation

$$\psi(A)(\omega)=U_\omega A(\omega)U^*_\omega,\quad \omega\varepsilon\Omega_o,\quad A\varepsilon\Gamma(\Omega_o,C^\infty)$$

under our assumption (ii) we have $\psi(A)\varepsilon\Gamma(\Omega_o,C^\infty)$ whenever $A=PR^{*p}Y^*XR^qP$, $0\le p,q\le n$, $X,Y\varepsilon S$. Applying Theorem A and Lemma 2 we deduce $\psi(A)\varepsilon\Gamma(\Omega_o,\tilde{C}^\infty)$ for any $A\varepsilon(\Omega_o,C^\infty)$ and

$$(*)\qquad P_\omega R^{*p}_\omega\varphi(Y)^*\varphi(X)R^q_\omega P_\omega=U_\omega R^{*p}_\omega Y^*XR^q_\omega U^*_\omega$$

for any $0\leq p,q$, $X,Y\in S$.

Let $\omega_o\in\Omega_o$ be given. Since $I\in S$, Lemma 1 implies

$$H=\bigvee_{X\in S}\ \bigvee_{j\geq 0} XR^j_{\omega_o}P_{\omega_o}H=\bigvee_{j\geq 0} R^j_{\omega_o}P_{\omega_o}H.$$

Let $U\in L(H)$ be defined by the equation

$$U(XR^j_{\omega_o}P_{\omega_o}x)=\varphi(X)\tilde{R}^j_{\omega_o}\tilde{P}_{\omega_o}U_{\omega_o}x$$

for any $X\in S$, $0\leq j$, $x\in H$. Using (*) we derive that U is a well defined unitary operator and $UX=\varphi(X)U$, $X\in S$.

THEOREM C. *Suppose* $S\subset\{T\}'$, $\varphi(S)\subset\{\tilde{T}\}'$. *The following conditions are equivalent:*

(i) φ *is the restriction to* S *of an inner automorphism in* $L(H)$;

(ii) *there exists a unitary operator* $V_\omega:\ker(\omega-T)^{n+1}\to\ker(\omega-\tilde{T})^{n+1}$ *such that*

$$\varphi(X)\,|\ker(\omega-\tilde{T})^{n+1}=V_\omega XV^*_\omega\,|\ker(\omega-\tilde{T})^{n+1}$$

for any $\omega\in\Omega$, $X\in S$.

PROOF. It is sufficient to remark that under our assumptions, the present condition (ii) is equivalent with (ii) in Theorem B, where $U_\omega=V_\omega P_\omega$.

REFERENCES

1. Apostol, C.: The correction by compact perturbation of the singular behavior of operators, *Rev. Roumaine Math. Pures Appl.* 21(1976), 155-175.

2. Cowen, M.J.; Douglas, R.G.: Complex geometry and operator theory, *Acta Math.* 141(1978), 187-261.

3. Dixmier, J.: *Les C*-algèbres et leurs representations*, Gauthier-Villars, Paris, 1969.

4. Takesaki, M.: *Theory of Operator Algebras. I*, Springer-Verlag, New York, 1979.

C.Apostol and M.Martin
Department of Mathematics,
INCREST,
Bdul Păcii 220, 79622 Bucharest,
Romania.

ON PERIODIC DISTRIBUTION GROUPS

Ioana Ciorănescu

We give a spectral characterization of the infinitesimal generator of a periodic distribution group generalizing some results of Harn Bart [1] on periodic groups of class (C_o).

1. INTRODUCTION

Let X be a Banach space and A a closed and densely defined operator on X; then A is said to be *well-posed for the abstract Cauchy problem* in the sense of distributions if there exists $E\in L(\mathcal{D};L(X))$ satisfying the following conditions:

(i) $\operatorname{supp} E\subset[0,+)$;

(ii) $E'-AE=\delta\otimes I_X$; $E'-EA=\delta\otimes I_{D(A)}$

where $\mathcal{D}$ is the test functions space of L. Schwartz, E' is the derivative of E, I_X and $I_{D(A)}$ are the identities on X and on the domain D(A) of A, respectively.

Following J.L. Lions we shall call E in the above definition a *distribution semi-group* and A its *infinitesimal generator* [8].

An $L(X)$-valued distribution E is called a *distribution group* if

(a) $E(\varphi*\psi)=E(\varphi)\,E(\psi)$, for every $\varphi,\psi\in\mathcal{D}$;

(b) $E=E_+ + E_-$ where E_+ and $\check{E}_-$ are distribution semigroups (where $\check{E}$ is defined by $\check{E}(\varphi)=E(\check{\varphi})$, $\varphi\in\mathcal{D}$ and $\check{\varphi}(t)=\varphi(-t)$).

A distribution group E is called *tempered* if E_+, $E\in L(S;L(X))$, S being the space of rapidly decreasing test functions.

By a result of Lions [8] the generator A of a tempered distribution group has purely imaginary spectrum; a complete characterization of the generator of a tempered distribution group was given in [4], namely we have:

THEOREM 1.1. *A densely defined and closed operator* A *with purely imaginary spectrum is the generator of a tempered distribution group if and only if there are* $n_o, m_o \in \mathbb{N}$ *such that*

(1.1) $$||R(\lambda;A)|| \leq \text{const.}(1+|\lambda|)^{n_o}|Re\lambda|^{-m_o} \text{ for } Re\lambda\neq 0.$$

Moreover we have

(1.2) $$R(\lambda;A)=\begin{cases} E_+(e^{-\lambda t}) & \text{for } Re\lambda>0 \\ -E_-(e^{-\lambda t}) & \text{for } Re\lambda<0 \end{cases}$$

and

(1.3) $$E(\varphi)=\frac{1}{2\pi}\lim_{\varepsilon\to 0_+}\int_{-\infty}^{+\infty}[R(\varepsilon+it;A)-R(-\varepsilon+it;A)]\hat{\varphi}(t)dt, \qquad \varphi\in\mathcal{D}$$ *(where* $\hat{\varphi}(t)=\int_{-\infty}^{+\infty}e^{ist}\varphi(s)ds$*).*

Let E be a tempered distribution group and consider

$$\sigma=\{E(\varphi);\ \varphi\in\mathcal{D}\} \text{ and } \mathcal{R}=\{R(\lambda;A);\ Re\lambda\neq 0\}.$$

Denoting by $\mathcal{B}^c$ the commutant of a set $\mathcal{B}\subset L(X)$ we can easily get from (1.2) and (1.3) that

(1.4) $$\sigma^c=\mathcal{R}^c \text{ and } \sigma^{cc}=\mathcal{R}^{cc}.$$

Let us put $\mathcal{B}=\sigma^{cc}=\mathcal{R}^{cc}$; then $\mathcal{B}$ is a strongly closed subalgebra of $L(X)$ containing the identity, $\mathcal{B}\supset\sigma\cup\mathcal{R}$ and the spectrum of each $B\in\mathcal{B}$ with respect to $\mathcal{B}$ coincides with $\sigma(\mathcal{B})$.

Let $M=\{m\}$ be the set of maximal ideals of $\mathcal{B}$ and $B\to B(m)$ the Gelfand representation of $\mathcal{B}$ in the space $C(M)$ of continuous functions on M; then for $B\in\mathcal{B}$, $\sigma(B)=B(M)=\{B(m);\ m\in M\}$.

As $\mathcal{B}\subset\mathcal{R}$, by a well-known result [7], there are $M_1, M_2\subset M$, such that

$$M=M_1\cup M_2,\quad M_1\cap M_2=\emptyset$$

and a function $\alpha\in C(M)$ such that

(1.5) $$R(\lambda;A)(m)=\begin{cases}(\lambda-\alpha(m))^{-1}, & m\in M_1 \\ 0, & m\in M_2\end{cases}, \qquad Re\lambda\neq 0$$

and $\sigma(A)=\alpha(M_1)$.

Let us put $A_n=nAR(n;A)$, $n\in\mathbb{N}$; there $A_n\in L(X)$, $\lim_{n\to\infty} R(\lambda;A_n)=$

$R(\lambda;A)$ and by a result of H.Fattorini [5]:

$$(1.6)\qquad E(\varphi)=\lim_{n\to+\infty}\int_{-\infty}^{+\infty} e^{tA_n}\varphi(t)dt, \qquad \varphi\in\mathcal{D}.$$

Then putting $\alpha_n(m)=A_n(m)$, $m\in M$, it is clear by (1.5) that $\alpha_n(m)\to\alpha(m)$ $(n\to\infty)$ uniformly on M_1 and using (1.6) we finally get

$$(1.7)\qquad E(\varphi)(m)=\int_{-\infty}^{+\infty} e^{t\alpha(m)}\varphi(t)dt, \qquad \varphi\in\mathcal{D}\ ,\ m\in M_1\ .$$

Let us remark that the relation (1.7) is valid for arbitrary distribution semi-groups (see [2]).

2. THE SPECTRAL CHARACTERIZATION OF PERIODIC DISTRIBUTION GROUPS

Let X be a Banach space and E an $L(X)$-valued distribution; we say that E is:

(α) *periodic* if $E(\varphi)=E(\tau_T\varphi)$, for some T>0 and every $\varphi\in\mathcal{D}$, where $\tau_T\varphi(t)=\varphi(t-T)$;

(β) *strongly periodic* if for every $x\in X$, the X-valued distribution E_x defined by $E_x(\varphi)=E(\varphi)x$, $\varphi\in\mathcal{D}$, is periodic;

(γ) *weakly periodic* if for every $x^*\in X^*$ and $x\in X$, the scalar distribution x^*Ex defined by $x^*Ex(\varphi)=x^*E(\varphi)x$, $\varphi\in\mathcal{D}$, is periodic.

Let us denote by P_T the space of infinitely differentiable functions of period T>0 and let us call a *T-unitary function* a function $\xi\in\mathcal{D}$ such that $\sum_{-\infty}^{+\infty}\xi(t-nT)=1$, $t\in\mathbb{R}$. Then each periodic distribution E can be extended to the space P_T by the formula $E(\Theta)=E(\xi\Theta)$, $\Theta\in P_T$, independently of the unitary function ξ (see [9]).

We have the following essential result which can be proved exactly as in the scalar case [9]:

$E\in L(\mathcal{D};L(X))$ is periodic of period T>0 if and only if

$$(2.1)\qquad E=\sum_{-\infty}^{+\infty} A_n e^{in\omega t},\quad \omega=\frac{2\pi}{T}$$

where the convergence holds in $L(S;L(X))$ and

$$(2.2)\qquad A_n=\frac{1}{T}E(e^{-in\omega t}),\qquad n\in\mathbb{Z}$$

are in $L(X)$ such that the sequence $\{||A_n||\}_{n\in\mathbb{Z}}$ is of slow growth *(that is* $||A_n|| \leq \text{const.}|n|^k$, *for a given* $k \in \mathbb{N}$).

The series (2.1) is called *the Fourier series of* E and the operators A_n given by (2.2) are called *the Fourier coefficients of* E.

It is clear that each periodic vector-valued distribution is tempered.

In the case of $L(X)$-valued functions the above three notions of periodicity are equivalent, as was proved in [1], Theorem 2.1. Using the Fourier expansion (2.1) and a similar argument as in [1], we obtain the following result:

PROPOSITION 2.1. *Let* $E \in L(\mathcal{D};L(X))$; *then the following three statements are equivalent:*

(α) *E is periodic;*

(β) *E is strongly periodic;*

(γ) *E is weakly periodic.*

Further we restrict ourselves for simplicity to the case when E has period 2π. Our main result is:

THEOREM 2.2. *A closed and densely defined operator* A *is the generator of a periodic distribution group of period* 2π *if and only if*

a) $\sigma(A) \subset i\mathbb{Z}$ *and consists of poles of the resolvent which satisfy*

$$||R(\lambda;A)|| \leq \text{const.}(1+|\lambda|)^{n_o}, \qquad \text{Re}\lambda > \varepsilon_o$$

for some $n_o \in \mathbb{N}$, $\varepsilon_o > 0$.

b) *the set of eigenvectors of* A *spans a dense subspace in* X.

PROOF. *Necessity.* Let A be the generator of the periodic distribution group E, of period 2π. Then using (1.7) and the periodicity of E, we have:

$$(2.3) \qquad \int_{-\infty}^{+\infty} e^{t\alpha(m)}\varphi(t)dt = \int_{-\infty}^{+\infty} e^{(t+2\pi)\alpha(m)}\varphi(t)dt, \qquad \varphi \in \mathcal{D}, \; m \in M_1 .$$

For each $m \in M$ there is $\varphi_m \in \mathcal{D}$ with $\int_{-\infty}^{+\infty} e^{t\alpha(m)}\varphi(t)dt \neq 0$ such that (2.3) gives $e^{2\pi\alpha(m)} = 1$, $\forall m \in M_1$, that is $\alpha(m) = ki$, $k \in \mathbb{Z}$, $m \in M_1$. As $\sigma(A) = \alpha(M_1)$, the first part from (a) results. The second part is a consequence of Theorem 1.1.

In order to prove the necessity of (b), let us recall the following result of D.Fujiwara [6]:

If A *is the generator of a tempered distribution group* E *then denoting by* $D_\infty=\bigcap_{n=0}^{\infty} D(A^n)$, *endowed with the Fréchet topology given by the norms* $\{\|A^n x\|\}_{n\in\mathbb{N}}$, *the restriction* $A|D_\infty$ *generates an equi-continuous group* $\{T_t\}_{t\in\mathbb{R}}$ *in* $L(D_\infty)$; *moreover, we have*

$$E(\varphi)x=\int_{\infty}^{+\infty}\varphi(t)T_t x\,dt, \qquad \varphi\in\mathcal{D}, \quad x\in D_\infty. \tag{2.4}$$

Then for $\lambda\in\mathbb{C}$ and $x\in D_\infty$ we put (as in [1]):

$$B_{\lambda,t}x=e^{\lambda t}\int_0^t e^{-\lambda s}T_s x\,ds.$$

A simple computation gives

$$(\lambda-A)B_{\lambda,t}x=e^{\lambda t}x-T_t x$$

that is

$$(\lambda-A)B_{\lambda,2\pi}x=(e^{2\pi\lambda}-1)x, \qquad x\in D_\infty .$$

Hence for $x\in D_\infty$ and λ outside $i\mathbb{Z}$, we have

$$R(\lambda;A)x=B_{\lambda,2\pi}/e^{2\pi\lambda}-1. \tag{2.5}$$

The above relation shows that on D_∞ the resolvent has simple poles at each $\lambda=mi$, $m\in\mathbb{Z}$. For $m\in\mathbb{Z}$, let P_m be the residue of $R(\lambda;A)$ at mi; it is well known that P_m is a non-zero projection called *the spectral projection associated with* mi *and* A.

From (2.5) we immediately get

$$P_m x=\frac{1}{2\pi}\int_0^{2\pi}e^{-mit}T_t x\,dt, \qquad x\in D_\infty .$$

Let ξ be a 2π-unitary function; then:

$$P_m x=\frac{1}{2\pi}\int_0^{2\pi}\sum_{-\infty}^{+\infty}\xi(t-2n\pi)e^{-mit}T_t x\,dt=\frac{1}{2\pi}\sum_{-\infty}^{+\infty}\int_n^{n+1}\xi(s)e^{-mis}T_s x\,ds=$$

$$=\frac{1}{2\pi}\int_{-\infty}^{+\infty}\xi(s)e^{-mis}T_s x\,ds, \qquad x\in D_\infty ,$$

so that by (2.4) we get:

$$P_m x = \mathcal{E}(e^{-mit})x, \quad x \in D_\infty.$$

But D_∞ is dense in X, hence

$$(2.6) \qquad P_m = \mathcal{E}(e^{-imt}).$$

Moreover, for each $x \in D_\infty$

$$T_t x = \sum_m e^{imt} P_m x, \quad t \in \mathbb{R}.$$

Taking $t=2\pi$, we get:

$$(2.7) \qquad x = \sum_m P_m x, \qquad x \in D_\infty .$$

Let us further denote by $R(B)$, respectively $N(B)$ the image, respectively the null space of the operator B. Then it is clear that $R(P_m|D_\infty) = R(P_m)$ and $N(mi-A) \subset D_\infty$, $\forall\, m \in \mathbb{Z}$. Thus a simple argument shows that $R(P_m) = N(mi-A)$ and so part (b) of the necessity follows from (2.7).

Sufficiency. By (a) it is clear that A generates a tempered distribution group $\mathcal{E}$. Take $x \in N(mi-A)$, $m \in \mathbb{Z}$; then $x \in D_\infty$ and clearly $T_t x = e^{mit}x$. By (2.4), we have:

$$\mathcal{E}(\varphi)x = \int_{-\infty}^{+\infty} e^{imt}\varphi(t)x\,dt, \quad \varphi \in \mathcal{D},\ x \in N(mi-A).$$

This means that $\mathcal{E}x$ is 2π-periodic for $x \in \bigcup_{m \in \mathbb{Z}} N(mi-A)$ and condition (b) implies the desired conclusion.

From the above proof, we see that also the following holds:

COROLLARY. *Let $\mathcal{E}$ be a periodic distribution group (of period 2π) and P_m the m-the Fourier coefficient of $\mathcal{E}$; then:*

(i) P_m *is a projection and coincide with the residue of* $R(\lambda;A)$ *at the point* mi;

(ii) $\sum_{m=-\infty}^{+\infty} P_m x = x$, $\forall\, x \in D_\infty$.

REMARK. The above theorem and corollary generalize Theorem 3.1 from [1]: in the case of periodic groups of class (C_o), $\sigma(A)$ consists of simple poles of $R(\lambda;A)$ at $\lambda=mi$, $m \in \mathbb{Z}$ and $\sum_{m=-\infty}^{+\infty} P_m x = x$

for all $x \in D(A)$, P_m being the residue of $R(\lambda;A)$ at mi.

3. AN EXEMPLE OF A PERIODIC DISTRIBUTION GROUP

Let $\sigma(t)=\frac{3\pi-t}{2}$ for $0\le t<2\pi$ and extended with period 2π on all $\mathbb{R}$; then

1) $\sigma(t)>0$, $\forall\ t\in\mathbb{R}$
2) σ is continuous on each interval $(2n\pi,\ 2(n+1)\pi)$
3) $\sigma\in L^{\infty}(\mathbb{R})$
4) the function $1/\sigma$ is periodic and has the same above three properties.

Let $C_{2\pi}$ be the space of bounded periodic functions on $\mathbb{R}$ which multiplied by σ are continuous on each interval of the form $(2n\pi,\ 2(n+1)\pi)$, $n\in\mathbb{Z}$, endowed with the usual supremum norm. We have

PROPOSITION 3.1. *The map defined by*

$$E(\varphi)f=\frac{\varphi*\sigma f}{\sigma}\ ,\quad \varphi\in\mathcal{D},\ f\in C_{2\pi} \tag{3.1}$$

is a periodic distribution group in $L(C_{2\pi})$ *with generator*

$$\begin{cases} Af=-\frac{d}{dt}(\sigma f)/\sigma \\ D(A)=\{f\in C_{2\pi}\ ,\ d/dt(\sigma f)\in C_{2\pi}\}. \end{cases} \tag{3.2}$$

PROOF. One can easily verify that $E\in L(\mathcal{D};L(C_{2\pi}))$ and that E is periodic; moreover $E(\varphi*\psi)=E(\varphi)E(\psi)$, $\varphi,\psi\in\mathcal{D}$. For $\varphi\in\mathcal{D}$, let us denote by

$$\varphi_+(t)=\begin{cases}\varphi(t) & t>0\\ 0 & t<0\end{cases}\quad\text{and}\quad \varphi_-(t)=\begin{cases}0 & t>0\\ \varphi(t) & t<0\ .\end{cases}$$

Then putting $E_+(\varphi)f=(\varphi_+*\sigma f)/\sigma$ and

$E_-(\varphi)f=(\varphi_-*\sigma f)/\sigma$ for $\varphi\in\mathcal{D}$, $f\in C_{2\pi}$, $E=E_++E_-$,

a simple computation shows that E_+ and $\check{E}_-$ are distribution semi--groups with generator A, respectively -A, defined by (3.2) (let us remark that A is closed and D(A) is dense in $C_{2\pi}$).

Let us put:

$$(R(\lambda;A)f)(s)=\frac{1}{\sigma(s)}\int_0^{+\infty} e^{-\lambda t}\sigma(s-t)f(s-t)dt,\quad \mathrm{Re}\lambda>0, \tag{3.3}$$

and let us estimate the right hand side of (3.3).

We recall that for $0<t<2\pi$ holds

$$\sigma(\pi)=\pi+\sin t+\frac{\sin 2t}{2}+\frac{\sin 3t}{3}+\ldots, \tag{3.4}$$

and that the equality (3.4) is valid a.e. on $\mathbb{R}$ and the convergence holds in $\mathcal{D}'$.

A simple computation gives

$$\int_0^{+\infty} e^{-\lambda t}\sin n(s-t)\,dt=\frac{\lambda\sin ns-n\cos ns}{\lambda^2+n^2}$$

and taking into account the positivity of σ and the relation (3.4), we obtain, for $\mathrm{Re}\lambda>0$

$$||R(\lambda;A)f||\leq \mathrm{const.}\frac{|\lambda|+1}{\mathrm{Re}\lambda^2}||f||.$$

(We used the formula $\sum_{n=1}^{\infty}\frac{\cos ns}{\alpha^2+n^2}=\frac{\pi}{2\alpha}\frac{\mathrm{ch}\alpha(\pi-s)}{\mathrm{sh}\,\alpha\pi}-\frac{1}{2\alpha^2}$, $0<s<2\pi$).

A similar estimation holds for $\mathrm{Re}\lambda<0$ and this implies that the distribution group E is not usual, that is it does not coincide with a group of continuous operators in $L(C_{2\pi})$. This follows also from the fact that the group $\{T_t\}_{t\in\mathbb{R}}$ generated by A on D_∞ is given by:

$$(T_t f)(s)=\frac{\sigma(s-t)f(s-t)}{\sigma(s)},\quad f\in C_{2\pi} \tag{3.5}$$

and it is clear that $D(T_t)\neq C_{2\pi}$.

Let us finally remark that choosing the function σ in a convenient way, many other periodic distribution groups can be constructed as above; by (3.5), it is clear that they are generalizing the group of translations. In a similar way general tempered distribution semi-groups in $L(L^2)$ were constructed in [3].

REFERENCES

1. Bart, H.: Periodic strongly continuous semigroups, *Ann.Mat. Pura Appl.*, 115 (1977), 311-318.

2. Ciorănescu, I.: Teoreme de reprezentare a unor clase de distribuţii vectoriale, *Stud.Cerc.Mat.* 24 (1972), 687-728.

3. Ciorănescu, I.: Un exemplu de semigrup distribuţie, *Stud. Cerc.Mat.* 26 (1974), 357-365.

4. Ciorănescu, I.: Analytic generator and spectral subspaces

for tempered distribution groups, *An.Univ.Craiova* 5 (1977), 11-26.

5. Fattorini, H.: A representation theorem for distribution semi-groups, *J.Differential Equations* 5 (1969), 72-105.

6. Fujiwara, D.: A characterization of exponenetial distribution semi-groups, *J.Math.Soc.Japan* 18 (1966), 267-275.

7. Hille, E.; Phillips, R.: *Functional analysis and semi-group*, Amer.Math.Soc.Coll.Publ. XXXI, 1957.

8. Lions, J.L.: Les semi-groupes distributions, *Portugal Math.* 19 (1960), 141-164.

9. Zemanian, A.H.: *Distribution theory and transform analysis*, Mc.Grow-Hill Book Comp., 1965.

Ioana Ciorănescu
Department of Mathematics,
INCREST,
Bdul Păcii 220, 79622 Bucharest,
Romania.

ON THE SMOOTHNESS OF ELEMENTS OF EXT[1)]

R.G. Douglas

For X a compact metrizable space Brown, Fillmore and I introduced in [2] the study of a certain class of C*-algebra extensions of $K(H)$ by $C(X)$, where $K(H)$ is the C*-algebra of compact operators on the complex separable Hilbert space H. In this note we want to consider some questions concerning the fine analytical structure of such extensions. The partial answers seem sufficient to suggest that further study would be worthwhile.

Recall that Ext (X) denotes the abelian group formed by equivalence classes of extensions of $K(H)$ by $C(X)$. One way of defining an extension is as a *-monomorphism $\tau: C(X) \to \mathcal{Q}(H)$, where $\mathcal{Q}(H) = L(H)/K(H)$ is the Calkin algebra for H. The fine structure in which we are interested exists, for example, when X is embedded in some Euclidean space $\mathbf{R}^n$. If $\{x_i\}_{i=1}^{n}$ denote the coordinate functions of $\mathbf{R}^n$ restricted to X, then one can choose an n-tuple of self-adjoint operators $(H_1, H_2, \ldots, H_n)$ in $L(H)$ such that $\tau(x_i) = \pi(H_i)$ for $i=1,2,\ldots,n$. Such an n-tuple will be said to be a representation for $[\tau]$ in Ext (X) with $X \subset \mathbf{R}^n$.

Representations for $[\tau]$ are not unique. Indeed if $K_1, K_2, \ldots, K_n$ are compact self-adjoint operators on H, then $(H_1+K_1, H_2+K_2, \ldots, H_n+K_n)$ is a representation if $(H_1, H_2, \ldots, H_n)$ is and all representations up to unitary equivalence are obtained in this manner. Key properties of a representation for $[\tau]$ in Ext(X) are that all commutators $[H_i, H_j]$ are compact and the joint essential spectrum is $X \subset \mathbf{R}^n$.

Not all representations for a $[\tau]$ in Ext (X) share the same properties. For example, $[\tau]$ is trivial if and only if the $\{H_i\}$ can be choosen such that all commutators $[H_i, H_j]=0$. In this

---

1) Research supported in part by a grant from the National Science Foundation, and the Institut Mittag Leffler.

note we are interested in how small the commutators of a representation for a fixed $[\tau]$ in Ext (X) can be taken to be.

DEFINITION. Let I be an operator ideal $F \subset I \subset K$, where F denotes the ideal of finite rank operators on H. An element $[\tau]$ in Ext(X) is said to be *I-smooth* if there is a representation $(H_1, H_2, \ldots, H_n)$ consisting of self-adjoint operators for which $[H_i, H_j]$ is in I, $1 \leq i, j \leq n$.

A similar condition could be defined for $X \subset \mathbf{C}^m$, where we take $\{z_i\}_{i=1}^m$ to be the restriction of the coordinate functions of $\mathbf{C}^m$ to X and consider m-tuples of operators $(T_1, T_2, \ldots, T_m)$ for which $\pi(T_i) = \tau(z_i)$, $i = 1, 2, \ldots, m$. If one requires that all the commutators $[T_i, T_j]$ and $[T_i, T_j^*]$ be in I for $1 \leq i, j \leq m$, then I-smoothness for $X \subset \mathbf{C}^m$ is the same as for $X \subset \mathbf{C}^m = \mathbf{R}^{2m}$. In case $X \subset \mathbf{R}^2$ it is convenient to consider a single operator T and its self--commutator $[T, T^*]$.

Although the notion of I-smoothness depends on the particular embedding, we shall see that if X is sufficiently regular an intrinsic meaning can be given. After doing this we shall formulate a more abstract definition of I-smoothness which is valid even for the non-commutative case.

In this note we consider only the case $I = C_1$, where C_1 is the ideal of trace class operators. In [2] the C_1-smooth elements of Ext (X) for $X \subset \mathbf{C}$ were described based on results of Berger--Shaw [1] and Helton-Howe [5]. Recall that Ext (X) can be identified with the (possibly infinite) product $\prod_{i \geq 1} \mathbf{Z}$, where i indexes the bounded components $\{O_i\}_{i \geq 1}$ of the complement of X in $\mathbf{C}$. Moreover, if (T) is a representation for an element a in Ext (X), then a in Ext (X) corresponds to $(\text{ind}\,(T - \lambda_i))_{i \geq 1}$, where λ_i is a point in O_i.

THEOREM. *The element a in* Ext (X) *is* C_1*-smooth if and only if* $\sum_{i \geq 1} |\text{ind}\,(T - \lambda_i)|\,\text{area}\,(O_i) < \infty$. *In particular all elements in* Ext (X) *are* C_1*-smooth if and only if* X *is finitely connected.*

This is a very satisfying result and it would be of interest to extend it both to other ideals, and to more general X. However, it seems too much to hope, at least at the present, that one can obtain such a definitive result for $X \subset \mathbb{R}^n$, $n>2$. Therefore we concentrate on the case when X is a finite complex. The result we obtain is a refinement of a result of Helton-Howe [6]. In [6] Helton-Howe identify a certain trace form defined for a C_1-smooth element a of Ext (X) with its image $ch_1(a)$ in $H_1(X)$, where ch_1 is the first Chern character. That shows that a C_1-smooth element is a torsion element if X is simply connected. We show that it is actually a trivial element if the dimension of X is no greater than three and conjecture that it is true in general. Since detailed arguments of certain points were omitted from [6] we sketch a complete proof. We begin with the following where π_1 denotes the fundamental group.

THEOREM. *If* X *is a finite complex such that* $\pi_1(X)=0$ *and* $X \subset \mathbb{R}^n$, *then a* C_1-*smooth element in* Ext (X) *has finite order.*

PROOF. Let $(H_1, H_2, \ldots, H_n)$ be a C_1-smooth self-adjoint representation for a in Ext (X), let E be the C*-algebra generated by $\{H_i\}_{i=1}^n$, I and K, and let $\varphi: E \to C(X)$ be the symbol map. Then it follows from Helton-Howe [6] that there exists a *-subalgebra A of E with C_1-commutators such that the algebra $C^\infty(X)$ of restriction of C^∞-functions on $\mathbb{R}^n$ to X is contained in $\varphi(A)$. Moreover, there exists a homology class h in $H_2(\Omega, X)$, the relative de Rham homology group, where Ω is some open set containing X, such that

$$\text{ind } (U) = \sum_{j,k=1}^{m} h(du_{jk} \wedge d\bar{u}_{jk})$$

for any operator U in $E \otimes M_m(\mathbb{C})$ for which the symbol $(\varphi \otimes 1_m)(U) = \{u_{jk}\}_{j,k=1}^m$ is unitary and has entries in $C^\infty(X)$.

Since $H_2(\Omega, X)$ is isomorphic to $H_1(X)$ and the latter group is isomorphic to the ordinary homology group with complex coefficients for X a finite complex, it follows that if $\pi_1(X)=0$, then $H_2(\Omega, X)=0$ and hence $h \equiv 0$. Therefore the homomorphism

γ_∞: Ext (X)→Hom (K^1(X), **Z**) satisfies $\gamma_\infty(a)=0$ since K^1(X) can be realized as the direct limit of smooth unitary valued functions on X. The result now follows from the universal coefficients theorem for Ext, since for X a finite complex kerγ_∞ is the torsion subgroup of Ext (X).

We next show that a C_1-smooth element in Ext (X) is actually trivial if dimX≤3 by an inductive argument based on the Mayer--Vietoris sequence for Ext. Let us state the precise case we will use.

LEMMA. *Let* X *be a finite complex,* Δ *be a simplex of maximal dimension, and* $i:\partial\Delta\to X\setminus\Delta$ *and* $j:X\setminus\Delta\to X$ *be inclusion maps. Then there is a map* ∂: Ext (X)→Ext (S(∂Δ)), *where* S *denotes suspension, such that*

$$\text{Ext }(\partial\Delta)\xrightarrow{i_*}\text{Ext }(X\setminus\Delta)\xrightarrow{j_*}\text{Ext }(X)\xrightarrow{\partial}\text{Ext }(S(\partial\Delta))$$

is exact.

THEOREM. *If* X *is a finite complex embedded in* $\mathbf{R}^n$ *such that* $\pi_1(X)=0$ *and* dimX≤3, *then the only* C_1*-smooth element of* Ext (X) *is the trivial element.*

PROOF. Let Δ be a simplex of maximal dimension in X and suppose dimΔ=3. If a in Ext (X) is C_1-smooth, then by the previous result it is a torsion element and hence $\partial a=0$, since Ext (S(∂Δ))=**Z** is torsion free. Therefore, there exists a' in Ext (X\Δ) such that $j_*(a')=a$. Moreover, since Ext (∂Δ)=0 it follows that a' is a torsion element. If $a'=0$, then $a=0$ and we are finished. If not we proceed until we have a torsion element b in Ext (X_2), where X_2 denotes the two-skeleton of X.

Now we observe that if dimΔ=2, then Ext (S(∂Δ))=0 and hence we can find an element b' in Ext (X_2\Δ) mapping to b. However, the b' obtained may not be a torsion element since Ext (∂Δ)=**Z**. Nevertheless, proceeding inductively we eventually obtain c in Ext (X_1), where X_1 denotes the one-skeleton of X, such that c

maps to a.

We complete the argument with the following.

LEMMA. *If* X *is a simply connected finite complex, then* $i_*:\text{Ext}\ (X_1)\to\text{Ext}\ (X)$ *is the zero map.*

PROOF. If $\varphi:T\to X_1$ is continuous, then $\varphi_*:\text{Ext}\ (\mathbf{T})\to\text{Ext}\ (X_1)$ and the range of all such maps φ generates Ext (X_1). Hence to prove $i_*=0$, it is enough to show that $i_*\varphi_*=0$ for each φ. However, because X is simply connected, there is a continuous extension of φ to $\tilde{\varphi}:\overline{\mathbf{D}}\to X$.

If $j:\mathbf{T}\to\overline{\mathbf{D}}$ is inclusion, then we have the commutative diagram

$$\begin{array}{ccc} \text{Ext}\ (\mathbf{T}) & \xrightarrow{j_*} & \text{Ext}\ (\overline{\mathbf{D}}) \\ {\scriptstyle \varphi_*}\downarrow & & \downarrow{\scriptstyle \tilde{\varphi}_*} \\ \text{Ext}\ (X_1) & \xrightarrow[i_*]{} & \text{Ext}\ (X) \end{array}$$

and $i_*\varphi_*=\tilde{\varphi}_*j_*=0$ since Ext $(\overline{\mathbf{D}})=0$.

Although we are unable to prove it we believe that the preceding result holds for an arbitrary finite complex. In fact, we believe that even more is true.

CONJECTURE. If X is a finite complex smoothly embedded in $\mathbf{R}^n$, then the collection of C_1-smooth elements of Ext (X) coincides with the range of $i_*:\text{Ext}\ (X_1)\to\text{Ext}\ (X)$, where X_1 is the one-skeleton of X.

Observe that i_* is usually not one-to-one and that Ext(X_1) can be quite large while $i_*\{\text{Ext}\ (X_1)\}$ is quite small. That the range of i_* consists of C_1-smooth elements can be proved, at least for a smoothly embedded X.

The extension of the theorem to an arbitrary finite complex X would follow if one could show that if a C_1-smooth element a in Ext (X) can be lifted to a' in Ext $(X\setminus\Delta)$, then a' can be taken to be C_1-smooth. I had erroneously thought that I had proved that. The full conjecture would follow if one could show, in addition, that the mapping ∂ in the Mayer-Vietoris sequence preserves C_1-smoothness. I believe that both statements are true.

Before continuing let us point out that C_1-smooth torsion elements exist. If in the construction of the torsion element in Ext($\mathbb{R}P_2$) [4] one is careful to embed $\mathbb{R}P_2$ in $\mathbb{R}^4$ so that the "middle circle" is smoothly embedded, then the symbols of the Toeplitz operators will be C^∞ and hence their commutators will be C_1. Thus all of Ext($\mathbb{R}P_2$) is C_1-smooth. Observe that this element comes from the one-skeleton.

Although the definition of C_1-smooth depends on a particular embedding, an intrinsic definition can be given, at least when X is a smooth compact manifold, based on the functional calculus of Helton-Howe [5]. Let X be a smooth compact manifold and $X \xrightarrow{f} \mathbb{R}^n$ be a smooth embedding. If $(H_1, H_2, \ldots, H_n)$ have C_1-commutators and E is the C*-algebra generated by $\{H_i\}_{i=1}^n$, then there is a *-subalgebra A of E having C_1-commutators and such that $C^\infty(X) \subset \varphi(A)$, where $\varphi: E \to C(X)$ is the symbol map. Therefore if $g: X \to \mathbb{R}^m$ is another smooth embedding of X, then $g_i = x_i(g)$ are in $C^\infty(X)$ and hence there exist $\{G_i\}_{i=1}^m \subset A$ such that $\varphi(G_i) = g_i$, $i=1,2,\ldots,m$. Thus $(G_1, G_2, \ldots, G_m)$ is a C_1-smooth representation for the element of Ext (X) represented by $(H_1, H_2, \ldots, H_n)$. Therefore for a smooth manifold, the notion of C_1-smooth depends on the differential structure and not the embedding. It would be interesting to know whether it does indeed depend on the particular differential structure.

The preceding suggests how one could generalize the problem to the non-commutative case. Let C be a separable C*-algebra and C^∞ be a norm-dense *-subalgebra of C. An element $\tau: C \to Q(H)$ is said to be I-smooth if there exists a *-subalgebra A of $L(H)$ such that all commutators of operators in A lie in I and $\pi(A) \supset \tau(C^\infty)$. When $C=C(X)$ and $C^\infty = C^\infty(X)$ this reduces to the previous definition.

It seems likely that K-homology "cycles" of higher dimensions permit different degrees of smoothness and that more general theorems involving the higher dimensional parts of the Chern character and C_k-smoothness await further investigations. One should also consider in this context the recent results of Voiculescu [7].

One last general question is whether the I-smooth elements in Ext(C) form a subgroup. They do in all the cases one can compute, but the most natural approach to the problem would require a refinement of Stinespring's theorem.

REFERENCES

1. Berger, C.A.; Shaw, B.I.: Intertwining, analytic structure, and the trace norm estimate, *Proc.Conf.on Operator Theory*, Springer-Verlag Lecture Notes 345, 1-6, 1973.

2. Brown, L.G.; Douglas, R.G.; Fillmore, P.A.: Unitary equivalence modulo the compact operators and extensions of C^*-algebras, *Proc.Conf. on Operator Theory*, Springer-Verlag Lecture Notes 345, 58-128, 1973.

3. Brown, L.G.; Douglas, R.G.; Fillmore, P.A.: Extensions of C^*-algebras and K-homology, *Ann.Math.* (2) 105 (1977), 265-324.

4. Douglas, R.G.: The relation of Ext to K-theory, *Convegno Teoria degli operatori indice e teoria K.* (Rome, Ottobre 1975), Symposia Matematica XX, Rome, 1977.

5. Helton, J.W.; Howe, R.: Integral operators: commutators, traces, index and homology, *Proc.Conf.on Operator Theory*, Springer-Verlag Lecture Notes 345, 141-209, 1973.

6. Helton, J.W.; Howe, R.: Traces of commutators of integral operators, *Acta Math.* 136 (1976), 271-305.

7. Voiculescu, D.: Some results on norm-ideal perturbations of Hilbert space operators, *J.Operator Theory* 2 (1979), 3-37.

R.G. Douglas
Department of Mathematics,
State University of New York,
Stony Brook, New York 11794,
U.S.A.

TRIVIALITY THEOREMS FOR HILBERT MODULES

Maurice J.Dupré[1] and Peter A.Fillmore

INTRODUCTION

In a recent paper of Kasparov [K] the theory of Hilbert modules over noncommutative C^*- algebras is used to establish a general theory of extensions of C^*-algebras that extends results of Brown, Douglas, and Fillmore [BDF], Fillmore [F], and Pimsner, Popa, and Voiculescu [PPV]. Since the category of Hilbert $C(X)$-modules is equivalent to the category of Hilbert bundles over X [DD;DG], many questions of topological interest can be recast in terms of Hilbert $C(X)$-modules which then give rise to questions about general Hilbert modules. In particular, Kasparov's stability theorem [K] (which plays an essential part in the proof that inverses exist in the general theory of EXT) is the noncommutative extension of a triviality theorem of Dixmier and Douady [DD, Th.4] (which itself provides the existence of classifying maps for arbitrary separable Hilbert bundles over paracompact spaces).

This has led us to look for noncommutative generalizations of some of the other triviality theorems for Hilbert bundles.Our main result is an extension of [DD,Prop.18]. It should be noted that the proofs given by Dixmier and Douady are topological in nature, combining local and contractibility arguments. For instance[DD, Th.4] uses the contractibility of the sphere of unit vectors in infinite dimensional Hilbert space as well as [DD, Prop.18], which itself depends on the contractibility of the unitary group of infinite dimensional Hilbert space in the strong operator topology. In contrast our proofs (and Kasparov's) are global and purely analytic.

Our crucial Lemma 2 generalizes [DD, Lemmas 9 and 11] and

1) Partially supported by the National Science Foundation.

replaces the original homotopy arguments by infinite dimensional "general position" arguments. The idea is to produce a nonvanishing vector field close to a given vector field by "sliding" it along a nonvanishing vector field correctly. If the two vector fields are orthogonal it is intuitively clear that this process results in a nonvanishing vector field. This is the situation in the stability theorem, where one can keep an infinite dimensional supply of unit vector fields perpendicular to the work area. However this is not possible in the more subtle situation of Lemma 2. Although Lemma 2 easily yields Kasparov's theorem, we begin with the simple direct proof possible when the group action (if any) is ignored.

Finally, in view of these results it seems reasonable to look for the eventual replacement of more topology and homotopy by noncommutative analysis.

PRELIMINARIES

Let A be a fixed unital C^*-algebra. Consider a complex vector space M which is a unital right A-module and is provided with an A-valued bilinear form (,) satisfying

1) $(\lambda x)a = \lambda(xa) = x(\lambda a)$
2) $(x,\lambda y) = \lambda(x,y)$
3) $(x,ya) = (x,y)a$
4) $(x,y)^* = (y,x)$
5) $(x,x) \geq 0$

for all $x,y \in M, \lambda \in \mathbb{C}$, and $a \in A$. Then a generalized Cauchy-Schwarz inequality

$$(x,y)^*(x,y) \leq \|(x,x)\|(y,y)$$

follows, either by applying states [P;R] or by the obvious generalization of the usual argument [K]. If we set

$$\|x\| = \|(x,x)\|^{\frac{1}{2}}$$

for $x \in M$, then as usual $\| \ \|$ is a seminorm on M such that

$$\|(x,y)\| \leq \|x\| \ \|y\| \text{ and } \|xa\| \leq \|x\| \ \|a\|$$

for all $x,y \in M$ and $a \in A$. Moreover all of this structure transfers to the quotient $M/\{x \mid (x,x)=0\}$, which satisfies

6) $(x,x) = 0$ only if $x = 0$

in addition to 1)-5). Such an object can then be completed in the norm, and if complete is called a *Hilbert A-module.*

The algebra A itself (or any closed right ideal) becomes a Hilbert A-module on setting $(a,b)=a^*b$. If M_α is a Hilbert A-module for each index α, then one obtains a Hilbert A-module $\bigoplus_\alpha M_\alpha$, the direct sum, by completing the algebraic direct sum in the inner product

$$(\bigoplus_\alpha x_\alpha, \bigoplus_\alpha y_\alpha)=\sum_\alpha (x_\alpha, y_\alpha).$$

If $M_\alpha=M$ for each $\alpha\varepsilon\Delta$, then we put

$$M^\Delta=\bigoplus_\alpha M_\alpha.$$

In particular $\mathcal{H}_A$ denotes the countably infinite direct sum of copies of A. Note that if $A=C(X)$ with X a compact Hausdorff space, then $\mathcal{H}_A\cong C(X,\mathcal{H})$ as Hilbert C(X)-modules (where $\mathcal{H}$ is separable infinite dimensional Hilbert space), and that $C(X,\mathcal{H})$ is the space $\Gamma(X\times\mathcal{H})$ of sections of the trivial Hilbert bundle. In general the sections of any Hilbert bundle over X form a Hilbert C(X)-module, and conversely [DD, Prop.4] any Hilbert C(X)-module arises in this fashion from a unique (up to isomorphism) Hilbert bundle.

THE TRIVIALITY THEOREMS

We say that a subset C of a Hilbert A-module M *generates* M provided that the set of all finite A-linear combinations of elements of C is dense in M. The set C is *orthonormal* if for all $x,y\varepsilon C$,

$$(x,y)=\begin{cases}1\varepsilon A, & x=y\\ 0\ , & x\neq y\end{cases}$$

and is an *orthonormal basis* if it is both generating and orthonormal.

The trivial module $\mathcal{H}_A$ of countably infinite rank defined above has an obvious orthonormal basis $\{e_1,e_2,\ldots\}$ and it is easy to see that if $\{f_1,f_2,\ldots\}$ is an orthonormal basis of a Hilbert A-module M, then $e_n\to f_n$ defines an isomorphism $\mathcal{H}_A\cong M$ of Hilbert A-modules.

We use $\perp$ to signify perpendicularity with respect to Hilbert A-module inner products. We say that $x\varepsilon M$ is *nonsingular* if $|x|=$

$=(x,x)^{\frac{1}{2}}$ is invertible in A, and we call x a *unit* if $|x|=1$ (so that an orthonormal basis consists of units).

LEMMA 1. *Let* M *be a Hilbert* A-*module with* $e_1,\ldots,e_n$ *orthonormal in* M, $x\in M$, *and* $\varepsilon>0$. *Suppose* $y\in M$ *is a unit with* $y\perp\{x,e_1,\ldots,e_n\}$. *Then there is* $e_{n+1}\in M$ *so that*

(1) $e_1,\ldots,e_n,e_{n+1}$ *are orthonormal*

(2) $e_{n+1}\in \text{span}_A\ \{e_1,\ldots,e_n,x,y\}$

(3) dist $(x, \text{span}_A\{e_1,\ldots,e_{n+1}\})\le\varepsilon$.

PROOF. Set $x'=x-\sum_{k=1}^{n} e_k(e_k,x)$ and set $x''=x'+\varepsilon y$. Then $|x''|^2=|x'|^2+\varepsilon^2\ge\varepsilon^2>0$ so x'' is nonsingular. Define $e_{n+1}=x''|x''|^{-1}$. Then $e_{n+1}\in\text{span}_A\{x',y\}$ which is orthogonal to $\{e_1,\ldots,e_n\}$ and hence $e_1,e_2,\ldots,e_n,e_{n+1}$ are orthonormal in M. Since $x'\in\text{span}_A\ \{x,e_1,\ldots,e_n\}$, we have (2) because $e_{n+1}\in\text{span}_A\ \{x',y\}$. If $w=e_{n+1}|x''|+\sum_{k=1}^{n} e_k(e_k,x)$, then $w\in\text{span}_A\{e_1,\ldots,e_{n+1}\}$ and $||w-x||=||x''-x'||=\varepsilon$.

THEOREM (Kasparov [K]). *If* M *is a countably generated Hilbert* A-*module, then* $M\oplus H_A\cong H_A$.

PROOF. Let $\{e_n\}$ be the standard orthonormal basis for H_A and $\{y_n\}$ a sequence which generates M. Identify M and H_A as submodules of $M\oplus H_A$, and let $\{x_n\}\subset\{e_n\}\cup\{y_n\}$ be a sequence that repeats each e_n and each y_n infinitely many times. Notice that for each m, $\{x_n:n\ge m\}$ generates $M\oplus H_A$. Inductively assume we have constructed orthonormal $\bar{e}_1,\ldots,\bar{e}_n$ and an integer $m(n)\ge n$ so that

(1) $\{\bar{e}_1,\ldots,\bar{e}_n\}\subseteq\text{span}_A\ \{x_1,\ldots,x_n,e_1,\ldots,e_{m(n)}\}$

(2) dist $(x_k,\text{span}_A\{\bar{e}_1,\ldots,\bar{e}_k\})\le 1/k$, $1\le k\le n$.

Since each x_i is a y_k or an e_j, there is $m>m(n)$ with $e_m\perp\{x_1,\ldots,x_{n+1}\}$. Since $e_m\perp\{e_1,\ldots,e_{m(n)}\}$, by (1) it follows that

$$e_m\perp\{x_{n+1},\bar{e}_1,\ldots,\bar{e}_n\}.$$

By Lemma 1, there is a unit $\bar{e}_{n+1}\in\text{span}_A\{\bar{e}_1,\ldots,\bar{e}_n,x_{n+1},e_m\}$ so that $\bar{e}_1,\ldots,\bar{e}_n,\bar{e}_{n+1}$ are orthonormal and dist $(x_{n+1},\text{span}_A\{\bar{e}_1,\ldots,\bar{e}_{n+1}\})\le\frac{1}{n+1}$. But from (1) and $\bar{e}_{n+1}\in\text{span}_A\{\bar{e}_1,\ldots,\bar{e}_n,x_{n+1},e_m\}$ we see that

$$\{\bar{e}_1,\ldots,\bar{e}_{n+1}\}\subseteq\text{span}_A\{x_1,\ldots,x_{n+1},e_1,\ldots,e_m\}.$$

Setting $m(n+1)=m$ completes the induction. We thus have an orthonormal sequence $\{\bar{e}_n\}$ satisfying (1) and (2). Since (2) guarantees that $\{\bar{e}_n\}$ generates $M\oplus H_A$, it follows that $M\oplus H_A \cong H_A$.

COROLLARY. *If* M *is countably generated and* Δ *is an infinite set, then* $M\oplus A^\Delta \cong A^\Delta$.

PROOF. Obviously $H_A \oplus A^\Delta \cong A^\Delta$ so $M\oplus A^\Delta \cong M\oplus(H_A\oplus A^\Delta)\cong H_A\oplus A^\Delta \cong A^\Delta$.

If M is a closed submodule of a Hilbert A-module N, and if

$$M^\perp = \{x\varepsilon N \mid x\perp M\},$$

it is not generally true that $M + M^\perp = N$. For example, if R is a closed essential right ideal of A, then $R^\perp = \{0\}$ but R need not be all of A.

Consider those Hilbert A-modules M for which there is a Hilbert A-module M' such that $M\oplus M' \cong A^n$ for some finite n (that is, M can be regarded as a submodule of A^n such that $M+M^\perp = A^n$). In the commutative case, realizing M and M' as $\Gamma(E)$ and $\Gamma(E')$ for some Hilbert bundles E and E' over X, and using

$$\Gamma(E)\oplus\Gamma(E') \cong \Gamma(E\oplus E'),$$

we get $E\oplus E' \cong X\times \mathbb{C}^n$. But then E is of finite rank and is therefore [DD, p.250] locally trivial. That is, E is an ordinary complex vector bundle. The converse is well-known, and hence we may regard the direct summands of A^n as the noncommutative analogues of complex vector bundles.

In the next lemma we use the fact that $(x,e_n)\to 0$ for all $x\varepsilon H_A$, where $\{e_n\}$ is the standard orthonormal basis. To see this, note that the set of such x is closed submodule (by the Cauchy-Schwarz inequality) that contains the basis.

LEMMA 2. *Let* M *be a Hilbert* A*-module of* H_A *such that* $M\cong A^n$ *for some finite* n. *Then the nonsingular elements of* $M^\perp$ *are dense in* $M^\perp$. *Also,* $H_A = M\oplus M^\perp$ *and* $M^\perp \cong H_A$.

PROOF. Let $g_1,\ldots,g_n$ be an orthonormal basis for M and let $\{e_n\}$ be the standard orthonormal basis for H_A. Let $\varepsilon\geq 0$ be given. For each m, set

$$e'_m = e_m - \sum_{k=1}^{n} g_k(g_k,e_m)$$

so $e'_m \varepsilon M^\perp$. Then

$$(e'_m, e'_m) = 1 - \sum_{k=1}^{n} (e_m, g_k)(g_k, e_m).$$

By the remark preceding the lemma it follows that $|e'_m| \to 1$, and therefore there is m_o such that e'_m is nonsingular whenever $m \geq m_o$. Now set $e''_m = e'_m |e'_m|^{-1}$, so that e''_m is a unit for $m \geq m_o$. Suppose $x \varepsilon M^\perp$ is given. Then

$$(e''_m, x) = |e'_m|^{-1}(e'_m, x) = |e'_m|^{-1}(e_m, x) \to 0.$$

Choose $m \geq m_o$ such that $\|(e''_m, x)\| < \varepsilon$ and set

$$x' = x + \varepsilon e''_m.$$

Since e''_m is a unit, $\|x' - x\| = \varepsilon$. We now demonstrate that x' is nonsingular. Set

$$u = x - e''_m(e''_m, x)$$

$$v = e''_m[(e''_m, x) + \varepsilon 1].$$

Then $u \perp v$ (since $u \perp e''_m$) and $x' = u + v$. Thus

$$|x'|^2 = |u|^2 + |v|^2 = |u|^2 + ((e''_m, x) + \varepsilon 1)^*((e''_m, x) + \varepsilon 1),$$

and the right hand term is invertible by the spectral radius formula, since $\|(e''_m, x)\| < \varepsilon$. It follows that $|x'|^2$ is itself invertible. Thus the nonsingular elements of $M^\perp$ are dense in $M^\perp$. Now let $\{x_n\}$ be a sequence in $\{e_m\}$ which repeats each e_m infinitely many times, and put $x = x_1 - \sum_{k=1}^{n} g_k(g_k, x_1)$. Then there is (take $\varepsilon=1$) a unit $g_{n+1} \varepsilon M^\perp$ with dist $(x, g_{n+1}A) \leq 1$, and hence dist $(x_1, \mathrm{span}_A \{g_1, \ldots, g_{n+1}\}) \leq 1$. Replace M by $\mathrm{span}_A\{g_1, \ldots, g_{n+1}\}$, x_1 by x_2, and $\varepsilon=1$ by $\varepsilon=1/2$, etc. In this way we obtain an orthonormal basis $\{g_k\}$ of H_A extending the basis $g_1, \ldots, g_n$ of M we began with. But then $\{g_k : k>n\}$ is an orthonormal basis of $M^\perp$.

MAIN THEOREM. *Let* M *be Hilbert* A-*module of* H_A *and assume there is some Hilbert* A-*module* N *with* $M \oplus N \cong A^n$ *with* n *finite. Then* $H_A = M \oplus M^\perp$ *and* $M^\perp \cong H_A$.

PROOF. Since $N \oplus M \cong A^n$, there is a surjective A-linear map $A^n \to N$ and hence N is finitely generated. Thus by Kasparov's theorem we have $N \oplus H_A \cong H_A$. Therefore altogether we have

$$A^n \cong N \oplus M \subseteq N \oplus H_A \cong H_A$$

so by Lemma 2, if K is the orthogonal complement of $N \oplus M$ in $N \oplus H_A$, then $K \cong H_A$ and $N \oplus M \oplus K = N \oplus H_A$. But clearly, $K = M^\perp$ is the orthogonal complement of M in H_A.

PROPOSITION 1. *If* N *is any Hilbert* A*-module, if* $M \subseteq N$ *is a Hilbert* A*-submodule and if* M *is a direct summand of* A^n *for some finite* n, *then* $M \oplus M^\perp = N$.

PROOF. Use the technique of the proof of the main theorem to reduce the problem to the case where $M \cong A^n$. Now let $g_1, \ldots, g_n$ be an orthonormal basis for M and if $x \in N$, put $x' = \sum_{k=1}^{n} g_k (g_k, x)$. Then $x' \in M$ and $x - x' \in M^\perp$, so $M + M^\perp = N$.

We note that Proposition 1 generalizes Proposition 17 of [DD]. Moreover, there are easy counterexamples to Proposition 1, and hence also to Lemma 2, if M is not a direct summand of A^n for n finite.

In fact with $M \cong N \cong H_A$ and A commutative the proposition can fail. Let H_0 be a subspace of codimension one in an infinite dimensional separable Hilbert space H. Then

$$M = \{f \in C([0,1], H) \mid f(0) \in H_0\}$$

is a Hilbert $C([0,1])$-module such that $M^\perp = 0$ in $C([0,1], H)$. Moreover we will have $M \cong C([0,1], H)$ if there exists a strongly continuous $U: [0,1] \to L(H)$ such that $U(t)$ is unitary for $t > 0$ and $U(0)$ is an isometry with range H_0. Such a function can be constructed using the observation that if $e_1, e_2, \ldots$ is an orthonormal basis and U_n is the unitary operator that permutes $e_1, \ldots, e_n$ cyclically and fixes the rest of the basis, then U_n converges strongly to the unilateral shift. Alternatively one may appeal to [DD, Theorem 5].

Let M be any Hilbert A-module. Set $(M,M) = \{(m,m') : m, m' \in M\}$. Then $\text{span}_{\mathbb{C}}(M,M)$ is a two-sided *-ideal of A whose closure we call the *support* of M, as in [DG]. If E is a Hilbert bundle over the compact space X, then the support of $\Gamma(E)$ is the ideal in $C(X)$ corresponding to the open set of all points where E has a nonzero fibre. Notice that M^Δ and M have the same support for any set Δ.

PROPOSITION 2. *If* M *has support* A, *then* M^n *has a unit for some finite* n.

PROOF. By polarization we have

$$\mathrm{span}_{\mathbb{C}}(M,M)=\mathrm{span}_{\mathbb{C}}|M|^2,$$

where $|M|^2=\{|m|^2 : m\in M\}$. Since M has support A, it follows that $\mathrm{span}_{\mathbb{C}}|M|^2$ is a dense two-sided ideal of A and hence

$$A = \mathrm{span}_{\mathbb{C}}|M|^2$$

because the group of nonsingular elements of A is open in A. It is now easy to see that 1=a−b where a and b are each sums of elements of $|M|^2$. But then $a=1+b\geq 1$ so a is nonsingular. Writing $a=\sum_{i=1}^{n}(x_i,x_i)$ with $x_i\in M$, we have

$$1= \sum_{i=1}^{n}(x_i a^{-\frac{1}{2}},x_i a^{-\frac{1}{2}})$$

and therefore $\bigoplus_i x_i a^{-\frac{1}{2}}$ is a unit of M^n.

Before proceeding, we note that if $M=N_1\oplus N_2$ then we have bounded A-linear projections $P_1:M\to N_1$ and $P_2:M\to N_2$ which are surjective. In particular, any direct summand of a countably generated Hilbert A-module is again countably generated.

COROLLARY. *Suppose* M *is countably generated and has support* A. *If* Δ *is an infinite set, then* $M^\Delta\cong A^\Delta$.

PROOF. We may assume that Δ is countably infinite. By Proposition 2 there is a finite n such that M^n has a unit, and then $M^n\cong N\oplus A$ for some N by Proposition 1. By the above remark N and also N^Δ are countably generated, and so using Kasparov's Theorem we have

$$M^\Delta\cong (M^n)^\Delta\cong (N\oplus A)^\Delta\cong N^\Delta\oplus A^\Delta = N^\Delta\oplus H_A\cong H_A = A^\Delta .$$

This corollary is the noncommutative analogue of [DD, Cor.3, page 260]. As a final remark, it is interesting to contemplate a noncommutative analogue of [DD, Theorem 5]. If M is countably generated and A is finitely generated, what extra hypothesis is needed to give $M\cong H_A$? If C(X) is finitely generated then X is finite dimensional. If in addition E is a Hilbert bundle over X such that $\Gamma(E)$ is countable generated, then E is separable. In order to apply [DD, Theorem 5] to conclude that E is trivial, we need to know in addition that every fibre of E is infinite dimensional. Presumably what is missing then is a suitable Hilbert module analogue of this condition.

BIBLIOGRAPHY

[BDF] Brown, L.G.; Douglas, R.G.; Fillmore, P.A.: Extensions of C^*-algebras and K-homology, *Ann.Mat.* 105(1977), 265-324.

[DD] Dixmier, J.; Douady, A.: Champs continus d'espace hilbertiennes, *Bull.Soc.Math.France* 91(1963), 227-283.

[D_1] Dupré, M.J.: Classifying Hilbert bundles. II, *J.Functional Analysis* 22(1976), 295-322.

[D_2] Dupré, M.J.: The classification and structure of C^*-algebra bundles, *Mem.Amer.Math.Soc.* No.222, Providence, 1979.

[DG] Dupré, M.J.; Gillette, R.M.: Automorphisms of C^*-algebras, preprint.

[F] Fillmore, P.A.: Extensions relative to semifinite factors, *Symposia Math.* 20(1976), 487-496.

[H] Husemoller, D.: *Fibre Bundles*, McGraw-Hill, N.Y., 1966.

[K] Kasparov, G.G.: Hilbert C^*- modules: theorems of Stinespring and Voiculescu, *J.Operator Theory* 4(1980), 133-150.

[P] Paschke, W.L.: Inner product modules over B^*-algebras, *Trans.Amer.Math.Soc.* 182(1973), 443-468.

[PPV] Pimsner, M.; Popa, S.; Voiculescu, D.: Homogeneous C^*-extensions of $C(X)\otimes K(H)$, *J.Operator Theory* 1(1979), 55-108.

[R] Rieffel, M.A.: Induced representations of C^*-algebras, *Adv.in Math.* 13(1974), 176-257.

M.J.Dupré
Department of Mathematics,
Tulane University,
New Orleans, Lousiana 70118,
U.S.A.

P.A.Fillmore
Department of Mathematics,
Dalhousie University,
Halifax, Nova Scotia B3H 4H8,
Canada

EXACT CONTROLLABILITY AND SPECTRUM ASSIGNMENT

Gheorghe Eckstein

Let X and U be two complex Hilbert spaces. We consider the linear (time invariant) system

(1) $$\frac{dx(t)}{dt} = Ax(t)+Bu(t),$$

where $A\varepsilon L(X)$, $B\varepsilon L(U,X)$ and $u\varepsilon L^2_{loc}(\mathbb{R}_+,U)$. X is called the *state space*, U the *input space* and $L^2_{loc}(\mathbb{R}_+,U)$ the *control space*. The Cauchy problem (1) with the initial condition $x(0)=x_o$, where $x_o\varepsilon X$, has the solution

(2) $$x(t;0,x_o,u(\cdot))=e^{tA}x_o + \int_0^t e^{(t-s)A}Bu(s)ds.$$

The state x_o is said *controllable* if there is a control $u(\cdot)$ and a "time" $T\varepsilon\mathbb{R}_+$ such that

$$x(T;0,x_o,u(\cdot))=0.$$

We will denote the system (1) by (A,B). The system (A,B) is called *exactly controllable* if every state $x_o\varepsilon X$ is controllable. In the mathematical literature there are many concepts of "controllability", some of them called "exact controllability" so that the reader must be careful which definition is taken into account (see [3] or [4]). If X is finite dimensional all the controllability concepts coincide and in this case the following theorem is valid:

THEOREM. *The system* (A,B) *is controllable iff for each* $\Lambda=\{\lambda_1,\lambda_2,\ldots\lambda_n\}\subset\mathbb{C}$ *(where* $n=\dim X$*) there is* $F\varepsilon L(X,U)$ *such that* $\sigma(A-BF)=\Lambda$.

This theorem is known as Wonham's theorem (see [8]). We must mention that this theorem appears in the earlier book [7]of V.Popov, so perhaps the theorem should be called Popov-Wonham theorem.

If U is finite dimensional and X is infinite dimensional then the spectrum of A-BF cannot be arbitrary (only point spectrum of A can be moved). There are attempts to obtain results concerning the spectrum assignment in the case when X is infinite dimensional and U finite dimensional, but A is supposed to be in very special classes of unbounded operators (see [2]). The aim of this paper is to prove the following

THEOREM A. *Let* X *be infinite dimensional and separable. The system* (A,B) *is exactly controllable iff for any nonempty compact set* $K\subset\mathbb{C}$ *there is* $F\in L(X,U)$ *such that* $\sigma(A-BF)=K$.

We shall include some known proofs to make easier the task of the reader.

§.1.PRELIMINARIES

We shall currently use the following recent characterisation of the exact controllability:

1.1.THEOREM (Korobov and Rabah [5]). *The system* (A,B) *is exactly controllable iff there is* $n\in\mathbb{N}$ *such that*

(3) $BU+ABU+\ldots+A^{n-1}BU=X$.

Note that this theorem can be stated in the following form:

1.2. COROLLARY. *The system* (A,B) *is exactly controllable iff there is* $n\in N$ *and* $C_k\in L(X,U)$, $k=0,1,\ldots,n-1$, *such that*

(4) $\sum_{k=0}^{n-1} A^k BC_k=I_X$.

PROOF. If $Y=U_o+U_1+\ldots+U_{n-1}$ (where each U_k is a copy of U) and $C\in L(Y,X)$ is the operator matrix $[B\ AB\ldots A^{n-1}B]$, the equality (3) means that C is surjective and (4) means that $D=[C_o^*C_1^*\ldots C_{n-1}^*]^*$ is a right-inverse for C. Obviously C is surjective iff it is right-invertible.

1.3. LEMMA. *The system* (A,B) *is exactly controllable iff for each* $F\in L(X,U)$ *the system* (A-BF,B) *is exactly controllable.*

PROOF. If (A,B) is exactly controllable then using Corollary 1.2 there are $n\in\mathbb{N}$ and the operators C_k such that

$$\sum_{k=0}^{n-1} A^k BC_k=I.$$

By induction one proves that there exist $D_{jk}\in L(X)$ such that

$$A^kB=[(A-BF)+BF]^kB=\sum_{j=0}^{k}(A-BF)^jBD_{jk},$$

where $D_{kk}=I$, $D_{ok}=D_{ok-1}+FA^{k-1}B$, $D_{jk}=D_{j-1,k-1}$ for $0<j<k$. From here, we get

$$I=\sum_{k=0}^{n-1}A^kBC_k=\sum_{j=0}^{n-1}(A-BF)^jB(\sum_{k=j}^{n-1}D_{jk}C_k).$$

Using again Corollary 1.2 , the system (A-BF,B) is exactly controllable. Conversely, if (A-BF,B) is exactly controllable then, as we have already proved, (A-BF-BF',B) is exactly controllable. Choosing F'=-F we complete the proof.

1.4.DEFINITION. Suppose $A\in L(X)$ and $B\in L(U,X)$. The operator A has B-*assignable spectrum* if for each nonempty compact set $K\subset\mathbb{C}$ there is $F\in L(X,U)$ such that $\sigma(A-BF)=K$.

1.5. LEMMA. *If* A *has* B-*assignable spectrum then, for each* $F\in L(X,U)$, A-BF *has* B-*assignable spectrum.*

PROOF. Let $K\subset\mathbb{C}$ be a nonempty compact set. Then for given F, there exists F' such that $\sigma(A-BF')=K$ and from here $\sigma(A-BF-B(F'-F))=$ $=K$.

The following statement is obvious:

1.6.PROPOSITION. *Let* $A\in L(X)$, $B\in L(U,X)$ *and* $S\in L(X,Y)$ *an invertible operator. The system* (A,B) *is exactly controllable iff the system* (SAS^{-1},SB) *is exactly controllable.* A *has* B-*assignable spectrum iff* SAS^{-1} *has* SB-*assignable spectrum.*

1.7. LEMMA. *If* $F\in L(X,U)$ *then for any* $n\in\mathbb{N}$

$$(A+BF)^n=A^n+\sum_{k=0}^{n-1}A^kBF(A+BF)^{n-k-1}.$$

PROOF. Standard induction.

Consider $L(X)\times L(U,X)$ endowed with the product topology of the norm-topologies.

1.8.PROPOSITION. *The set*

$$\{(A,B)\in L(X)\times L(U,X)\mid (A,B)\ \textit{is an exactly controllable system}\}$$

is open.

PROOF. If (A,B) is exactly controllable, using Corollary 1.2 there are $n\in N$ and the operators C_k such that

$$\sum_{k=0}^{n-1} A^k B C_k = I_X$$

which means that the operator matrix $[B\ AB \ldots A^{n-1}B]$ is right-invertible. Since the set of right-invertible operators is open, the statement is obvious.

Note that if (A,B) satisfies (3) for a certain n, then for (A_1,B_1) in a neighbourhood of (A,B), the equality (3) holds for the same n.

1.9. THEOREM. *If the system* (A,B) *is exactly controllable then there is a closed subspace* $\mathcal{U}_0$ *of* $\mathcal{U}$ *such that* $B\mathcal{U}_0$ *is closed and the system* $(A,B|_{\mathcal{U}_0})$ *is exactly controllable.*

PROOF. By Proposition 1.8 there exists $\varepsilon>0$ such that $\|B-B_1\|<\varepsilon$ implies that the system (A,B_1) is also exactly controllable. Let $\{E_t\}_{t\geq 0}$ be the spectral scale of $|B|=(B^*B)^{\frac{1}{2}}=\int_0^\infty t\,dE_t$.

Let $\mathcal{U}_0=(I-E_{\varepsilon/2})\mathcal{U}$ and $B_1=B(I-E_{\varepsilon/2})$. We have $\|B-B_1\|\leq\varepsilon/2$ and

$$\|B_1u\|=\|Bu\|=\||B|u\|\geq\varepsilon/2\|u\| \quad \forall u\in\mathcal{U}_0,$$

so that $B\mathcal{U}_0$ is closed. The system (A,B_1) is exactly controllable and it is obvious that the system $(A,B_1|_{(\mathrm{Ker}B_1)^\perp})$ is also exactly controllable. But $\mathrm{Ker}\,B_1=\mathcal{U}\ominus\mathcal{U}_0$ and $B_1|_{\mathcal{U}_0}=B|_{\mathcal{U}_0}$, so the proof is finished.

Note that both systems (A,B) and $(A,B|_{\mathcal{U}_0})$ satisfy (3) for the same n.

1.10. REMARKS. If X is infinite dimensional and the system (A,B) is exactly controllable then $\mathcal{U}$ must be infinite dimensional. If $B\mathcal{U}$ is not closed then the above $\mathcal{U}\ominus\mathcal{U}_0$ is infinite dimensional.

1.11. From now on we suppose that X is infinite dimensional, *separable* and that $B\mathcal{U}=X_1$ is a closed subspace of X. Then the exact controllability of the system (A,B) can be restated in the following way:

$$X_1+AX_1+\ldots+A^{n-1}X_1=X$$

for sufficiently large n. Using a well-known theorem of R.G.Douglas (see[1]), the B-assignability of spectrum can be also reformulated as:

For every nonempty compact set $K\subset\mathbb{C}$ there is $F\in L(X)$ such that $FX\subset X_1$ and $\sigma(A-F)=K$.

1.12.LEMMA. *Let* $X_1\oplus X_2\oplus X_3$ *be an orthogonal decomposition of* X *and* A *an operator such that* $AX_1\subset X_1\oplus X_2$ *and* $P_{X_2}AX_1=X_2$. *Then for any* $F\in L(X)$, *such that* $FX\subset X_2$ *and* $FX_1=\{0\}$, *there is an invertible* $S\in L(X)$ *such that* $S|_{X_1}=I_{X_1}$ *and such that for every* $G\in L(X)$ *satisfying* $GX\subset X_1$, *there exists* $H\in L(X)$ *for which* $HX\subset X_1$ *and*

$$(*)\qquad A+F+G=S^{-1}(A+H)S.$$

PROOF. The operator A has the matrix

$$\begin{pmatrix} A_{11} & A_{12} & A_{13} \\ A_{21} & A_{22} & A_{23} \\ 0 & A_{32} & A_{33} \end{pmatrix}$$

where A_{21} maps X_1 *onto* X_2 ($A_{ij}=P_{X_i}A|_{X_j}$). Let B_{12} be a right-inverse for A_{21}. If F is like in the hypothesis then it has the matrix

$$\begin{pmatrix} 0 & 0 & 0 \\ 0 & F_{22} & F_{23} \\ 0 & 0 & 0 \end{pmatrix}.$$

Put

$$S=\begin{pmatrix} I_{X_1} & B_{12}F_{22} & B_{12}F_{23} \\ 0 & I_{X_2} & 0 \\ 0 & 0 & I_{X_3} \end{pmatrix}.$$

Obviously S is invertible and $S|_{X_1}=I_{X_1}$.

If

$$G=\begin{pmatrix} G_{11} & G_{12} & G_{13} \\ 0 & 0 & 0 \\ 0 & 0 & 0 \end{pmatrix}$$

is given, let H be the operator with matrix

$$\begin{pmatrix} H_{11} & H_{12} & H_{13} \\ 0 & 0 & 0 \\ 0 & 0 & 0 \end{pmatrix},$$

where

$$H_{11}=G_{11}+B_{12}F_{22}A_{21}$$

$$H_{12}=G_{12}+B_{12}F_{22}A_{22}+B_{12}F_{23}A_{32}-A_{11}B_{12}F_{22}-G_{11}B_{12}F_{22}$$

$$H_{13} = G_{13}+B_{12}F_{22}A_{23}+B_{12}F_{23}A_{33}-A_{11}B_{12}F_{23}-G_{11}B_{12}F_{23}.$$

By straightforward computation one verifies that

$$S(A+F+G) = (A+H)S$$

and this proves (*).

1.13. LEMMA. *Let* $X=X_o \oplus X_1$, *where* X_1 *is infinite dimensional and* $A\in L(X)$ *an operator for which* X_1 *is invariant. Suppose that* M_o *is a closed subspace of* X_1 *such that* $M_o+AM_o+\ldots+A^kM_o$ *is closed for each* k *and* $M_o+AM_o+\ldots+A^{n-1}M_o=X_1$. *Then there exists* $G\in L(X)$ *satisfying* $GX\subset X_o$ *such that the subspace* $M_o+(A+G)M_o+\ldots+(A+G)^kM_o$ *is closed for each* k *and* $M_o+(A+G)M_o+\ldots+(A+G)^nM_o=X$.

PROOF. Let $Y_k=M_o+AM_o+\ldots+A^kM_o$; obviously $Y_{k+1}\supset Y_k$. Denoting $M_{k+1}=Y_{k+1}\ominus Y_k$ we have $X=X_o\oplus M_o\oplus M_1\oplus\ldots\oplus M_{n-1}$. Since $M_o+AY_k=Y_{k+1}$ and $M_k\subset Y_k$ we have $AM_k\subset M_o\oplus M_1\oplus\ldots\oplus M_{k+1}$, thus $P_{M_{k+1}}AM_k=M_{k+1}$. If M_{n-1} is infinite dimensional, choose G such that $GM_{n-1}=X_o$ and $GM_{n-1}^{\perp}=\{0\}$. Obviously $(A+G)^kM_o=A^kM_o$ for $k\le n-1$, thus $M_o+(A+G)M_o+\ldots+(A+G)^kM_o=$ $=Y_k$ for $k\le n-1$. Moreover, since $M_{n-1}\subset Y_{n-1}=X_1$, we have $X_1+(A+G)X_1\supset$ $\supset X_1+(A+G)M_{n-1}=X_1+GM_{n-1}=X_o+X_1=X$ and this leads to $M_o+(A+G)M_o+\ldots$ $\ldots+(A+G)^nM_o=X$. If M_{n-1} is finite dimensional, the construction of G is slightly different. Let ℓ be the largest index for which M_ℓ is infinite dimensional. Note that $X_1\ominus Y_\ell=M_{\ell+1}\oplus\ldots\oplus M_{n-1}$ is finite dimensional. Then $N=\mathrm{Ker}(P_{M_{\ell+1}}A|_{M_\ell})$ is infinite dimensional, so there is $G\in L(X)$ such that $GN=X_o$ and $G(N^{\perp})=\{0\}$. Obviously $\alpha G(\alpha\neq 0)$ has the same properties, so the norm of G can be supposed arbitrarily small. The operator with matrix $[I_{M_o}\ A|_{M_o}\ldots A^{n-1}|_{M_o}]$

maps $M_o \oplus M_o \oplus \dots \oplus M_o$ (n copies) onto X_1, thus, since the set of surjective operators is open, the operator $[I_{M_o}\ P_{X_1}(A+G)|_{M_o} \dots\dots \dots P_{X_1}(A+G)^{n-1}|_{M_o}]$ will be also onto if $||G||$ is sufficiently small, and consequently

$$X_o+M_o+(A+G)M_o+\dots+(A+G)^{n-1}M_o \supset X_1.$$

We have $(A+G)^k M_o = A^k M_o$ for $k \le \ell$, so that

$$(M_o+(A+G)M_o+\dots+(A+G)^k M_o = Y_k \quad \text{for } k \le \ell.$$

$Y_\ell+(A+G)Y_\ell = Y_{\ell+1} \oplus X_o$ is closed and of finite codimension, what implies that every superspace is also closed; thus

$$M_o+(A+G)M_o+\dots+(A+G)^k M_o$$

are closed linear manifolds containing X_o for $k>\ell$. But this implies

$$M_o+(A+G)M_o+\dots+(A+G)^{n-1}M_o \supset X_1+X_o=X.$$

1.14.THEOREM. *Let* X_1 *be a closed subspace of* X *and* $A \in L(X)$ *such that for some* n

$$X_1+AX_1+\dots+A^{n-1}X_1=X.$$

Then there exist $F \in L(X)$, *satisfying* $FX \subset X_1$, X_o *a closed subspace of* X_1 *and* $m(n) \in \mathbb{N}$ *such that:*

(i) $$Y_k = X_o+(A-F)X_o+\dots+(A-F)^k X_o$$

is closed for each k,

(ii) $$Y_{m(n)-1} = X.$$

PROOF. We proceed by induction. For n=1 we put F=0, $X_o=X_1$ and m(1)=1. Suppose that the assertion is true for n-1. Let $F_1=P_{X_1}A$ and denote $A_1=A-F_1$. We have $A_1 X \perp X_1$ and $X_1+A_1X_1+\dots+A_1^{n-1}X_1 = X$. If all $X_1+A_1X_1+\dots+A_1^k X_1$ are closed, then we let $X_o=X_1$, F=0 and m(n)=n. If $X_1+A_1X_1+\dots+A_1^k X_1$ is not closed for some k, then $X \ominus X_1$ is infinite dimensional. If A_1X_1 is not closed, using Theorem 1.9 (for the system $(A_1|_{X\ominus X_1}, A_1|_{X_1})$, there is $X_1' \subset X_1$ a closed subspace for which A_1X_1' is closed(thus $X_1 \ominus X_1'$ is infinite dimensional), such that

$$A_1X_1'+A_1(A_1X_1')+\dots+A_1^{n-2}(A_1X_1') = X \ominus X_1.$$

In virtue of the induction hypothesis, there exist $F_2 \in L(X \ominus X_1)$, satisfying $F_2(X \ominus X_1) \subset A_1 X_1'$, and a closed subspace M_o of $A_1 X_1'$ such that

$$M_o + A_2 M_o + \ldots + A_2^{m(n-1)-1} M_o = X \ominus X_1 \quad \text{and}$$

$$M_o + A_2 M_o + \ldots + A_2^k M_o \text{ is closed for each } k,$$

where $A_2 = A_1 - F_2$ (we consider F_2 defined on whole X letting $F_2 X_1 = \{0\}$). Let $X_o = (A_2|_{X_1'})^{-1} M_o$. Then

$$X_o + A_2 X_o + \ldots + A_2^{m(n-1)} X_o = (X \ominus X_1) \oplus X_o \quad \text{and}$$

$$X_o + A_2 X_o + \ldots + A_2^k X_o \text{ is closed for each } k.$$

By Lemma 1.13 there is $G \in L((X \ominus X_1) \oplus X_1')$, satisfying $GX \subset X_1' \ominus X_o$ (again we define $G(X_1 \ominus X_1') = \{0\}$), such that $A_2 - G$ verifies $X_o + (A_2 - G)X_o + \ldots + (A_2 - G)^k X_o$ are still closed and $X_o + (A_2 - G)X_o + \ldots + (A_2 - G)^{m(n-1)+1} X_o = (X \ominus X_1) \oplus X_1'$. For the space $X_1' \oplus (X \ominus X_1)$ and the operator $A_1 - F_2 - G$ the hypothesis of Lemma 1.12 are fulfilled; thus, there exists $H \in L((X \ominus X_1) \oplus X_1')$ such that $A_1 - H$ (being similar to $A_1 - F_2 - G$) verifies

$$X_o + (A_1 - H)X_o + \ldots + (A_1 - H)^{m(n-1)+1} X_o = (X \ominus X_1) \oplus X_1' \quad \text{and}$$

$$X_o + (A_1 - H)X_o + \ldots + (A_1 - H)^k X_o \text{ is closed for each } k.$$

Using again Lemma 1.13 we find $F_3 \in L(X)$, satisfying $F_3 X \subset X_1 \oplus X_1'$, such that

$$X_o + (A_1 - H - F_3)X_o + \ldots + (A_1 - H - F_3)^k X_o \text{ are closed} \quad \text{and}$$
$$X_o + (A_1 - H - F_3)X_o + \ldots + (A_1 - H - F_3)^{m(n-1)+2} X_o = X.$$

If, at the beginning, $A_1 X_1$ is closed, the proof is similar but easier: we start with X_1 instead of X_1' and $F_3 = 0$. Note that $m(n) \leq m(n-1) + 3$, hence $m(n) \leq 3n - 2$.

1.15. COROLLARY. *If* (A,B) *is exactly controllable then there are* $F \in L(X,U)$ *and a closed subspace* X_o *of* BU *such that for a suitable orthogonal decomposition* $X_o \oplus X_1 \oplus \ldots \oplus X_m$ *of* X *the corresponding matrix* $(A_{ij})_{0 \leq i,j \leq m}$ *of* $A - BF$ *satisfies:*

$$A_{j+1,j} X_j = X_{j+1} \quad \textit{for } j = 0, 1, \ldots, m-1.$$

$$A_{ij} = 0 \quad \textit{for } i - j \geq 1.$$

PROOF. Theorem 1.14 implies that there are $m \in \mathbb{N}$, $F \in L(X,U)$, satisfying $F\mathcal{X}\subset B\mathcal{U}$, and $\mathcal{X}_o\subset B\mathcal{U}$ such that

$$\mathcal{Y}_k=\mathcal{X}_o+(A-BF)\mathcal{X}_o+\ldots+(A-BF)^k\mathcal{X}_o$$

is closed for each k and $\mathcal{Y}_m=\mathcal{X}$. Denoting $A'=A-BF$ and $\mathcal{X}_k=\mathcal{Y}_k\ominus\mathcal{Y}_{k-1}$ (for $k\geq 1$) we have

$$A'\mathcal{Y}_k\subset\mathcal{Y}_{k+1} \quad\text{and}\quad \mathcal{X}_o+A'\mathcal{Y}_k=\mathcal{Y}_{k+1}.$$

From here, if $i-j>1$, we get $P_{\mathcal{X}_i}A|_{\mathcal{X}_j}=0$. Moreover,

$$\mathcal{X}_{j+1}=P_{\mathcal{X}_{j+1}}\mathcal{Y}_{j+1}=P_{\mathcal{X}_{j+1}}(A'\mathcal{Y}_j+\mathcal{X}_o)=P_{\mathcal{X}_{j+1}}A'\mathcal{Y}_j=P_{\mathcal{X}_{j+1}}A'\mathcal{X}_j$$

so $A_{1+j,j}$ are surjective.

1.16.PROPOSITION. *Let* $\mathcal{X}=\mathcal{X}_o\oplus\mathcal{X}_1\oplus\ldots\oplus\mathcal{X}_m$ *and* $A\in L(\mathcal{X})$ *be an operator for which the corresponding matrix* $(A_{ij})_{i,j\leq m}$ *satisfies:*

$$A_{j+1,j} \quad \text{are surjective,}$$

$$A_{ij}=0 \quad \text{if } i-j>1.$$

Let $C_{ij}=\delta_{i,j+1}A_{ij}$ *and* C *be the operator with matrix* $(C_{ij})_{i,j\leq m}$. *Then there exists an invertible* $S\in L(\mathcal{X})$, *satisfying* $S|_{\mathcal{X}_o}=I_{\mathcal{X}_o}$, *such that for any* $D\in L(\mathcal{X})$ *which satisfies* $D\mathcal{X}\subset\mathcal{X}_o$, *there is* $F\in L(\mathcal{X})$ *such that* $F\mathcal{X}\subset\mathcal{X}_o$ *and*

$$(A+F)S=S(C+D). \tag{**}$$

PROOF. Each $A_{j+1,j}$ being onto, is right invertible. Let $A^r_{j,j+1}\in L(\mathcal{X}_{j+1},\mathcal{X}_j)$ be such that $A_{j+1,j}A^r_{j,j+1}=I_{\mathcal{X}_{j+1}}$. Let $S=(S_{ij})_{i,j\leq m}$ be an operator such that $S_{ii}=I_{\mathcal{X}_i}$ and $S_{ij}=0$ for $i>j$. Then S is invertible and $S|_{\mathcal{X}_o}=I_{\mathcal{X}_o}$. We have to choose S_{ij} for $i<j$. Let $D=(D_{ij})_{i,j\leq m}$ given such that $D\mathcal{X}\subset\mathcal{X}_o$. Let $\{E_{ij}\}$ be the equation obtained from the i,j-entries in the matrix representation of (**):

$$\{E_{ij}\}:\ \sum_{\ell=0}^{m}(A_{i\ell}+F_{i\ell})S_{\ell j}=\sum_{\ell=0}^{m}S_{i\ell}(C_{\ell j}+D_{\ell j}) \qquad i,j\leq m.$$

We have $D_{\ell j}=0$ for $\ell\neq 0$ and we choose $F_{ij}=0$ for $i\neq 0$. If $j\leq i-1$ then $\{E_{ij}\}$ is an identity. The equation $\{E_{mm}\}$ is

$$A_{m,m-1}S_{m-1,m}+A_{mm}=0$$

which is obviously satisfied by $S_{m-1,m}=-A^r_{m-1,m}A_{mm}$. Suppose that

$S_{p-1,j}$ are chosen such that $\{E_{pj}\}$ are satisfied for all $p>i\geq 1$. Then the equation $\{E_{ij}\}$ is

$$A_{i,i-1}S_{i-1,j}+\sum_{\ell=i}^{m} A_{i\ell}S_{\ell j}=S_{i,j+1}A_{j+1,j}$$

and we can choose

$$S_{i-1,j}=A^{r}_{i-1,i}(S_{i,j+1}-\sum_{\ell=i}^{m} A_{i\ell}S_{\ell j}).$$

We obtain an operator S which satisfies all the equations $\{E_{ij}\}$ for $i\geq 1$ (it is easy to see that these equations are not depending on D). It remains to find F. The equations $\{E_{oo}\}$ is

$$A_{oo}+F_{oo}=D_{oo}$$

and from here $F_{oo}=D_{oo}-A_{oo}$. Suppose $F_{oo},F_{o1},\dots,F_{o,k-1}$ are such that $\{E_{oj}\}$ are fulfilled for $j\leq k-1$. Then the equation

$$\{E_{ok}\}:\quad (A_{oo}+F_{oo})S_{ok}+\dots+(A_{o,k-1}+F_{o,k-1})S_{k-1,k}+$$

$$+A_{ok}+F_{ok}=D_{ok}+S_{o,k+1}A_{k+1,k}$$

gives us F_{ok}. So the statement is proved.

§.2. THE MAIN RESULTS

2.1. For the beginning, let us examine the following easy case: Let K be a (k+1)-dimensional space with $\{e_o,e_1,\dots,e_k\}$ as orthonormal basis and let T be the truncated right shift, i.e. the operator which has the matrix

$$\begin{pmatrix} 0 & 0 & 0 & \dots & 0 & 0 \\ 1 & 0 & 0 & \dots & 0 & 0 \\ 0 & 1 & 0 & \dots & 0 & 0 \\ \vdots & & & & \vdots & \vdots \\ 0 & & \dots & & 1 & 0 \end{pmatrix}.$$

If F is the rank-one operator which has the matrix

$$\begin{pmatrix} a_o & a_1 & \dots & a_k \\ 0 & 0 & \dots & 0 \\ \vdots & \vdots & & \vdots \\ 0 & 0 & \dots & 0 \end{pmatrix}$$

then the characteristic polynomial of T+F is

$$\lambda^{k+1}-a_o\lambda^k+\ldots+(-1)^{k+1}a_k.$$

For a fixed λ_0, let $a_s=\binom{k+1}{s}\lambda_0^s$; denoting by F_{λ_0} the corresponding F, we have $\sigma(T+F)=\{\lambda_0\}$ and it is easy to see that

$$||F||\leq(k+1)^{k+1}(\max\{1,|\lambda_0|\})^k.$$

Let now $\mathcal{Y}=\bigoplus_{\alpha\in\mathbb{N}}\mathcal{K}_\alpha$, where each $\mathcal{K}_\alpha$ is finite dimensional with orthonormal basis $\{e_{\alpha 0},e_{\alpha 1},\ldots,e_{\alpha k_\alpha}\}$. Suppose $0\leq k_\alpha\leq m$ for each α. In every $\mathcal{K}_\alpha$ consider the truncated right shift T_α. Let $T=\bigoplus_{\alpha\in\mathbb{N}}T_\alpha\in\mathcal{L}(\mathcal{Y})$ and $K\subset\mathbb{C}$, a nonempty compact set. Choose a sequence $\{\lambda_\alpha\}_{\alpha\in\mathbb{N}}$ which is dense in K and for each α put $F_\alpha=F_{\lambda_\alpha}\in\mathcal{L}(\mathcal{K}_\alpha)$. Then, since

$$||F_\alpha||\leq(m+1)^{m+1}\{\max_{\lambda\in K\cup\{1\}}|\lambda|\}^m,$$

the operator $F=\bigoplus_{\alpha\in\mathbb{N}}F_\alpha$ is bounded and

$$\sigma(T+F)=\sigma(\bigoplus_{\alpha\in\mathbb{N}}(T_\alpha+F_\alpha))=\text{closure }\{\lambda_1,\lambda_2,\ldots\}=K.$$

Denoting by $\mathcal{Y}_0$ the subspace of $\mathcal{Y}$ which has $\{e_{\alpha_0}\}_{\alpha\in\mathbb{N}}$ as orthonormal basis, we have $F\mathcal{Y}\subset\mathcal{Y}_0$ and

$$\mathcal{Y}_0+T\mathcal{Y}_0+\ldots+T^m\mathcal{Y}_0=\mathcal{Y}.$$

We have obtained the spectrum assignment theorem for this particular case. In what follows, we shall see that the general case can be reduced to this particular one.

2.2.THEOREM. *If* (A,B) *is exactly controllable then there is* $F\in\mathcal{L}(\mathcal{X},\mathcal{U})$ *such that* A-BF *is nilpotent.*

PROOF. By Corollary 1.15 there exist $F_1\in\mathcal{L}(\mathcal{X},\mathcal{U})$ and an orthogonal decomposition $\mathcal{X}_o\oplus\mathcal{X}_1\oplus\ldots\oplus\mathcal{X}_m$ of $\mathcal{X}$ such that the matrix of the operator $A-BF_1$ satisfies the hypothesis of Proposition 1.16. Using the notations from 1.16, the operator C attached to $A-BF_1$ is nilpotent. Choosing D=0, in virtue of Proposition 1.16, there exists $F'\in\mathcal{L}(\mathcal{X})$ such that $A-BF_1-F'$ is similar to C and $F'\mathcal{X}\subset\mathcal{X}_0$. But, since $F'\mathcal{X}\subset\mathcal{X}_0\subset B\mathcal{U}$, F' can be factorised as BF_2, where $F_2\in\mathcal{L}(\mathcal{X},\mathcal{U})$; thus putting $F=F_1+F_2$, the operator A-BF is nilpotent.

2.3. Let us examine closer the above operator C. In the decomposition $X_0 \oplus X_1 \oplus \dots \oplus X_m$, C has the matrix

$$(6) \qquad \begin{pmatrix} 0 & 0 & 0 & \dots\dots & 0 & 0 \\ C_{10} & 0 & 0 & \dots\dots & 0 & 0 \\ 0 & C_{21} & 0 & \dots\dots & 0 & 0 \\ \vdots & & & & & \\ \vdots & & & & & \\ 0 & 0 & 0 & \dots\dots & C_{m,m-1} & 0 \end{pmatrix}$$

where $C_{j+1,j}$ are onto. Let $Y_k = X_0 \ominus \operatorname{Ker}(C^k|_{X_0})$. We have $X_0 = Y_0 \supset Y_1 \supset \dots \supset Y_m$ and C^k maps Y_k one-to-one onto X_k. Let $Y = \bigoplus_{k=0}^{m} Y_k$. For $x \in Y_k$ we denote by $\overset{\ell}{x}$ the vector $(0 \oplus 0 \oplus \dots \oplus x \oplus \dots \oplus 0)$ (x on the $\ell+1$ seat). Let $Z = \bigoplus_{k=0}^{m} (C^k|_{Y_k}) \in L(Y,X)$; then Z is invertible and $Z^{-1}CZ|\overset{k}{Y_k} = P_{Y_{k+1}}|_{Y_k}$. Moreover, $Z\overset{0}{Y_0} = X_0$. Let $E_k = Y_k \ominus Y_{k+1}$ and $T = Z^{-1}CZ$. Then $Y = (\overset{0}{E_0} \oplus \overset{0}{E_1} \oplus \dots \oplus \overset{0}{E_m}) \oplus (\overset{1}{E_1} \oplus \dots \oplus \overset{1}{E_m}) \oplus \dots \oplus (\overset{m-1}{E_{m-1}} \oplus \overset{m-1}{E_m}) \oplus \overset{m}{E_m} = \overset{0}{E_0} \oplus (\overset{0}{E_1} \oplus \overset{1}{E_1}) \dots \oplus (\overset{0}{E_m} \oplus \overset{1}{E_m} \oplus \dots \oplus \overset{m}{E_m})$. Each subspace $H_k = (\overset{0}{E_k} \oplus \overset{1}{E_k} \oplus \dots \oplus \overset{k}{E_k})$ reduces T and $T|_{H_k}$ has the matrix

$$\begin{pmatrix} 0 & 0 & \dots & 0 & 0 \\ I & 0 & \dots & 0 & 0 \\ 0 & I & \dots & 0 & 0 \\ \vdots & & & & \\ 0 & 0 & & I & 0 \end{pmatrix}.$$

Obviously, each H_k is the orthogonal sum of $\dim E_k$ $(k+1)$-dimensional subspaces which reduces T, and the restriction of T at each of them is a truncated right shift having the ambulant subspace contained in Y_0. We have $Y = \bigoplus_{\alpha \in \mathbb{N}} K_\alpha$ where $\dim K_\alpha \le m+1$ and $T = \bigoplus_{\alpha \in \mathbb{N}} T_\alpha$, each T_α being a truncated right shift in K_α.

2.4. THEOREM. *If the system* (A,B) *is exactly controllable then* A *has* B-*assignable spectrum.*

PROOF. Using the previous results, there exist $X_0 \subset BU$, $F_1 \in L(X,U)$ and an invertible $S \in L(X)$ satisfying $S|_{X_0} = I_{X_0}$ and such that the operator $C=S^{-1}(A-BF_1)S$ has the matrix of form (6). Cf. 2.3 we find Y and $Z\in L(Y,X)$ such that $T=Z^{-1}CZ$ is the orthogonal sum of the truncated right shifts T_α. Let $K\subset\mathbb{C}$ be a nonempty compact set. According 2.1, there is $F_K\in L(Y)$, satisfying $F_K Y\subset Y_0$, such that $\sigma(T-F_K)=K$. Letting $F_2'=ZF_KZ^{-1}$ we have $C-F_2'=Z(T-F_K)Z^{-1}$, and letting $F_2''=SF_2'S^{-1}$, $A-BF_1-F_2''=SZ(T-F_K)Z^{-1}S^{-1}$ thus $\sigma(A-BF_1-F_2'')=$ $=K$. Since $F_2''X=SZF_KZ^{-1}S^{-1}X=SZF_KY\subset SZY_0=SX_0=X_0\subset BU$, using the Douglas'Theorem, $F_2''=BF_2$ where $F_2\in L(X,U)$. Putting $F=F_1+F_2$,

$$\sigma(A-BF)=K.$$

2.5. THEOREM. *If* A *has* B-*assignable spectrum then the system* (A,B) *is exactly controllable.*

PROOF. *Let* $F\in L(X,U)$ *be such that* $\sigma(A-BF)=\{a\}$, where $|a|>\|A\|$. Since we have

$$(A-BF)^n-A^n=(A-BF)^n(I-(A-BF)^{-n}A^n), \text{and}$$

$$\lim_{m\to\infty}\|(A-BF)^{-m}A^m\|=0,$$

we can find $n\geq 1$ such that $(A-BF)^n-A^n$ is invertible. But by Lemma 1.7 ,

$$(A-BF)^n-A^n=\sum_{k=0}^{n-1} A^kBM_k, \quad M_k\in L(X,U)$$

and we derive

$$I=\sum_{k=0}^{n-1} A^kBC_k, \quad C_k=M_k((A-BF)^n-A^n)^{-1}.$$

Now the theorem follows by Corollary 1.2.

Theorems 2.4 and 2.5 gives us Theorem A.

REFERENCES

1. Douglas, R.G.: On majoration, factorisation and range inclusion of operators in Hilbert space, *Proc.Amer.Math.Soc.* 17(1966),413-415.

2. Feintuch, A.; Rosenfeld, M.: On pole assignment for a class of infinite dimensional linear systems, *SIAM J.Control.Opt.* 16(1978),270-276.

3. Fuhrmann, P.: Exact controllability and observability and realisation theory in Hilbert space, *J.Math.Anal.Appl.*53 (1976), 377-392.

4. Helton, J.W.: Discrete time systems, operator models and scattering theory, *J.Functional Analysis* 16(1974),15-38.

5. Korobov, V.I.; Rabah, R.: Exact controllability in Banach spaces (Russian), *Diferentialnîe Uravnenie* 15(1979), 2142-2150.

6. Megan, M.: Stability and observability for linear discrete time systems in Hilbert spaces, *Bull.Math.Soc.Math.R.S.R.*, to appear.

7. Popov, V.M.: *Hiperstabilitatea sistemelor automate*, Editura Academiei R.S.R., Bucureşti, 1966. (French translation: Dunod, Paris, Bibliotheque de l'automaticien No-37, 1973).

8. Wonham, V.M.: On pole assignment in multi-input controllable linear systems, *IEEE Trans.Autom.Control* 12 (1967), 660-665.

Gh.Eckstein
Faculty of Natural Sciences,
University of Timişoara,
Bdul Pârvan 4,
Timişoara 1900,
Romania.

GENERALIZED DERIVATIONS

L.A. Fialkow

1. INTRODUCTION

The present paper is a discussion of open problems concerning generalized derivations, together with some of the basic results obtained until now, for the sake of some perspective. Properties of generalized derivations have applications concerning linear operator equations, similarity of operator matrices, quasisimilarity, and commutator theory among other topics.

Let H_1 and H_2 denote infinite dimensional complex Hilbert spaces, and let $L(H_2,H_1)$ denote the space of all bounded operators from H_2 to H_1. For a Banach space X, let $L(X)$ denote the algebra of all bounded linear operators on X.

For $A \in L(H_1)$ and $B \in L(H_2)$, let $T(A,B)$ denote the operator on $L(H_2,H_1)$ defined by $T(A,B)(X)=AX-XB$. In the case when $H_1=H_2$ and $A=B$, we denote $T(A,A)$ by δ_A, the inner derivation induced by A; for this reason $T(A,B)$ may be considered the "generalized derivation" induced by A and B.

If $H_1=H_2$ $(\equiv H)$ and $(I, |||\cdot|||)$ is a norm ideal in $L(H)$, then $T_I(A,B)$ denotes the restriction of $T(A,B)$ to I, and $T_I(A,B)$ is bounded, since

$$|||AX-XB||| \le (||A||+||B||)|||X||| \quad (X \in I).$$

In [6], Calkin proved that if I is any 2-sided ideal in $L(H)$, then the center of $L(H)/I$ is trivial; it follows readily from this result that the range of $T(A,B)$ is contained in I if and only if there exists a (necessarily unique) scalar $\lambda \in \mathbb{C}$ such that $A-\lambda$, $B-\lambda \in I$. In this case, if I is also a norm ideal with norm $|||\cdot|||$, then $T(A,B)$ induces an operator $\mathrm{T}_I(A,B): L(H) \to I$ by $\mathrm{T}_I(A,B)(X)=AX-XB$; T_I is bounded, since

$$|||AX-XB|||=|||(A-\lambda)X-X(B-\lambda)||| \le (|||A-\lambda|||+|||B-\lambda|||)||X||.$$

In the sequel we will discuss norm and spectral properties of $T(A,B)$, $T_I(A,B)$, and $\mathrm{T}_I(A,B)$.

2. THE NORM

For $T \in L(H)$, let $d(T) = \inf_{\lambda \in \mathbb{C}} ||T-\lambda||$, the distance from T to the scalar multiples of the identity. In [15], J.Stampfli proved that $||T(A,B)|| = \inf_{\lambda \in \mathbb{C}}(||A-\lambda|| + ||B-\lambda||)$; in particular, $||\delta_A|| = 2d(A)$. The calculation of d(A) for particular operators is difficult, but a few results are known. If A is hyponormal, then d(A) is equal to the radius of the smallest disk containing $\sigma(A)$ (the spectrum of A) [15]. For the standard Volterra operator V, a calculation of J.Deddens (unpublished) implies that $d(V) \approx 0.54954$, so that $d(V) < ||V||$. Moreover, there exist nilpotent operators N, acting on finite dimensional spaces, for which $d(N) < ||N||$.

The problem of evaluating $||T_I(A,B)||$ remains open; here we will consider the norm of $\delta_I(A) \equiv T_I(A,A)$. In general, the value of $||\delta_I(A)||$ depends on I as well as on A, but there do exist operators A, called S-*universal operators*, for which $||\delta_I(A)|| = ||\delta_A|| = 2d(A)$ for *every* norm ideal I. In [8] it is proved that a subnormal operator A is S-universal if and only if $\operatorname{diam}(\sigma(A))$ is equal to the diameter of the smallest disk containing $\sigma(A)$.

QUESTION 2.1. Is the same result valid for hyponormal operators?

The answer is affirmative for hyponormal weighted shifts (not all of which are subnormal); indeed, every hyponormal weighted shift is S-universal [8]. Question 2.1 would have an affirmative answer if it could be shown that $||\delta_{C_2}(A)|| \le \operatorname{diam}(\sigma(A))$ for A hyponormal; the inequality is valid for A subnormal.

An example of [8] shows that an infinite direct sum of finite dimensional nilpotent operators may be S-universal, but it is unknown whether there exists a nonzero quasinilpotent operator that is S-universal. For an arbitrary operator $A \in L(H)$ and for each norm ideal I, $\operatorname{diam}(W(A)) \le ||\delta_I(A)|| \le 2d(A)$, where W(A) denotes the numerical range of A [8]. Thus a sufficient condition for A to be S-universal is that $\operatorname{diam}(W(A)) = 2d(A)$. If the converse is true, the characterization of S-universal operators would be complete, and this would be a first step in the evaluation of the norm of $\delta_I(A)$.

QUESTION 2.2. Is $A\in L(H)$ S-universal if and only if $\operatorname{diam}(W(A))=2d(A)$?

3. THE RANGE

In this section we discuss several properties of the range of $T(A,B)$; at the outset we note that other studies of the range, from a more C^*-algebraic viewpoint, have been pursued by several authors, e.g. [1]. The range of an inner derivation has been studied in considerable detail; we list three typical results.

THEOREM 3.1. (Stampfli [16]). *$R(\delta_A)$ (the range of δ_A) contains no unitarily invariant subset; in particular, $R(\delta_A)$ does not contain every rank one operator.*

THEOREM 3.2. (Apostol [3]). *The following are equivalent:*

i) *$R(\delta_A)$ is norm closed in $L(H)$;*

ii) *A is similar to a Jordan model;* iii) *A is algebraic and $R(p(A))$ is norm closed for every polynomial $p(z)$.*

THEOREM 3.3. (Stampfli [16]). *$L(H)/R(\delta_A)^-$ is infinite dimensional; in particular, $R(\delta_A)$ is not norm dense.*

We seek appropriate analogues of these results for the operators $T(A,B)$, $T_I(A,B)$, and $T_I(A,B)$. We begin with analogues of Theorem 3.1. In the sequel, $\sigma_r(T)$ and $\sigma_l(T)$, will denote, respectively, the right spectrum and left spectrum of a Hilbert space operator T.

THEOREM 3.4. [8]. *The following are equivalent:*

i) *$\operatorname{Ran}(T(A,B))$ contains each rank one operator;*

ii) *$T(A,B)$ is surjective;*

iii) *$T_I(A,B)$ is surjective for every norm ideal I;*

iv) *$T_K(A,B)$ is surjective for some norm ideal K;*

v) *$T(A,B)$ has a bounded right inverse in $L(L(H))$;*

vi) *$T_I(A,B)$ has a bounded right inverse in $L(I)$ for every norm ideal I;*

vii) *$T_K(A,B)$ has a bounded right inverse in $L(K)$ for some norm ideal K;*

viii) $\sigma_r(A)\cap\sigma_l(B)=\emptyset$ [7].

A direct analogue of this result for the case when $T(A,B)$ is bounded below (or left invertible) is given in [8]. Using these results, it can also be shown that $T_I(A,B)$ is neither surjective nor bounded below [12]. In [12] it is also shown that $T_I(A,B)$ has closed range if and only if $A-\lambda$ and $B-\lambda$ are finite rank operators for some $\lambda\in\mathbb{C}$.

The problems of range closure for $T(A,B)$ and $T_I(A,B)$ remain open. In the next section we solve these problems under the additional hypothesis that $T(A,B)$ has finite nullity or deficiency. For the present we mention two partial results.

THEOREM 3.5. (Anderson-Foiaş [2]). *If* A *and* B *are normal,* $R(T(A,B))$ *is closed if and only if* $\sigma(A)\cap\sigma(B)$ *contains no topological limit point of* $\sigma(A)\cup\sigma(B)$.

THEOREM 3.6. [4][10]. *If* A *and* B *are compact, then* $R(T(A,B))$ *is closed if and only if* A *and* B *are finite rank operators.*

We next turn our attention to the case when $T(A,B)$ has dense range. In the sequel $\sigma_{re}(T)$ and $\sigma_{le}(T)$ will denote the right and left essential spectra of T. J.P. Williams [17] proved that $R(T(A,B))$ is dense in the weak operator topology if and only if there exists no nonzero finite rank operator X such that BX=XA; the range is ultraweakly dense if and only if there exists no nonzero trace class operator X such that BX=XA. The next result complements Theorem 3.3.

THEOREM 3.7. [9]. *The following are equivalent:*

i) $R(T(A,B))$ *is norm dense;*

ii) $\sigma_{re}(A)\cap\sigma_{le}(B)=\emptyset$ *and there exists no nonzero trace class operator* X *such that* BX=XA;

iii) *Given* $Y\in L(H)$ *and* $\varepsilon>0$, *there exists* $X\in L(H)$ *such that* $K\equiv AX-XB-Y$ *is compact and* $||K||<\varepsilon$.

QUESTION 3.8. Can X be chosen such that AX-XB-Y is a trace class (or finite rank) operator of arbitrarily small trace norm?

It seems difficult to characterize the case when BX=XA admits a nonzero trace class solution. When A and B are normal, a nonzero operator solution exists if and only if some reducing part of A is unitarily equivalent to a reducing part of B. It follows that a nonzero trace class solution exists if and only if A and B have a common eigenvalue (in which case a rank one solution exists).

PROBLEM 3.9. For operators within specific classes, e.g. hyponormals, weighted shifts, etc., give concrete necessary or sufficient conditions for the existence of nonzero trace class intertwinings.

The case when $\mathcal{T}_{C_p}$ or T_{C_p} $(1 \le p \le \infty)$ has dense range has been characterized in [9] and [12]; the corresponding characterization for arbitrary norm ideals is an open problem.

4. THE SEMI-FREDHOLM DOMAIN

For an operator T on a Banach space $\mathcal{X}$, let $\operatorname{def}(T)=\dim(X/\overline{\mathcal{R}(T)})$ (the deficiency of T) and let $\operatorname{nul}(T)=\dim(\ker(T))$ (the nullity of T). T is *semi-Fredholm* if $\mathcal{R}(T)$ (the range of T) is norm closed and def(T) or nul(T) is finite; in this case, the index of T is defined by $\operatorname{ind}(T)=\operatorname{nul}(T)-\operatorname{def}(T)$. The semi-Fredholm domain of T is the set $\rho_{SF}(T)=\{\lambda \in \mathbb{C}: T-\lambda \text{ is semi-Fredholm}\}$; we set $\sigma_{SF}(T)= =\mathbb{C}\setminus \rho_{SF}(T)$. T is *Fredholm* if $\mathcal{R}(T)$ is closed and both nul(T) and def(T) are finite. Let $\sigma_e(T)=\{\lambda \in \mathbb{C}: T-\lambda \text{ is not Fredholm}\}$, the (Fredholm) essential spectrum of T. Thus $\sigma_{SF}(T) \subset \sigma_e(T) \subset \sigma(T)$ and in this section we describe these sets (and the index function) for $\mathcal{T}(A,B)$ and $\mathcal{T}_I(A,B)$.

The first result in this direction is due to Rosenblum [14], who proved that $\sigma(\mathcal{T}(A,B))=\sigma(A)-\sigma(B)\equiv\{\alpha-\beta: \alpha\in\sigma(A),\ \beta\in\sigma(B)\}$; thus $\mathcal{T}(A,B)$ is invertible if and only if $\sigma(A)\cap\sigma(B)=\emptyset$. The case when $\mathcal{T}(A,B)$ is surjective or bounded below was characterized by Davis and Rosenthal [7] (cf. Theorem 3.4.). These authors also studied the more general operator $S(X)=\sum_{i=1}^{n} A_i X B_i$, where $\{A_1,\ldots,A_n\}$ and $\{B_1,\ldots,B_n\}$ are sets of commuting Banach space operators (or merely elements of a Banach algebra [13]).

For $T\in\mathcal{L}(\mathcal{H})$, let $\sigma_{oo}(T)=\{\lambda\in\sigma(T):\lambda \text{ is isolated in } \sigma(T) \text{ and } T-\lambda \text{ is Fredholm}\}$. For $\lambda\in\sigma_{oo}(T)$, let $n_T(\lambda)$ denote the dimension of the Riesz subspace for T corresponding to $\{\lambda\}$; in this case, $n_T(\lambda)=\dim\{x\in\mathcal{H}: (T-\lambda)^k x=0 \text{ for some } k>0\}$ and $0<n_T(\lambda)<\infty$. The essential spectrum of $T(A,B)$ may be described as follows.

THEOREM 4.1. [10][11].

i) $\sigma_e(T(A,B)) = (\sigma_e(A)-\sigma(B)) \cup (\sigma(A)-\sigma_e(B))$;

ii) *$T(A,B)$ is Fredholm if and only if* $\sigma_e(A)\cap\sigma(B) = \sigma(A)\cap\sigma_e(B)=\emptyset$. *In this case, either* $\sigma(A)\cap\sigma(B)=\emptyset$, *in which case $T(A,B)$ is invertible, or* $\sigma(A)\cap\sigma(B)$ *is finite and the distinct points of* $\sigma(A)\cap\sigma(B)$ *may be listed as* $\alpha_1,\ldots,\alpha_n,\beta_1,\ldots,\beta_p$, *where* $\{\alpha_1,\ldots,\alpha_n\}\subset \sigma_{oo}(A)$ *and* $\{\beta_1,\ldots,\beta_p\}\subset\sigma_{oo}(B)$. *(The decomposition of* $\sigma(A)\cap\sigma(B)$ *is not necessarily unique and either the* α_i's *or the* β_j's *may be absent.) Then* $\mathrm{ind}(T(A,B)) = -\sum_{i=1}^{n} n_A(\alpha_i)\,\mathrm{ind}(B-\alpha_i) + \sum_{j=1}^{p} n_B(\beta_j)\,\mathrm{ind}(A-\beta_j)$.

The next results describe the semi-Fredholm domain of T.

THEOREM 4.2. [11].

i) *$T(A,B)$ is semi-Fredholm and* $\mathrm{ind}(T(A,B))<+\infty$ *if and only if* $\sigma_{le}(A)\cap\sigma_r(B)=\sigma_l(A)\cap\sigma_{re}(B)=\emptyset$;

ii) *$T(A,B)$ is semi-Fredholm and* $\mathrm{ind}(T(A,B))>-\infty$ *if and only if* $\sigma_{re}(A)\cap\sigma_l(B)=\sigma_r(A)\cap\sigma_{le}(B)=\emptyset$;

iii) $\sigma_{SF}(T(A,B)) = [(\sigma_{le}(A)-\sigma_r(B))\cup(\sigma_l(A)-\sigma_{re}(B))]\cap \cap[(\sigma_{re}(A)-\sigma_l(B))\cup(\sigma_r(A)-\sigma_{le}(B))]$.

COROLLARY 4.3.

i) *$T(A,B)$ is semi-Fredholm and* $\mathrm{ind}\,(T(A,B))=-\infty$ *if and only if* $\sigma_{le}(A)\cap\sigma_r(B)=\sigma_l(A)\cap\sigma_{re}(B)=\emptyset$ *and* $(\sigma_e(A)\cap\sigma(B))\cup \cup(\sigma(A)\cap\sigma_e(B))\neq\emptyset$.

ii) *$T(A,B)$ is semi-Fredholm and* $\mathrm{ind}\,(T(A,B))=+\infty$ *if and only if* $\sigma_{re}(A)\cap\sigma_l(B)=\sigma_r(A)\cap\sigma_{le}(B)=\emptyset$ *and* $(\sigma_e(A)\cap\sigma(B))\cup \cup(\sigma(A)\cap\sigma_e(B))\neq\emptyset$.

To see how the last cases can arise, let U denote a unilateral shift of infinite multiplicity and let B denote any operator whose spectral radius is less than 1. Then $T(U,B)$ and $T(B,U)$ are semi-Fredholm, $\mathrm{ind}(T(U,B))=-\infty$, and $\mathrm{ind}(T(B,U))=+\infty$. Note that since $T(A,B)-\lambda=T(A-\lambda,B)$, the preceding results actually describe $\mathrm{ind}(T(A,B)-\lambda)$ for all $\lambda\in\rho_{SF}(T(A,B))$.

Many of the spectral properties of $T_I(A,B)$ are identical to those of $T(A,B)$. Brown and Pearcy [5] showed that $\sigma(T_I(A,B))=\sigma(T(A,B))$ and the analogues for left and right spectra appear in [8] (see Theorem 3.4 above). A parallel result also holds for essential spectra.

THEOREM 4.4. *For each norm ideal* I, $\sigma_{SF}(T_I(A,B))=\sigma_{SF}(T(A,B))$ *and* $\text{ind}(T_I(A,B)-\lambda)=\text{ind}(T(A,B)-\lambda)$ *for each* $\lambda\in\rho_{SF}(T_I(A,B))$; *in particular,* $\sigma_e(T_I(A,B))=\sigma_e(T(A,B))$.

The proof of this result entails systematic modifications of the proofs of Theorems 4.1 and 4.2, so we will omit the details. The idea of the proof is as follows. When T is not semi-Fredholm (but has closed range) the proof that nul(T) (resp.def(T)) is infinite follows from showing that $\text{nul}(T)$ $(\text{def}(T))\geq\dim(L(H,K))$ for certain nontrivial Hilbert spaces H and K at least one of which is infinite dimensional. Since the space of finite rank operators in $L(H,K)$ is also infinite dimensional, it follows that $\text{nul}(T_I)(\text{def}(T_I))$ is infinite. In the case when T is semi--Fredholm, the null space or defect space (whichever is finite dimensional) may be identified with an algebraic direct sum of spaces of the form $L(H,K)$ where H or K is finite dimensional. Since these spaces consist entirely of finite rank operators, they also correspond to a decomposition of the null space or defect space of T_I. From this it follows that T_I is also semi--Fredholm and that T and T_I have the same index functions.

The operator $T_I(A,B)$ is never semi-Fredholm. Indeed, T_I has closed range if and only if $A-\lambda$ and $B-\lambda$ are both finite rank operators (for some $\lambda\in\mathbb{C}$), and in this case it is easy to verify that $\text{nul}(T_I)=\text{def}(T_I)=\infty$.

The results of this section show that $T(B,A)$ has many spectral properties in common with those of the Banach space adjoint of $T(A,B)$. This observation and several results of [9] suggest the following question.

QUESTION 4.5. If $T(A,B)$ has dense range, is $T(B,A)$ injective?

5. CONCLUSION

The proofs of many (though not all) of the results discussed in this paper use Hilbert space techniques in essential ways. Indeed, these results suggest that certain other Banach space operators may also be studied by Hilbert space methods. The operators nearest at hand are of the form $X \to \sum_{i=1}^{n} A_i X B_i$, where $\{A_i\}$ and $\{B_i\}$ are families of (commuting) operators on a Banach space or elements of a Banach algebra.

Definitive results concerning the spectra of such operators have been obtained [13], and partial results on the left and right spectra and on the approximate point and defect spectra have also appeared. Apparently, the literature contains no results concerning the norm, range closure, density of the range, restriction to ideals, or essential spectra of these operators, and such areas of investigation may prove interesting. Even in the Hilbert space case, the extension from $T(A,B)$ to these more general operators seems to be nontrivial.

REFERENCES

1. Anderson, J.H.; Bunce, J.W.; Deddens, J.A.; Williams, J.P.: C*-algebras and derivation ranges: d-symmetric operators, *Acta Sci.Math. (Szeged)* 40 (1978), 211-227.

2. Anderson, J.A.; Foiaş, C.: Properties which normal operators share with normal derivations and related operators, *Pacific J.Math.* 61 (1975), 313-325.

3. Apostol, C.: Inner derivations with closed range, *Rev.Roumaine Math.Pures Appl.* 21 (1976), 249-265.

4. Apostol, C.; Stampfli, J.: On derivation ranges, *Indiana Univ.Math.J.* 25 (1976), 857-869.

5. Brown, A.; Pearcy, C.: On the spectra of derivations on norm ideals, preprint.

6. Calkin, J.: Two-sided ideals and convergence in the ring of bounded operators in Hilbert spaces, *Ann.of Math.* 42 (1941), 839-873.

7. Davis, C.; Rosenthal, P.: Solving linear operator equations, *Canad.J.Math.* 26 (1974), 1384-1389.

8. Fialkow, L.: A note on norm ideals and the operator X→AX-XB, *Israel J.Math.* 32 (1979), 331-348.

9. Fialkow, L.: A note on the range of the operator X→AX-XB, *Illinois J.Math.*, to appear.

10. Fialkow, L.: Elements of spectral theory for generalized derivations, *J.Operator Theory* 3 (1980), 89-113.

11. Fialkow, L.: Elements of spectral theory for generalized

derivations.II: the semi-Fredholm domain, preprint.

12. Fialkow, L.; Loebl, R.: On generalized derivations and norm ideals, preprint.

13. Lumer, G.; Rosenblum, M.: Linear operator equations, *Proc. Amer.Math.Soc.* 10 (1959), 32-41.

14. Rosenblum, M.: On the operator equation BX-XY=Q, *Duke Math. J.* 23 (1956), 263-269.

15. Stampfli, J.: The norm of a derivation, *Pacific J.Math.* 33 (1970), 737-747.

16. Stampfli, J.: Derivations on $B(H)$: The range, *Illinois J. Math.* 17 (1973), 518-524.

17. Williams, J.P.: On the range of a derivation, *Pacific J.Math.* 28 (1971), 273-279.

L.A. Fialkow
Department of Mathematics,
Western Michigan University,
Kalamazoo, MI 49008,
U.S.A.

COMMUTANTS MODULO THE COMPACT OPERATORS OF CERTAIN CSL ALGEBRAS

Frank Gilfeather[1)] and David R.Larson[1)]

In recent years several papers have appeared which focus on the structure of the commutant modulo compacts or essential commutant of certain algebras of operators on Hilbert space. For von Neumann algebras B.Johnson and S.Parrott [6]have shown that for all, but possibly ones containing certain type II_1 direct summands, the essential commutant is the algebraic commutant plus the compact operators. Subsequently characterizations have been given for the essential commutant of the analytic Toeplitz operators [3], nest algebras [2] and nest subalgebras of von Neumann algebras [4].

In this paper we are concerned with the essential commutant of certain non-selfadjoint algebras with commutative subspace lattices. A is called a <u>finite</u> <u>width</u> CSL algebra if A=Alg$L$ where L is the commutative subspace lattice formed by the join of a finite number of mutually commuting nests [1]. Under a condition (†), given in Section 1, we first show that finite width CSL algebras determined by continuous nests satisfying this have essential commutants equal to scalar multiples of I plus the compact operators. This condition (†) is the natural extension to finite width algebras of the order property for nest algebras and naturally excludes the extreme case when one nest is the complement of another.

In Sections 2 and 3 we investigate the structure of the essential commutant of width two CSL algebras. The essential commutant is determined for all width two CSL algebras satisfying a condition (*) which is the "essential" version of (†). In Sec-

---

1) Partially supported by the National Science Foundation.

tion 2 we show that the essential commutant of most of these algebras decomposes as scalar multiples of the identity plus compacts. However, in difference to the Johnson and Parrot result and the nest algebra results, certain width two CSL algebra satisfying (*) have essential commutants which do not decompose as the algebraic commutant plus compacts. The essential commutant of these cases are completely analyzed in Section 3. Since the pathology described above occurs for width two CSL algebras these are the algebras primarily focused on in this paper.

§1. PRELIMINARIES AND BASIC RESULTS

All operators will be bounded linear operators on separable Hilbert space. All subspaces will be closed and all projections will be self-adjoint. We write $L(H)$ for the set of bounded operators and $LC(H)$ for the set of compact operators on H. Let L be a collection of subspaces of H containing $\{0\}$ and H and closed under pairwise intersections and joins (closed linear spans). L is *commutative* if the projections on members of L pairwise commute, L is a *nest* (usually denoted by N) if it is totally ordered and finally L has *width n* if it is the join of n pairwise commuting nests. The term *subspace lattice* will denote a lattice L of projections closed in the strong topology and all lattices in this paper will be subspace lattices.

An algebra A is *reflexive* if $A=\mathrm{AlgLat}A$ where as usual $\mathrm{Lat}A$ denotes the subspace lattice for a set A and $\mathrm{Alg}P$ is the invariant set of operators for a set of projections P. Subspace lattices L need not be reflexive ($L=\mathrm{LatAlg}L$) however, commutative ones are reflexive [1] and in particular nests N are reflexive. Given two projections E and F and an algebra A we write $E<<F$ if $EL(H)F\subset A$ and we say E and F are strictly ordered.

We shall often disregard the distinction between a projection and its range space. Thus we consider a subspace lattice as consisting of projections or subspaces and we may use the same notation to indicate either. This occurs most often in the technical arguments. We shall let Π denote the canonical projection of $L(H)$ onto the Calkin algebra and let $\sigma(T)$ and $\sigma_e(T)$ denote the spectrum and essential spectrum of an operator T. Finally, esscom$A$ will be the essential commutant of A and A' the algebraic commutant of A.

We first consider two general results pertinent to the investigation of the essential commutant of an algebra $A=\mathrm{Alg}L$ where L is a commutative subspace lattice (following A.Hopenwasser A will be called a CSL algebra). For a commutative subspace lattice L we define the *core* of L (denoted by C_L) to be the von Neumann algebra generated by L.

LEMMA 1.1. *Let L be a commutative subspace lattice and $A=\mathrm{Alg}L$. Then $A'=W^*(L_r)$, where $W^*(L_r)$ is the von Neumann algebra generated by the complemented projections L_r in L.*

PROOF. Since $L_r \subset A'$ clearly $W^*(L_r) \subset A'$. Conversely if $T \varepsilon A'$, then $T \varepsilon (A \cap A^*)'$. However, $(A \cap A^*)' = C_L$ so T is a normal operator. Let $E(\cdot)$ be the spectral measure for T, then $E(\delta) \varepsilon A'$ for every Borel set δ and thus $E(\delta)$ and $I-E(\delta)=E(\delta)^{\perp} \varepsilon \mathrm{Lat}A=L$.

Using Johnson and Parrot's theorem [6] one can reduce essential commutant questions for CSL algebras to questions involving operators in C_L. The following lemma shows that the essential commutant of A is a C*- algebra.

LEMMA 1.2. *Let A be a CSL algebra with invariant subspace lattice L. Then* esscom$A$ *is the sum of the compact operators and a C*-subalgebra of C_L.*

PROOF. Let $T \varepsilon$ esscom$A$. Then T essentially commutes with the von Neumann algebra $D=A\ A^*$. Since $D'=C_L$ and D is a type I von Neumann algebra, we may apply Johnson and Parrot's result to T and D [6]. Thus $T=T_0+K$ where $T_0 \varepsilon C_L$ and K_0 is compact. Since $\Pi(T)$ is normal and commutes with $A/LC(H)$ so does $\Pi(T^*)$. Thus the subalgebra E of C_L consisting of operators in esscom$A$ is self adjoint. Since $E+LC(H)$ is clearly in esscom$A$ the proof is complete.

The following lemma extends certain lemmas in [4] and is in fact a corollary of one of them.

LEMMA 1.3. *Let L be a commutative subspace lattice, $A=\mathrm{Alg}L$, and $E \ll F$ be orthogonal strictly ordered core projections. If*

$T\varepsilon A'$, *then* $T(E+F)=\alpha(E+F)$, *for some scalar* α.

PROOF. We restrict T, the algebra A and L to the space $(E+F)H$ and call the restriction $\hat{T},\hat{A},\hat{L}$ respectively. Then every $\hat{P}\varepsilon\hat{L}$ is either $\leq\hat{E}$ or $\geq\hat{E}$. Since $\hat{E}\varepsilon C_{\hat{L}}$ it follows that $\hat{E}\varepsilon\hat{L}$ and is a comparable element of $\hat{L}$. Applying (2.3) in [4] it follows that $\hat{A}'$ is trivial.

Now we shall consider CSL algebras of finite width. By placing a condition on the generating nests we can determine that the algebra has trivial commutant and hence that the generated lattice has no complemented members. Let $A=A_{N_1}\cap\ldots\cap A_{N_n}$ where $N_1,\ldots,N_n$ are commuting nests and $L=\bigvee_{i=1}^{n} N_i$. Then A and L are reflexive and $A=\mathrm{Alg}L$. Let (†) be the following condition on $N_1,\ldots,N_n$:

(†) If the product $P_1 \ldots P_n=0$ for $P_i\varepsilon N_i$, then $P_i=0$ for some i.

We use the proceding lemma to show that $A'=\mathbb{C}I$ and hence $L_r=\{0,I\}$.

PROPOSITION 1.4. *If* $N_1,\ldots,N_n$ *satisfy* (†), *then* $A=A_{N_1}\cap\ldots\cap A_{N_n}$ *has trivial commutant.*

PROOF. First assume that for some i_0 we have $0^+=\inf\{P\varepsilon N_{i_0}: P>0\}$ is equal to 0. Since (†) holds we can, if necessary, enlarge the N_i and not change L so that $0^+=0$ for each N_i. Let $P_{im}\to 0$ as $m\to\infty$ for each i and let $E_m=P_{1m}\ldots P_{nm}$ and $F_m=P_{1m}^{\perp}\ldots P_{nm}^{\perp}$. By Lemma 1.3, $T\varepsilon A'$ implies that $T(E_m+F_m)=\alpha_m(E_m+F_m)$. However, $F_m\to I$ strongly and $\alpha_m=\alpha$ for all m so $T=\alpha I$. Next if $0^+=P_{i1}\neq 0$ for each nest N_i, set $P_1=P_{11}\ldots P_{n1}$. The condition (†) implies that $P_1\neq 0$ and it is easy to see that P_1 is a comparable element for $L=\vee N_i$. The result now follows from Lemma 2.3 in [4].

Below are several technical lemmas which are repeatedly used in the sequel. Recall that for an algebra two projections E and F are strictly ordered $E\gg F$ if $FL(H)E\subset A$. For these lemmas we shall be assuming that A is a CSL algebra and $L=\mathrm{Lat}A$.

LEMMA 1.5. *Let* $\{F_i\}\cup\{E_i\}$ *be a set of pairwise orthogonal nonzero core projections with* F_i *finite dimensional. Assume that for each i there exists a* k_i *with* $E_j >> \Sigma F_i$ *for* $j \geq k_i$. *Let* $T \varepsilon$ esscom$A$, $E = \Sigma E_i$ *and* $F = \Sigma F_i$. *Then* $\sigma_e(FT|FH) = \{\alpha\}$, *for some scalar* α, *and* $TE - \alpha E$ *is a compact operator.*

PROOF. Let $\alpha \varepsilon \sigma_e(FT|FH)$. There exists by Wolf's theorem an infinite rank projection $P \leq F$ with $PTP - \alpha P$ compact (cf. Theorem 1.1 in [5]). Since $F_1 + \ldots + F_k$ is finite rank for all k a partial isometry S can be constructed with initial domain EH and final domain in PH so that $S \varepsilon A$. Since $ST - TS \varepsilon LC(H)$ thus also $S^*ST - S^*TS \varepsilon LC(H)$. However, $S^*ST - S^*TS = ET - S^*PTPS = ET - \alpha E + K$ for $K \varepsilon LC(H)$. The choice of α was arbitrary and E is infinite rank so $\sigma_e(FT|FH)$ must be a singleton.

REMARK. If $\sigma_e(FT|FH) = \{\alpha\}$ and T is a normal operator, then we may drop the requirement that F_i be finite dimensional in the above lemma. The conclusion then is that $T(E+F) - \alpha(E+F) \varepsilon LC(H)$.

LEMMA 1.6. *Let* $\{F_i\}$, $\{E_i\}$ *and* T *be as in* (1.5) *but allow* E_i *to be zero and assume* $F_1 >> F_2 >> \ldots$. *Then* $T(E+F) - \alpha(E+F) \varepsilon LC(H)$.

PROOF. By Lemma 1.5 we have $TE - \alpha E \varepsilon LC(H)$. Now divide $\{F_i\}$ into two sets according to even or odd index. Applying (1.5) to each of these parts and interchanging them we have $TF - \alpha F \varepsilon LC(H)$.

LEMMA 1.7. *Let* $E << F$ *where* E *and* F *are orthogonal infinite rank core projections and let* $T \varepsilon$ esscom$A$. *Then* $T(E+F) - \alpha(E+F) \varepsilon LC(H)$.

PROOF. Let $\alpha \varepsilon \sigma_e(ET|EH)$ and P be an infinite rank projection with $P \leq E$ and $PTP - \alpha P \varepsilon LC(H)$. There exists a partial isometry S with initial domain F and final domain P. Since $E << F$ then $S \varepsilon A$ and hence $ST - TS \varepsilon LC(H)$. Thus $S^*ST - S^*TS \varepsilon LC(H)$ and $FT - \alpha F \varepsilon LC(H)$. Moreover, $\sigma_e(ET|EH)$ must be a singleton. Applying the argument to A^*, $L^{\perp}$ and T^* we may conclude that $ET^* - \bar{\alpha} E \varepsilon LC(H)$ and hence that $T(E+F) - \alpha(E+F) \varepsilon LC(H)$.

REMARK. The requirement in Lemma 1.7 and 1.3 that E and F be orthogonal is unnecessary. If $E << F$ then $E_1 << F_1$ for any subprojections E_1 of E and F_1 of F. Moreover if $E_0 << E_0$ for a core projection E_0, then $A'|E_0H$ is just the scalars on E_0H and if E_0 has infinite rank the analogous result is true for the esscom$A$.

LEMMA 1.8. *Let* $E_1 >> E_2 >> \dots$ *or* $E_1 << E_2 << \dots$ *where* $E_i \neq 0$ *are mutually orthogonal core projections. If* $T \varepsilon \mathrm{esscom}A$ *then* $T(\Sigma E_i) - \alpha(\Sigma E_i) \varepsilon LC(H)$.

PROOF. If $E_1 << E_2 << \dots$ and all the projections E_i are finite rank we apply Lemma 1.6. If one E_k is infinite rank then apply Lemma 1.7 to ΣE_i for $l \leq k$ and ΣE_i for $i > k$. If the strict order is reversed we consider the CSL algebra A^* with $\mathrm{Lat}A^* = L^{\perp}$ and $T^* \varepsilon \mathrm{esscom}A^*$. We have the same core projections however the strict ordering is reversed.

REMARK. The device of considering $A^*, L^{\perp}$ and $T^* \varepsilon \mathrm{esscom}A^*$ to prove something about $T \varepsilon \mathrm{esscom}A$ is used several times. The effect is that one reverses strict order between core projections so one can apply the above lemmas or consider fewer cases.

The first application of these lemmas is to show that a finite width CSL algebra satisfying (†) and with continuous nests has trivial essential commutant.

PROPOSITION 1.9. *Let* $A = A_{N_1} \cap \dots \cap A_{N_n}$ *where* $N_1, \dots, N_n$ *are continuous mutually commuting nests satisfying* (†) . *Then* $\mathrm{esscom}A = \mathbb{C}I + LC(H)$.

PROOF. Let $\{P_{ik}\}_{k=1}^{\infty}$ be a sequence of nonzero members of N_i converging to zero in the strong operator topology (as projections). Let $F_k = P_{1k} \dots P_{nk}$ and $E_k = P_{1k}^{\perp} \dots P_{nk}^{\perp}$. Then $F_k \neq 0, F_k \to 0$, $E_k \to I$ and $E_k >> F_k$. Moreover, since all N_i are continuous each E_k and F_k is infinite rank. If $T \varepsilon \mathrm{esscom}A$, then by Lemma 1.2, $T - T_0 \varepsilon$ $\varepsilon LC(H)$ for $T_0 \varepsilon C_L \cap \mathrm{esscom}A$. Now apply Lemma 1.7 to T_0. Thus $T_0(E_k + F_k) - \alpha_0(E_k + F_k) \varepsilon LC(H)$. However, since N_i is continuous $C'_{N_i} \cap LC(H) = \{0\}$ so $C_L \cap LC(H) = \{0\}$. Since $T_0(E_k + F_k) - \alpha(E_k + F_k) \varepsilon C_L$ it must be zero. Thus $T_0(E_k + F_k) = \alpha I$ and consequently $T_0 = \alpha I$.

That all N_i are continuous can be replaced with simply requiring one N_i to be continuous. Since if some N_j is not continous it can be enlarged to become continuous without affecting

L and hence A. This is possible because no finite rank projection can commute with N_i.

That this proposition does not hold in general without condition (†) is seen by leeting $N_1=N$ and $N_2=N^{\perp}$ for some nontrivial nest N. The following example shows that condition (†) is too weak for general results concerning trivial essential commutants.

EXAMPLE 1.10. Let E_1, E_2, E_3 be mutually orthogonal projections with $E_1+E_2+E_3=I$, E_1 and E_2 infinite rank and E_3 finite rank. Let $N=\{0,E_1+E_3,I\}$ and $M=\{0,E_2+E_3,I\}$. Then N and M satisfy (†) while clearly E_1 and E_2 essentially reduce $A=A_N\cap A_M$.

§2. ESSENTIAL COMMUTANTS OF WIDTH TWO CSL ALGEBRAS

Motivated by Proposition 1.9 which shows that esscom$A$ is trivial for certain nests which satisfy (†) and by (1.10) which shows that (†) clearly is not sufficient, we are naturally led to consider the following essential version of (†). Given commuting nests $N_1,\ldots N_k$ we say they satisfy (*) if:

(*) Whenever $P_i \varepsilon N_i$ and $\Pi(P_1)\Pi(P_2)\ldots\Pi(P_n)=0$ then $\Pi(P_i)=0$ for some i.

If one of the nests N_i is continuous then by (1.9) and the remark following it, the condition (*) reduces to (†) and (1.9) implies that esscom$A$ is trivial. However, in §3 we see that esscom$A$ can be nontrivial even when (*) is satisfied and when L has no essentially reducing members. Such nontrivial essential commutants occur in the width two case.

In this section and the following section we completely analyze the essential commutant of a width two CSL algebra satisfying (*). We consider the cases where the essential commutant is trivial here and analyze the exceptional case in Section 3. Some of these results generalize to finite width cases however the width two algebras seem to illustrate the technical problems and obstructions involved in this investigation. Thus the balance of the paper only concerns width two CSL algebras satisfying condition (*).

In what follows $A=\text{Alg } L$ where $L=N\vee M$ and N and M are commuting nests. To analyze esscom$A$ we shall for the most part consider only $C_L \cap \text{esscom}A$. Moreover, the results in this section concern when $C_L \cap \text{esscom}A = \mathbb{C}I$ so we might as well (and sometimes do) consider $C_L \cap \text{esscom}A^*$. Again we remark that this has the effect of reversing the order of the nests and changing strict order relations but does not effect the core nor the essential commutant of the algebra.

LEMMA 2.1. *Suppose* $\pi(N)=\pi(M)=\{0,I\}$ *and either* $\pi^{-1}(I)\cap(N\cup M)$ or $\pi^{-1}(0)\cap(N\cup M)$ *is finite. Then* $\text{esscom}A = \mathbb{C}I + LC(H)$.

PROOF. Taking orthogonal complements of N and M in the first case we may assume that $I=P_0>P_1>\ldots$ and $I=Q_0>Q_1>\ldots$ where $\{P_i\}=N$, $\{Q_i\}=M$ and each nonzero projection has finite corank. Let $E_i = P_i - P_{i+1}$ and $F_i = Q_i - Q_{i+1}$. Since $P_i^\perp$ is finite dimensional $P_i^\perp \le Q_{k_i}^\perp$ for some k_i. But $Q_{k_i}^\perp P_i^\perp >> P_i Q_{k_i}$ for the algebra A and thus $P_i^\perp >> Q_{k_i}$. Whence $E_i \le P_{i+1}^\perp >> Q_{k_{i+1}} = \Sigma F_j$ for $j \ge k_{i+1}$.

The next case involves one nest which is trivial in the Calkin algebra and the other which is nontrivial there. By trivial in the Calkin algebra we mean $\pi(N)=\{0,I\}$.

LEMMA 2.2. *If one nest is trivial in the Calkin algebra and the other nontrivial then* esscom$A$ *is scalars plus compacts.*

PROOF. Assume $\pi(N)$ is trivial and by taking complements if necessary assume $I=P_0>P_1>P_2>\ldots$, where $\{P_n\}=N\setminus\{0\}$. Thus $P_i^\perp$ are all finite rank and $P_n \to 0$ strongly. Let $Q \in M$ with Q, $Q^\perp$ both infinite dimensional. Set $R_i = P_i - P_{i+1}$ and define $E_i = Q^\perp R_i$ and $F_i = QR_i$. The proof is completed by applying Lemma 1.5 when $T \in \text{esscom}A$ is assumed to be normal.

The final case involving N and M when one or both are trivial in the Calkin algebra is the exceptional case which we postpone until Section 3. Precisely in §3 we will have $\pi^{-1}(I)\cap N$ and $\pi^{-1}(0)\cap M$ are finite or vice versa while $\pi(N)=\pi(M)=\{0,I\}$. Now we consider cases when neither N nor M is trivial in the Calkin algebra.

For the subsequent results we let N_f denote the nonzero finite rank projections in N and $\# N_f$ for the cardinality of this set.

LEMMA 2.3. *Let* $\# N_f$ *and* $\# M_f$ *be finite. Then* esscom$A$ *is scalar plus compact.*

PROOF. By restricting to the intersection of the complements of the largest finite projections in N and M we may assume that $N_f = M_f = \emptyset$. Now condition (*) implies that $\Pi(P)\Pi(Q)=0$ implies $P=0$ or $Q=0$. The proof now proceeds in several cases.

Case 1. Assume that both N and M have immediate successors to 0, that is, $0^+ = \inf\{P \mid P>0, P\in N\} \neq 0$ and respectively for M. Let $P\in N$ and $Q\in M$ be the immediate successors of 0 in N and M respectively. By our reduction we have PQ infinite rank and clearly $PQ \ll P^\perp Q^\perp + P^\perp Q + PQ^\perp$. If this sum is finite rank we have our conclusion otherwise we can apply Lemma 1.7 to show esscom$A$ is trivial.

Case 2. Now assume $0^+ = P \neq 0$ in N while $0^+ = 0$ in M. Let Q_n be a strictly decreasing sequence in M with $Q_0 = I$ and $Q_n \to 0$ strongly. Let $R_n = Q_n - Q_{n+1}$ and $E_n = R_n P$. If $T \in$ esscom$A$ by (1.8) we have $TP = \alpha P + K$ where K is compact. Considering the fact that $R_n P \gg R_{n+1} P$ and using the remarks following (1.5) and (1.2) we conclude this case.

Case 3. Assume $0^+ = 0$ for both nests N and M. Let P_n and Q_n be decreasing sequences of projections in N and M respectively with $P_0 = Q_0 = I$ and $P_n \to 0$ and $Q_n \to 0$ strongly. Let $R_n = P_n - P_{n+1}$ and $S_n = Q_n - Q_{n+1}$ and notice that $R_n S_m \gg R_k S_\ell$ if $n>k$ and $m>\ell$. For all $R_n S_m$ there is an k,ℓ with $R_n S_m \gg R_k S_\ell \neq 0$ since in fact $P_n Q_m$ is infinite rank and $P_n Q_m = \Sigma R_k S_\ell$ where the sum is over $k>n$ and $\ell>m$. If $T \in$ esscom$A$ and if T is normal then applying (1.8) to one infinite nonzero chain $R_{n_1} S_{m_1} \gg R_{n_2} S_{m_2} \gg \ldots$, and then applying the remark following (1.5) we conclude this case and the result.

The final case of "simple" essential commutant follows.

LEMMA 2.4. *Let* $\Pi(N)$ *and* $\Pi(M)$ *be nontrivial and* $\# N_f$ *or* $\# M_f$ *be infinite. Then* esscom$A$ *is scalars plus compacts.*

PROOF. We shall assume $\# N_f$ is denumerable and set $P_\infty = P = \sup\{P_f \mid P_f \in N_f\}$. Let Q be in M so that $\Pi(Q) \neq 0$ or I. By our assumptions P_∞, $P_\infty^\perp$, Q and $Q^\perp$ are all infinite dimensional as well as is $P_\infty Q$ by our standing hypothesis (*). Let T be a normal operator in esscomA and $0=P_0<P_1$ ... the elements of N_f and $R_i=P_i-P_{i-1}$.

Since $P^\perp Q^\perp+PQ^\perp=Q^\perp$ is infinite either $P^\perp Q^\perp$ or $PQ^\perp$ or both are infinite rank projections. If $P^\perp Q^\perp$ is infinite rank then (1.7) implies that $T(PQ+P^\perp Q^\perp)=(a+K_1)(PQ+P^\perp Q^\perp)$ where K_1 is compact. We next consider the case where $PQ^\perp$ is infinite rank. The projections $PQ^\perp=\Sigma R_iQ^\perp$ and $PQ=\Sigma R_iQ$ with $R_iQ^\perp>>R_jQ$ for $i\geq j$. Considering the complemented case then the strict orders reverse for these core projections and now $R_iQ^\perp<<R_jQ$ for $i\geq j$ and all the projections are finite rank. Applying (1.5) and the remark following it, the operator $T^*(PQ+PQ^\perp)=T^*P=(b+K_2)P$ where K_2 is compact. If $P^\perp Q^\perp$ were infinite rank then $\bar{b}=a$ where a appears above. Thus $T(P+P^\perp Q^\perp)=(aI+K_3)(P+P^\perp Q^\perp)$ where K_3 is compact.

Finally, we need to consider $P^\perp Q$ if it has infinite rank. If $\# M_f<\infty$ then by 2.8 case 2 we may assume $Q=0^+=0$; thus $P^\perp Q>>PQ$. Now if Q is the first infinite rank projection in M, that is, $Q=Q_\infty=\sup\{M|M\varepsilon M_f\}$. We set $0=Q_0<Q_1<\ldots$ the elements of M_f and $S_i=Q_i-Q_{i-1}$. Now just as above $\{PS_i\}$ and $\{P^\perp S_i\}$ are finite rank and $P^\perp S_i>>P\ S_j$ for $i\geq j$. Again as above we consider the complemented case and there strict orders reverse for A^*. That is *now* $PQ=\Sigma PS_i$ and $P^\perp Q=\Sigma P^\perp S_i$ and $P^\perp S_i<<P\ S_j$ for $i\geq j$. Thus applying (1.5) and its remark we conclude that $T^*(P^\perp Q+PQ)=T^*Q\ (bI+K_4)Q$ where K_4 is compact and $\bar{b}=a$ since $TPQ=(aI+K_3)PQ$. This case completes the proof.

We combine the preceeding results into a theorem. Let A be a width two CSL algebra with N and M the commuting nests which determine A.

THEOREM 2.5. Suppose either $\Pi^{-1}(I)\cap(N\cup M)$ *or* $\Pi^{-1}(0)\cap(N\cup M)$ *are finite if both N and M are trivial in the Calkin algebra. Further, let N and M satisfy the condition* (*), *that is,* $\Pi(P)\Pi(Q)=0$ *for* $P\varepsilon N$, $Q\varepsilon M$ *implies* $\Pi(P)=0$ *or* $\Pi(Q)=0$. *Then* esscomA *is scalars plus compacts.*

§3. EXCEPTIONAL CASE

In this section we describe the essential commutant of a width two CSL algebra A for which $\Pi^{-1}(I)\cap N$ is finite, $\Pi^{-1}(0)\cap M$ is finite and $\Pi(N)=\Pi(M)=\{0,I\}$. Without loss of generality we can immediately reduce to the case when $\Pi(N-\{I\})=$

$=\{0\}$ and $\Pi(M-\{0\})=\{I\}$, that is N consists only of finite rank projections and I and M consists of finite co-rank projections and $\{0\}$. Clearly these algebras satisfy (*) in Section 2 and describing their essential commutant will complete the program for all width two CSL algebras satisfying (*).

The analysis of the essential commutant of these width two CSL algebras is done in Theorem 3.4. However, we first present a more transparent case in which N and M "overlap" in a simple manner. The general result is patterned after the simpler one and uses it in one step.

For this section we shall let A_0 be the width two CSL algebra determined by the two nests $N=\{P_i\}$ where $0=P_0<P_1<\ldots$ and $M=\{Q_i\}$ with $\ldots<Q_2<Q_1<Q_0=I$ and each P_i and $Q_i^\perp$ is finite rank. Furthermore, assume $P_{i-1}<Q_i^\perp<P_i$ for all $i\geq 1$. We let $L_0=N\vee M$ and $A_0=\mathrm{Alg}\,L_0$. If we set $R_{2n}=Q_nP_n$, $R_{2n-1}=Q_n^\perp-P_{n-1}$ and $R_{2n+1}=Q_{n+1}^\perp-P_n$. Then A_0 is completely determined by the relationships between these minimal core projections as follows: $R_{2n-1}<<R_{2n-1}$ and $R_{2n}<<R_{2n-1}+R_{2n+1}$. Thus an operator $A\varepsilon A_0$ if and only if

(1) $AR_{2n} \subset R_{2n}$ and

(2) $AR_{2n+1} \subseteq R_{2n}+R_{2n+1}+R_{2n+2}$.

Arveson has shown that every commutative subspace lattice admits a representation as the lattice of increasing subsets of some standard partially ordered measure space [1]. We can easily see that L_0 is order isomorphic to the lattice of increasing subsets of the natural numbers $\mathbb{N}$ with the ordering $\succ$ given by $2n\succ 2n+1$. Specifically let $A\subset\mathbb{N}$ be an increasing set, that is, if $2n+1\varepsilon A$, then $2n+1\pm 1\varepsilon A$. Let $P\varepsilon L_0$ be the projection on span $\{R_i : i\varepsilon A\}$. Clearly every $P\varepsilon L_0$ arises this way. Thus L_0 is isomorphic to $\hat{L}=\{A\subset\mathbb{N} : 2n+1\pm 1\varepsilon A$ if $2n+1\varepsilon A$ and this is an order isomorphism where set inclusion determines the order on $\hat{L}$.

The following proposition shows that the essential commutant of A_0 is nontrivial and in fact contains no nontrivial projections.

PROPOSITION 3.1. *Esscom*$A_0=C_0+LC(H)$ *where* C_0 *is the* C*-*subalgebra* $\{\Sigma\alpha_iR_i : \{\alpha_i\}$ *bounded and* $\alpha_i-\alpha_{i+1}\to 0\}$ *of* C_L.

PROOF. Let $\{\alpha_i\}$ be a bounded sequence of complex scalars and $T_0=\Sigma\alpha_i R_i$. Using 1) and 2) above we compute AT_0-T_0A for $A\varepsilon A_0$ and get $(AT_0-T_0A)R_{2n}=0$ while

(3) $(AT_0-T_0A)R_{2n-1}=(\alpha_{2n-1}-\alpha_{2n-2})R_{2n-2}AR_{2n-1}+(\alpha_{2n-1}-\alpha_{2n})R_{2n}AR_{2n-1}$.

In equation (3) we can choose A in A_0 so that $||R_{2n}AR_{2n-1}||=1$ while $R_{2n-2}AR_{2n-1}=0$ for all n. Thus if $T_0\varepsilon\text{esscom}A_0$ it is necessary that $\alpha_{2n-1}-\alpha_{2n}\to 0$. Similarly we conclude that $\alpha_{2n-1}-\alpha_{2n-2}\to 0$ as $i\to\infty$. Conversely if T is of the form T_0+K where $T_0=\Sigma\alpha_i R_i$ and $\alpha_i-\alpha_{i+1}\to 0$ then combining equations (1) and (2) with (3) we may conclude that $T_0\varepsilon\text{esscom}A_0$.

The exceptional case in (2.5) will be considered next. First, however, we give a condition on N and M which determines when L_r is trivial.

LEMMA 3.2. *Let* $\Pi(N-\{I\})=\{0\}$, $\Pi(M-\{0\})=\{I\}$ *and* $L=N\vee M$. *Then* $N\cap M^\perp$ *generate* $W^*(L_r)$.

PROOF. Let $N=\{0=P_0<P_1<\ldots\}$ and $M=\{I=Q_0>Q_1>\ldots\}$. Notice that $E_i=P_i-P_{i-1}$ and $F_i=Q_i-Q_{i+1}$ are the minimal core projections in N and M respectively and $R_{ij}=E_iF_j$ are the minimal core projections in $L=N\vee M$. The set $\{R_{ij}\}$ has an important order property relative to the algebra $A=\text{Alg}L$. That is, $R_{ij}<<R_{nm}$ if and only if $i\le n$ and $j\ge m$ whence $R_{ij}L(H)R_{nm}\subset A$.

Let $L\varepsilon L_r$, that is, L and $L^\perp$ are in L. Since R_{ij} are minimal members of C_L each $R_{ij}\le L$ or $L^\perp$. Let $R_{1k}\le L$ for some k with $R_{1k}\ne 0$. Then since $R_{1\ell}>>R_{1k}$ or $R_{1k}<<R_{1\ell}$ for all ℓ it follows that $R_{1\ell}\le L$ for all ℓ. Let i_0 be the first index for which $0\ne R_{i_0k}\le L^\perp$. As for i=1 it follows that $R_{i_0\ell}\le L^\perp$ for all ℓ. Let $k_0=\max\{k:R_{ik}\ne 0, 1\le i<i_0\}$ and choose i_1 so that $R_{i_1k_0}\ne 0$ for $i_1<i_0$. Then $R_{i_1k_0}\varepsilon L$. Let $j\le k_0$ and $i\ge i_0$, then $R_{i_1k_0}<<R_{ij}$ and $R_{ij}\varepsilon L$ as well. But $0\ne R_{i_0k}\le L^\perp$ so $k>k_0$. Similarly $R_{ij}\le L$ if $i\ge i_0$ and $j\le k$ so in particular $R_{ij}=0$ if $i\ge i_0$ and $j\le k_0$.

We now have $R_{ij}=0$ if $i\ge i_0$ and $j\le k_0$ and $R_{ij}=0$ if $i<i_0$ and $k>k_0$. However, $P_{i_0-1}=\Sigma R_{ij}$ where $i<i_0$ while $Q_{k_0+1}=\Sigma R_{ij}$ where $j>k_0$ and thus $P_{i_0-1}+Q_{k_0+1}=I$ while $P_{i_0-1}Q_{k_0+1}=0$. Thus $P_{i_0-1}\le L$ and $P_{i_0-1}\varepsilon N\cap M^\perp$. Either $Q_{k+1}=L^\perp$ and $P_{i_0-1}=L$ or applying the same argument to the compression and invoking induction we obtain $L\varepsilon W^*(N\cap M^{\perp})$.

We now come to the description of the essential commutant of the exceptional case in (2.5).

PROPOSITION 3.3. *Let* A *be a width two* CSL *algebra and* $\mathrm{Lat}A=L=N\vee M$ *where* N *and* M *are commuting nests. Assume* $\Pi(N-\{I\})=\{0\}$ *and* $\Pi(M-\{0\})=\{I\}$ *and* $N\cap M^{\perp}=\{0,I\}$. *Then there exists mutually orthogonal finite rank core projection* $\{F_i\}$ *with* $I=\Sigma F_i$ *so that* $T\varepsilon\mathrm{ess\,com}A$ *iff there exists a bounded sequence* $\{a_i\}$ *with* $a_{i+1}-a_i\to 0$ *and* $T-\Sigma a_i F_i$ *is compact.*

PROOF. Let $N=\{0=P_0<P_1<\dots\}$ and $M=\{I=Q_0>Q_1>\dots\}$ and consider R_{ij} as in the proof of (3.2). That is, $R_{ij}=E_iF_j$ where $E_i=P_i-P_{i-1}$ and $F_j=Q_j-Q_{j+1}$. Since $Q_j\to 0$ strongly and P_i is finite dimensional eventually $P_iQ_j=0$ so that eventually $E_iQ_j=0$. Similarly since $P_i\to I$ and F_j are finite dimensional $P_iF_j=F_j$ or $E_iF_j=0$. Thus if we define $k_i=\max\{j:R_{ij}\neq 0\}$ and $\ell_j=\max\{i:R_{ij}\neq 0\}$ we have k_i and $\ell_j\to\infty$ as $i,j\to\infty$.

The proof consists of identifying certain core projections made up of blocks of $\{R_{ij}\}$ so that the algebra A is contained in a new width two CSL algebra A_0 whose minimal core projections are these blocks. A_0 will satisfy (3.1) and we shall then show that $\mathrm{esscom}A=\mathrm{esscom}A_0$.

Define inductively $r_{-1}=s_{-1}=0$, $r_0=1$, $s_0=\ell_1$, $r_k=\max\{k_j:s_{k-2}<j\leq s_{k-1}\}$ and $s_k=\max\{\ell_i:r_{k-1}<i\leq r_k\}$. Since $N\cap M^{\perp}=\{0,1\}$ it follows that $1<r_1<r_2<\dots$ and $\ell_1<s_1<s_2\ \dots$. The indices $\{r_i\}$ and $\{s_i\}$ will determine the new core projections as mentioned above, however, first we indicate some properties of R_{ij} with i,j having various values. First if j is between s_{k-2} and s_{k-1} $(\leq s_{k-1})$ and $i>r_k$ then $R_{ij}=0$ and if $i\leq r_k$ and $j>s_k$ then $R_{ij}=0$ also. Moreover, for each R_{ij} with $r_k<i\leq r_{k+1}$ and $s_{k-1}<j\leq s_k$ there is at least one $0\neq R_{i_kj_k}$ with $r_{k-1}<i_k\leq r_k$ and $j_k=s_k$. Thus $R_{i_kj_k}>>R_{ij}$ for all $r_k<i\leq r_{k+1}$ and $s_{k-1}<j\leq s_k$. Let $U_{k+1}=\Sigma R_{ij}$ where $r_k<i\leq r_{k+1}$ and $s_{k-1}<j\leq s_k$ for $k=0,1,\dots$ The important fact we have is that $R_{i_kj_k}>>U_{k+1}$ for $k=0,1,\dots$. This will enable us to generate members of A in order to determine the structure of $T\varepsilon\text{esscom}\mathcal{A}$. Let $V_{k+1}=\Sigma R_{ij}$ with $r_k<i\leq r_{k+1}$ and $s_k<j\leq s_{k+1}$. The second important fact is that $R_{i_kj_k}\leq V_{k-1}$ and not only do we have that $R_{i_kj_k}>>U_{k+1}$ but moreover $R_{i_kj_k}>>R_{ij}$ for at least one nonzero projection in U_k. This will "tie" U_k and U_{k-1} together. Next we need to observe that by the definition of the indices r_k and s_k, *each* R_{ij} in V_k is >> some R_{ij} in U_k.

Next we observe that the projections (or subspaces) U_k and V_k are mutually orthogonal and sum to the identity. Moreover, they determine a width two CSL algebra $\mathcal{A}_0$ using the relations $V_k>>U_k+U_{k+1}$ (this is not in general true for $\mathcal{A}$). However, $\mathcal{A}\subseteq\mathcal{A}_0$ is given by (3.1). Thus we need only show that $T\varepsilon\text{esscom}\mathcal{A}$ has the form given in (3.1) relative to the projections V_k and U_k. That is if $T\varepsilon C_{\mathcal{L}}$ and $T\varepsilon\text{esscom}\mathcal{A}$, then $T=\Sigma\alpha_kU_k+\beta_kV_k$ where $\alpha_k-\beta_k$ and $\beta_k-\alpha_{k+1}\to 0$ as $k\to\infty$.

For T in $C_{\mathcal{L}}$ and in $\text{esscom}\mathcal{A}$ we may write $T=\Sigma\alpha_{ij}R_{ij}$ for scalars α_{ij}. We need to show that T can be modified by a compact operator so that the same constant can be used for each R_{ij} in the same U_k or V_k. Finally, we need to give the relationship between those constants as mentioned above. For each U_k choose one R_{ij} with $0\neq R_{ij}\leq U_k$ and set $R_k=U_{ij}$ and $\alpha_k=\alpha_{ij}$ for this choice. Let γ_k be $\max|\alpha_{ij}-\alpha_k|$ where the max is taken over the α_{ij} for which $R_{ij}\leq U_k$ and let S_k be the R_{ij} where this maximum occurs. We must show that $\gamma_k-\alpha_k\to 0$. Define a map A_k from $R_{i_kj_k}$ to R_k and S_k taking a unit vector f_k in $R_{i_kj_k}$ to the sum g_k+h_k where g_k and h_k are unit vectors in R_k and S_k respectively. Let $A=\Sigma A_k$ and by the strict ordering properties of the R_{ij} we have that $A\varepsilon\mathcal{A}$. Since TA-AT is compact we conclude that $||(TA-AT)f_k||\to 0$, that is, $\gamma_k-\alpha_k\to 0$. Therefore, T is a compact perturbation of T_0 where $T_0U_k=\alpha_kU_k$ and $|\alpha_k-\alpha_{i_kj_k}|\to 0$.

Next set $\beta_k=\alpha_{i_kj_k}$ and let $\sigma_k=\max|\alpha_{ij}-\beta_k|$ where the max is taken over α_{ij} corresponding to the R_{ij} in V_k and denote this R_{ij} by P_k. As we remarked above $P_k>>R_{ij}$ for some $R_{ij}\leq U_k$ and $R_{i_kj_k}>>R_{i'j'}$ for some $R_{i'j'}$ in U_k. Thus we can define a map A_k taking a unit vector f_k in $R_{i_kj_k}$ and a unit vector g_k in P_k to unit vectors in $R_{i'j'}$ and R_{ij} respectively (maybe the same vector if $(i',j')=(i,j)$). Letting $A=\Sigma A_k$ we have $A\in\mathcal{A}$. Since T_0A-AT_0 is compact we conclude that $\|(T_0A-AT_0)(f_k+g_k)\|\to 0$, that is, $\sigma_k-\beta_k\to 0$ and $\beta_k-\alpha_k\to 0$. Thus T_0 can be perturbed by a compact operator so that restricted to V_k it is simply β_kV_k. The proof is now complete since we may set $F_{2k}=U_k$ and $F_{2k+1}=V_k$ and $a_{2k}=\alpha_k$ while $a_{2k+1}=\beta_k$.

REMARK. The above result shows that there are no essentially reducing projections for $\mathcal{A}$. Thus the C*-algebra consisting of esscom$\mathcal{A}$ is not norm generated by its projections. This is in contrast to our previous results and examples concerning essential commutants.

Our final result concerns the general "exceptional" case to Theorem 2.5. Using (3.2) we reduce this case to the above proposition. Let $\mathcal{N}\cap\mathcal{M}^{\perp}=\{0=L_0<L_1<\ldots\}$. If $\{L_i\}$ is a finite set then we obtain the conclusion of (3.3). The lattice $\mathcal{L}_n=\mathcal{L}|(L_n-L_{n-1})$ is just the join of the restrictions $\mathcal{N}_n$ and $\mathcal{M}_n$ of $\mathcal{N}$ and $\mathcal{M}$ to L_n-L_{n-1}. It is easy to see that $\mathcal{N}_n\cap\mathcal{M}_n^{\perp}=\{0,I_n\}$. Let $J(n)$ be the length of the sequence $r_k(n)$ generated in the above proof by the restrictions of $\mathcal{L}$, $\mathcal{N}$, $\mathcal{M}$ and $\mathcal{A}$ to L_n-L_{n-1}. Call $J(n)$ the *order* of L_n-L_{n-1}. $J(n)$ is finite and measures the length of the sequence of V's obtained in describing the algebra $(L_n-L_{n-1})\mathcal{A}|(L_n-L_{n-1})H$. Let $T\in C_{\mathcal{L}}\cap$esscom$\mathcal{A}$. If $J(n)$ is bounded as $n\to\infty$ it follows that T is a compact perturbation of $\Sigma a_i(L_i-L_{i-1})$. In case $J(n)\to\infty$ we get our final result.

THEOREM 3.4. *Let $\mathcal{A}$ be a width two* CSL *algebra as in* (3.3) *except that* $\mathcal{N}\cap\mathcal{M}^{\perp}=\{0=L_0<L_1<\ldots\}$ *and* $J(n)$ *is the order of* L_i-L_{i-1}. *If* $J(n)$ *is bounded then* esscom$\mathcal{A}$ *is* $W^*(\mathcal{N}\cap\mathcal{M}^{\perp})=\mathcal{A}'$ *plus the compact operators. If* $J(n)\to\infty$ *then there are mutually orthogonal finite rank core projections* $\{F_i\}$ *with* $I=\Sigma F_i$ *so that* esscom$\mathcal{A}$ *is the sum of* $\mathcal{A}'$, *the compact operators and* C*-*algebra consisting of* $\Sigma\alpha_iF_i$ *where* $\{\alpha_i\}$ *is a bounded sequence and* $\alpha_i-\alpha_{i-1}\to 0$.

PROOF. Let $\{F_{ni}\}$ consist of the $\{U_k\}$ and $\{V_k\}$ determined as in the above proof on each restriction of $\mathcal{A}$ to L_n-L_{n-1}. If

$T\in C_L \cap \mathrm{esscom}A$, then T can be represented as $T=\Sigma\alpha_{ni}F_{ni}$. As in the above proof we see that given $\varepsilon>0$, there exists a N_ε so that $|\alpha_{ni}-\alpha_{n,i+1}|<\varepsilon$ if $i>N_\varepsilon$ and $i,i+1\leq J(n)$. Thus by adding to T the operator $\Sigma b_n(L_n-L_{n-1})$ we may modify the α_{ni} so that $\alpha_{n,J(n)}= =\alpha_{n+1,1}$.

Now using dictionary order we relable the F_{in} and α_{in} as F_k and α_k. Thus $T=\Sigma\alpha_k F_k+\Sigma b_n(L_n-L_{n-1})$ and $\alpha_k-\alpha_{k-1}\to 0$ as $k\to\infty$.

REFERENCES

1. Arveson, W.: Operator algebras and invariant subspaces, *Ann. of Math.* 100(1974), 433-532.
2. Christensen, E.; Peligrad, C.: Commutants of nest algebras modulo the compact operators, preprint.
3. Davidson, K.R.: On operators commuting with Toeplitz operators modulo the compact operators, *J.Functional Analysis* 24(1977), 291-302.
4. Gilfeather, F.; Larson, D.R.: Nest subalgebras of von Neumann algebras: Commutants modulo compacts and distance estimates, preprint.
5. Fillmore, P.A.; Stampfli, J.G.; Williams, J.P.: On the essential numerical range, the essential spectrum, and a problem of Halmos, *Acta Sci.Math.(Szeged)* 33(1972),179-192.
6. Johnson, B.E.; Parrott, S.K.: Operators commuting with a von Neumann algebra modulo the set of compact operators, *J.Functional Analysis* 11(1972), 39-61.

Frank Gilfeather and David R.Larson
Department of Mathematics and Statistics,
University of Nebraska-Lincoln
Lincoln, Nebraska 68588
U.S.A.

SIMILARITY OF OPERATOR BLOCKS AND CANONICAL FORMS. II. INFINITE DIMENSIONAL CASE AND WIENER-HOPF FACTORIZATION.

I. Gohberg, M.A. Kaashoek, F. van Schagen

The concept of block-similarity introduced in part I and its extension to the infinite dimensional case developed here provide a unified approach to state feedback theory for systems, the theory of Kronecker indices and Wiener-Hopf factorization problems. In this part we concentrate on the connections with the factorization theory.

INTRODUCTION

This paper is a continuation of [4], in which we considered the problem of classifying blocks of matrices up to similarity. The theory developed in [4] provides a general framework for state feedback theory and the theory of Kronecker indices. In the present paper we show that Wiener-Hopf factorization problems can also be treated on the basis of the block-similarity theory. Theorems about Wiener-Hopf factorization that were recently proved ([5, 10, 6]) appear in this paper as corollaries of our general approach. For example, the connection between factorization indices and Kronecker indices, as established in [5] (see also [2]), we obtain in this way. Also the necessary and sufficient conditions for Wiener-Hopf factorization of operator polynomials given in [10] and the formulas for the factorization indices in [6] we derive in this paper by applying the block-similarity theorems.

To obtain some of the results mentioned above it was necessary to generalize the block-similarity approach to the infinite dimensional case. At the same time the infinite dimensional form of the block-similarity theorems allowed us to consider other applications in infinite dimensional spaces. For instance, we show that with minor modifications the connection between factorization indices and Kronecker indices, given in [5], holds for any operator polynomial that admits Wiener-Hopf factorization.

The present paper consists of three chapters. In Chapter I we give the infinite dimensional version of the block-similarity theory. The main theorems are proved for two extremal cases. The next chapter deals with Wiener-Hopf factorization for operator polynomials. The connections with Kronecker equivalence, state feedback equivalence and block-similarity are established. The applications referred to in the previous paragraphs also appear in this chapter. In the final chapter the main results of Chapter 2 are extended to analytic operator functions. The formulas for linearization, as given in [1, 3], are used to obtain explicit expressions for the factors appearing in the Wiener-Hopf factorization.

The next paper in this series will be a short paper dealing with the reconstruction of a rational matrix assuming that the eigenvalue and eigenvector structure of both the function and its inverse are given. Further plans concern the perturbation theory for blocks of operators and stability problems.

I. INFINITE DIMENSIONAL VERSION OF THE BLOCK-SIMILARITY THEORY

1. Preliminaries about blocks

Let P and Q be bounded projections of the Banach space X. By a (P,Q)-*block* A we shall mean a bounded operator $A: \operatorname{Im} Q \to \operatorname{Im} P$ together with the projections P and Q. Thus a (P_1,Q_1)-block A_1 is equal to a (P_2,Q_2)-block A_2 whenever $P_1 = P_2$, $Q_1 = Q_2$ and $A_1 = A_2$.

Let $T: X \to X$ be a bounded linear operator. A (P,Q)-block A

is said to be a (P,Q)-block of T if A = PTQ, where PTQ is considered as an operator from Im Q into Im P. As in [4] we say that the (P_1,Q_1)-block A_1 is *similar* to the (P_2,Q_2)-block A_2 if there exists an invertible bounded operator S on X such that

(1) $\quad S[\mathrm{Ker}\ P_1] = \mathrm{Ker}\ P_2, \quad S[\mathrm{Im}\ Q_1] = \mathrm{Im}\ Q_2,$

(2) $\quad (P_2SP_1)A_1 = A_2(Q_2SQ_1).$

Assuming (1) we can rewrite (2) as

(3) $\quad (SA_1-A_2S)x \in \mathrm{Ker}\ P_2 \quad (x \in \mathrm{Im}\ Q_1).$

For i = 1,2 let A_i be a (P_i,Q_i)-block of some operator T_i acting on the Banach space X_i. By the *direct sum* $A_1 \oplus A_2$ of the blocks A_1 and A_2 we shall mean the operator

$$A_1 \oplus A_2: \mathrm{Im}\ Q_1 \oplus \mathrm{Im}\ Q_2 \to \mathrm{Im}\ P_1 \oplus \mathrm{Im}\ P_2,$$

considered as a $(P_1 \oplus P_2,\ Q_1 \oplus Q_2)$-block. Using direct sums we can build blocks and decompose complicated blocks into elementary ones. We shall describe two kinds of standard elementary blocks.

Let Y be a Banach space. Let $X = Y^n$ and V be the operator on X defined by

$$V(y_1,\ldots,y_n) = (0,y_1,\ldots,y_{n-1}).$$

Define P and Q to be the projections

$$P(y_1,\ldots,y_n) = (0,y_2,\ldots,y_n),$$
$$Q(y_1,\ldots,y_n) = (y_1,\ldots,y_{n-1},0).$$

We shall call the (P,I)-block of V a *blockshift of the first kind* and the (I,Q)-block of V a *blockshift of the third kind* (see also [4]). Blockshifts of the second kind, which we also considered in [4], will not be used in the present paper. The space Y we shall call the *base space* of the blockshift and the number n-1 will be called its *index*.

In the operator case one can formulate decomposition theorems like those of [4], Section I.3, provided one assumes the subspaces occuring in the proofs to be closed and complemented whenever that is necessary. Here we shall consider only the extremal cases that either P or Q is equal to the identity operator on X.

2. Main theorems for (P,I)-blocks

LEMMA 2.1. *Let* P *be a bounded projection of the Banach space* X, *and let* A *be a* (P,I)-*block. Put* $F_0 = \{0\}$, $F_1 = \operatorname{Ker} P$ *and* $F_j = F_1 \oplus AF_{j-1}$ *for* $j \geq 2$. *If for* $1 \leq j \leq \ell$ *the map*

$$\Delta_j = \operatorname{row}(A^{i-1}(I-P))_{i=1}^{j}: X^j \to X$$

has a generalized inverse, then there exist closed subspaces U_{ij}, $1 \leq i \leq j \leq \ell$, *in* X *such that*

(i) $F_i = F_{i-1} \oplus U_{ii} \oplus \ldots \oplus U_{i\ell}$, $1 \leq i \leq \ell$;

(ii) $AU_{ii} = \{0\}$, $1 \leq i < \ell$;

(iii) $AU_{ij} = PU_{i+1\,j}$, $1 \leq i \leq j-1 \leq \ell-1$;

(iv) *the operators* $A|U_{ij}$ *and* $P|U_{i+1\,j}$ *are injective and have closed range for* $1 \leq i \leq j-1 \leq \ell-1$.

PROOF. To prove the lemma we first show that the operators

(4) $$A|F_k: F_k \to F_{k+1}, \quad j = 1,\ldots,\ell-1,$$

have a generalized inverse. From the definition of F_{k+1} it is clear that $\operatorname{Im}(A|F_k)$ is complemented in F_{k+1}. So we have to show that $(\operatorname{Ker} A) \cap F_k$ is complemented in F_k. This will be done in a number of steps.

Note that $\operatorname{Im} \Delta_j = F_j$. Let Δ_j^+ be a generalized inverse of Δ_j, and consider

$$S_j = (I - \Delta_{j-1}\Delta_{j-1}^+)A^{j-1}(I-P): \operatorname{Ker} P \to X.$$

For $j = 1$ we have $S_j = (I-P)$. From

$$F_j = \operatorname{Im} \Delta_j = \operatorname{Im} \Delta_{j-1} + \operatorname{Im} A^{j-1}(I-P)$$

it is clear that $\operatorname{Im} S_j = (I - \Delta_{j-1}\Delta_{j-1}^+)F_j$. It follows that

$$F_j = F_{j-1} \oplus \operatorname{Im} S_j,$$

and hence $\operatorname{Im} S_j$ is complemented in X. Observe that

$$\operatorname{Ker} S_j = \{x \in \operatorname{Ker} P \mid A^{j-1}x \in F_{j-1}\}.$$

So $\{0\} = \operatorname{Ker} S_1 \subset \operatorname{Ker} S_2 \subset \ldots \subset \operatorname{Ker} S_\ell \subset \operatorname{Ker} P$. We shall prove that

(5) $$\operatorname{Ker} P = \operatorname{Ker} S_j \oplus \operatorname{Im} (I-P)\pi_j\Delta_j^+S_j.$$

Here $\pi_j : X^j \to X$ is the canonical projection of X^j onto the last coordinate space.

To prove (5), take $x \in \operatorname{Ker} P$ and consider $z = \Delta_j^+ S_j x$. Put $y_0 = \pi_j z$. Then

$$z = \begin{pmatrix} y \\ y_0 \end{pmatrix},$$

where $y \in X^{j-1}$. Since $S_j x \in F_j$, we have $\Delta_j \Delta_j^+ S_j x = S_j x$. But then

$$S_j x = \Delta_j \Delta_j^+ S_j x = [\Delta_{j-1} \quad A^{j-1}(I-P)] \begin{pmatrix} y \\ y_0 \end{pmatrix}$$

$$= \Delta_{j-1} y + A^{j-1}(I-P) y_0 .$$

Now use that $S_j x = (I - \Delta_{j-1}\Delta_{j-1}^+) A^{j-1}(I-P)x$. One obtains that

$$S_j x = S_j (I-P) y_0 . \tag{6}$$

So $x - (I-P)y_0 \in \operatorname{Ker} S_j$, and thus $\operatorname{Ker} S_j + \operatorname{Im}(I-P)\pi_j \Delta_j^+ S_j = \operatorname{Ker} P$. Next, take $u \in \operatorname{Ker} S_j \cap \operatorname{Im}(I-P)\pi_j \Delta_j^+ S_j$. So $u = (I-P)\pi_j \Delta_j^+ S_j x$ for some $x \in \operatorname{Ker} P$. From formula (6) we know that $S_j x = S_j (I-P) y_0 = S_j u = 0$. But then u must be zero. This proves formula (5).

From formula (5) it follows that $\operatorname{Ker} S_{j-1}$ is complemented in $\operatorname{Ker} S_j$. So there exist closed subspaces $M_1, \ldots, M_\ell$ of Ker P such that

$$\operatorname{Ker} P = \operatorname{Ker} S_\ell \oplus M_\ell, \quad \operatorname{Ker} S_{j+1} = \operatorname{Ker} S_j + M_j, \ j=1,\ldots,\ell-1.$$

For $j = 1, \ldots, \ell$ put

$$Z_j = \begin{pmatrix} M_1 \oplus \cdots \oplus M_\ell \\ \vdots \qquad \vdots \\ M_j \oplus \cdots \oplus M_\ell \end{pmatrix} = \left\{ \begin{pmatrix} x_1 \\ \vdots \\ x_j \end{pmatrix} \in X^j \mid x_i \in M_i \oplus \cdots \oplus M_\ell \right\}.$$

From the definition of the spaces M_j it is clear that Δ_j maps Z_j in a one-one manner onto F_j.

Note that $A^j(I-P)[M_j] \subset F_j$ if $j < \ell$. As Δ_j maps Z_j in a one-one manner onto F_j, there exist bounded linear operators

$$E_{ij} : M_j \to M_i \oplus \cdots \oplus M_\ell, \quad i = 1, \ldots, j,$$

such that the following diagram is commutative:

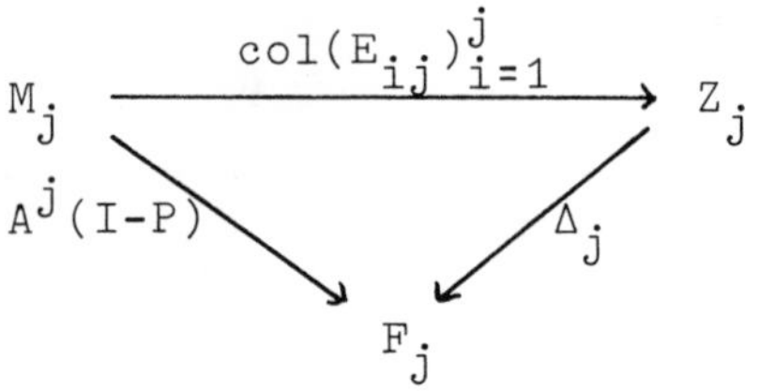

In other words, for $x \in M_j$ $(1 \leq j < \ell)$ we have

(7) $$A^j(I-P)x = (I-P)E_{1j}x + A(I-P)E_{2j}x + \dots + A^{j-1}(I-P)E_{jj}x.$$

As $\mathrm{Im}\, A \subset \mathrm{Im}\, P$, this implies that $E_{1j} = 0$. Define

$$T_j = \begin{pmatrix} -E_{2j} \\ \vdots \\ -E_{jj} \\ I \end{pmatrix} : M_j \to Z_j .$$

Formula (7) implies that

(8) $$A\Delta_j(T_j x) = 0 \quad (x \in M_j).$$

Take a fixed k with $1 \leq k < \ell$. Let $y \in (\mathrm{Ker}\, A) \cap F_k$. We know that y is of the form

$$y = \Delta_k \begin{pmatrix} x_1 \\ \vdots \\ x_k \end{pmatrix},$$

where $x_i \in M_i \oplus \dots \oplus M_\ell$. Assume $x_i = 0$ for $j < i \leq k$. The fact that $Ay = 0$ implies that $x_j \in \mathrm{Ker}\, S_{j+1}$. On the other hand $x_j \in M_j \oplus \dots \oplus M_\ell$. So we must have $x_j \in M_j$. Put

$$y_j = \Delta_k \begin{pmatrix} T_j \\ 0 \\ \vdots \\ 0 \end{pmatrix} x_j = \Delta_j T_j x_j .$$

Then $y_j \in (\mathrm{Ker}\, A) \cap F_k$, and hence $y - y_j \in (\mathrm{Ker}\, A) \cap F_k$. Furthermore, from the definition of T_j it is clear that $y-y_j$ is of the form:

$$y - y_j = \Delta_k \begin{pmatrix} \hat{x}_1 \\ \vdots \\ \hat{x}_{j-1} \\ 0 \\ \vdots \\ 0 \end{pmatrix}$$

with $\hat{x}_i \in M_i \oplus \ldots \oplus M_\ell$ for $i = 1,\ldots,j-1$. So we can repeat the reasoning. It follows that

(9) $$(\mathrm{Ker}\ A) \cap F_k = \Delta_1 T_1[M_1] \oplus \ldots \oplus \Delta_k T_k[M_k].$$

Let W_k be the subspace of Z_k spanned by the vectors

$$\begin{pmatrix} -E_{2j} \\ \vdots \\ -E_{jj} \\ I \\ 0 \\ \vdots \\ 0 \end{pmatrix} x, \quad x \in M_j,\ j = 1,\ldots,k.$$

We have proved that $\Delta_k W_k = (\mathrm{Ker}\ A) \cap F_k$. Obviously,

$$Z_k = W_k \oplus \begin{pmatrix} M_2 \oplus \cdots\cdots \oplus M_\ell \\ \vdots \quad\quad \vdots \\ M_{k+1} \oplus \cdots \oplus M_\ell \end{pmatrix}.$$

As Δ_k maps Z_k in a one-one manner onto F_k it is clear that $\Delta_k[W_k]$ has a closed complement in F_k. Thus $(\mathrm{Ker}\ A) \cap F_k$ is complemented in F_k. So we have proved that the operators (4) have generalized inverses.

We start now with the construction of the spaces U_{ij}. As $F_{\ell-1}$ is complemented in F_ℓ there exists a closed subspace $U_{\ell\ell}$ such that $F_\ell = F_{\ell-1} \oplus U_{\ell\ell}$. As $\mathrm{Ker}\ P \subset F_{\ell-1}$, the operator $P|U_{\ell\ell}$ is injective and has closed range. Now assume we have constructed closed subspaces U_{ij}, $k \le i \le j \le \ell$, of X such that

(i)' $F_i = F_{i-1} \oplus U_{ii} \oplus \ldots \oplus U_{i\ell}$, $k+1 \le i \le \ell$;

(ii)' $AU_{ii} = 0$, $k+1 \le i < \ell$;

(iii)' $AU_{ij} = PU_{i+1\,j}$, $k+1 \le i \le j-1 \le \ell-1$;

(iv)' $A|U_{ij}$ and $P|U_{i+1\,j}$ are injective and have closed range for $k+1 \leq i \leq j-1 \leq \ell-1$.

From $F_{k+1} = F_k \oplus U_{k+1\,k+1} \oplus \dots \oplus U_{k+1\,\ell}$ and Ker $P \subset F_k$ it is clear that $P|U_{k+1\,k+1},\dots,P|U_{k+1\,\ell}$ are injective and have closed range. Put $W_{k+1\,j} = PU_{k+1\,j}$ for $k \leq j-1 \leq \ell-1$, and set $W_{k+1} = W_{k+1\,k+1} \oplus \dots \oplus W_{k+1\,\ell}$. Observe that $PF_{k+1} = PF_k \oplus W_{k+1}$. Also $PF_{k+1} = P(\text{Ker } P \oplus AF_k) = PAF_k = AF_k$, and similarly $PF_k = AF_{k-1}$. It follows that

$$AF_k = PF_{k+1} = PF_k \oplus W_{k+1} = AF_{k-1} \oplus W_{k+1}.$$

From formula (9) we know that

$$(\text{Ker } A) \cap F_k = (\text{Ker } A) \cap F_{k-1} \oplus \Delta_k T_k[M_k].$$

Put $U_{kk} = \Delta_k T_k[M_k]$. Then $AU_{kk} = 0$. Next, let A_k^+ be a generalized inverse of $(A|F_k)\colon F_k \to F_{k+1}$. Define $U_{kj} = A_k^+ W_{k+1\,j}$ for $j = k+1,\dots,\ell$. Clearly, U_{kj} is closed and $A|U_{kj}$ is injective and has closed range for $k \leq j-1 \leq \ell-1$. Further

$$AU_{kj} = AA_k^+ W_{k+1\,j} = W_{k+1\,j} = PU_{k+1\,j}$$

for $k \leq j-1 \leq \ell-1$. It remains to show that

$$F_k = F_{k-1} \oplus U_{kk} \oplus U_{k\,k+1} \oplus \dots \oplus U_{k\ell}$$

Take $x \in F_k$. Then $Ax = Af_{k-1} + w_{k+1} + \dots + w_\ell$ with $f_{k-1} \in F_{k-1}$ and $w_j \in W_{k+1\,j}$. Let $u_j = A_k^+ w_j \in U_{kj}$. Then $Au_j = w_j$ and

$$x - f_{k-1} - \sum_{j=k+1}^{\ell} u_j \in (\text{Ker } A) \cap F_k.$$

But $(\text{Ker } A) \cap F_k \subset F_{k-1} + U_{kk}$. So $x \in F_{k-1} + U_{kk} + \dots + U_{k\ell}$. Next assume that

$$(10) \qquad f_{k-1} + u_k + u_{k+1} + \dots + u_\ell = 0,$$

where $f_{k-1} \in F_{k-1}$ and $u_j \in U_{kj}$. By applying A to the vectors in (10), one sees that

$$Af_{k-1} + Au_{k+1} + \dots + Au_\ell = 0.$$

But this implies that $f_{k-1} \in (\text{Ker } A) \cap F_{k-1}$ and $u_j = 0$ for $j = k+1,\dots,\ell$. Inserting this in (10), yields $f_{k-1} + u_k = 0$. So $u_k \in U_{kk} \cap (\text{Ker } A) \cap F_{k-1} = \{0\}$. Hence all the terms in (10) must be zero. The lemma is proved.

Let us mention that many of the arguments used in the preceding proof are similar to those used by Rowley in [10], Section 4. From Lemma 2.1 we shall now deduce the main decomposition theorem for (P,I)-blocks.

THEOREM 2.2. *Let P be a bounded projection of the Banach space X, and let A be a (P,I)-block. In order that the block A is similar to a direct sum of blockshifts of the first kind it is necessary and sufficient that there exists $\ell \geq 1$ such that the map*

$$\Delta_j = \text{row}(A^{i-1}(I-P))_{i=1}^{j} : X^j \to X$$

has a generalized inverse for $1 \leq j \leq \ell$ and is surjective for $j = \ell$.

PROOF. First suppose that in the space X_0 the (P_0,I)-block A_0 is a direct sum of blockshifts of the first kind. Then it is clear that there exists a number ℓ such that

$$\Delta_{0j} = \text{row}(A_0^{i-1}(I-P_0))_{i=1}^{j} : X_0^j \to X_0$$

has a generalized inverse for $i \leq j \leq \ell$ and is surjective for $j = \ell$. Now suppose that the (P,I)-block A is similar to the (P_0,I)-block A_0. So let $S: X \to X_0$ be an invertible bounded linear operator such that

$$S[\text{Ker } P] = \text{Ker } P_0, \qquad P_0(SA - A_0S) = 0.$$

By induction one proves that

$$(11) \qquad \Delta_{0j} \begin{pmatrix} (I-P_0)S(I-P) & \cdot & \cdots & \cdot & (I-P_0)SA^{j-1}(I-P) \\ & & \cdot & & \cdot \\ & & & \cdot & \vdots \\ & & & & \cdot \\ & & & & (I-P_0)S(I-P) \end{pmatrix} = S\Delta_j .$$

Let Ω_j be the second operator matrix in (11). Obviously Ω_j maps $(\text{Ker } P)^j$ in a one-one manner onto $(\text{Ker } P_0)^j$. Since $(\text{Im } P_0)^j \subset \text{Ker } \Delta_{0j}$, the operator $\Delta_{0j} \mid (\text{Ker } P_0)^j$ has a generalized inverse for $1 \leq j \leq \ell$ and is surjective for $j = \ell$. So we conclude that the same must be true for $\Delta_j \mid (\text{Ker } P)^j$.

Again we have $(\mathrm{Im}\, P)^j \subset \mathrm{Ker}\, \Delta_j$. It follows that Δ_j has the desired properties.

Now, conversely, suppose that Δ_j has a generalized inverse for $1 \le j \le \ell$ and is surjective for $j = \ell$. So in the notations of Lemma 2.1 we have $X = \mathrm{Im}\, \Delta_\ell = F_\ell$. Therefore

$$X = \bigoplus_{i=1}^{\ell} \bigoplus_{j=i}^{\ell} U_{ij} = \bigoplus_{j=1}^{\ell} \bigoplus_{i=1}^{j} U_{ij}, \quad \mathrm{Ker}\, P = \bigoplus_{j=1}^{\ell} U_{1j}$$

Define the projection P_1 by putting $\mathrm{Ker}\, P_1 = \mathrm{Ker}\, P$ and $\mathrm{Im}\, P_1 = \bigoplus_{i=2}^{\ell} \bigoplus_{j=i}^{\ell} U_{ij}$. Then the (P_1,I)-block P_1A is similar to the (P,I)-block A. Now note that for $i+1 \le j \le \ell$, $1 \le i \le \ell-1$ we have

$$P_1A[U_{ij}] = P_1P[U_{i+1\,j}] = P_1U_{i+1\,j} = U_{i+1\,j},$$

and $P_1A|U_{ij}\colon U_{ij} \to U_{i+1\,j}$ is a bounded bijective operator. Put $U_j = U_{1j}$, and define $S\colon \bigoplus_{j=1}^{\ell} U_j^j \to X = \bigoplus_{j=1}^{\ell} \left(\bigoplus_{i=1}^{j} U_{ij}\right)$ by setting

$$S|U_j^j = \begin{pmatrix} I & & & & \\ & P_1A & & & \\ & & \cdot & & \\ & & & \cdot & \\ & & & & (P_1A)^{j-1} \end{pmatrix} | U_j^j .$$

Then S is invertible and

$$S^{-1}(P_1A)S \mid U_j^j = \begin{pmatrix} 0 & \cdot & \cdot & \cdot & 0 \\ I & \cdot & & & \cdot \\ & \cdot & \cdot & & \cdot \\ & & \cdot & \cdot & \cdot \\ & & & I & 0 \end{pmatrix} | U_j^j .$$

It follows that S establishes a block-similarity between P_1A and a direct sum of blockshifts of the first kind.

A (P,I)-block A is said to be of *finite type* if there exists a positive integer ℓ such that $\Delta_j = \mathrm{row}(A^{i-1}(I-P))_{i=1}^{j}$ has a generalized inverse for $1 \le j \le \ell$ and is surjective for $j = \ell$. According to the previous theorem a (P,I)-block A is similar to a direct sum $A_1 \oplus \ldots \oplus A_r$ of blockshifts of the first kind. Let Y_i be the base space of the blockshift A_j, and let ν_j be its index. If two indices ν_α and ν_β are equal, then

$A_\alpha \oplus A_\beta$ is again a blockshift of the first kind, its base is equal to $Y_\alpha \oplus Y_\beta$ and its index is $\nu = \nu_\alpha = \nu_\beta$. So without loss of generality we may assume that $\nu_1 < \nu_2 < \dots < \nu_r$. The set $\{(Y_1,\nu_1),\dots,(Y_r,\nu_r)\}$ we call the *characteristics* of the (P,I)-block A. This terminology is justified by the following theorem.

THEOREM 2.3. *Let* A *be a* (P,I)*-block and* A' *a* (P',I)*-block, both of finite type. Then* A *and* A' *are similar if and only if they have the same characteristics.*

Note. The sets of characteristics $\{(V_i,\nu_i) \mid i = 1,\dots,k\}$ and $\{(V_i',\nu_i') \mid i = 1,\dots,k'\}$ will be called *equal* if $k = k'$, the Banach spaces V_i and V_i' are isomorphic and $\nu_i = \nu_i'$ for all i.

PROOF. Equal sets of characteristics define similar direct sums of blockshifts of the first kind. As A (A') is similar to the direct sum of blockshifts of the first kind, defined by the characteristics of A (A'), and similarity is a transitive relation we have that A and A' are similar.

To prove the converse, let $(Y_1,\nu_1),\dots,(Y_r,\nu_r)$ be a set of characteristics for the (P,I)-block A. We have to show that this set is uniquely determined by A. Let A_j be the blockshift of the first kind with base space Y_j and index ν_j, and let $A_0 = A_1 \oplus \dots \oplus A_r$ be the block direct sum with corresponding projection P_0. Then, by definition, A and A_0 are block-similar with similarity $S: X \to X_0$, say. Put $\Delta_j = \mathrm{row}(A^{i-1}(I-P))_{i=1}^{j}$ and $\Delta_{0j} = \mathrm{row}(A_0^{i-1}(I-P_0))_{i=1}^{j}$. From formula (11) we see that $S\,\mathrm{Im}\,\Delta_j = \mathrm{Im}\,\Delta_{0j}$. Further, if $Ax = 0$, then $A_0Sx = P_0A_0Sx = P_0(A_0S - SA)x = 0$. So $S\,\mathrm{Ker}\,A \subset \mathrm{Ker}\,A_0$. Using the symmetry of the similarity notion we may conclude that $S\,\mathrm{Ker}\,A = \mathrm{Ker}\,A_0$. So we have

$$(12)\qquad S[\mathrm{Ker}\,A \cap \mathrm{Im}\,\Delta_j] = \mathrm{Ker}\,A_0 \cap \mathrm{Im}\,\Delta_{0j}.$$

Now one easily checks that

$$\mathrm{Ker}\,A_0 \cap \mathrm{Im}\,\Delta_{0j} = \mathrm{Ker}\,A_0 \cap \mathrm{Im}\,\Delta_{0j-1} \oplus \begin{cases} Y_i & \text{if } j = \nu_i+1, \\ (0) & \text{otherwise.} \end{cases}$$

According to formula (12) this implies that the numbers $\nu_1,\dots,\nu_r$ are uniquely determined by the block A. Also, one sees that the spaces $Y_1,\dots,Y_r$ are uniquely determined up to an isomorphism by A. The proof is complete.

From the last part of the proof of the previous theorem one deduces without difficulty the following corollary.

COROLLARY 2.4. *Let* A *be a* (P,I)*-block of finite type. Put* $\Delta_j = \text{row}(A^{i-1}(I-P))_{i=1}^{j}$ *for* $j \geq 1$ *and* $\Delta_0 = 0$. *Let* $\omega_1 < \dots < \omega_r$ *be the positive integers* j *such that the quotient space*

$$Y_j = \frac{\text{Ker } A \cap \text{Im } \Delta_j}{\text{Ker } A \cap \text{Im } \Delta_{j-1}} \neq (0).$$

Then $(Y_{\omega_1},\omega_1-1),\dots,(Y_{\omega_r},\omega_r-1)$ *is the set of characteristics of the block* A.

Let $(Y_1,\nu_1),\dots,(Y_r,\nu_r)$ be the set of characteristics of the (P,I)-block A. Then A is similar to the (P_0,I)-block of the operator T_0, where

$$T_0 = \left(\begin{array}{c|c|c} \begin{matrix} 0 & & & \\ I_1 & \ddots & & \\ & \ddots & \ddots & \\ & & I_1 & 0 \end{matrix} & & \\ \hline & \ddots & \\ \hline & & \begin{matrix} 0 & & & \\ I_r & \ddots & & \\ & \ddots & \ddots & \\ & & I_r & 0 \end{matrix} \end{array}\right) \begin{matrix} \}\ \nu_1+1 \\ \\ \\ \}\ \nu_r+1 \end{matrix} \left(\begin{array}{c|c|c} \begin{matrix} 0 & 0 & \cdots & 0 \\ 0 & I_1 & & \\ \vdots & & \ddots & \\ 0 & & & I_1 \end{matrix} & & \\ \hline & \ddots & \\ \hline & & \begin{matrix} 0 & 0 & \cdots & 0 \\ 0 & I_r & & \vdots \\ \vdots & & \ddots & \\ 0 & \cdots & & I_r \end{matrix} \end{array}\right) = P_0$$

Here $I_1,\dots,I_r$ denote the identity operators on $Y_1,\dots,Y_r$, respectively.

We end this section with a theorem that will be used later on.

THEOREM 2.5. *Let* X *and* Y *be Banach spaces, and let* $A: X \to X$ *and* $B: Y \to X$ *be bounded linear operators. Suppose that*

$$[B \ AB \ \dots \ A^{j-1}B]: Y^j \to X$$

has a generalized inverse for $1 \leq j \leq \ell$ *and is surjective for* $j = \ell$. *Then there exist closed subspaces* $U_0,\dots,U_\ell$ *of* Y *with* $Y = \bigoplus_{j=0}^{\ell} U_j$, *and there exist bounded operators*

$$N: \bigoplus_{j=1}^{\ell} U_j^j \to X, \qquad F: X \to Y$$

such that N *is invertible and*

(i) $N^{-1}B: \bigoplus_{j=0}^{\ell} U_j \to \bigoplus_{j=1}^{\ell} U_j^j$ *has the matrix*

$$\begin{pmatrix} 0 & I_1 & 0 & 0 & & 0 \\ \cdot & 0 & I_2 & & & \\ \cdot & \cdot & 0 & 0 & & \\ & & 0 & I_3 & & \\ \cdot & \cdot & \cdot & 0 & & \\ & & & 0 & & \\ \cdot & & & & & 0 \\ \cdot & \cdot & \cdot & & & I_\ell \\ & & & & & 0 \\ & & & & & \\ 0 & 0 & 0 & 0 & \cdot & 0 \end{pmatrix};$$

(ii) $N^{-1}(A-BF)N: \bigoplus_{j=1}^{\ell} U_j^j \to \bigoplus_{j=1}^{\ell} U_j^j$ *has the matrix*

$$\begin{pmatrix} 0 & & & \\ & \begin{matrix} 0 & 0 \\ I_2 & 0 \end{matrix} & & \\ & & \begin{matrix} 0 & 0 & 0 \\ I_3 & 0 & 0 \\ 0 & I_3 & 0 \end{matrix} & \\ & & & \ddots \\ & & & & \begin{matrix} 0 & \cdot & \cdots & \cdot & 0 \\ I_\ell & \ddots & & & \vdots \\ 0 & \ddots & \ddots & & \vdots \\ \vdots & & \ddots & \ddots & \vdots \\ 0 & \cdots & 0 & I_\ell & 0 \end{matrix} \end{pmatrix}. \tag{13}$$

In (i) *and* (ii) *the symbol* I_j *denotes the identity operator on* U_j. *Note that it might happen that* $U_j = (0)$ *for some* j.

PROOF. Let P be a projection of X such that Ker P = Im B. Consider the (P,I)-block PA of the operator A. We first prove that

$$\Delta_{0j} = \operatorname{row}((PA)^{i-1}(I-P))_{i=1}^{j}: X^j \to X$$

has a generalized inverse for $1 \le j \le \ell$ and is surjective for $j = \ell$. Put $\Omega_j = \text{row}(A^{i-1}B)_{i=1}^{j}$. As B has a generalized inverse, there exists a closed subspace M such that $Y = \text{Ker}\, B \oplus M$. The fact that $(\text{Ker}\, B)^j \subset \text{Ker}\, \Omega_j$ implies that Ω_j and $\Omega_j \mid M^j$ have the same invertibility properties. Let B^+ be a generalized inverse of B such that $BB^+ = I-P$ and $\text{Im}\, B^+ = M$. As B^+ maps Im B in a one-one manner onto M it is clear that $[BB^+ \; ABB^+ \; \dots \; A^{j-1} BB^+] \mid (\text{Im}\, B)^j$ has a generalized inverse for $j = 1,\dots,\ell$ and is surjective for $j = \ell$. Now use formula (11) with $S = I$, $A_0 = PA$ and $P_0 = P$. It follows that $\Delta_{0j} \mid (\text{Ker}\, P)^j : (\text{Ker}\, P)^j \to X$ has a generalized inverse for $j = 1,\dots,\ell$ and is surjective for $j = \ell$. As $(\text{Im}\, P)^j \subset \text{Ker}\, \Delta_{0j}$, the operator Δ_{0j} must have the same properties.

Now, like in the proof of Theorem 2.2 we have

$$X = \bigoplus_{j=1}^{\ell} \bigoplus_{i=1}^{j} U_{ij}, \qquad \text{Im}\, B = \text{Ker}\, P = \bigoplus_{j=1}^{\ell} U_{jj}.$$

Let P_1 be the projection of X with $\text{Ker}\, P_1 = \text{Im}\, B$ and $\text{Im}\, P_1 = \bigoplus_{j=2}^{\ell} \bigoplus_{i=2}^{j} U_{ij}$. Put $A_0 = P_1PA = P_1A$. Lemma 2.1 gives

$$A_0[U_{ii}] = (0) \quad (1 \le i \le \ell),$$

$$A_0[U_{ij}] = U_{i+1\, j} \quad (1 \le i \le j-1 \le \ell-1).$$

Let B^+ be a generalized inverse of B. Then BB^+ is a projection of X onto Im B. So we have

$$A_0 = A - (I-P_1)A = A - BB^+(I-P_1)A.$$

Put $F = B^+(I-P_1)A$. Then $A_0 = A - BF$. Further, define $U_j = B^+[U_{1j}]$ for $j = 1,\dots,\ell$ and $U_0 = \text{Ker}\, B$. Then $Y = \bigoplus_{j=0}^{\ell} U_j$. Further, define $N: \bigoplus_{j=1}^{\ell} U_j^j \to X = \bigoplus_{j=1}^{\ell} \bigoplus_{i=1}^{j} U_{ij}$ by setting

$$N \mid U_j^j = \begin{pmatrix} B & & & \\ & P_1AB & & \\ & & \ddots & \\ & & & (P_1A)^{j-1}B \end{pmatrix} \mid U_j^j.$$

Now it is simple to check that $U_0,\dots,U_\ell$, F and N have the desired properties.

3. Main theorems for (I,Q)-blocks

LEMMA 3.1. *Let Q be a bounded projection of the Banach space X, and let A be a (I,Q)-block. Put* $D_0 = X$, $D_1 = \operatorname{Im} Q$ *and* $D_j = \{x \in D_{j-1} \mid Ax \in D_{j-1}\}$ *for* $j \geq 2$. *If for* $1 \leq j \leq \ell$ *the map*

$$\Omega_j = \operatorname{col}((I-Q)(AQ)^{i-1})_{i=1}^{j} : X \to X^j$$

has a generalized inverse. Then there exist closed subspaces U_{ij}, $1 \leq i \leq j \leq \ell$, *in X such that*

(i) $D_{i-1} = D_i \oplus U_{ii} \oplus \dots \oplus U_{i\ell}$ $(1 \leq i \leq \ell)$;

(ii) $A[U_{ij}] = U_{i-1\,j}$ *and* $A|U_{ij}$ *is injective* $(2 \leq i \leq j \leq \ell)$.

PROOF. For $1 \leq j \leq \ell$ define

$$S_j : D_{j-1} \to \operatorname{Ker} Q, \quad S_j x = (1-Q)(AQ)^{j-1}x. \tag{14}$$

We shall prove that $S_1,\dots,S_\ell$ have generalized inverses. Consider $\Omega_j^0 : X \to (\operatorname{Ker} Q)^j$, defined by $\Omega_j^0 x = \Omega_j x$. Note that $D_j = \operatorname{Ker} \Omega_j^0$ and that Ω_j^0 has a generalized inverse for $j = 1,\dots,\ell$. So D_j is a complemented subspace of X. As $D_j \subset D_{j-1}$ this implies that there exists a closed subspace W such that

$$D_{j-1} = D_j \oplus W. \tag{15}$$

Further note that for $x \in D_{j-1}$ we have $x, Ax, \dots, A^{j-1}x \in \operatorname{Im} Q$ and $(AQ)^{j-1}x = A^{j-1}x$. This gives $D_j = \operatorname{Ker} S_j$. So $\operatorname{Ker} S_j$ is complemented.

Next let V be a closed complement of D_{j-1} in X. So X = $X = D_j \oplus W \oplus V$. By applying Ω_j^0, we see that $\Omega_j^0[W]$ is complemented in $\Omega_j^0[X]$. But $\Omega_j^0[X]$ is complemented in $(\operatorname{Ker} Q)^j$. So $\Omega_j^0[W]$ is complemented in $(\operatorname{Ker} Q)^j$. Now observe that

$$\Omega_j^0 x = \begin{pmatrix} \Omega_{j-1}^0 x \\ S_j x \end{pmatrix}.$$

So for $x \in W \subset D_{j-1}$ we have that $\Omega_j^0 x = \begin{pmatrix} 0 \\ S_j x \end{pmatrix}$. So $S_j[W] = \operatorname{Im} S_j$ is complemented in Y, and hence we proved that S_j has a generalized inverse.

The construction of the spaces U_{ij} is carried out by induction. First we take $U_{\ell\ell}$ such that $D_{\ell-1} = D_\ell \oplus U_{\ell\ell}$ (see (15)). Next take $2 \leq k \leq \ell$ and assume that we have U_{ij} $(k \leq i \leq j \leq \ell)$ such that (i)' $D_{i-1} = D_i \oplus U_{ii} \oplus \dots \oplus U_{i\ell}$ $(k \le i \le \ell)$

(ii)" $A[U_{ij}] = U_{i-1\,j}$ and $A|U_{i-1\,j}$ is injective $(k+1 \le i \le \ell)$.

We shall construct the spaces $U_{k-1\,k-1}, \dots, U_{k-1\,\ell}$. Put U_{ij} $(k \le i \le j \le \ell)$ such that (i) and (ii) hold for $k \le i \le j \le \ell$. Put

$$V = U_{kk} \oplus U_{k\,k+1} \oplus \dots \oplus U_{k\ell}.$$

We know that V is closed in X and $D_{k-1} = D_k \oplus V$. Because $\operatorname{Ker} S_k = D_k$ has a generalized inverse, the space $S_k[V] = \operatorname{Im} S_k$ is complemented in Ker Q. Note that for $x \in D_{k-1}$ we have $S_k x = S_{k-1}Ax$. So $S_k[V] = S_{k-1}A[V]$ is complemented in $\operatorname{Im} S_{k-1} \subset$ $\subset \operatorname{Ker} Q$. Choose a closed subspace U in $\operatorname{Im} S_{k-1}$ such that

$$\operatorname{Ker} Q = S_{k-1}A[V] \oplus U \oplus W = \operatorname{Im} S_{k-1} \oplus W.$$

Let S_{k-1}^{+} be a generalized inverse of S_{k-1} with $\operatorname{Ker} S_{k-1}S_{k-1}^{+} = W$. Let Q_{k-1} be the projection of Ker Q along $S_{k-1}A[V] \oplus W$ onto U. Then $S_{k-1}^{+}Q_{k-1}$ is a generalized inverse to $Q_{k-1}S_{k-1}$ as one easily checks. So $\operatorname{Ker}(Q_{k-1}S_{k-1})$ is a complemented subspace of D_{k-2}. Now $\operatorname{Ker}(Q_{k-1}S_{k-1}) = A[V] + \operatorname{Ker} S_{k-1} = A[V] + D_{k-1}$. Choose a closed subspace $U_{k-1\,k-1}$ such that

$$D_{k-2} = (D_{k-1} + A[V]) \oplus U_{k-1\,k-1}.$$

Next we prove $D_{k-1} \cap A[V] = \{0\}$. Indeed, if for $x \in V$ we have $Ax \in D_{k-1}$, then $S_k x = S_{k-1}Ax = 0$. So $x \in (\operatorname{Ker} S_k) \cap V = D_k \cap V =$ $= \{0\}$. Now to finish the proof we show that

$$A|V \colon V \to D_{k-2}$$

is one-one and has closed range. Because if this is known we can choose $U_{k-1\,j} = A[U_{kj}]$, $k \le j \le \ell$. So choose a sequence $(x_n)_{n\in\mathbb{N}}$ in V such that $\|x_n\| = 1$ $(n = 1,2,\dots)$ and $\lim_{n\to\infty} Ax_n = 0$. Let $S_k^{\sim}$ be a generalized inverse to S_k such that $\operatorname{Im} S_k^{\sim}S_k = V$. Then

$$x_n = S_k^{\sim}S_k x_n = S_k^{\sim}S_{k-1}Ax_n \to 0 \quad (n \to \infty),$$

which contradicts $\|x_n\| = 1$ for all n. So $A|V$ is one-one and has closed range.

THEOREM 3.2. *Let Q be a bounded projection of the Banach space X, and let A be a (I,Q)-block. In order that the block A is similar to a direct sum of shifts of the third kind it is necessary and sufficient that there exists* $\ell \geq 1$ *such that the map*

$$\Omega_j = \mathrm{col}((I-Q)(AQ)^i)_{i=0}^{j-1}: X \to X^j$$

has a generalized inverse for $1 \leq j \leq \ell$ *and is injective for* $j = \ell$.

PROOF. First suppose that in the space X_0 the (I,Q_0)-block A_0 is a direct sum of blockshifts of the third kind. Then it is clear that there exists a number ℓ such that

$$\Omega_{0j} = \mathrm{col}((I-Q_0)(A_0Q_0)^{i-1})_{i=1}^{j}: X_0 \to X_0^j$$

has a generalized inverse for $1 \leq j \leq \ell$ and is injective for $j = \ell$. Now suppose that the (I,Q)-block A is similar to the (I,Q_0)-block A_0. So let $S: X \to X_0$ be an invertible bounded operator such that

$$S(\mathrm{Im}\, Q) = \mathrm{Im}\, Q_0, \qquad (SA - A_0S)Q = 0.$$

Then we have

$$(16)\qquad \begin{bmatrix} (I-Q_0)S & & & \\ (I-Q_0)A_0Q_0S & (I-Q_0)S & & \\ \vdots & \ddots & \ddots & \\ (I-Q_0)(A_0Q_0)^{j-1}S & \cdots & (I-Q_0)A_0Q_0S & (I-Q_0)S \end{bmatrix} \Omega_j = \Omega_{0j}S.$$

We conclude that $\Omega_j^0: X \to (\mathrm{Ker}\, Q)^j$ defined by $\Omega_j^0 x = \Omega_j x$ has a generalized inverse for $1 \leq j \leq \ell$ and is injective for $j = \ell$. So the same holds true for Ω_j.

Next suppose that Ω_j has a generalized inverse for $1 \leq j \leq \ell$ and is surjective for $j = \ell$. Using the notations of Lemma 3.1 we have $D_\ell = \mathrm{Ker}\, \Omega_\ell = \{0\}$. Therefore

$$X = \bigoplus_{i=1}^{\ell} \bigoplus_{j=i}^{\ell} U_{ij} = \bigoplus_{j=1}^{\ell} \bigoplus_{i=1}^{j} U_{ij}$$

and

$$\mathrm{Im}\, Q = \bigoplus_{i=2}^{\ell} \bigoplus_{j=i}^{\ell} U_{ij} = \bigoplus_{j=2}^{\ell} \bigoplus_{i=2}^{j} U_{ij}.$$

Further, for $2 \le i \le j \le \ell$ we have $A|U_{ij}: U_{ij} \to U_{i-1\,j}$ is a bounded bijective operator. Put $U_j = U_{jj}$, and define $S: \bigoplus_{j=1}^{\ell} U_j^j \to X = \bigoplus_{j=1}^{\ell} \bigoplus_{i=1}^{j} U_{j-i+1,j}$ by setting

$$S|U_j^j = \begin{pmatrix} I \\ A \\ \vdots \\ A^{j-1} \end{pmatrix} \mid U^j$$

Clearly S is invertible. Further, if Q' is the projection of X onto Im Q along $\bigoplus_{j=1}^{\ell} U_{1j}$, then

$$S^{-1}(AQ')S|U_j^j = \begin{pmatrix} 0 & \cdots & \cdots & 0 \\ I & \ddots & & \vdots \\ & \ddots & \ddots & \vdots \\ & & I & 0 \end{pmatrix} \mid U_j^j.$$

It follows that the (I,Q')-block AQ' is block-similar to a direct sum of blockshifts of the third kind. But the (I,Q)-block A and the (I,Q')-block AQ' are also block-similar. Hence the proof is complete.

A (I,Q)-block A is said to be of *finite type* if there exists a positive integer ℓ such that $\Omega_j = \mathrm{col}((I-Q)(AQ)^{i-1})_{i=1}^{j}$ has a generalized inverse for $1 \le j \le \ell$ and is injective for $j = \ell$.. So a (I,Q)-block A of finite type is always similar to a direct sum $A_1 \oplus \dots \oplus A_s$ of blockshifts of the third kind. Let Z_j be the base space of the blockshift A_j, and let κ_j be its index. Without loss of generality we may assume that $\kappa_1 < \kappa_2 < \dots < \kappa_s$. The set

$$\{(Z_1,\kappa_1),\dots,(Z_s,\kappa_s)\}$$

we call the *characteristics* of the (I,Q)-block A. The next theorem is the analogue of Theorem 2.3 in the previous section.

THEOREM 3.3. *Let* A *be a* (I,Q)*-block and* A' *a* (I,Q')*-block, both of finite type. Then* A *and* A' *are similar if and only if they have the same characteristics.*

PROOF. The proof of the "if part" is the same as for

Theorem 2.3. To prove the converse, let $(Z_1,\kappa_1),\ldots,(Z_s,\kappa_s)$ be a set of characteristics for the (I,Q)-block A. We have to show that this set is uniquely determined by A. Let A_j be the block-shift of the third kind with base space Z_j and index κ_j, and let $A_0 = A_1 \oplus \ldots \oplus A_s$ be the block direct sum with the corresponding projection Q_0. Then, by definition, A and A_0 are block-similar with similarity $S\colon X \to X_0$, say. Let D_j and D_{0j} be the spaces introduced in Lemma 3.1 for A and A_0, respectively.

Using the special form the block A_0 has, one easily deduces that

$$(17)\qquad D_{0j-1} = (D_{0j} + A_0 D_{0j}) \oplus \begin{cases} Z_i & \text{if } j = \kappa_i+1, \\ (0) & \text{otherwise.} \end{cases}$$

Next we shall prove that

$$(18)\qquad S[D_j] = D_{0j}, \quad S[D_j + AD_j] = D_{0j} + AD_{0j}.$$

In order to do this, it is sufficient to prove that

$$S[D_j] \subset D_{0j}, \quad SA[D_j] \subset A_0 D_{0j}.$$

But these inclusions are easy to check by induction on j. From formulas (17) and (18) it is clear that the numbers $\kappa_1,\ldots,\kappa_s$ are uniquely determined by the block A. Also one sees that up to an isomorphism the spaces $Z_1,\ldots,Z_s$ are uniquely determined by A. The theorem is proved.

The following corollary is an immediate consequence of formulas (17) and (18) above.

COROLLARY 3.4. *Let* A *be a* (I,Q)-*block of finite type. Put* $\Omega_j = \mathrm{col}((I-Q)(AQ)^{i-1})_{i=1}^{j}$ *for* $j \geq 1$ *and* $\Omega_0 = I$. *Let* $\omega_1 < \omega_2 < \ldots$ $\ldots < \omega_s$ *be the positive integers* j *such that the quotient space*

$$Z_j = \frac{\mathrm{Ker}\ \Omega_{j-1}}{\mathrm{Ker}\ \Omega_j + A\ \mathrm{Ker}\ \Omega_j} \neq (0).$$

Then $(Z_{\omega_1},\omega_1-1),\ldots,(Z_{\omega_s},\omega_s-1)$ *is the set of characteristics of the block* A.

THEOREM 3.5. *Let* X *and* Y *be Banach spaces, and let* $A\colon X \to X$ *and* $C\colon X \to Y$ *be bounded linear operators. Suppose that* $\mathrm{col}(CA^{i-1})_{i=1}^{j}\colon X \to Y^j$ *has a generalized inverse for* $1 \leq j \leq \ell$ *and is injective for* $j = \ell$. *Then there exist closed subspaces* $U_0, \ldots, U_\ell$ *of* Y *with* $Y = \bigoplus_{j=0}^{\ell} U_j$, *and there exist bounded operators*

$$N: \bigoplus_{j=1}^{\ell} U_j^j \to X, \quad G: X \to Y$$

such that N *is invertible and*

(i) $CN: \bigoplus_{j=1}^{\ell} U_j^j \to \bigoplus_{j=0}^{\ell} U_j$ *is represented by the matrix*

$$\begin{bmatrix} 0 & \cdot & \cdot & \cdot & \cdot & & & & & & & \\ I_1 & 0 & \cdot & \cdot & \cdot & \cdot & & & & & & \\ 0 & 0 & I_2 & 0 & \cdot & \cdot & \cdot & \cdot & \cdot & & & \\ & & & 0 & 0 & I_3 & 0 & \cdot & \cdot & \cdot & & \\ & & & & & & & & & & & \\ 0 & & \cdot & & \cdot & & \cdot & & 0 & 0 & 0 & \cdots & I_\ell \end{bmatrix},$$

(ii) $N^{-1}(A-CG)N: \bigoplus_{j=1}^{\ell} U_j^j \to \bigoplus_{j=1}^{\ell} U_j^j$ *is represented by the matrix* (13).

In (i) *and* (ii) *the symbol* I_j *denotes the identity operator on* U_j. *Note that it might happen that* $U_j = (0)$ *for some* j.

PROOF. Let Q be a projection such that $\operatorname{Im} Q = \operatorname{Ker} C$. Consider the (I,Q)-block AQ of A. First we prove that

$$(19) \qquad \operatorname{col}((I-Q)(AQ)^{i-1})_{i=1}^{j}: X \to X^j$$

has a generalized inverse for $1 \le j \le \ell$ and is injective for $j = \ell$. Note that $\operatorname{col}(CA^{i-1})_{i=1}^{j}: X \to (\operatorname{Im} C)^j$ has a generalized inverse for $1 \le j \le \ell$ and is injective for $j = \ell$. Now choose a generalized inverse C^+ of C such that $C^+C = (I-Q)$. Then $C^+|\operatorname{Im} C: \operatorname{Im} C \to X$ is injective and has complemented range. So $C^+.\operatorname{col}(CA^{i-1})_{i=1}^{j} = \operatorname{col}(I-Q)A^{i-1})_{i=1}^{j}$ has complemented kernel and range for $1 \le j \le \ell$ and is injective for $j = \ell$. It follows that $\operatorname{col}((I-Q)A^{i-1}Q)_{i=1}^{j}: \operatorname{Im} Q \to X^j$ has a generalized inverse for $1 \le j \le \ell$ and is injective for $j = \ell$. Next one can use an identity as in formula (16) (with $Q = Q_0$, $A_0 = AQ$ and $S = I$) to conclude that the operator (19) has the desired invertibility properties.

Next we apply Lemma 3.1 and conclude that

$$X = \bigoplus_{j=1}^{\ell} \bigoplus_{i=1}^{j} U_{ij}, \quad \operatorname{Ker} C = \operatorname{Im} Q = \bigoplus_{j=2}^{\ell} \bigoplus_{i=2}^{j} U_{ij}.$$

Further $AQ[U_{ij}] = U_{i-1\,j}$ and $AQ|U_{ij}$ is injective. Define $U_j = C(AQ)^{j-1}[U_{jj}]$. Note that U_j is closed and

$$E_j = C(AQ)^{j-1}|U_{jj}\colon U_{jj} \to U_j$$

is bijective, because U_{1j} is in a closed linear complement of Ker C. Let $N\colon \bigoplus_{j=1}^{\ell} U_j^j \to X = \bigoplus_{j=1}^{\ell} \bigoplus_{i=1}^{j} U_{j-i+1\,j}$ be defined by

$$N|U_j^j = \begin{pmatrix} E_j^{-1} \\ (AQ)E_j^{-1} \\ \vdots \\ (AQ)^{j-1}E_j^{-1} \end{pmatrix} \Big| \; U_j^j.$$

Then (i) holds true and $N^{-1}(AQ)N$ is represented by the matrix (13). Let C^+ be a generalized inverse of C such that $C^+C = I-Q$. Then

$$AQ = A - A(I-Q) = A - (AC^+)C.$$

So we take $G = AC^+$. Also we have $\operatorname{Im} C = \bigoplus_{j=1}^{\ell} U_j$. Finally, we choose U_0 to be Ker C^+.

II. WIENER-HOPF FACTORIZATION OF OPERATOR POLYNOMIALS

1. Preliminaries

We begin with recalling the definition of Wiener-Hopf factorization. Let Γ be a closed rectifiable Jordan curve in the complex plane. The bounded inner domain of Γ we denote by Ω, and for simplicity we shall assume that $0 \in \Omega$. In this chapter Y will denote a complex Banach space. Let $L_1(\lambda)$ and $L_2(\lambda)$ be operator polynomials on Y, i.e., polynomials whose coefficients are bounded linear operators on Y. We call $L_1(\lambda)$ and $L_2(\lambda)$ *left Wiener-Hopf equivalent* with respect to Γ if $L_1(\lambda)$ and $L_2(\lambda)$ are invertible for each $\lambda \in \Gamma$ and

(1) $\qquad L_2(\lambda) = E_-(\lambda)L_1(\lambda)E_+(\lambda), \quad (\lambda \in \Gamma),$

where $E_+(\lambda)$ $(E_-(\lambda))$ is holomorphic on Ω (on $\mathbb{C}_\infty \setminus \bar{\Omega}$), continuous up to the boundary Γ, and for each λ in $\bar{\Omega}$ (in $\mathbb{C}_\infty \setminus \Omega$) the operator $E_+(\lambda)$ ($E_-(\lambda)$) is invertible. We call (1) a *left Wiener-Hopf factorization* of $L_2(\lambda)$ if in the right hand side of (1) the middle term $L_1(\lambda) = D(\lambda) = \Sigma_{i=1}^r \lambda^{\nu_i} P_i$, where $0 \le \nu_1 \le \dots \le \nu_r$ are integers and $P_1,\dots,P_r$ are mutually disjoint projections of Y such that $\Sigma_{i=1}^r P_i = I_Y$. For obvious reasons we prefer for finite dimensional Y to choose $\mathrm{Im}\, P_i$ 1-dimensional, and in that case $\nu_1 \le \dots \le \nu_r$ are called the *left Wiener-Hopf factorization indices*. In the infinite dimensional case we shall assume that $0 \le \nu_1 < \nu_2 < \dots < \nu_r$.

We call $L_1(\lambda)$ and $L_2(\lambda)$ *right Wiener-Hopf equivalent* with respect to Γ if $L_1(\lambda)$ and $L_2(\lambda)$ are invertible for each $\lambda \in \Gamma$ and

$$L_2(\lambda) = E_+(\lambda)L_1(\lambda)E_-(\lambda), \quad (\lambda \in \Gamma),$$

where $E_+(\lambda)$ and $E_-(\lambda)$ are as above. One defines *right Wiener-Hopf factorization* and *right Wiener-Hopf factorization indices* in the same way as it is done for the "left" case.

In this chapter our main concern is to find necessary and sufficient conditions for Wiener-Hopf factorization of operator polynomials. Our main tool will be the notion of Γ-spectral pairs as introduced in [7]. First we shall repeat the main definitions. A pair of operators (A,B) is called a *left admissible pair* if $A: X \to X$ and $B: Y \to X$. Here X is an auxiliary Banach space which is called the *base space* of the pair (A,B). A left admissible pair (A,B) is said to be a *left partial Γ-spectral pair* for the operator polynomial $L(\lambda) = \Sigma_{i=0}^{\ell} \lambda^i L_i$ if

(a) $\sigma(A) \subset \Omega$,

(b) $\Sigma_{i=0}^{\ell} A^i B L_i = 0$,

(c) $\mathrm{row}(A^{i-1}B)_{i=1}^{\ell}$ is right invertible.

The condition (b) is equivalent to the requirement that the function $(\lambda-A)^{-1}BL(\lambda)$ has an analytic continuation on Ω.

In a similar way one defines the notion of a right partial Γ-spectral pair (C,A) for $L(\lambda)$. In this case $C: X \to Y$ and $A: X \to X$, and instead of conditions (b) and (c) one has to require

(b)' $\Sigma_{i=0}^{\ell} L_i CA^i = 0$,

(c)' $\mathrm{col}(CA^{i-1})_{i=1}^{\ell}$ is left invertible.

Let (A,B) and (A',B') be left admissible pairs with base space X and X', respectively. We say that (A,B) and (A',B') are *similar* if there exists an invertible operator $S: X \to X'$ such that

$$A = SA'S^{-1}, \quad B = SB'.$$

The pair (A',B') is called a *restriction* of (A,B) if there exists an A-invariant subspace Z of X such that Z is complemented in X and the pair (A',B') is similar to $(PA|\mathrm{Im}\, P, PB)$, where P may be any projection of X along Z. The right admissible pair (C',A') is said to be a *restriction* of the right admissible pair (C,A) if there exists an A-invariant subspace Z in X such that Z is complemented in X and the pairs (C',A') and $(C|Z, A|Z)$ are similar, i.e.,

$$C' = (C|Z)S, \quad A' = S^{-1}(A|Z)S$$

for some invertible operator $S: X' \to Z$.

An admissible pair (A,B) is called a *left Γ-spectral pair* for $L(\lambda)$ if first of all (A,B) is a left partial Γ-spectral pair for $L(\lambda)$ and secondly any other left partial Γ-spectral pair for $L(\lambda)$ is a restriction of (A,B). The notion of a *right Γ-spectral pair* for $L(\lambda)$ is defined in a similar way. Given a left Γ-spectral pair (A,B) for $L(\lambda)$ one can always find (see [10]) an operator $C: X \to Y$ such that (C,A) is a right Γ-spectral pair for $L(\lambda)$ and the following extra condition is satisfied:

(d) $L(\lambda)^{-1} - C(\lambda-A)^{-1}B$ has an analytic continuation on Ω.

Such a triple (C,A,B) is called a *Γ-spectral triple* for $L(\lambda)$ (cf. [10]).

We give some examples of Γ-spectral triples. Let $L(\lambda) = \lambda^{\ell}I + \lambda^{\ell-1}L_{\ell-1} + \dots + \lambda L_1 + L_0$ be a monic operator polynomial. Put $X = Y^{\ell}$ and define

(2) $$A = \begin{pmatrix} 0 & I & & & \\ & & \cdot & & \\ & & & \cdot & \\ & & & & \cdot \\ & & & & I \\ -L_0 & \cdot & \cdot & \cdot & -L_{\ell-1} \end{pmatrix}, \quad B = \begin{pmatrix} 0 \\ 0 \\ \vdots \\ 0 \\ I \end{pmatrix}, \quad C = [I \quad 0 \; \ldots \; 0].$$

If Γ is such that $\sigma(A) \subset \Omega$, then one easily checks that (C,A,B) is a Γ-spectral triple. If $\sigma(A) \cap \Gamma = \emptyset$ and P is the Riesz projection given by Γ and A, i.e.,

$$P = \frac{1}{2\pi i} \int_\Gamma (\lambda - A)^{-1} d\lambda,$$

then $(C|\operatorname{Im} P, A|\operatorname{Im} P, PB)$ is a Γ-spectral triple for $L(\lambda)$.

A Γ-spectral triple (C,A,B) for $L(\lambda)$ has a certain "maximality" condition (see [9]), namely

(3) $$I_X = \frac{1}{2\pi i} \int_\Gamma (\lambda-A)^{-1} B L(\lambda) C (\lambda-A)^{-1} d\lambda.$$

This formula will play an important role in the next section. To prove it one multiplies the right hand side of (3) on the right by $A^n B$. Note that

$$C(\lambda-A)^{-1}A^n B = - \sum_{j=1}^{n} \binom{n}{j} \lambda^{n-j} C(A-\lambda)^{j-1} B + \lambda^n C(\lambda-A)^{-1} B.$$

Now use (d) and the fact that $(\lambda-A)^{-1}BL(\lambda)$ has an analytic continuation on Ω. One obtains

$$\left(\frac{1}{2\pi i} \int_\Gamma (\lambda-A)^{-1} B L(\lambda) C (\lambda-A)^{-1} d\lambda\right) A^n B = A^n B.$$

But then one can apply condition (c) to derive formula (3).

2. Main theorem about Wiener-Hopf equivalence

Let $\lambda A_1 + B_1$ be a pencil of bounded linear operators from X_1 to X_1' and $\lambda A_2 + B_2$ be a pencil of bounded linear operators from X_2 to X_2'. These pencils will be called *strictly equivalent* (in the sense of Kronecker) if there exist invertible bounded operators $S: X_1 \to X_2$ and $T: X_1' \to X_2'$ such that $T(\lambda A_1 + B_1) = (\lambda A_2 + B_2)S$.

THEOREM 2.1. *For* $i = 1,2$ *let* (A_i, B_i) *be a left* Γ*-spectral pair for the operator polynomial* $L_i(\lambda)$ *and let* X_i *be its base space. Further, let* P_i *be the projection of* $X_i \oplus Y$ *along* $(0) \oplus Y$ *onto* $X_i \oplus (0)$*, and put*

$$Z_i = \begin{pmatrix} A_i & B_i \\ 0 & 0 \end{pmatrix} : X_i \oplus Y \to X_i \oplus Y.$$

Then the following statements are equivalent.

(i) *The operator polynomials* $L_1(\lambda)$ *and* $L_2(\lambda)$ *are left Wiener-Hopf equivalent with respect to* Γ.

(ii) *The* (P_1,I)*-block of* Z_1 *is similar to the* (P_2,I)*-block of* Z_2.

(iii) *The linear pencils* $[\lambda+A_1 \;\; B_1]$ *and* $[\lambda+A_2 \;\; B_2]$ *are strictly equivalent.*

(iv) *The pairs* (A_1,B_1) *and* (A_2,B_2) *are feed-back equivalent, i.e., there exist an operator* $F: X_1 \to Y$ *and invertible operators* $N: X_1 \to X_2$ *and* $M: Y \to Y$ *such that*

(4) $$N^{-1}A_2N = A_1 - B_1M^{-1}F, \quad B_2M = NB_1.$$

PROOF. (ii) $\Rightarrow$ (iii). Let

$$S = \begin{pmatrix} S_{11} & S_{12} \\ S_{21} & S_{22} \end{pmatrix} : X_1 \oplus Y \to X_2 \oplus Y$$

give the similarity between (P_1,I)-block of Z_1 and (P_2,I)-block of Z_2. Then

$$S_{11}[\lambda+A_1 \;\; B_1] = [\lambda+A_2 \;\; B_2]S$$

establishes the desired strict equivalence. To see this one can apply the same arguments as in the finite dimensional case (see [4]).

(iii) $\Rightarrow$ (iv). Next, assume $E[\lambda+A_1 \;\; B_1] = [\lambda+A_2 \;\; B_2]F$ where

$$E: X_1 \to X_1, \quad F = \begin{pmatrix} F_{11} & F_{12} \\ F_{21} & F_{22} \end{pmatrix} : X_1 \oplus Y \to X_2 \oplus Y$$

are invertible operators. By comparing coefficients one sees that $E = F_{11}$, $F_{12} = 0$ and

$$EA_1 = A_2E + B_2F_{21}, \quad EB_1 = B_2F_{22}.$$

So formula (4) holds with $N = E$, $M = F_{22}$ and $F = F_{21}$.

(iv) $\Rightarrow$ (ii). If formula (4) holds true, then it is simple to check that the operator

$$S = \begin{pmatrix} N & 0 \\ F & M \end{pmatrix} : X_1 \oplus Y \to X_2 \oplus Y$$

defines a similarity between the (P,I)-block of Z_1 and the (P_2,I)-block of Z_2.

(iv) ⇒ (i). Assume formula (4) holds true. Let $C_1\colon X_1 \to Y$ and $C_2\colon X_2 \to Y$ be operators such that (C_1,A_1,B_1) is a Γ-spectral triple for $L_1(\lambda)$ and (C_2,A_2,B_2) is a Γ-spectral triple for $L_2(\lambda)$. We define

$$(5) \qquad E_-(\lambda) = M + F(\lambda-A_1)^{-1}B_1.$$

Observe that $E_-(\lambda)^{-1} = M^{-1} - M^{-1}FN^{-1}(\lambda-A_2)^{-1}B_2$ (see [1], Section 1.1). As both $\sigma(A_1)$ and $\sigma(A_2)$ are subsets of Ω, the function $E_-(\lambda)$ has the desired properties. Next consider

$$(6) \qquad E_+(\lambda) = L_1(\lambda)^{-1}E_-(\lambda)^{-1}L_2(\lambda).$$

First we show that $E_+(\lambda)$ has an analytic continuation on Ω. The fact that (A_2,B_2) is a Γ-spectral pair for $L_2(\lambda)$ implies that the functions $E_-(\lambda)^{-1}L_2(\lambda)$ and

$$C_1(\lambda-A_1)^{-1}B_1E_-(\lambda)^{-1}L_2(\lambda) = C_1N^{-1}(\lambda-A_2)^{-1}B_2L_2(\lambda)$$

have an analytic continuation on Ω. Also, $L_1(\lambda)^{-1} - C_1(\lambda-A_1)^{-1}B_1$ has an analytic continuation on Ω. Now

$$E_+(\lambda) = [L_1(\lambda)^{-1} - C_1(\lambda-A_1)^{-1}B_1]E_-(\lambda)^{-1}L_2(\lambda) + C_1(\lambda-A_1)^{-1}B_1E_-(\lambda)^{-1}L_2(\lambda).$$

So $E_+(\lambda)$ has an analytic continuation on Ω. In the same way one sees that $E_+(\lambda)^{-1} = L_2(\lambda)^{-1}E_-(\lambda)L_1(\lambda)$ is analytic on Ω. So $E_+(\lambda)$ has the desired properties. Of course we have

$$(7) \qquad L_2(\lambda) = E_-(\lambda)L_1(\lambda)E_+(\lambda), \qquad \lambda \in \Gamma,$$

and so (i) is proved.

(i) ⇒ (iv). Suppose $L_1(\lambda)$ and $L_2(\lambda)$ are left Wiener-Hopf equivalent with respect to Γ, and let the Wiener-Hopf equivalence be given by (7). Define $N\colon X_1 \to X_2$, $M\colon Y \to Y$ and $F\colon X_1 \to Y$ by

$$(8) \qquad N = \frac{1}{2\pi i}\int_\Gamma (\omega-A_2)^{-1}B_2L_2(\omega)E_+(\omega)^{-1}C_1(\omega-A_1)^{-1}d\omega,$$

$$(9) \qquad F = \frac{1}{2\pi i}\int_\Gamma E_-(\omega)L_1(\omega)C_1(\omega-A_1)^{-1}d\omega,$$

(10) $M = E_-(\infty)$.

We have to show (4) for this choice of N, F and M. To do this we define

$$H(\lambda) = -L_1(\lambda)^{-1} + C_1(\lambda - A_1)^{-1}B_1.$$

Then $H(\lambda)$ is analytic on a neighbourhood of $\Omega \cup \Gamma$. Now let Γ' be a closed rectifiable Jordan curve in Ω such that $L_1(\lambda)$ and $L_2(\lambda)$ are invertible on Γ' and $\sigma(A_1)$ and $\sigma(A_2)$ are contained in the inner domain of Γ'. Define

$$N_1 = \frac{1}{2\pi i} \int_{\Gamma'} (\lambda - A_1)^{-1}B_1L_1(\lambda)E_+(\lambda)C_2(\lambda - A_2)^{-1}d\lambda.$$

We shall see that $N_1 = N^{-1}$. Now

$$NN_1 = \left(\frac{1}{2\pi i}\right)^2 \int_{\Gamma'} \int_{\Gamma} (\omega - A_2)^{-1}B_2L_2(\omega)E_+(\omega)^{-1}C_1 \frac{1}{\lambda - \omega} \circ$$
$$\circ \left((\omega - A_1)^{-1} - (\lambda - A_1)^{-1}\right)B_1L_1(\lambda)E_+(\lambda)C_2(\lambda - A_2)^{-1}d\omega d\lambda.$$

As

$$\left(\frac{1}{2\pi i}\right)^2 \int_{\Gamma'} \int_{\Gamma} (\omega - A_2)^{-1}B_2L_2(\omega)E_+(\omega)^{-1}\left(\frac{H(\omega) - H(\lambda)}{\lambda - \omega}\right) \circ$$
$$\circ\ L_1(\lambda)E_+(\lambda)C_2(\lambda - A_2)^{-1}d\omega d\lambda = 0,$$

we have

$$NN_1 = \left(\frac{1}{2\pi i}\right)^2 \int_{\Gamma'} \int_{\Gamma} (\omega - A_2)^{-1}B_2L_2(\omega)E_+(\omega)^{-1} \frac{1}{\lambda - \omega} \circ$$
$$\circ\ \left(L_1(\omega)^{-1} - L_1(\lambda)^{-1}\right)L_1(\lambda)E_+(\lambda)C_2(\lambda - A_2)^{-1}d\omega d\lambda =$$
$$= \left(\frac{1}{2\pi i}\right)^2 \int_{\Gamma'} \int_{\Gamma} (\omega - A_2)^{-1}B_2E_-(\omega) \frac{1}{\lambda - \omega} \left(L_1(\lambda) - L_1(\omega)\right) \circ$$
$$\circ\ E_+(\lambda)C_2(\lambda - A_2)^{-1}d\omega d\lambda =$$
$$= \left(\frac{1}{2\pi i}\right)^2 \int_{\Gamma'} \int_{\Gamma} (\lambda - \omega)^{-1}(\omega - A_2)^{-1}B_2 \circ$$
$$\circ\ \left(E_-(\omega)L_1(\lambda)E_+(\lambda) - L_2(\omega)E_+^{-1}(\omega)E_+(\lambda)\right) C_2(\lambda - A_2)^{-1}d\omega d\lambda =$$
$$= \frac{1}{2\pi i} \int_{\Gamma'} (\lambda - A_2)^{-1}B_2L_2(\lambda)C_2(\lambda - A_2)^{-1}d\lambda = I_{X_2}$$

(see (3)). Here we used that (C_2, A_2, B_2) is a Γ'-spectral triple of $L_2(\lambda)$ and that $(\lambda - \omega)^{-1}(\omega - A_2)^{-1}B_2E_-(\omega)$ is analytic outside and has a second order zero at ∞. In a similar way one proves

$N_1N = I_{X_1}$. So $N_1 = N^{-1}$. Next we consider

$$NB_1 = \frac{1}{2\pi i}\int_\Gamma (\omega-A_2)^{-1}B_2L_2(\omega)E_+(\omega)^{-1}C_1(\omega-A_1)^{-1}B_1d\omega =$$
$$= \frac{1}{2\pi i}\int_\Gamma (\omega-A_2)^{-1}B_2L_2(\omega)E_+(\omega)^{-1}\big(L_1(\omega)^{-1} + H(\omega)\big)d\omega =$$
$$= \frac{1}{2\pi i}\int_\Gamma (\omega-A_2)^{-1}B_2E_-(\omega)d\omega = B_2E_-(\infty) = B_2M.$$

Finally,

$$A_2N - NA_1 = \frac{1}{2\pi i}\int_\Gamma (A_2-\omega)(\omega-A_2)^{-1}B_2L_2(\omega)E_+(\omega)^{-1}C_1(\omega-A_1)^{-1}d\omega +$$
$$+ \frac{1}{2\pi i}\int_\Gamma (\omega-A_2)^{-1}B_2L_2(\omega)E_+(\omega)^{-1}C_1(\omega-A_1)^{-1}(\omega-A_1)d\omega =$$
$$= \frac{1}{2\pi i}\int_\Gamma -B_2L_2(\omega)E_+(\omega)^{-1}C_1(\omega-A_1)^{-1}d\omega +$$
$$+ \frac{1}{2\pi i}\int_\Gamma (\omega-A_2)^{-1}B_2L_2(\omega).E_+(\omega)^{-1}C_1d\omega =$$
$$= -B_2F.$$

So (iv) is proved.

Observe that the proof of Theorem 2.1 gives more than just the equivalence of the four statements (i) - (iv). In fact we have shown that explicit formulas (see (8), (9), (10) may be given for the operators F, N and M in formula (4) whenever the functions $E_+(\lambda)$ and $E_-(\lambda)$ in (7) are known. Conversely, if the operators F, N and M in formula (4) are known, then the functions $E_-(\lambda)$ and $E_+(\lambda)$ defined by (6) and (7) establish the Wiener-Hopf equivalence between $L_1(\lambda)$ and $L_2(\lambda)$.

The next theorem may be viewed as the transposed version of Theorem 2.1. We omit its proof.

THEOREM 2.2. *For* i = 1,2 *let* (C_i,A_i) *be a right* Γ*-spectral pair for the operator polynomial* $L_i(\lambda)$ *and let* X_i *be its base space. Further, let* Q_i *be the projection of* $X_i \oplus Y$ *along* $(0)\oplus Y$ *onto* $X_i \oplus (0)$, *and put*

$$Z_i = \begin{pmatrix} A_i & 0 \\ C_i & 0 \end{pmatrix} : X_i \oplus Y \to X_i \oplus Y.$$

Then the following statements are equivalent:

(i) *The operator polynomials* $L_1(\lambda)$ *and* $L_2(\lambda)$ *are right*

Wiener-Hopf equivalent.

(ii) *The* (I,Q_1)*-block of* Z_1 *is similar to the* (I,Q_2)*-block of* Z_2.

(iii) *The linear pencils* $\begin{pmatrix}\lambda+A_1\\ C_1\end{pmatrix}$ *and* $\begin{pmatrix}\lambda+A_2\\ C_2\end{pmatrix}$ *are strictly equivalent.*

(iv) *The pairs* (C_1,A_1) *and* (C_2,A_2) *are output-injection equivalent, i.e., there exist an operator* $K\colon Y \to X_1$ *and invertible operators* $N\colon X_1 \to X_2$ *and* $M\colon Y \to Y$ *such that*

(11) $$N^{-1}A_2N = A_1 - KMC_1, \quad C_2N = MC_1.$$

3. Wiener-Hopf factorization

In the two theorems of this section we give (in terms of Γ-spectral pairs) necessary and sufficient conditions in order that an operator polynomial admits a Wiener-Hopf factorization with respect to Γ. The first theorems of this type are due to B. Rowley [10]. We add to his results the description of the characteristics, and we prove the theorems on the basis of the general Wiener-Hopf equivalence theorems of the previous section.

Let $A\colon X \to X$ and $B\colon Y \to X$ be bounded linear operators. We call the pair (A,B) of *finite type* if there exists a positive integer ℓ such that

$$\Delta_j = \operatorname{row}(A^{i-1}B)_{i=1}^{j}\colon Y^j \to X$$

has a generalized inverse for $1 \le j \le \ell-1$ and is left invertible for $j = \ell$. Let P denote the projection of $X \oplus Y$ along $(0) \oplus Y$ onto $X \oplus (0)$. Then the (P,I)-block of the operator

$$T = \begin{pmatrix} A & B \\ 0 & 0 \end{pmatrix} : X \oplus Y \to X \oplus Y$$

is a block of finite type if and only if the pair (A,B) is of finite type. This one can derive easily from the identities

$$(PT)^i(I-P) = \begin{pmatrix} 0 & A^{i-1}B \\ 0 & 0 \end{pmatrix}, \ i \ge 1.$$

Using these connections we define the *characteristics* of the pair (A,B) to be the characteristics of the (P,I)-block of T.

THEOREM 3.1. *Let* $L(\lambda)$ *be an operator polynomial, and let* (A,B) *be a left* Γ*-spectral pair for* $L(\lambda)$. *Then* $L(\lambda)$ *admits with respect to* Γ *a left Wiener-Hopf factorization*

$$(12)\qquad L(\lambda) = E_-(\lambda)\left(\Sigma_{i=1}^{r} \lambda^{\nu_i} P_i\right)E_+(\lambda)$$

if and only if the pair (A,B) *is of finite type. Further, if in* (12) *the projections* $P_1,\ldots,P_r$ *are different from zero and* $\nu_1 < \nu_2 < \ldots < \nu_r$, *then the set*

$$\{(\operatorname{Im} P_1,\nu_1),\ldots,(\operatorname{Im} P_r,\nu_r)\}$$

is equal to the set of characteristics of the pair (A,B).

PROOF. First suppose that $L(\lambda)$ admits a left Wiener-Hopf factorization with respect to Γ. So assume (12) holds. Without loss of generality we may assume that the projections $P_1,\ldots,P_r$ are different from zero and $\nu_1 < \nu_2 < \ldots < \nu_r$. Put $X_0 = \bigoplus_{i=1}^{r} (\operatorname{Im} P_i)^{\nu_i}$, and let the operators $A_0\colon X_0 \to X_0$, $B_0\colon Y \to X_0$ and $C_0\colon X_0 \to Y$ be defined by

$$(13)\quad A_0 = \begin{pmatrix} \begin{matrix} 0 & & & \\ I_1 & \ddots & & \\ & \ddots & \ddots & \\ & & I_1 & 0 \end{matrix} & & \\ & \ddots & \\ & & \begin{matrix} 0 & & & \\ I_r & \ddots & & \\ & \ddots & \ddots & \\ & & I_r & 0 \end{matrix} \end{pmatrix} \begin{matrix} \left.\vphantom{\begin{matrix}0\\0\\0\\0\end{matrix}}\right\} \nu_1 \\ \\ \left.\vphantom{\begin{matrix}0\\0\\0\\0\end{matrix}}\right\} \nu_r \end{matrix} \begin{pmatrix} \begin{matrix} I_1 & & 0 \\ 0 & & \vdots \\ \vdots & & \vdots \\ 0 & & \vdots \end{matrix} \\ \begin{matrix} 0 & & 0 \\ \vdots & & I_r \\ \vdots & & 0 \\ 0 & & 0 \end{matrix} \end{pmatrix} = B_0,$$

$$C_0 = \begin{pmatrix} 0 & \cdots & 0 & I_1 & 0 & \cdots & \cdots & 0 \\ & & & & & & & \\ 0 & \cdots & \cdots & 0 & 0 & \cdots & 0 & I_r \end{pmatrix}.$$

Here I_j denotes the identity map on Im P_j. Further, if $\nu_1 = 0$, then the matrix A_0 starts with a block operating on $(\mathrm{Im}\ P_2)^{\nu_2}$ and B_0 and C_0 start with a zero column and a zero row, respectively. The triple (C_0, A_0, B_0) is a Γ-spectral triple for $\Sigma_{i=1}^{r} \lambda^{\nu_i} P_i$.

From Theorem 2.1 we know that there exist an operator $F: X \to Y$ and invertible operators $N: X \to X_0$ and $M: Y \to Y$ such that $A_0 N = NA - B_0 F$ and $B_0 M = NB$. By induction one proves

$$(14)\quad [B_0 A_0 B_0 \dots A_0^{j-1} B_0] \begin{bmatrix} M & FB & FAB & & FA^{j-2}B \\ 0 & M & FB & \cdot & \\ & & M & \cdot & \cdot \\ & & & \ddots & \cdot \\ & & & \cdot & FAB \\ & & & & FB \\ & & & & M \end{bmatrix} = N[B\ AB \dots A^{j-1}B].$$

As (A_0, B_0) is a pair of finite type, formula (14) shows that (A,B) is a pair of finite type.

To identify the characteristics of the pair (A,B), let P_0 be the projection of $X_0 \oplus Y$ along $(0) \oplus Y$ onto $X_0 \oplus (0)$. According to Theorem 2.1 the (P,I)-block of the operator

$$\begin{bmatrix} A & B \\ 0 & 0 \end{bmatrix} : X \oplus Y \to X \oplus Y$$

is similar to the (P_0,I)-block of the operator

$$(15)\quad \begin{bmatrix} A_0 & B_0 \\ 0 & 0 \end{bmatrix} : X_0 \oplus Y \to X_0 \oplus Y.$$

So these two blocks have the same characteristics. Using Corollary I.2.4 one easily checks that the characteristics of the (P_0,I)-block of the operator (15) are $\{(\mathrm{Im}\ P_1, \nu_1), \dots$ $\dots, (\mathrm{Im}\ P_r, \nu_r)\}$. So the characteristics of the pair (A,B) are $\{(\mathrm{Im}\ P_1, \nu_1), \dots, (\mathrm{Im}\ P_r, \nu_r)\}$.

Now, conversely assume that (A,B) is a pair of finite type.

So we can apply Theorem I.2.5 to get a decomposition $Y = \overset{\ell}{\underset{i=0}{\oplus}} U_i$. Define P_i to be the projection of Y onto U_i along $\underset{j \neq i}{\oplus} U_j$. Let N and F be as in Theorem I.2.5, and define $A_0 = N^{-1}(A-BF)N$ and $B_0 = N^{-1}B$. Choose $C_0 : \overset{\ell}{\underset{j=1}{\oplus}} U_j^j \to Y$ in such a way that C_0 is represented by the matrix occuring in Theorem I.3.5(i). Then $L(\lambda)$ is left Wiener-Hopf equivalent to $D(\lambda) = \sum_{i=0}^{\ell} \lambda^i P_i$, because the pair (A_0,B_0) is a left Γ-spectral pair for $D(\lambda)$ and this pair is feed-back equivalent to the pair (A,B). So $L(\lambda)$ admits a left Wiener-Hopf factorization with respect to Γ.

To formulate the analogous theorem for right Wiener-Hopf factorization we have to consider right Γ-spectral pairs. A pair (C,A) is said to be *of finite type* if there exists a positive integer ℓ such that

$$\Omega_j = \operatorname{col}(CA^{i-1})_{i=1}^{j} : X \to Y^j$$

has a generalized inverse for $1 \leq j \leq \ell-1$ and is left invertible for $j = \ell$. This condition is equivalent to the requirement that the (I,Q)-block of the operator

$$T = \begin{pmatrix} A & 0 \\ C & 0 \end{pmatrix} : X \oplus Y \to X \oplus Y$$

is a block of finite type. Here Q is the projection of $X \oplus Y$ along $(0) \oplus Y$ onto $X \oplus (0)$. Using this connection, we define the *characteristics* of the pair (C,A) to be the characteristics of the (I,Q)-block of T.

The next theorem may be viewed as the transposed version of Theorem 3.1. We omit the proof.

THEOREM 3.2. *Let* $L(\lambda)$ *be an operator polynomial, and let* (C,A) *be a right* Γ*-spectral pair for* $L(\lambda)$. *Then* $L(\lambda)$ *admits with respect to* Γ *a right Wiener-Hopf factorization*

$$L(\lambda) = E_+(\lambda)\left(\Sigma_{i=1}^{r} \lambda^{\kappa_i} P_i\right)E_-(\lambda)$$

if and only if the pair (C,A) *is of finite type. Further, if the projections* $P_1,\ldots,P_r$ *are different from zero and* $\kappa_1 < \ldots < \kappa_r$, *then* $\{(\operatorname{Im} P_1,\kappa_1),\ldots,(\operatorname{Im} P_r,\kappa_r)\}$ *is equal to the set of characteristics of the pair* (C,A).

Let (A,B) be a left Γ-spectral pair for $L(\lambda) = \Sigma_{j=0}^{\ell} \lambda^j L_j$. From Theorem 3.1 we know that $L(\lambda)$ admits a left Wiener-Hopf factorization with respect to Γ if and only if the pair (A,B) is a pair of finite type. We mention here that this condition may be formulated in terms of the moments of $L(\lambda)^{-1}$ with respect to Γ. To see this, choose C such that (C,A,B) is a Γ-spectral triple for $L(\lambda)$ with respect to Γ. By conditions (a) and (d) in Section 1 we have

$$R_{-j} = \frac{1}{2\pi i} \int_{\Gamma} \lambda^{j-1} L(\lambda)^{-1} d\lambda = CA^{j-1}B, \quad j \geq 1.$$

It follows that

$$(16) \quad \begin{bmatrix} C \\ CA \\ \vdots \\ CA^{\ell-1} \end{bmatrix} [B \ AB \ \dots \ A^{j-1}B] = \begin{bmatrix} R_{-1} & \cdots & R_{-j} \\ \vdots & & \vdots \\ R_{-\ell} & \cdots & R_{-\ell-j+1} \end{bmatrix}.$$

Now recall that $\mathrm{col}(CA^{i-1})_{i=1}^{\ell}$ is left invertible. So $\Omega_j = \mathrm{row}(A^{i-1}B)_{i=1}^{j}$ has a generalized inverse if and only if the operator matrix in the right hand side of (16) has a generalized inverse. As Ω_ℓ is right invertible (see condition (c) of Section 1), we conclude that (A,B) is a left Γ-spectral pair for $L(\lambda)$ if and only if the following operator matrices

$$(17) \qquad [R_{-\alpha-\beta+1}]_{\alpha=1,\beta=1}^{\ell \quad j}, \quad j = 1,\dots,\ell-1,$$

have generalized inverses. By combining this with Theorem 3.1, one sees (cf. [10], Theorem 6.6) that $L(\lambda) = \Sigma_{j=0}^{\ell} \lambda^j L_j$ admits a left Wiener-Hopf factorization with respect to Γ if and only if the operator matrices (17) have generalized inverses. In a similar way one can prove (cf. [10], Theorem 6.1) that $L(\lambda) = \Sigma_{j=0}^{\ell} \lambda^j L_j$ admits a right Wiener-Hopf factorization with respect to Γ if and only if the operator matrices

$$[R_{-\alpha-\beta+1}]_{\alpha=1,\beta=1}^{j \quad \ell}, \quad j = 1,\dots,\ell-1,$$

have generalized inverses.

4. Wiener-Hopf factorization and Kronecker's strict equivalence

For $i = 1,2$ let $\lambda E_i + F_i$ be a pencil of bounded linear operators acting from X_i to X_i'. The direct sum $(\lambda E_1+F_1) \oplus \oplus (\lambda E_2+F_2)$ is defined to be the pencil $\lambda(E_1 \oplus E_2) + (F_1 \oplus F_2)$ of operators acting from $X_1 \oplus X_2$ to $X_1' \oplus X_2'$.

THEOREM 4.1. *Let* $[\lambda I + A \quad B]$ *be a pencil of bounded linear operators acting from* $X \oplus Y$ *to* X. *Then the following conditions are equivalent.*

(i) *The pair* (A,B) *is a pair of finite type and its set of characteristics is equal to* $\{(Y_1,\nu_1),\ldots,(Y_r,\nu_r)\}$.

(ii) *The pencil* $[\lambda I + A \quad B]$ *is strictly equivalent to a direct sum* $N_1(\lambda) \oplus \ldots \oplus N_r(\lambda)$, *where for* $i = 1,\ldots,r$

$$N_i(\lambda) = \begin{pmatrix} \lambda I_i & I_i & 0 & & 0 \\ 0 & \ddots & \ddots & \ddots & \\ & \ddots & \ddots & \ddots & 0 \\ 0 & & 0 & \lambda I_i & I_i \end{pmatrix} : Y_i^{\nu_i+1} \to Y_i^{\nu_i}$$

and $0 \le \nu_1 < \ldots < \nu_r$. *Here* $Y^0 = (0)$.

PROOF. Suppose that the pair (A,B) is of finite type. Let $(Y_1,\nu_1),\ldots,(Y_r,\nu_r)$ be the characteristics of (A,B). Then there exist a bijective bounded linear operator $N\colon \bigoplus_{i=1}^{r} Y_1^{\nu_i} \to X$ and a bounded linear operator $F\colon Y \to X$ such that the operator matrices of $A_0 = N^{-1}(A-BF)N$ and $B_0 = N^{-1}B$ are given by (13). Now

$$N^{-1}(\lambda I+A \quad B)\begin{pmatrix} N & 0 \\ -FN & I \end{pmatrix} = (\lambda I + A_0 \quad B_0).$$

We obtain (ii) by a simple reordering of the colums of $(\lambda I + A_0 \quad B_0)$.

Conversely, suppose (ii). First reorder the columns of $N_1(\lambda) \oplus \ldots \oplus N_2(\lambda)$ in such a way that one obtains a pencil $[\lambda I + A_0 \quad B_0]$. Obviously (A_0,B_0) is a pair of finite type and its set of characteristics is equal to $\{(Y_1,\nu_1),\ldots,(Y_r,\nu_r)\}$. Further, we have $[\lambda I + A \quad B]S = N[\lambda I + A_0 \quad B_0]$. By comparing coefficients one can see that S can be written as

$$S = \begin{pmatrix} N & 0 \\ -FN & I \end{pmatrix}.$$

So $A_0 = N^{-1}(A-BF)N$ and $B_0 = N^{-1}B$, and thus the pairs (A,B) and (A_0,B_0) are feed-back equivalent. But then we conclude that the pair (A,B) is of finite type and has the desired characteristics (cf. Theorem 2.1).

If $Y_1,\dots,Y_r$ and $\nu_1 < \dots < \nu_r$ are as in statement (ii) of the previous theorem, then set $\{(Y_1,\nu_1),\dots,(Y_r,\nu_r)\}$ is called the set of *right Kronecker characteristics* of the pencil $[\lambda I + A \;\; B]$. Let P be the projection of $X \oplus Y$ along $(0) \oplus Y$ onto $X \oplus (0)$. From Theorem 4.1 it is clear that the right Kronecker characteristics of the pencil $[\lambda I + A \;\; B]$ are equal to the characteristics of the (P,I)-block of the operator

$$Z = \begin{pmatrix} A & B \\ 0 & 0 \end{pmatrix} : X \oplus Y \to X \oplus Y.$$

By using Theorem I.2.3 and the equivalence of statements (ii) and (iii) in Theorem 2.1, one obtains:

THEOREM 4.2. *Suppose that the pairs* (A_1,B_1) *and* (A_2,B_2) *are of finite type. Then the pencils* $[\lambda I_1 + A_1 \;\; B_1]$ *and* $[\lambda I_2 + A_2 \;\; B_2]$ *are strictly equivalent if and only if they have the same right Kronecker characteristics.*

The next theorem follows from Theorem 3.1 and the definition of the right Kronecker characteristics.

THEOREM 4.3. *Let* (A,B) *be a left* Γ*-spectral pair of the operator polynomial* $L(\lambda)$. *Suppose that the pair* (A,B) *is of finite type. Let*

$$L(\lambda) = E_-(\lambda)\left(\Sigma_{i=1}^{r} \lambda^{\nu_i} P_i\right)E_+(\lambda), \qquad \lambda \in \Gamma, \tag{19}$$

be a left Wiener-Hopf factorization with respect to Γ. *Then the set* $\{(\operatorname{Im} P_1,\nu_1),\dots,(\operatorname{Im} P_r,\nu_r)\}$ *is equal to the set of right Kronecker characteristics of the pencil* $[\lambda I + A \;\; B]$.

The following theorem, due to Gohberg and Lerer [5], see also [2], can now be obtained as a special case of Theorem 4.3.

THEOREM 4.4. *Let* (A,B) *be a left* Γ*-spectral pair of the matrix polynomial* $L(\lambda)$. *Then the left Wiener-Hopf factorization indices of* $L(\lambda)$ *with respect to* Γ *are equal to the right*

Kronecker indices of the pencil $[\lambda I + A \quad B]$.

PROOF. Just note that the Kronecker indices are obtained from the Kronecker characteristics by repeating $\dim(\mathrm{Im}\, P_i)$ times the number ν_i and that the Wiener-Hopf factorization indices are obtained by repeating the number ν_i in (19) $\dim(\mathrm{Im}\, P_i)$ times.

We leave it to the reader to introduce the left Kronecker characteristics and to prove the analogues of Theorems 4.1-4.4 for linear pencils of the form

$$\begin{pmatrix} \lambda I + A \\ C \end{pmatrix}$$

Also the connections with right Wiener-Hopf factorization are left to the reader.

5. The finite dimensional case

In this section we derive the Gohberg-Lerer-Rodman theorem about factorization indices for a rational matrix polynomial $\Sigma_{j=-s}^{t} \lambda^j L_j$ (see [6]) as a consequence of the general Wiener-Hopf equivalence theorems of Section 2. First we observe that for a matrix polynomial the operators appearing in a left or right Γ-spectral pair always act between finite dimensional spaces. This fact allows us for matrix polynomials to add to the list of equivalent properties of Theorem 2.1 a fifth equivalent property.

THEOREM 5.1. *For* $i = 1,2$ *let* (A_i, B_i) *be a left* Γ*-spectral pair for the* $n\times n$ *matrix polynomial* $L_i(\lambda)$ *and let* X_i *be its base space. Further, let* P_i *be a projection of* X_i *with* $\mathrm{Ker}\, P_i = \mathrm{Im}\, B_i$. *Then* $L_1(\lambda)$ *and* $L_2(\lambda)$ *are left Wiener-Hopf equivalent with respect to* Γ *if and only if the* (P_1, I)*-block of* A_1 *is similar to the* (P_2, I)*-block of* A_2.

PROOF. Use the equivalence of the statements (a) and (b) in Theorem IV.2.1 of [4] and apply Theorem 2.1.

Let $L(\lambda) = \Sigma_{j=-s}^{t} \lambda^j L_j$ be a rational $r\times r$ matrix polynomial, and assume that $\det L(\lambda) \neq 0$ for $\lambda \in \Gamma$. Then $L(\lambda)$ admits a left Wiener-Hopf factorization with respect to Γ:

$$(20)\qquad L(\lambda) = E_-(\lambda)\begin{pmatrix} \lambda^{\kappa_1} & & \\ & \ddots & \\ & & \lambda^{\kappa_r} \end{pmatrix} E_+(\lambda), \qquad \lambda \in \Gamma.$$

The next theorem, due to Gohberg, Lerer and Rodman [6], describes the left factorization indices $\kappa_1 \le \ldots \le \kappa_r$ in terms of the moments of $L(\lambda)^{-1}$ with respect to Γ. The factorization (20) is called a *canonical* factorization if all indices κ_j are equal to zero.

THEOREM 5.2. *Let* $L(\lambda) = \Sigma_{j=-s}^{t} \lambda^j L_j$ *be a rational* $r\times r$ *matrix polynomial with* $\det L(\lambda) \neq 0$ *for* $\lambda \in \Gamma$, *and let* $\kappa_1 \le \ldots \le \kappa_r$ *be its left factorization indices with respect to* Γ. *Then for* $i = 1,\ldots,r$ *one has*

$$(21)\qquad \kappa_i+s = |\{j \mid r + 1 + r_{j-1} - r_j \le i,\ 1 \le j \le s+t\}|,$$

where $|\Omega|$ *denotes the number of elements in the set* Ω, $r_0 = 0$ *and*

$$r_j = \operatorname{rank}[R_{-\alpha-\beta+s+1}]_{\alpha=1,\beta=1}^{s+t\ j}, \quad R_{-\alpha} = \frac{1}{2\pi i}\int_\Gamma \lambda^{\alpha-1}L(\lambda)^{-1}d\lambda.$$

In particular $L(\lambda)$ *admits a canonical left Wiener-Hopf factorization with respect to* Γ *if and only if*

$$(22)\qquad r_j = \begin{cases} jr & \text{for } j = 1,\ldots,s, \\ sr & \text{for } j = s+1,\ldots,s+t. \end{cases}$$

PROOF. Let $L_1(\lambda) = \lambda^s L(\lambda) = \Sigma_{i=0}^{t+s} \lambda^i L_{i-s}$, and let (A,B) be a left Γ-spectral pair for $L_1(\lambda)$. Let

$$(23)\qquad L_1(\lambda) = E_-(\lambda)D(\lambda)E_+(\lambda), \quad D(\lambda) = \operatorname{diag}(\lambda^{\nu_i})_{i=1}^r,$$

be a left Wiener-Hopf factorization with respect to Γ. By comparing (20) and (23) one sees that $\nu_i = \kappa_i+s$. Let (A_0,B_0) be as in (13), and assume that $\dim \operatorname{Im} P_j = 1$. So in (13) the symbol I_j may be replaced by a simple 1. Then (A_0,B_0) is a left Γ-spectral pair of $D(\lambda)$. Let $q_j = \operatorname{rank}(B_0,\ldots,A_0^{j-1}B_0)$ for $j \ge 1$ and $q_0 = 0$. From (13) one easily sees that

$$\nu_i = \{j \mid r + 1 + q_{j-1} - q_j \le i,\ \ j = 1,\ldots,s+t\}.$$

Theorem 2.1 gives that there exist operators N, M and F (N and M invertible) such that $A_0N = NA - B_0F$ and $B_0M = NB$. So formula (14) holds. This proves that $q_j = \mathrm{rank}[B\ AB\ \dots\ A^{j-1}B]$. Now let C be such that (C,A,B) is a Γ-spectral triple for $L_1(\lambda)$. Then $\mathrm{col}\,(CA^{j-1})_{j=1}^{s+t}$ is left invertible. So

$$q_j = \mathrm{rank}\begin{pmatrix} C \\ CA \\ \vdots \\ CA^{s+t-1}\end{pmatrix}[B\ AB\ \dots\ A^{j-1}B] = \mathrm{rank}\begin{pmatrix} CB & \dots & CA^{j-1}B \\ \vdots & & \vdots \\ CA^{s+t-1}B & \dots & CA^{j+s+t-2}B\end{pmatrix}.$$

From conditions (a) and (d) in Section 1 we may conclude that

$$CA^{\alpha}B = \frac{1}{2\pi i}\int_\Gamma \lambda^{\alpha}L_1(\lambda)^{-1}d\lambda = \frac{1}{2\pi i}\int_\Gamma \lambda^{\alpha-s}L(\lambda)^{-1}d\lambda = R_{-\alpha+s-1}.$$

So $q_j = r_j$, and formula (21) has been proved.

To prove the second part of the theorem we first observe that

$$r \geq r_1 - r_0 \geq r_2 - r_1 \geq \dots \geq (r_{s+t} - r_{s+t-1}) \geq 0.$$

These inequalities follow from the fact that $r_j = q_j = \mathrm{rank}\,[B\ AB\ \dots\ A^{j-1}B]$. Now take $\kappa_1 = \dots = \kappa_r = 0$ in (21). For i = 1 this yields $r_j - r_{j-1} = r$ for $j = 1,\dots,s$, and for $i = r$ one obtains $r_j - r_{j-1} = 0$ for $j = s+1,\dots,s+t$. But then formula (22) is clear. The converse is trivial.

By employing Theorem 2.2 one can also prove the analogue of Theorem 5.2 for right Wiener-Hopf factorization. A similar remark holds true for Theorem 5.1.

6. The Fredholm case

In this section we consider factorization problems for a rational operator polynomial $L(\lambda) = \Sigma_{i=-s}^{t}\lambda^i L_i$. Throughout we assume that the coefficients $L_{-s},\dots,L_t$ are bounded linear operators on the Banach space Y.

THEOREM 6.1. *Suppose that* $L(\lambda) = \Sigma_{i=-s}^{t}\lambda^i L_i$ *admits a left Wiener-Hopf factorization with respect to* Γ*:*

(24) $$L(\lambda) = E_-(\lambda)\Big(\sum_{i=-s}^{t}\lambda^i P_i\Big)E_+(\lambda), \quad \lambda \in \Gamma.$$

Here $P_{-s},\dots,P_t$ *are mutually disjoint (possibly zero) projections such that* $P_{-s} + \dots + P_t = I_Y$. *Let* (A,B) *be a left* Γ*-spectral pair for* $\lambda^s L(\lambda)$ *with base space* X *and consider the operator*

$$\Delta_s = \mathrm{row}(A^{i-1}B)_{i=1}^{s} : Y^s \to X.$$

Then for each $i \neq 0$ *the projection* P_i *is of finite rank if and only if* Δ_s *is a Fredholm operator. More generally, we have*

(a) $\dim \mathrm{Ker}\, \Delta_s = \sum_{j=1}^{s} j \,\mathrm{rank}\, P_{-j}$,

(b) $\mathrm{codim}\, \mathrm{Im}\, \Delta_s = \sum_{j=1}^{t} j \,\mathrm{rank}\, P_j$.

PROOF. Let (A_0,B_0) be a left Γ-spectral pair for $\Sigma_{i=0}^{s+t} \lambda^i P_{i-s}$. We may assume that A_0 and B_0 are as in formula (13). Put $\Delta_{0s} = \mathrm{row}\,(A_0^{i-1}B_0)_{i=1}^{s}$. Formulas (a) and (b) are easy to check for Δ_{0s} instead of Δ_s. As $\lambda^s L(\lambda)$ and $\Sigma_{i=0}^{s+t} \lambda^i P_{i-s}$ are Wiener-Hopf equivalent, we may apply Theorem 2.1 to show that the pair (A,B) and (A_0,B_0) are feed-back equivalent. But then we have for Δ_s and Δ_{0s} formula (14), which implies that $\dim \mathrm{Ker}\, \Delta_s = \dim \mathrm{Ker}\, \Delta_{0s}$ and $\mathrm{codim}\, \mathrm{Im}\, \Delta_s = \mathrm{codim}\, \mathrm{Im}\, \Delta_{0s}$.

In the diagonal term of the right hand side of (24) the exponent of λ has the same range as the exponent of λ in $L(\lambda)$. This does not pose an extra condition on $L(\lambda)$. In fact if $L(\lambda)$ admits a left Wiener-Hopf factorization with respect to Γ, then the diagonal term is always as in (24).

The next theorem is the analogue of Theorem 6.1 for right Wiener-Hopf factorization and may be proved similarly.

THEOREM 6.2. *Suppose that* $L(\lambda) = \Sigma_{i=-s}^{t} \lambda^i L_i$ *admits a right Wiener-Hopf factorization with respect to* Γ:

$$L(\lambda) = E_+(\lambda)\Big(\sum_{i=-s}^{t} \lambda^i Q_i\Big)E_-(\lambda), \qquad \lambda \in \Gamma.$$

Here $Q_{-s},\dots,Q_t$ *are mutually disjoint (possibly zero) projections such that* $Q_{-s} + \dots + Q_t = I_Y$. *Let* (C,A) *be a right* Γ*-spectral pair of* $\lambda^s L(\lambda)$, *and consider*

$$\Omega_s = \mathrm{col}(CA^{i-1})_{i=1}^{s} : X \to Y^s.$$

Then for each $j \neq 0$ *the projection* Q_j *is of finite rank if and only if* Ω_s *is a Fredholm operator. More generally we have*

(a) $\dim \operatorname{Ker} \Omega_s = \sum_{j=1}^{t} j \operatorname{rank} Q_j$,

(b) $\operatorname{codim} \operatorname{Im} \Omega_s = \sum_{j=1}^{s} j \operatorname{rank} Q_{-j}$.

THEOREM 6.3. *Suppose that* $L(\lambda) = \Sigma_{j=-s}^{s} \lambda^j L_j$ *admits a left and a right Wiener-Hopf factorization with respect to the unit circle* γ*:*

$$L(\lambda) = E_-(\lambda)(\sum_{i=-s}^{s} \lambda^i P_i)E_+(s) = F_+(\lambda)(\sum_{i=-s}^{s} \lambda^i Q_i)F_-(\lambda). \tag{25}$$

Then for each $i \neq 0$ *the projections* P_i *and* Q_i *are of finite rank if and only if the operator*

$$H_s = \begin{pmatrix} R_{s-1} & \cdots & R_0 \\ \vdots & & \vdots \\ R_0 & \cdots & R_{1-s} \end{pmatrix} : Y^s \to Y^s \tag{26}$$

is Fredholm. Here

$$R_{-j} = \frac{1}{2\pi i} \int_\gamma \lambda^{j-1} L(\lambda)^{-1} d\lambda. \tag{27}$$

PROOF. Let (C_1,A_1,B_1) be a Γ-spectral triple of $\lambda^s L(\lambda)$, and let (C_2,A_2,B_2) be a Γ-spectral triple of $\lambda^s L(\frac{1}{\lambda})$. Suppose that for each $i \neq 0$ the projections P_i and Q_i are of finite rank. Then we know from Theorems 6.1 and 6.2 that $\Omega_s = \operatorname{col}(C_1 A_1^i)_{i=0}^{s-1}$ and $\Delta_s = \operatorname{row}(A_1^i B_1)_{i=0}^{s-1}$ are Fredholm. So $\Omega_s \Delta_s$ is a Fredholm operator. Further $\Omega_s \Delta_s = H_s$, because

$$C_1 A_1^\alpha B_1 = \frac{1}{2\pi i} \int_\gamma \lambda^\alpha C_1(\lambda - A_1)^{-1} B_1 d\lambda =$$

$$= \frac{1}{2\pi i} \int_\gamma \lambda^\alpha \lambda^{-s} L(\lambda)^{-1} d\lambda = R_{s-\alpha-1}.$$

Secondly, suppose that H_s is a Fredholm operator. Then $\operatorname{Ker} \Delta_s$ is finite dimensional and $\operatorname{Im} \Omega_s$ has finite codimension. This gives that $P_{-s},\ldots,P_{-1}$ and $Q_{-s},\ldots,Q_{-1}$ are finite dimensional. Now note that

$$\begin{aligned} L(\tfrac{1}{\lambda}) &= E_-(\tfrac{1}{\lambda})(\Sigma_{i=-s}^{s} \lambda^i P_{-i})E_+(\tfrac{1}{\lambda}), \\ L(\tfrac{1}{\lambda}) &= F_+(\tfrac{1}{\lambda})(\Sigma_{i=-s}^{s} \lambda^i Q_{-i})F_-(\tfrac{1}{\lambda}), \end{aligned} \tag{27}$$

and these factorizations are, respectively, a left and a right Wiener-Hopf factorization of $L(\frac{1}{\lambda})$ with respect to γ. Observe that

$$C_2A_2^{\alpha}B_2 = \frac{1}{2\pi i}\int_{\gamma} \lambda^{\alpha-s}L(\tfrac{1}{\lambda})^{-1}d\lambda = \frac{1}{2\pi i}\int_{\gamma} \lambda^{-\alpha+s-2}L(\lambda)^{-1}d\lambda = R_{-s+\alpha+1}.$$

So one sees that $H_s = \mathrm{col}(C_2A_2^{s-i})_{i=1}^{s} \circ \mathrm{row}(A_2^{s-i}B_2)_{i=1}^{s}$. As H_s is Fredholm, it follows that $\ker(\mathrm{row}(A_2^{i-1}B_2)_{i=1}^{s})$ is finite dimensional and $\mathrm{Im}\ \mathrm{col}(C_2A_2^{i-1})_{i=1}^{s}$ has finite codimension. So from (27) and Theorems 6.1 and 6.2 we may conclude that $P_1,\dots,P_s$ and $Q_1,\dots,Q_s$ are of finite rank.
This completes the proof of the theorem.

We conclude with a few remarks. Suppose that $L(\lambda) = \Sigma_{j=-s}^{t} \lambda^j L_j$ admits a left Wiener-Hopf factorization as in formula (24), and let us assume that for each $i \neq 0$ the projections P_i are of finite rank. Then the numbers rank P_i $(i \neq 0)$ determine uniquely the left Wiener-Hopf equivalence class of $L(\lambda)$. Indeed, consider two diagonal terms:

$$D(\lambda) = \sum_{i=-s}^{t} \lambda^i P_i, \qquad D'(\lambda) = \sum_{i=-s}^{t} \lambda^i P_i',$$

and assume rank P_i = rank $P_i' < \infty$ for $i \neq 0$. Then also rank $(I-P_0)$ = rank $(I-P_0') < \infty$, and hence for each i we can find an invertible operator S_i such that

$$S_iP_iS_i^{-1} = P_i, \quad i = -s,\dots,t.$$

Put $E = \Sigma_{j=-s}^{t} P_j'S_jP_j$. Then E is invertible and $ED(\lambda) = D(\lambda)'E$.

Factorizations of the type appearing in Theorem 6.3 have been studied by Gohberg and Leiterer in [8]. They proved that for a rational operator polynomial $L(\lambda) = \Sigma_{j=-s}^{s} \lambda^j L_j$ we have Wiener-Hopf factorizations as in (25) with P_i and Q_i of finite rank for each $i \neq 0$ if and only if the block Toeplitz operators

$$\begin{pmatrix} L_0 & \cdot & \cdot & L_s & & \\ \cdot & \cdot & & & \cdot & \\ \cdot & & \cdot & & & \cdot \\ L_{-s} & & & \cdot & & \\ & \cdot & & & & \\ & & \cdot & & & \end{pmatrix} \quad \text{and} \quad \begin{pmatrix} L_0 & \cdot & \cdot & L_{-s} & & \\ \cdot & \cdot & & & \cdot & \\ \cdot & & \cdot & & & \cdot \\ L_s & & & \cdot & & \\ & \cdot & & & & \\ & & \cdot & & & \end{pmatrix},$$

acting on $\ell_1(Y)$, are Fredholm operators.

Let R_{-j} be as in (27), and for α and β positive integers consider the operator matrix

$$H_{\alpha\beta} = [R_{s-\mu-\nu+1}]_{\mu=1,\nu=1}^{\alpha \quad \beta} .$$

From the remarks made at the end of Section 3 one may deduce that $L(\lambda) = \Sigma_{j=-s}^{s} \lambda^j L(\lambda)$ admits Wiener-Hopf factorizations as in (25) if and only if for $j = 1,\ldots,2s-1$ the operator matrices $H_{2s,j}$ and $H_{j,2s}$ have generalized inverses.

III. FACTORIZATION OF ANALYTIC OPERATOR FUNCTIONS

1. Preliminaries

In this chapter we deal with Wiener-Hopf factorization for analytic operator functions. Let Γ be a simple closed rectifiable Jordan curve in $\mathbb{C}$ with bounded inner domain Ω. As before $0 \in \Omega$. We shall consider operator functions

$$W: \bar{\Omega} \to L(Y)$$

that are analytic on Ω and continuous up to the boundary. Further we assume that $W(\lambda)$ is invertible for all λ on the boundary Γ. Throughout this chapter Y is a fixed complex Banach space.

A triple (C,A,B) of bounded linear operators

(1) $\quad A: X \to X, \quad B: Y \to X, \quad C: X \to Y$

is called a Γ-*spectral triple* for the operator function W if

(α) $\sigma(A) \subset \Omega$,

(β) $W(\lambda)C(\lambda-A)^{-1}$ has an analytic extension on Ω,

(γ) $\cap_{j=0}^{\infty} \operatorname{Ker} CA^j = (0)$,

(δ) $W(\lambda)^{-1} - C(\lambda-A)^{-1}B$ has an analytic extension on Ω.

In (1) the space X is a complex Banach space which may differ for different W. We refer to X as the *base space* of the triple.

It may be verified that for operator polynomials the definition of a Γ-spectral triple as given in Chapter II coincides with the one given here. The definition as used in the present section is taken from [9].

The existence of a Γ-spectral triple for an arbitrary W may be derived from the realization theorem proved in [1], Section 2.3. First of all, we know from Theorem 2.4 in [1] that W can be written as

$$W(\lambda) = I + S(\lambda-V)^{-1}R, \quad \lambda \in \Omega, \tag{2}$$

where V is a bounded linear operator on an auxiliary Banach space $\mathcal{A}$ such that

$$\sigma(V) \cap \Omega = \emptyset, \tag{3}$$

and R: $Y \to \mathcal{A}$ and S: $\mathcal{A} \to Y$ are bounded linear operators. Now put $T = V - RS$. Then (cf. [1], Corollary 2.7)

$$W(\lambda)^{-1} = I - S(\lambda-T)^{-1}R, \quad \lambda \in \Omega \setminus \sigma(T), \tag{4}$$

and

$$\sigma(T) \cap \Omega = \{\lambda \in \Omega \mid W(\lambda) \text{ is not invertible}\}. \tag{5}$$

It follows that $\sigma(T) \cap \Omega$ is an open and closed subset of $\sigma(T)$, and hence we may consider the corresponding Riesz projection Π, i.e.,

$$\Pi = \frac{1}{2\pi i} \int_\gamma (\lambda I-T)^{-1} d\lambda,$$

where γ is a contour in Ω around $\sigma(T) \cap \Omega$.

LEMMA 1.1. *Put* $X = \operatorname{Im} \Pi$, *and define*

$$C = -S\Pi\colon X \to Y, \quad A = \Pi T \Pi\colon X \to X, \quad B = \Pi R\colon Y \to X.$$

Then the triple (C,A,B) *is* Γ*-spectral triple for* W.

PROOF. From the definition of Π it is clear that $\sigma(A) = \sigma(T) \cap \Omega$. In particular we have $\sigma(A) \subset \Omega$. For $\lambda \in \Omega \setminus \sigma(T)$ we have

$$\begin{aligned} W(\lambda)C(\lambda-A)^{-1} &= -W(\lambda)S(\lambda-T)^{-1}\Pi \\ &= -S(\lambda-T)^{-1}\Pi - S(\lambda-V)^{-1}RS(\lambda-T)^{-1}\Pi \\ &= -S(\lambda-T)^{-1}\Pi - S(\lambda-V)^{-1}[V-\lambda+\lambda-T](\lambda-T)^{-1}\Pi \\ &= -S(\lambda-V)^{-1}\Pi. \end{aligned}$$

As $\sigma(V) \cap \Omega = \emptyset$, we see that $W(\lambda)C(\lambda-A)^{-1}$ has a holomorphic extension on Ω.

Put $M = \cap_{j=0}^{\infty} \operatorname{Ker} CA^j$. Obviously, $M \subset \cap_{j=0}^{\infty} \operatorname{Ker} ST^j$. So V and

T coincide on M and both operators leave M invariant. As $M \subset \operatorname{Im} \Pi$, we have $\sigma(T|_M) \subset \Omega$. Hence $\sigma(V|_M) \subset \Omega$. Let γ be contour in Ω around $\sigma(V|_M)$. Then for each $x \in M$

$$x = \frac{1}{2\pi i} \int_\gamma (\lambda - V|_M)^{-1} x d\lambda = \frac{1}{2\pi i} \int_\gamma (\lambda - V)^{-1} x d\lambda = 0.$$

So $\bigcap_{j=0}^{\infty} \operatorname{Ker} CA^j = (0)$.

Finally, for $\lambda \in \Omega \setminus \sigma(A)$ one has

$$W(\lambda)^{-1} - C(\lambda - A)^{-1} B = I - S(\lambda - T)^{-1}(I - \Pi)R,$$

and hence this function has an analytic extension on Ω. The lemma is proved.

The operators V, R and S appearing in formula (2) and the auxiliary space A can be chosen in different ways. One way, which is described in Section 2.3 of [1], is the following. For A one takes the space $C(\Gamma, Y)$ of all Y-valued continuous functions on Γ endowed with the supremum norm. The operator R is defined to be the canonical embedding from Y into $A = C(\Gamma, Y)$, that is, $(Ry)(z) = y$ for each $y \in Y$ and $z \in \Gamma$. Further one defines

$$(Vf)(z) = zf(z), \quad Sf = \frac{1}{2\pi i} \int_\Gamma [I - W(\xi)] f(\xi) d\xi.$$

For this choice of V, R and S formulas (2) and (3) hold true (cf., also [3], Section 2.2).

Although spectral triples for W may be constructed in many different ways they are all similar in the following sense. Let (C_1, A_1, B_1) and (C_2, A_2, B_2) be Γ-spectral triples for W, and let X_1 and X_2 be the corresponding base spaces. Then there exists an invertible operator $J: X_1 \to X_2$ such that

$$A_1 = J^{-1} A_2 J, \quad B_1 = J^{-1} B_2, \quad C_1 = C_2 J.$$

This is proved in [9]. Further, for any Γ-spectral triple for W we have (see also [9])

$$I_X = \frac{1}{2\pi i} \int_\Gamma (\lambda - A)^{-1} B W(\lambda) C (\lambda - A)^{-1} d\lambda.$$

2. Main theorem about Wiener-Hopf equivalence

Let $W_1, W_2 : \bar{\Omega} \to L(Y)$ be two operator functions of the type considered in the first paragraph of the previous section. The functions W_1 and W_2 are said to be *left Wiener-Hopf equivalent* with respect to Γ if

$$(6) \qquad W_2(\lambda) = E_-(\lambda)W_1(\lambda)E_+(\lambda), \quad \lambda \in \Gamma,$$

where E_+ (E_-) is holomorphic on Ω (on $\mathbb{C}_\infty \setminus \bar{\Omega}$), continuous up to the boundary Γ, and for each λ in $\bar{\Omega}$ (in $\mathbb{C}_\infty \setminus \Omega$) the operator $E_+(\lambda)$ ($E_-(\lambda)$) is invertible. We call (6) a *Wiener-Hopf factorization* of W_2 if in (6) we have that

$$W_1(\lambda) = D(\lambda) = \Sigma_{j=1}^{r} \lambda^{\nu_j} P_j,$$

where $0 \le \nu_1 \le \nu_2 \le \dots \le \nu_r$ are integers and $P_1,\dots,P_r$ are mutually disjoint projections of Y such that $\Sigma_{j=1}^{r} P_j$ is the identity operator on Y.

The following theorem is the analogue of Theorem II.2.1. It can be proved in exactly the same way as in the operator polynomial case.

THEOREM 2.1. *For* $i = 1,2$ *let* (C_i,A_i,B_i) *be a* Γ*-spectral triple for the operator function* W_i *and let* X_i *be its base space. Further, let* P_i *be the projection of* $X_i \oplus Y$ *along* $(0) \oplus Y$ *onto* $X_i \oplus (0)$*, and put*

$$Z_i = \begin{pmatrix} A_i & B_i \\ 0 & 0 \end{pmatrix} : X_i \oplus Y \to X_i \oplus Y.$$

Then the following statements are equivalent:

(i) *The operator functions* W_1 *and* W_2 *are left Wiener-Hopf equivalent with respect to* Γ.

(ii) *The* (P_1,I)*-block of* Z_1 *is similar to the* (P_2,I)*-block of* Z_2.

(iii) *The linear pencils* $[\lambda+A_1 \;\; B_1]$ *and* $[\lambda+A_2 \;\; B_2]$ *are strictly equivalent.*

(iv) *The pairs* (A_1,B_1) *and* (A_2,B_2) *are feed-back equivalent, i.e., there exist an operator* $F\colon X_1 \to Y$ *and bounded invertible operators* $N\colon X_1 \to X_2$ *and* $M\colon Y \to Y$ *such that*

$$(7) \qquad N^{-1}A_2N = A_1 - B_1M^{-1}F, \quad B_2M = NB_1.$$

More precisely, if condition (i) *is satisfied and the Wiener-*

Hopf equivalence is given by formula (6), *then in formula* (7) *one may take*

$$F = \frac{1}{2\pi i}\int_\Gamma E_-(\lambda)W_1(\lambda)C_1(\lambda-A_1)^{-1}d\lambda, \quad M = E_-(\infty),$$

$$N = \frac{1}{2\pi i}\int_\Gamma (\lambda-A_2)^{-1}B_2W_2(\lambda)E_+(\lambda)^{-1}C_1(\lambda-A_1)^{-1}d\lambda.$$

Conversely, if condition (iv) *is satisfied, then formula* (6) *holds true with*

$$E_-(\lambda) = M + F(\lambda-A_1)^{-1}B_1.$$

In a similar way one can state an analogous theorem about right Wiener-Hopf factorization for analytic operator functions (cf. Theorem II.2.2). We omit the details.

3. Wiener-Hopf factorization with explicit formulas

First of all we have the following analogue of Theorem II.3.1. Again the proof is the same as in the polynomial case.

THEOREM 3.1. *Let* (C,A,B) *be a* Γ*-spectral triple for the analytic operator function* W *and let* X *be its main space. Then with respect to* Γ *the function* W *admits a left Wiener-Hopf factorization*

$$W(\lambda) = E_-(\lambda)\left(\Sigma_{i=1}^{r}\ \lambda^{\nu_i}P_i\right)E_+(\lambda) \tag{8}$$

if and only if the pair (A,B) *is of finite type. Further, if in* (8) *the projections* $P_1,\dots,P_r$ *are different from zero and* $\nu_1 < \nu_2 < \dots < \nu_r$, *then the set*

$$\{(\operatorname{Im} P_1,\nu_1),\dots,(\operatorname{Im} P_r,\nu_r)\}$$

is equal to the set of characteristics of the pair (A,B).

Of course there is a similar theorem for right Wiener-Hopf factorization (cf. Theorem II.3.2).

In the remainder of this section we shall assume that the operator function W is as in formula (2) of Section 1, and our aim is to specify Theorem 3.1 for such a function. In particular we shall give explicit formulas for the factors $E_-(\lambda)$ and $E_+(\lambda)$ appearing in (8).

THEOREM 3.2. *Assume*

$$W(\lambda) = I + S(\lambda - V)^{-1}R, \qquad \lambda \in \Omega,$$

where $V: A \to A$ *is a bounded linear operator with no spectrum in* Ω. *Let* γ *be a contour in* Ω *around the part of* $\sigma(V-RS)$ *in* Ω, *and put*

$$\Delta_j = \operatorname{row}\left(\frac{1}{2\pi i}\int_\gamma \lambda^{\nu-1}[\lambda - (V-RS)]^{-1}R\,d\lambda\right)_{\nu=1}^{j} : Y^j \to A.$$

Then W *admits a left Wiener-Hopf factorization with respect to* Γ *if and only if for some integer* $\ell \geq 1$ *the operators* $\Delta_1, \ldots, \Delta_\ell$ *have generalized inverses and*

(9) $$\operatorname{Im} \Delta_\ell = \operatorname{Im}\left(\frac{1}{2\pi i}\int_\gamma [\lambda - (V-RS)]^{-1}d\lambda\right).$$

Furthermore, in that case there exist mutually disjoint projections $P_0, P_1, \ldots, P_\ell$ *of* Y *and bounded linear operators* $F, G: A \to Y$ *such that with*

(10) $$E_-(\lambda) = I - F[\lambda - (V-RS-RF)]^{-1}R,$$

(11) $$E_+(\lambda) = P_0 + (P_0 S + P_0 F + G)(\lambda - V)^{-1}R$$

we have the following left Wiener-Hopf factorization of W *with respect to* Γ:

$$W(\lambda) = E_-(\lambda)\left(\Sigma_{j=0}^{\ell} \lambda^j P_j\right)E_+(\lambda).$$

PROOF. Put $T = V-RS$. We have already mentioned that $\sigma(T) \cap \Omega$ is an open and closed subset of $\sigma(T)$ (cf. formula (5)). Let Π be the Riesz projection corresponding to $\sigma(T) \cap \Omega$. So

$$\Pi = \frac{1}{2\pi i}\int_\gamma [\lambda - (V-RS)]^{-1}d\lambda.$$

Put $X = \operatorname{Im} \Pi$, and let (C,A,B) be the triple introduced in Lemma 1.1. If $\tau: X \to A$ is the canonical embedding, then

$$\tau \circ [\operatorname{row}(A^{\nu-1}B)_{\nu=1}^{j}] = \Delta_j.$$

So Δ_j has a generalized inverse if and only if $\operatorname{row}(A^{\nu-1}B)_{\nu=1}^{j}$ has a generalized inverse. Further, formula (9) holds if and only if $\operatorname{row}(A^{\nu-1}B)_{\nu=1}^{\ell}$ is surjective. So the first part of the theorem follows from Theorem 3.1.

Next, assume that W admits a left Wiener-Hopf factorization

with respect to Γ. So we may assume that the pair (A,B) satisfies the conditions of Theorem I.2.5. Then there exist closed subspaces $U_0, U_1, \ldots, U_\ell$ of Y such that $Y = U_0 \oplus U_1 \oplus \ldots \oplus U_\ell$ and there exist bounded linear operators

$$F_0: X \to Y, \quad N: \bigoplus_{j=1}^{\ell} U_j^j \to X$$

such that N is invertible and the action of the operators $N^{-1}(A-BF_0)N$ and $N^{-1}B$ is given by:

$$(12) \qquad N^{-1}(A-BF)N(u_{j1},\ldots,u_{jj}) = (0,u_{j1},\ldots,u_{jj-1})$$

for $(u_{j1},\ldots,u_{jj}) \in U_j^j$, $1 \le j \le \ell$,

$$(13) \qquad N^{-1}Bu_j = (u_j,0,\ldots,0) \in U_j^j$$

for $u_j \in U_j \subset Y$, $1 \le j \le \ell$, and $U_0 = \operatorname{Ker} B$.

Let P_j be the projection of Y onto U_j along the spaces U_i, $i \ne j$. Define $G_0: X \to Y$ by

$$(14) \qquad G_0N(u_{j1},\ldots,u_{jj}) = u_{jj} \in U_j \subset Y.$$

Formulas (12), (13) and (14) imply that

$$(15) \qquad P_0 + G_0[\lambda - (A-BF_0)]^{-1}B = \Sigma_{j=0}^{\ell} \lambda^{-j} P_j.$$

Put $D(\lambda) = \Sigma_{j=0}^{\ell} \lambda^j P_j$. So the left hand side of (15) is equal to $D(\lambda)^{-1}$. The triple $(B, A-BF_0, G_0)$ is a Γ-spectral triple for $D(\lambda)$. Applying Theorem 2.1, we have the Wiener-Hopf factorization:

$$(16) \qquad W(\lambda) = E_-(\lambda)D(\lambda)E_+(\lambda), \quad \lambda \in \Gamma,$$

where $E_-(\lambda) = I - F_0[\lambda - (A-BF_0)]^{-1}B$.

Observe that $E_-(\lambda)^{-1} = I + F_0[\lambda-A]^{-1}B$. Recall the definitions of A and B (see Lemma 1.3), and define $F: \mathcal{A} \to Y$ by $F = F_0 \circ \Pi$. Then $E_-(\lambda)^{-1} = I + F(\lambda-T)^{-1}R$. It follows that $E_-(\lambda) = I - F(\lambda - (T-RF))^{-1}R$ is given by formula (10).

To obtain a good formula for $E_+(\lambda)$ we first compute $D(\lambda)^{-1}E_-(\lambda)^{-1}$. We have

$$D(\lambda)^{-1}E_-(\lambda)^{-1} = \{P_0 + G_0[\lambda - (A-BF)]^{-1}B\} \circ$$
$$\circ \{I + F_0(\lambda-A)^{-1}B\} =$$

$$= P_0 + P_0F_0(\lambda-A)^{-1}B + G_0[\lambda - (A-BF_0)]^{-1}B +$$
$$+ G_0[\lambda - (A-BF_0)]^{-1}BF_0(\lambda-A)^{-1}B =$$
$$= P_0 + (P_0F_0 + G_0)(\lambda-A)^{-1}B.$$

Define $G: A \to Y$ by $G = G_0 \circ \Pi$, and recall that $\tau(\lambda-A)^{-1}B = \Pi(\lambda-T)^{-1}R$. It follows that

$$D(\lambda)^{-1}E_-(\lambda)^{-1} = P_0 + (P_0F + G)(\lambda-T)^{-1}R. \tag{17}$$

Next we insert formula (17) in (16), and we use that W is given by formula (2). This yields

$$E_+(\lambda) = D(\lambda)^{-1}E_-(\lambda)^{-1}W(\lambda)$$
$$= \{P_0 + (P_0F + G)(\lambda-T)^{-1}R\}\circ\{I + S(\lambda-V)^{-1}R\}$$
$$= P_0 + P_0S(\lambda-V)^{-1}R + (P_0F + G)[\lambda - (V-RS)]^{-1}R +$$
$$+ (P_0F + G)[\lambda - (V - RS)]^{-1}RS(\lambda-V)^{-1}R$$
$$= P_0 + (P_0S + P_0F + G)(\lambda-V)^{-1}R.$$

So $E_+(\lambda)$ is given by formula (11), and the proof is finished.

Theorem 3.2 can be made more concrete by specifying the operators V, R and S appearing in the expression

$$W(\lambda) = I + S(\lambda-V)^{-1}R, \quad \lambda \in \Omega.$$

For example, if one chooses V, R and S as is done in the paragraph after the proof of Lemma 1.1, then the operators Δ_j appearing in Theorem 3.2 and the spaces appearing in (9) may be described explicitly.

REFERENCES

1. Bart, H., Gohberg, I., Kaashoek, M.A.: Minimal factorization of matrix and operator functions. OT1. Basel, Birkhäuser Verlag, 1979.

2. Fuhrmann, P.A., Willems, J.C.: Factorization indices at infinity for rational matrix functions. Integral Equations and Operator Theory 2 (3) (1979) 187-301.

3. Gohberg, I., Kaashoek, M.A., Lay, D.C.: Equivalence, linearization and decompositions of holomorphic operator functions. J. Funct. Anal. 28 (1978), 102-144.

4. Gohberg, I., Kaashoek, M.A., van Schagen, F.: Similarity of operator blocks and canonical forms. I. General results, Feedback equivalence and Kronecker indices. Integral

Equations and Operator Theory 3 (3) (1980), 350-396.

5. Gohberg, I., Lerer, L.: Factorization indices and Kronecker indices of matrix polynomials. Integral Equations and Operator Theory 2 (2) (1979), 199-243.

6. Gohberg, I., Lerer, L., Rodman, L.: Factorization indices for matrix polynomials. Bull. Amer. Math. Soc. 84 (2) (1978) 275-277.

7. Gohberg, I., Lerer, L., Rodman, L.: Stable factorizations of operator polynomials and spectral divisions simply behaved at infinity. I and II. J. of Math. Analysis and Appl. 74 (1980), 401-431; 75 (1980), 1-40.

8. Gohberg, I., Leiterer, J.: General theorems on the factorization of operator-valued functions with respect to a contour. I. Holomorphic functions (Russian), Acta Sci. Math. (Szeged) 34 (1973), 103-120.

9. Kaashoek, M.A., van der Mee, C.V.M., Rodman, L.: Analytical equivalence of holomorphic operator functions and linearization. (In preparation).

10. Rowley, B.: Wiener-Hopf factorization of operator polynomials. Integral Equations and Operator Theory 3 (3) (1980), 437-462.

I. Gohberg,
Department of Mathematics,
Tel-Aviv University
Ramat-Aviv, Israel

M.A. Kaashoek and F. van Schagen,
Wiskundig Seminarium,
Vrije Universiteit,
Amsterdam, The Netherlands

UNITARY ORBITS OF POWER PARTIAL ISOMETRIES AND APPROXIMATION BY BLOCK-DIAGONAL NILPOTENTS

Domingo A. Herrero

1. INTRODUCTION

Let $L(H)$ be the algebra of all (bounded linear) operators acting on the complex separable Hilbert space H. $T\in L(H)$ is called *block-diagonal* (*quasidiagonal*) if there exists an increasing sequence $\{P_n\}_{n=1}^{\infty}$ of finite rank (orthogonal) projections such that $P_n\to 1$ strongly, as $n\to\infty$, and $P_nT=TP_n$ for all n ($\|TP_n-P_nT\|\to 0$, as $n\to\infty$, resp.). The classes (BD) and (QD) of all block-diagonal and all quasidiagonal, respectively, operators were introduced and studied by P.R.Halmos in [10], where it is shown that if $T\in$ (QD), then given $\varepsilon>0$, there exists $K\in K$ (the ideal of all compact operators) and $B\in$ (BD) such that $\|K\|<\varepsilon$ and $T=B+K$; moreover, (QD) is closed in $L(H)$ and $(BD)^-=(QD)$ (the upper bar will always denote norm-closure).

Let $(N)_k=\{T\in L(H): T^k=0\}$ be the set of all nilpotent operators of order at most k ($k=1,2,3,\ldots$) and let $(N)=\bigcup_{k=1}^{\infty}(N)_k$ (the set of all nilpotent operators), $(BDN)_k=(BD)\cap(N)_k$, $(BDN)=(BD)\cap(N)$, $(QDN)_k=(QD)\cap(N)_k$ and $(QDN) = (QD)\cap(N)$.

The closure $(N)^-$ of (N) was completely characterized in [2], in terms of the different parts of the spectrum $\sigma(T)$ of an operator T in this set. In particular, $(N)^-$ contains every quasinilpotent operator. Clearly, $(BDN)^-\subset(BD)^-\cap(N)^-=(QD)\cap(N)^-$.

PROBLEM 1. Is $(BDN)^-=(QD)\cap(N)^-$?

The above question has been raised by L.R.Williams in [19], where it is conjectured that the answer must be negative. In [15], the author obtained several results which suggest that, on the contrary, the answer could be affirmative.

This article is a sequel of [15] and deals with several partial answers to Problem 1 and related questions.

C.Apostol and N.Salinas [3] proved that if Q is a quasinilpotent operator acting on an infinite dimensional Hilbert space, then dist $[Q,(N)_{4k}]\leq 4(1+\|Q\|)\|Q^k\|^{1/(k+1)}$. Combining the arguments of [1] and [3], an upper estimate is obtained for dist $[T,(N)_{2k}]$ for an arbitrary operator $T\epsilon L(H)$, in terms of $\|T\|$, $\|T^k\|$ and the spectral radius $sp(\pi(T))$ of the canonical projection $\pi(T)$ of T in the quotient Calkin algebra $A(H)=L(H)/K(H)$. (If $\sigma_e(T)=\sigma(\pi(T))$ denotes the essential spectrum of T, then $sp(\pi(T))=\max\{|\lambda|:\lambda\epsilon\sigma_e(T)\}$.)

In order to establish the other results, we shall need some extra notation: If $A_\upsilon\epsilon L(H_\upsilon)$ and $\{A_\upsilon\}_{\upsilon\epsilon\Gamma}$ is a bounded family of operators, then $A=\bigoplus_{\upsilon\epsilon\Gamma}A_\upsilon$ will denote the direct sum of the A_υ's acting in the usual fashion on $H=\bigoplus_{\upsilon\epsilon\Gamma}H_\upsilon$, the *orthogonal* direct sum of the spaces H_υ. In particular, if $B\epsilon L(H_o)$ and $0\leq\alpha\leq\infty$, then $B^{(\alpha)}$ will denote the direct sum of α copies of B acting on the direct sum $H_o^{(\alpha)}$ of α copies of H_o.

Minor modifications of the approach of C.Apostol and N.Salinas yielded the following result in [15]: If $Q\epsilon(QD)$ is quasinilpotent, then $Q\oplus 0\epsilon(BDN)^-$. A new modification of the same argument shows that if Q has the above form and $R\epsilon L(\mathbb{C}^n)$ is nilpotent, then $Q\oplus R^{(\infty)}\epsilon(BDN)^-$. In connection with these questions, the author was led to the following

PROBLEM 2. Let $T\epsilon(QD)$ and let $t=\pi(T)$. Does $C^*(t)$, the C^*-algebra generated by t and $e=\pi(1)$, always admit a unital *-representation ρ such that $\rho(t)$ is quasidiagonal?

An affirmative answer to the above question would immediately imply that $(BDN)^-$ contains all quasidiagonal quasinilpotent operators.

In Section 3 it is shown that $(BDN)_k$ is never closed (for $k\geq 2$) and $(BDN)_k^-=(QDN)_k$; furthermore, given $T\epsilon(QDN)_k$ and $\epsilon>0$, there exists $K\epsilon K$, $\|K\|<\epsilon$, such that $T-K\epsilon(BDN)_k$, $k=1,2,3,\ldots$.

Recall that $T\epsilon L(H)$ is a *power partial isometry* (ppi) if T^n

is a partial isometry for all n=1,2,... [13]. Section 4 is devoted to obtain (lower and upper) estimates for the distance from a given ppi A to the unitary orbit $\mathcal{U}(B)=\{UBU^*: U\in L(H)$ is unitary$\}$ of another ppi B. These results are used in Section 5 to settle a problem of L.R.Williams:

Given $f,g\in H$, define $f\otimes g\in L(H)$ by $f\otimes g(x)=\langle x,g\rangle f$. Let $q_k\in L(\mathbb{C}^k)$ be the Jordan nilpotent defined by $q_k=\sum_{j=2}^{k} e_{j-1}\otimes e_j$ $(k=1,2,3,\ldots)$; then $J=\bigoplus_{k=1}^{\infty} q_k$ is a ppi in $H=\bigoplus_{k=1}^{\infty}\mathbb{C}^k$. In [19], L.R.Williams gave a heuristic argument to support his conjecture that $(BDN)^-\neq(QD)\cap(N)$, by showing that, in a certain sense, J "tends to be far from (BDN)". It will be shown here that J is actually the (norm) limit of a sequence $\{Q_n\simeq[\bigoplus_{k=1}^{n-1} q_k]\oplus q_n^{(\infty)}\}_{n=1}^{\infty}$ ($A\simeq B$ means that A and B are unitarily equivalent operators) of block-diagonal power partial isometries.

An operator $T\in L(H)$ is called *n-normal* if it admits a representation as an n x n matrix of pairwise commuting normal operators (with respect to a suitable decomposition $H=\bigoplus_{j=1}^{n} H_j$, $H_j\simeq H$ for all j=1,2,...,n, of H), and *algebraically n-normal* if $T\simeq\bigoplus_{j=1}^{n} T_k$, where T_k is k-normal for each k. (T_k can, eventually, act on a subspace of finite dimension d_k, $0\leq d_k<\infty$.)

It is well-known that, given $A\in(\mathrm{Nor})_k=\{T\in L(H): T$ is algebraically k-normal$\}$ (k=1,2,...) and $\varepsilon>0$, there exists $B\in(BD)\cap(\mathrm{Nor})_k=$ $=(\mathrm{BDNor})_k$ (every operator in this set can be written as an infinite direct sum of operators acting on spaces of dimension at most k) such that $A-B\in K$ and $\|A-B\|<\varepsilon$ [17].

Since the operator Q_n (described above) belongs to $(\mathrm{BDNNor})_n=$ $=(BDN)\cap(\mathrm{Nor})_n$ and many operators in $(QD)\cap(N)^-$ are actually limits of operators in $(\mathrm{BDNNor})=\bigcup_{k=1}^{\infty}(\mathrm{BDNNor})_k$ (see [15]), it is natural to raise the following

PROBLEM 3. Characterize $(\mathrm{BDNNor})^-$. Is $(\mathrm{BDNNor})^-=(BDN)^-$? Is $(QD)=[\bigcup_{k=1}^{\infty}(\mathrm{Nor})_k]^-$?

The author wishes to thank Professors Constantin Apostol and Lázaro Recht for many helpful discussions.

2. VARIATIONS ON A THEME OF C.APOSTOL AND N.SALINAS

Let H be an infinite dimensional Hilbert space and assume that $T\varepsilon L(H)$ and λ belongs to the boundary $\partial\sigma_e(T)$ of the essential spectrum of T. Then, a minor modification of the constructions of [18] and [1] shows that $U(T)^-$ contains an operator

$$T_1=\begin{pmatrix} C_2 & 0 & 0 & B_2 \\ 0 & \lambda & B_1 & 0 \\ 0 & 0 & C_1 & 0 \\ 0 & 0 & 0 & \lambda \end{pmatrix}$$

(with respect to a suitable decomposition $H=\bigoplus_{j=1}^{4} H_j, H_j\simeq H$, $j=1,2,3,4$), and it is completely apparent that λ can be chosen so that $|\lambda|= = \min\{|\mu|:\mu\varepsilon\partial\sigma_e(T)\}\leq sp(t)\leq sp(T)$ and dist $[T,(N)_{2k}]=$ dist $[T_1, (N)_{2k}]$ for all $k=1,2,3...$.

Let $T_2\varepsilon L(H)$ be the operator obtained from T_1 by replacing the λ's by 0's. Then [3, Lemma 2.1], for every $\alpha>0$, $\beta>sp(T)=\max\{sp(C_1),sp(C_2)\}$ and every positive integer k, we have

$$\max_{j=1,2} \text{dist}[C_j\oplus 0,(N)_k]\leq\alpha\max_{j=1,2}\{||C_j||+\beta+\frac{||C_j^k||}{\alpha\beta^{k-1}}\}\leq\alpha||T||+\beta+\frac{||T^k||}{\alpha\beta^{k-1}}.$$

Thus, if $T\neq 0$, $k\geq 2$, $\beta=[(k-1)^2||T||.||T^k||]^{1/(k+1)}$,

$$\alpha=\beta/[(k-1)||T||]$$

and $\eta>0$, we can find operators $Q_j\varepsilon(N)_k(j=1,2)$ such that

$$\max_{j=1,2}||C_j\oplus 0-Q_j||<\{(k+1)/[(k-1)^{\frac{k-1}{k+1}}]\}(||T||.||T^k||)^{\frac{1}{k+1}}+\eta.$$

Let

$$T_\eta=\begin{pmatrix} Q_1 & \begin{pmatrix} 0 & B_2 \\ B_1 & 0\end{pmatrix} \\ 0 & Q_2\end{pmatrix}\varepsilon L(H);$$

then $T_\eta\varepsilon(N)_{2k}$ and $||T-T_\eta||<|\lambda|+\{(k+1)/[(k-1)^{\frac{k-1}{k+1}}]\}(||T||.||T^k||)^{\frac{1}{k+1}}+\eta$.

Since η can be chosen arbitrarily small, we obtain

THEOREM 2.1. *If H is a separable infinite dimensional Hilbert space and $T\in L(H)$, then*

$$\mathrm{dist}[T,(N)_{2k}]\leq sp(t)+C(k)(||T||\cdot||T^k||)^{\frac{1}{k+1}}\leq$$
$$\leq[C(k)+1](||T||\cdot||T^k||)^{\frac{1}{k+1}},$$

where $C(k)=(k+1)/[(k-1)^{(k-1)/(k+1)}]\leq 3$, for all $k=2,3,\ldots$.

(Observe that $sp(t)\leq sp(T)\leq||T^{k+1}||^{\frac{1}{k+1}}\leq(||T||\cdot||T^k||)^{\frac{1}{k+1}}$, whence we obtain the second inequality.)

Lemma 2.1 of [3] admits the following mild improvement.

LEMMA 2.2. *Let H be a Hilbert space of infinite dimension and let $T,R\in L(H)$. If $R\in(N)_m$ then for every $\alpha>0$, $\beta>sp(T)$ and every positive integer k, there exists $L\in L(H\oplus H)$ such that $L^{k+m-1}=0$ and*

$$||(T\oplus R)-L||<\alpha||T||+\beta+\frac{||T^k||}{\alpha\beta^{k-1}}.$$

PROOF. Observe that $H=H_o\oplus H_1$, where $H_o=\ker R\simeq H$. Thus

$$T\oplus R=\begin{pmatrix}T&0&0\\0&0&A\\0&0&B\end{pmatrix}=\begin{bmatrix}T\oplus 0&C\\0&B\end{bmatrix}$$

with respect to $H\oplus H_o\oplus H_1$, where $C=\begin{bmatrix}0\\A\end{bmatrix}$ and $B^{m-1}=0$.

According to [3, Lemma 2.1], there exists $Q\in L(H\oplus H_o)$ such that $Q^k=0$ and $||(T\oplus 0)-Q||<\alpha||T||+\beta+\frac{||T^k||}{\alpha\beta^{k-1}}$. Set

$$L=\begin{pmatrix}Q&C\\0&B\end{pmatrix}.$$

It is completely apparent that $||(T\oplus R)-L||=||(T\oplus 0)-Q||$ and

$$L^r=\begin{pmatrix} Q_r & \sum_{j=0}^{r-1} Q^jCB^{r-j-1} \\ 0 & B^r \end{pmatrix}$$

for all $r=2,3,\ldots$. In particular, if $r=k+m-1$, then either $j\geq k$, or $j<k$ and $r-j\geq m$; in either case, $Q^jCB^{r-j-1}=0$ for all $j=0,1,\ldots,k+m-2$, whence it readily follows that $L\varepsilon(N)_{k+m-1}$.

Similarly, [15 , Lemma 5.10] admits the following improvement. (The proof follows exactly the same scheme as the above one and will be omitted.)

LEMMA 2.3. *If* $A\varepsilon L(\mathbb{C}^d)$, $0<d<\infty$, $R\varepsilon L(\mathbb{C}^p)$ *is a nilpotent of order at most* m *,* α *and* β *are real numbers such that* $\alpha>0$ *and* $\beta>sp(A)$, *and* k *is a positive integer, then there exists a nilpotent* $L\varepsilon L(\mathbb{C}^d\oplus\mathbb{C}^{((k-1)dp)})$ *of order at most* $k+m-1$ *such that*

$$||A\oplus R^{((k-1)d)}-L||<2\alpha\sqrt{2}||A||+(1+2\alpha\sqrt{2})\{\alpha||A||+\beta+\frac{||A^k||}{\alpha\beta^{k-1}}\} .$$

REMARK. If $R^m=0$, but $R^{m-1}\neq 0$, for some $m, 1<m<p$, then R is similar to $\bigoplus_{k=1}^{m} q_k^{(\alpha_k)}$, $\sum_{k=1}^{m} k\alpha_k=p$ and therefore $\dim\ker R=n=\sum_{k=1}^{m}\alpha_k\geq p/m$. It readily follows that, in this case, instead of $(k-1)d$ copies of R, we only need $[((k-1)d+1)/n]$ copies, where $[r]$ denotes the integral part of the real number r.

LEMMA 2.4. *Assume that* $Q\varepsilon(QD)$ *is quasinilpotent. Given* $\varepsilon>0$, *there exists* $K\varepsilon K$ *such that* $||K||<\varepsilon$ *and* $Q-K$ *is unitarily equivalent to an infinite direct sum of nilpotent operators acting on finite dimensional spaces.*

PROOF. Since $Q\varepsilon(QD)$, there exists $K_1\varepsilon K$ such that $||K_1||<\varepsilon/2$ and $Q-K_1=\bigoplus_{n=1}^{\infty} A_n\,\varepsilon(BD)$. By using the upper semicontinuity of the spectrum [16], it is easily seen that K_1 can be chosen so that $\sup sp(A_n)\leq sp(\bigoplus_{n=1}^{\infty} A_n)<\varepsilon/2$. Since K_1 is compact, it follows that $sp(A_n)\to 0$ $(n\to\infty)$.

Clearly, for each n, we can choose a nilpotent operator B_n

acting on the same finite dimensional space as A_n such that $||A_n-B_n||\leq sp(A_n)$. Hence, $B=\bigoplus_{n=1}^{\infty} B_n$ is a direct sum of nilpotents acting on finite dimensional spaces, $K_2=B-A=\bigoplus_{n=1}^{\infty}(B_n-A_n)\in K$, $||K_2||<\varepsilon/2$, $K=Q-B=K_1+K_2\in K$ and $||K||<\varepsilon/2+\varepsilon/2=\varepsilon$.

THEOREM 2.5. *If* $Q\in L(H)$ *is a quasidiagonal quasinilpotent and the* C^**-algebra* $C^*(q)$ *admits a unital *-representation* ρ *into* $L(H_\rho)$ *such that either* $0<\dim H_\rho<\infty$ *or* H_ρ *is infinite dimensional and* $\rho(q)$ *is quasidiagonal, then* $Q\in(BDN)^-$.

PROOF. If H_ρ is finite dimensional, we choose $R=\rho(q)\in L(H_\rho)$. Assume that H_ρ is infinite dimensional and let $N=\rho(q)\in(QD)$. By Lemma 2.4, given $\varepsilon>0$ there exists $L=\bigoplus_{n=1}^{\infty} L_n\in(BD)$ such that the L_n's are nilpotent operators acting on finite dimensional spaces and $||N-L||<\varepsilon/4$. In this case, we choose $R=L_1$.

By Voiculescu's theorem [18] , in the first case $U(Q)^-$ contains an operator $T'\simeq Q\oplus R^{(\infty)}$ such that $||Q-T'||<\varepsilon/2$; in the second one, $U(Q)^-$ contains an operator $T''\simeq Q\oplus N^{(\infty)}$ such that $||Q-T''||<\varepsilon/4$, so that if we choose $T'\simeq Q\oplus L^{(\infty)}\simeq Q\oplus \dot{L}^{(\infty)}\oplus R^{(\infty)}$ conveniently (by replacing the direct summand $N^{(\infty)}$ by $L^{(\infty)}$), then $||Q-T'||\leq||Q-T''||+||N-L||<\varepsilon/2$.

By Lemma 2.4, there exists $Q'\in(BD)$ such that Q' is quasinilpotent and $||Q-Q'||<\varepsilon/2$. Let T be the operator obtained from T' by replacing Q by Q'. In either case, $T\simeq\{\bigoplus_{n=1}^{\infty} T_n\}\oplus R^{(\infty)}$, where T_n is a nilpotent acting on a subspace of finite dimension d_n, for all $n=1,2,3,\ldots$. Clearly, for each $k=2,3,\ldots$, we have $T\simeq\bigoplus_{n=1}^{\infty}[T_n\oplus R^{((k-1)d_n)}]$.

By Lemma 2.3 (take α and β as in the proof of Theorem 2.1), there exists a constant C (independent of k) such that

$$||[T_n\oplus R^{((k-1)d_n)}]-Q_{n,k}||\leq C[||T\oplus R||\cdot||T^k||]^{1/(k+1)},$$

for a suitably chosen $Q_{n,k}\in(N)_{k+m-1}$ acting on the (finite dimensional!) space of $T_n\oplus R^{((k-1)d_n)}$.

It readily follows that $L(H \oplus H)$ contains a sequence $\{Q_k\}_{k=1}^{\infty}$, $Q_k \in (BDN)_{k+m-1}$, $Q_k \simeq \bigoplus_{n=1}^{\infty} Q_{n,k}$ such that

$$||T-Q_k|| \leq C[||T \oplus R||.||T^k||]^{1/(k+1)} \to 0 \quad (k \to \infty).$$

Hence, $T \in (BDN)^-$. Since $||Q-T|| < \varepsilon$ and ε can be chosen arbitrarily small, we conclude that $Q \in (BDN)^-$.

3. APPROXIMATION OF QUASIDIAGONAL NILPOTENTS

The main topic of Section 2 was the approximation of an arbitrary operator T, in terms of $||T||$ and $||T^k||$, by nilpotents of *order strictly larger* than k, in infinite dimensional spaces.

What can be said about approximation by nilpotents of order k in spaces of arbitrary (finite or infinite) dimension? The results of [6, Section 4] provide a partial answer.

PROPOSITION 3.1. ([6, Corollary 1]). *If* $T \in L(H)$ $(0 < \dim \leq \infty)$, $||T|| \leq 1$ *and* $||T^k|| \leq \varepsilon$, *then* dist $[T,(N)_k] \leq \delta_k(\varepsilon)$, *where* $\delta_1(\varepsilon) = \varepsilon$, $\delta_2(\varepsilon) = 2\sqrt{\varepsilon}$ *and* $\delta_k(\varepsilon) = \sqrt{\varepsilon} + \delta_{k-1}((k-1)\sqrt{\varepsilon})$, *for all* $k \geq 3$.

THEOREM 3.2. (i) *If* $Q \in (QD)$ *is quasinilpotent and* $||Q^k|| \to 0$ $(k \to \infty)$ *fast enough, then* $Q \in (BDN)^-$.

(ii) *If* $k \geq 2$, $(BDN)_k$ *is not closed and* $(BDN)_k^- = (QDN)_k$. *Furthermore, given* $T \in (QDN)_k$ *and* $\varepsilon > 0$, *there exists* $B \in (BDN)_k$ *such that* $T-B$ *is compact and* $||T-B|| < \varepsilon$.

(iii) *Given* $T \in (QDN)_k \cap (Nor)_k$ *and* $\varepsilon > 0$, *there exists* $B \in (BDNNor)_k$ *such that* $T-B$ *is compact and* $||T-B|| < \varepsilon$.

PROOF. (i) Clearly, we can directly assume that $||Q|| = 1$. Let $||Q^m|| = \varepsilon_m$. According to Lemma 2.4, given $\eta_m > 0$ we can find $A_m = \bigoplus_{n=1}^{\infty} A_{mn}$ in (BD) such that $||Q-A_m|| < 1/m$, $||A_m|| \leq ||Q|| + 1/m$, $Q-A_m \in K$, A_{mn} is a nilpotent acting on a finite dimensional space (for each m and n, m,n=1,2,3,...) and $||(A_m)^m|| < \varepsilon_m + \eta_m$. If η_m is small enough, then (by Proposition 3.1) there exist operators B_{mn} such that $(B_{mn})^m = 0$ and $||A_{mn} - B_{mn}|| < 2\delta_m(\varepsilon_m)$. Thus, if $\varepsilon_m \to 0$ $(m \to \infty)$, fast enough to guarantee that $\delta_m(\varepsilon_m) \to 0$ $(m \to \infty)$, it readily follows that $Q \in (BDN)^-$.

(ii) Observe that if H = "multiplication by x" in $L^2([0,1], dx)$

and $\varepsilon>0$, then the Weyl-von Neumann theorem (see, e.g., [16],[18]) implies that $H-D$ is compact and $||H-D||<\varepsilon$, for a suitable diagonal hermitian operator $D=\text{diagonal}\ \{\lambda_1,\lambda_2,..\}$. Clearly, if $k\geq 2$, then

$$q_k\otimes D = \begin{pmatrix} 0 & D & 0 & . & . & . & 0 & 0 \\ 0 & 0 & D & . & . & . & 0 & 0 \\ 0 & 0 & 0 & . & . & . & 0 & 0 \\ . & . & . & . & . & & . & . \\ . & . & . & & . & . & . & . \\ . & . & . & & & & . & . \\ 0 & 0 & 0 & . & . & . & 0 & D \\ 0 & 0 & 0 & . & . & . & 0 & 0 \end{pmatrix} = \bigoplus_{n=1}^{\infty} \lambda_n q_k \in (BDN)_k ,$$

$q_k\otimes H-q_k\otimes D\in K$ and $||q_k\otimes H-q_k\otimes D||=||H-D||<\varepsilon$, whence we readily obtain that $q_k\otimes H\in (BDN)_k^-$.

But $q_k\otimes H\notin (BDN)_k$, because every non-zero reducing subspace of this operator has the form $L^2(\Gamma,dx)^{(k)}$ (for some measurable subset Γ of $[0,1]$ of positive measure) and therefore, it is an infinite dimensional subspace of $L^2([0,1],dx)^{(k)}$.

Hence, $(BDN)_k$ is not closed in $L(H)$.

It is obvious that $(BDN)_k^-\subset (QDN)_k$. Let $Q\in (QDN)_k$, $||Q||=1$, and let $\varepsilon>0$. By Lemma 2.4, there exist compact operators K_m such that $||K_m||<1/m$ and $B_m=Q-K_m = \bigoplus_{n=1}^{\infty} B_{mn}$, where B_{mn} is a nilpotent acting on a finite dimensional space for each m and n, m,n=1,2,... . Furthermore, replacing (if necessary) B_{mn} by $(1-\varepsilon_{mn})B_{mn}$ $(0\leq\varepsilon_{mn}\to 0, n\to\infty)$, we can directly assume that $||B_m||\leq 1$ for all m=1,2,... .

By Proposition 3.1, there exist operators C_{mn} such that $(C_{mn})^k=0$ and $||B_{mn}-C_{mn}||<\delta_k(||(B_{mn})^k||)\to\delta_k(||Q^k||)=0$ $(k\to\infty)$. Thus, if $C_m= \bigoplus_{n=1}^{\infty} C_{mn}$, then $C_m\in (BDN)_k$ and $||Q-C_m||\leq||K_m||+\sup_n||B_{mn}-C_{mn}||<$ $<1/m+\delta_k(||(B_m)^k||)\to 0$ $(m\to\infty)$.

Define $B=C_m$, where m is the first index such that $||Q-C_m||<\varepsilon$

and let P_t be the orthogonal projection of H onto the finite dimensional subspace H_t corresponding to $\bigoplus_{n=1}^{t} C_{mn}$ (or $\bigoplus_{n=1}^{t} B_{mn}$); then $P_t \to 1$ (strongly) and $||K_m - P_t K_m P_t|| \to 0$, as $t \to \infty$. We have

$$Q = B_m + K_m = \begin{bmatrix} \bigoplus_{n=1}^{t} B_{mn} + P_t K_m | H_t & P_t K_m | H_t^{\perp} \\ (1-P_t) K_m | H_t & \bigoplus_{n=t+1}^{\infty} B_{mn} + (1-P_t) K_m | H_t^{\perp} \end{bmatrix}$$

(with respect to the decomposition $H = H_t \oplus H_t^{\perp}$).

Since $||P_t K_m | H_t^{\perp}|| + ||(1-P_t) K_m | H_t|| + ||(1-P_t) K_m | H_t^{\perp}|| = ||P_t K_m (1-P_t)|| + ||(1-P_t) K_m P_t|| + ||(1-P_t) K_m (1-P_t)|| \leq 3 ||K_m - P_t K_m P_t|| \to 0\ (t \to \infty)$ and $Q^k = 0$, an elementary argument of continuity indicates that

$$\sup\{||(B_{mn})^k||:\ n > t\} = ||(\bigoplus_{n=t+1}^{\infty} B_{mn})^k|| \to 0\ (t \to \infty).$$

It follows from Proposition 3.1 that $||B_{mn} - C_{mn}|| \to 0$ $(n \to \infty)$, and therefore $Q - B = K_m + \bigoplus_{n=1}^{\infty} (B_{mn} - C_{mn}) \in K$.

(iii) follows by the same arguments (see also [17]).

4. HAUSDORFF DISTANCES BETWEEN UNITARY ORBITS OF POWER PARTIAL ISOMETRIES

Recall that an operator $T \in L(H)$ is a partial isometry if there exist two subspaces M (initial space) and N (final space) of H of the same dimension such that T maps M isometrically onto N and ker T = $M^{\perp}$. This is equivalent to say that T^*T is an orthogonal projection of H (onto M), or that TT^* is an orthogonal projection (onto N)[12].

The set of all orthogonal projections is closed in $L(H)$ and using this fact it is not difficult to check that the set (PPI) of all power partial isometries is also closed. A fortiori, if T is a ppi, then $U(T)^{-} \subset$ (PPI).

THEOREM 4.1. *T is a ppi if and only if it has the form*

(4.1) $$T \simeq \{\bigoplus_{k=1}^{\infty} q_k^{(\alpha_k)}\} \oplus S^{(\alpha)} \oplus S^{*(\beta)} \oplus V,$$

where S *is a forward shift of multiplicity one,* S^* (*≃the adjoint of* S) *is a backward shift of multiplicity one,* V *is a unitary operator acting on a subspace* H_V *and either*

$$\dim H_V + \sum_{k=1}^{\infty} \alpha_k = \infty \qquad \text{or} \qquad \alpha+\beta>0.$$

Furthermore, T, $\sigma(T)$ *and* $\sigma_e(T)$ *have exactly one of the following forms*

(i) $\sigma(T) \subset \partial D$, *where* ∂D *denotes the boundary of the open unit disc* $D=\{\lambda : |\lambda| < 1\}$, *iff* T *is unitary;*

(ii) $\sigma(T)=\sigma_e(T)=\{0\}$ *iff* $T = \bigoplus_{k=1}^{n} q_k^{(\alpha_k)}$. *(Clearly, in this case* $\alpha_k=\infty$ *for some* k, $1 \le k \le n$.)

(iii) $\{0\} \subsetneq \sigma(T) \subset \{0\} \cup \partial D$ *iff* $T = Q \oplus V$, *where* Q *has the form of* (ii) *and* V *is unitary and both operators* (Q *and* V) *act on non-zero subspaces. There are three possible subcases:* $\sigma_e(T)=\{0\}$ (*iff* $\dim H_V$ *is finite*), $\sigma_e(T) \subset \partial D$ (*iff* Q *acts on a finite dimensional space*) *or* $\sigma_e(T) \supsetneq \{0\}$ (*iff* Q *and* V *act on infinite dimensional spaces*).

Otherwise, $\sigma(T)=D^-$, $\sigma_e(T) \supset \partial D$ *and*

(iv) $\sigma_e(T)=\partial D$ *iff* $\alpha+\beta+\sum_{k=1}^{\infty}\alpha_k<\infty$ *and* $\alpha+\beta>0$;

(v) $\sigma_e(T)=\{0\} \cup \partial D$ *iff* $T = \{\bigoplus_{k=1}^{n} q_k^{(\alpha_k)}\} \oplus S^{(\alpha)} \oplus S^{*(\beta)} \oplus V$, $\sum_{k=1}^{n}\alpha_k=\infty$ *and* $0<\alpha+\beta<\infty$.

In the remaining cases, $\sigma(T)=\sigma_e(T)=D^-$ *and*

(vi) *The left essential spectrum* $\sigma_{le}(T)$ *of* T *coincides with* ∂D *iff* $\beta+\sum_{k=1}^{\infty}\alpha_k<\infty$ *and* $\alpha=\infty$;

(vii) *The right essential spectrum* $\sigma_{re}(T)$ *of* T *coincides with* ∂D *iff* $\alpha+\sum_{k=1}^{\infty}\alpha_k<\infty$ *and* $\beta=\infty$;

(viii) $\sigma_{le}(T)=\{0\} \cup \partial D$ *iff* $T = \{\bigoplus_{k=1}^{n} q_k^{(\alpha_k)}\} \oplus S^{(\alpha)} \oplus S^{*(\beta)} \oplus V$, $\alpha = \sum_{k=1}^{n}\alpha_k=\infty$ *and* $\beta<\infty$;

(ix) $\sigma_{re}(T)=\{0\} \cup \partial D$ *iff* T *has the form of* (viii), $\beta=\sum_{k=1}^{n}\alpha_k=\infty$ *and*

$\alpha<\infty$; *or*

(x) $\sigma_{le}(T)=\sigma_{re}(T)=D^-$ *iff either* $\alpha=\beta=\infty$ *or* $\alpha_k\neq 0$ *for infinitely many values of* k.

The first part of Theorem 4.1 (i.e., the structure of the ppi's) was obtained by P.R.Halmos and L.J.Wallen in [13]. The classification (i)-(x) is a trivial consequence of formula (4.1).

We are interested in estimating the distance from a given ppi T to the set of operators that are unitarily equivalent to another ppi L, i.e.,

$$\text{dist}\,[T,\mathcal{U}(L)]\overset{\text{def}}{=}\inf\,\{\|T-L'\|:L'\in\mathcal{U}(L)\}.$$

It is easily seen that, given A,B in $\mathcal{L}(\mathcal{H})$, we have

$$\text{dist}[A,\mathcal{U}(B)]=\text{dist}[B,\mathcal{U}(A)]=\text{dist}[\mathcal{U}(A),\mathcal{U}(B)]\overset{\text{def}}{=}\inf\{\|A'-B'\|:A'\in\mathcal{U}(A),B'\in\mathcal{U}(B)\}.$$

Moreover, $\text{dist}[\mathcal{U}(A),\mathcal{U}(B)]$ actually coincides with the *Hausdorff distance* $d_H[\mathcal{U}(A),\mathcal{U}(B)]$ between unitary orbits (or their closures). In order to simplify the notation, we shall write

$$\{A;B\}=\text{dist}[\mathcal{U}(A),\mathcal{U}(B)].$$

It is immediate that $\{A;B\}=\{A^*;B^*\}$. The interested reader can consult [8], [9],[18] for the structure of the closure of a unitary orbit. Following [8], we shall say that A and B are *approximately unitarily equivalent* ($A\simeq_a B$) if $\mathcal{U}(A)^-=\mathcal{U}(B)^-$. Clearly, $\simeq_a$ is an equivalence relation and $(\mathcal{L}(\mathcal{H})/\simeq_a,\{.,.\})$ is a metric space.

PROPOSITION 4.2. $(\mathcal{L}(\mathcal{H})/\simeq_a,\{.,.\})$ *is a complete metric space.*

PROOF. It only remains to prove that this metric space is complete. Let $\{\mathcal{U}(A_n)^-\}_{n=1}^\infty$ be a Cauchy sequence. Passing, if necessary, to a subsequence, we can assume that $\sum_{n=1}^\infty\{A_n;A_{n+1}\}<\infty$.

By hypothesis, there exist unitary operators $\{U_n\}_{n=1}^\infty$ such that $\|A_n-U_nA_{n+1}U_n^*\|<2\{A_n;A_{n+1}\}$. Hence $\{A_1,U_1A_2U_1^*,(U_1U_2)A_3(U_1U_2)^*,\ldots,(U_1U_2U_3\ldots U_n)A_{n+1}(U_1U_2U_3\ldots U_n)^*,\ldots\}$ is a Cauchy sequence in $\mathcal{L}(\mathcal{H})$.

Let

$$A=(\text{norm})\text{-}\lim_{n\to\infty}(U_1U_2\ldots U_n)A_{n+1}(U_1U_2\ldots U_n)^*.$$

It is straightforward to check that $\lim_{n\to\infty}\{A_n;A\}=0$.

LEMMA 4.3. (1) *If* $||A||, ||B|| \leq 1$ *and* $||A^k x|| = 1$, *but* $B^k x = 0$ (*in particular, if* $B^k = 0$) *for some unitary vector* $x \in H$ *and some* $k \geq 1$, *then* $||A-B|| \geq 1/k$.

(2) *If* $||a|| = ||a^k|| = 1$, $||b|| \leq 1$ *and* $b^k = 0$, *then* $||A-B|| \geq ||a-b|| \geq 1/k$.

PROOF. (1) $1 = ||(A^k - B^k)x|| \leq ||A^k - B^k|| \leq \sum_{j=0}^{k-1} ||A^{k-j}B^j - A^{k-j-1}B^{j+1}|| \leq \sum_{j=0}^{k-1} ||A||^{k-j} ||A-B|| ||B^j|| \leq k||A-B||$.

(2) follows by exactly the same argument.

REMARK. If we merely assume that $||A|| = ||A^k x|| = 1$ and $B^k x = 0$ (i.e., we do not put any restriction on $||B||$), then the conclusion is: $||A-B|| \geq 2^{1/k} - 1$. Indeed, if $||A-B|| < \delta$, then $||B|| \leq 1 + \delta$ and a formal repetition of the above proof shows that

$$1 \leq ||A-B|| \sum_{j=0}^{k-1} ||B||^j \leq \delta \sum_{j=0}^{k-1} (1+\delta)^j = (1+\delta)^k - 1,$$

so that $(1+\delta)^k \geq 2$, i.e., $\delta \geq 2^{1/k} - 1$. Since $1/2k < 2^{1/k} - 1 < 1/k$ for all $k > 1$ ($k(2^{1/k} - 1) \to 1 - 1/e$, as $k \to \infty$), both estimates are of the same order.

LEMMA 4.4. *If* T, L *are unitary operators, then*

$$d_H[\sigma_e(T), \sigma_e(L)] \leq \{T;L\} \leq d_H[\sigma_e(T); \sigma_e(L)] + \max\{\text{dist}[\lambda, \sigma_e(T) \cup \sigma_e(L)] : \lambda \in [\sigma(T) \cup \sigma(L)] \setminus [\sigma_e(T) \cup \sigma_e(L)]\}. \tag{4.4}$$

Furthermore, if $\{\lambda_n\}_{n=1}^{\infty}$, $\{\mu_n\}_{n=1}^{\infty} \in \mathbf{C}^{(\infty)}$, $\{\lambda_n\}^- = \sigma(T)$, $\{\mu_n\}^- = \sigma(L)$, $\text{card}\{\lambda_n : \lambda_n = \lambda\} = \text{nul}(\lambda - T)$ *for each isolated point* λ *of* $\sigma(T)$ *and* $\text{card}\{\mu_n : \mu_n = \mu\} = \text{nul}(\mu - L)$ *for each isolated point* μ *of* $\sigma(L)$, *then*

$$\{T;L\} = \inf_{\tau}\{\sup_n |\lambda_n - \mu_{\tau(n)}|\},$$

where the infimum is taken over all bijections τ *of the set of all natural numbers.*

PROOF. Let T_o (L_o) be the diagonal unitary operator defined by $T_o e_n = \lambda_n e_n$ ($L_o e_n = \mu_n e_n$) with respect to the orthonormal basis

$\{e_n\}_{n=1}^{\infty}$. Then, the Weyl-von Neumann theorem implies that $T\simeq_a T_o$ and $L\simeq_a L_o$, so that $\{T;L\}=\{T_o;L_o\}$ [16], [18].

The formula $\{T_o;L_o\}=\inf_{\tau}\{\sup_n|\lambda_n-\mu_{\tau(n)}|\}$ can be easily obtained by the "redistribution" of the spectral measure of L_o, and (4.4) is a trivial consequence of this formula.

PROPOSITION 4.5. $((PPI)/\simeq_a,\{.;.\})$ *is a complete metric space of diameter* 2. *The elements of this metric space (i.e., the closures of the unitary orbits of* ppi's) *admit the following classification. (The cases* (i)-(x) *correspond to the classification given in Theorem* 4.1.)

Let T *be a* ppi, *then*

(i) *If* T *is unitary, then* $U(T)^-=\{L\varepsilon(PPI):\sigma(L)=\sigma(T),\sigma_e(L)=\sigma_e(T)$ *and* $\mathrm{nul}\,(\lambda-L)=\mathrm{nul}\,(\lambda-T)$ *for all* $\lambda\varepsilon\sigma(L)\backslash\sigma_e(L)\}$, *where* $\mathrm{nul}\,A=\dim\ker A$;

(ii) *If* $T=\bigoplus_{k=1}^{n} q_k^{(\alpha_k)}$, *then* $U(T)$ *is closed;*

(iii) *If* $T=\{\bigoplus_{k=1}^{n} q_k^{(\alpha_k)}\}\oplus V$, *then* $U(T)^-=\{L^*\{\bigoplus_{k=1}^{n} q_k^{(\alpha_k)}\}\oplus V'$: $V'\varepsilon U(V)^-\}$;

(iv)-(ix) *If* $T=\{\bigoplus_{k=1}^{n} q_k^{(\alpha_k)}\}\oplus S^{(\alpha)}\oplus S^{*(\beta)}\oplus V$, *where* $\alpha+\beta>0$ *and* $\min\{\alpha,\beta\}<\infty$, *then* $U(T)^-=U(\{\bigoplus_{k=1}^{n} q_k^{(\alpha_k)}\}\oplus S^{(\alpha)}\oplus S^{*(\beta)})^-$;

(x') *If* $T=\{\bigoplus_{k=1}^{n} q_k^{(\alpha_k)}\}\oplus S^{(\infty)}\oplus S^{*(\infty)}\oplus V$, *then* $U(T)^-=U(\{\bigoplus_{k=1}^{n} q_k^{(\alpha_k)}\}\oplus S^{(\infty)}\oplus S^{*(\infty)})^-$;

(x") *If* $T=\{\bigoplus_{k=1}^{\infty} q_k^{(\alpha_k)}\}\oplus S^{(\alpha)}\oplus S^{*(\beta)}\oplus V$, *where* $\alpha_k\neq 0$ *for infinitely many values of* k, *then* $U(T)^-=U(\bigoplus_{k=1}^{\infty} q_k^{(\alpha_k)})^-$.

Furthermore, if R *is a* ppi *such that* $R\simeq_a T$, *then the number of direct summands* q_k, $k=1,2,3,\ldots$, $(S,S^*$, *resp.) in* R *is equal to the number of direct summands* q_k, $k=1,2,3,\ldots$, $(S,S^*$, *resp.) in* T, *for each* k *and either* $\partial D\subset\sigma_e(R)=\sigma_e(T)$, *or* $\partial D\not\subset\sigma_e(R)=\sigma_e(T)$ *and the unitary direct summand* V' *of* R *and the unitary direct summand* V *of* T *are approximately unitarily equivalent (except in* (x"), *resp.).*

PROOF. It is clear that $((PPI)/\simeq_a,\{.;.\})$ is a complete metric space and that

$$\operatorname{diam}((PPI)/\simeq_a)=\sup\{\{T;L\}:T,L\in(PPI)\}\leq\sup\{\|T-L\|:T,L\in(PPI)\}\leq 2.$$

On the other hand, if $\alpha+\beta>0$, $\min\{\alpha,\beta\}<\infty$, F is a nilpotent ppi acting on a finite dimensional space, V is unitary and $\|V(F\oplus S^{(\alpha)}\oplus S^{*(\beta)})V^*-A\|<1$, then A is a semi-Fredholm operator of index $\beta-\alpha$ (see [16] for definition and properties). Similarly, if $\|V-B\|<1$, then B must be invertible.

Thus, if $T=F\oplus S^{(\alpha)}\oplus S^{*(\beta)}$ and either L is unitary, or $\alpha\neq\beta$ and $L=G\oplus V$, where G is a nilpotent ppi acting on a finite dimensional space and V is unitary, or $L=F\oplus S^{(\alpha')}\oplus S^{*(\beta')}$, $\alpha'+\beta'>0$ and $\min\{\alpha',\beta'\}<\infty$, but $\operatorname{ind} L\neq\operatorname{ind} T$, then $\{T;L\}=2$. Hence $\operatorname{diam}((PPI)/\simeq_a)=2$.

Let $T=\{\bigoplus_{k=1}^{\infty} q_k^{(\alpha_k)}\}\oplus S^{(\alpha)}\oplus S^{*(\beta)}\oplus V$ and $R=\{\bigoplus_{k=1}^{\infty} q_k^{(\beta_k)}\}\oplus S^{(\alpha')}\oplus$ $\oplus S^{*(\beta')}\oplus V'$ be two ppi's, and observe that

$$P_k=(1/2)(T^{*k}T^k+T^kT^{*k}-1)(T^{*k}T^k+T^kT^{*k}-2)$$

is an orthogonal projection of H such that ran P_k contains the subspace corresponding to the direct summand $\bigoplus_{j=1}^{k} q_j^{(\alpha_j)}$ of T, is contained in the subspace corresponding to the direct summand $\bigoplus_{j=1}^{k+m} q_j^{(\alpha_j)}$ (where m is the largest integer smaller than k/2) and, moreover,

$$(1-P_k)T(1-P_k)\simeq Q\oplus 0,$$

where Q acts on a subspace of the subspace corresponding to the direct summand $\bigoplus_{j=k+1}^{k+m} q_j^{(\alpha_j)}$ and $Q\simeq\bigoplus_{j=k+1}^{k+m} q_{2k-j}^{(\alpha_j)}$ is a nilpotent of order n=k-2 (if k is odd) or n=k-1 (if k is even).

Then $P_{k,1}=(Q^{n-1}+Q^*)^n\oplus 0$ is the orthogonal projection of H onto the subspace corresponding to the direct summand $q_{2k-(k+1)}^{(\alpha_{k+1})}=$ $=q_n^{(\alpha_{k+1})}$ and $(1-P_{k,1})(Q\oplus 0)(1-P_{k,1})=(1-P_{k,1})(1-P_k)T(1-P_k)(1-P_{k,1})\simeq$

$$\simeq\{\bigoplus_{j=k+2}^{k+m} q_{2k}^{(\alpha_j)}\}\oplus 0.$$

By induction, we can obtain pairwise orthogonal projections $(1-P_k)$, $P_{k,1}, P_{k,2}, \ldots, P_{k,m}$ such that $L_k = P_k - \sum_{r=1}^{m} P_{k,r}$ is the orthogonal projection onto the subspace corresponding to the direct summand $\bigoplus_{j=1}^{k} q_j^{(\alpha_j)}$ and $L_k - L_{k-1}$ $(L_0 = 0)$ is the orthogonal projection onto the subspace corresponding to the direct summand $q_k^{(\alpha_k)}$, so that $(L_k - L_{k-1}) = k\alpha_k$.

It is easily seen that $L_k - L_{k-1} = p_k(T, T^*)$ for a suitable polynomial $p_k(.,.)$ in two non-commutative variables.

If $\beta_1 \neq \alpha_1$, then we can take $p_1(T,T^*) = 1/2(T^*T + TT^* - 1)(T^*T + TT^* - 2)$. Since rank $p_1(T,T^*) \neq$ rank $p_1(R_1, R_1^*)$ for any $R_1 \simeq R$, it readily follows that

$$1 \leq \| p_1(T,T^*) - p_1(R_1, R_1^*) \| \leq 6 \| T - R_1 \|,$$

so that $\{T;R\} \geq 1/6$.

If $\beta_j = \alpha_j$ for $j = 1,2,3,\ldots k-1$, but $\beta_k \neq \alpha_k$ (for some $k > 1$), then $1 \leq \| p_k(T,T^*) - p_k(R_1, R_1^*) \|$ forces the inequality $\{T;R\} \geq C_k$ for some *computable* positive constant C_k depending only on k. (Namely, $C_k \geq [|p_k| \deg(p_k)]^{-1}$, where $\deg(p_k)$ is the degree of $p_k(.,.)$ and $|p_k|$ is the sum of the moduli of its coefficients.)

Thus, if $R \simeq_a T$, then $\beta_k = \alpha_k$ for all $k = 1,2,\ldots$. Assume that $\beta_k = \alpha_k$ for all k. If $\alpha_k \neq 0$ for infinitely many values of k, then the results of [8] and [11] indicate that $T \simeq_a \bigoplus_{k=1}^{\infty} q_k^{(\alpha_k)} \simeq_a R$.

Assume that $\beta_k = \alpha_k$ for $k = 1,2,\ldots,m$ $(m \geq 1)$, and $\beta_k = \alpha_k = 0$ for all $k > m$. If $\alpha = \alpha'$ and $\beta = \beta'$ and $\alpha + \beta > 0$, then we conclude as above that $T \simeq_a \{ \bigoplus_{k=1}^{m} q_k^{(\alpha_k)} \} \oplus S^{(\alpha)} \oplus S^{*(\beta)} \simeq_a R$. If $\beta \neq \beta'$, then nul $(\lambda - T) \neq$ $\neq$ nul $(\lambda - R)$ for all $\lambda \in D \setminus \{0\}$. On the other hand, $\| (\lambda - \bigoplus_{k=1}^{m} q_k^{(\alpha_k)})^{-1} \| =$

$$= \| \sum_{j=0}^{m-1} \lambda^{-j-1} [\bigoplus_{k=1}^{m} q_k^{(\alpha_k)}]^j \| \leq \sum_{j=0}^{m=1} |\lambda|^{-j-1} = (|\lambda|^{-m} - 1)/(|\lambda|^{-1} - 1) \text{ for}$$

all $\lambda \in D \setminus \{0\}$.

Assume that $\beta > \beta'$ and $R_1 = WRW^*$ for some unitary operator W;

then there exists a unitary vector $x\varepsilon\ker(2^{-1/m}-T)$ such that $x\perp\ker(2^{-1/m}-R_1)$ and therefore

$$||T-R_1||\geq||(2^{-1/m}-R_1)x||=||([2^{-1/m}-\bigoplus_{k=1}^{m} q_k^{(\alpha_k)}]\oplus[2^{-1/m}-S^{(\alpha')}\oplus$$

$$\oplus S^{*(\beta')}\oplus V']Wx||\geq\min[2^{1/m}-1,\inf\{||(2^{-1/m}-S^{(\alpha')}\oplus S^{*(\beta')}\oplus V')y||:$$

$$:||y||=1,y\perp\ker(2^{-1/m}-S^{(\alpha')}\oplus S^{*(\beta')}\oplus V')\}]=\min[2^{1/m}-1,1-2^{-1/m}]=$$

$$=2^{1/m}-1.$$

Hence, $\{T;R\}\geq 2^{1/m}-1$.

If either $\beta\leq\beta',\alpha\neq\alpha'$ and $\alpha+\beta>0$, or $\alpha=\beta=0$ and $\alpha'+\beta'>0$, then we similarly conclude (replacing, if necessary, T and R by T^* and R^*, respectively) that $\{T;R\}\geq 2^{1/m}-1$.

If $\alpha=\beta=\alpha'=\beta'=0$ and V and V′ act on isomorphic Hilbert spaces then $||(\lambda-\bigoplus_{k=1}^{m} q_k^{(\alpha_k)})^{-1}||\leq m$ for all $\lambda\varepsilon\partial D$. Replacing, if necessary, V and V′ by suitable operators $V_1\simeq_a V$ and $V_1'\simeq_a V'$ and interchanging, if necessary, the roles of V_1 and V_1', we can find a point $\lambda\varepsilon\partial D$ and a unitary vector x such that $Vx=\lambda x$ and $||(\lambda-V'')x||\geq\delta$ for all $V''\simeq V'$, where $\delta=\{V;V'\}>0$. (Unless, of course, $V\simeq_a V'$, in which case, $R\simeq_a T$. To see this, analyze the proof of Lemma 4.5: either $\lambda\notin\sigma(V')$, or λ is isolated in $\sigma(V')$, $\mathrm{nul}(\lambda-V')<\mathrm{nul}(\lambda-V)$ and $x\perp\ker(\lambda-V')$.)

Hence,

$$||T-R''||\geq||[(\lambda-T)-(\lambda-R'')]x||=||(\lambda-R'')x||\geq\min[1/m,\inf\{||(\lambda-V'')y||:$$

$$:||y||=1,\ y\perp\ker(\lambda-V'')\}]\geq\min[1/m,\delta],$$

for all $R''\simeq_a R$. Hence, $\{T;R\}\geq\min[1/m,\{V;V'\}]>0$.

If $\alpha=\beta=\alpha'=\beta'=0$, but $\dim \mathcal{H}_{V'}\neq\dim \mathcal{H}_V$, then a minor modification of the same argument shows that $\{T;R\}\geq 1/m$.

Assume that $\alpha_k=\beta_k=0$ for all $k=1,2,\ldots$. If $\alpha'\neq\alpha$ or $\beta'\neq\beta$ (in particular, if T is unitary, but R is not unitary), then it follows from Lemma 4.3 that $\{T;R\}\geq 1$. Thus, any two different types (from (i) to (x")) correspond to different elements of $((PPI)/\simeq_a)$.

(i) is contained in Lemma 4.3, (ii) is contained in [18] and the remaining results follows from (i), (ii) and [8] , [11] and [18].

According to [18], $\mathcal{U}(A)^{-} \subset \mathcal{U}(A)+\mathcal{K}$ for all $A \in \mathcal{L}(\mathcal{H})$; furthermore, if $A' \in \mathcal{U}(A)^{-}$, then given $\varepsilon>0$ there exists V unitary such that $A'-VAV^* \in \mathcal{K}$ and $||A'-VAV^*||<\varepsilon$. Thus, if we identify two ppi's, T and L, whenever $L \in \mathcal{U}(T)+\mathcal{K}$ $(=\mathcal{U}(T)^{-}+\mathcal{K})$, then we shall obtain the following coarser classification.

COROLLARY 4.6. *Let* T *be a* ppi; *then*

(i) *If* T *is unitary, then* $T \in \mathcal{U}(W)+\mathcal{K}$, *where* W *is an arbitrary unitary operator such that* $\sigma(W)=\sigma_e(W)=\sigma_e(T)$;

(ii) *If* $T=\{\bigoplus_{k=1}^{n} q_k^{(\alpha_k)}\}=\{\bigoplus_{j=1}^{p} q_{k_j}^{(\infty)}\} \oplus F$, *where* F *is a nilpotent acting on a subspace of finite dimension* d, $0 \le d < \infty$, *then there exists a unique* m, $0 \le m < GCD\{k_1,k_2,\ldots,k_p\}$ *such that* $\mathcal{U}(T)+\mathcal{K} = \mathcal{U}(\{\bigoplus_{j=1}^{p} q_{k_j}^{(\infty)}\} \oplus 0_m)+\mathcal{K}$, *where* 0_m *denotes the* 0 *operator acting on a subspace of dimension* m, *and* $t \simeq \pi(\bigoplus_{j=1}^{p} q_{k_j}^{(\infty)})$ in the Calkin algebra;

(iii) *If* $T=\{\bigoplus_{j=1}^{p} q_{k_j}^{(\infty)}\} \oplus F \oplus V$, *where* F *acts on a subspace of finite dimension and* $\dim \mathcal{H}_V=\infty$, *then* $T \in \mathcal{U}(\{\bigoplus_{j=1}^{p} q_{k_j}^{(\infty)}\} \oplus W)+\mathcal{K}$, *where* W *is a unitary operator such that* $\sigma(W)=\sigma_e(W)=\sigma_e(V)$;

(iv)-(ix) *If* $T=\{\bigoplus_{j=1}^{p} q_{k_j}^{(\infty)}\} \oplus F \oplus S^{(\alpha)} \oplus S^{*(\beta)} \oplus V$, *where* F *acts on a finite dimensional space*, $\alpha+\beta>0$ *and* $\min\{\alpha,\beta\}<\infty$, *then* $T \in \mathcal{U}(\{\bigoplus_{j=1}^{p} q_{k_j}^{(\infty)}\} \oplus M^{(\gamma)})+\mathcal{K}$, *where* M=S *and* $\gamma=\beta-\alpha$ (*if* $\alpha<\beta$), *or* M=U *is the bilateral shift of multiplicity one and* $\gamma=1$ (*if* $\alpha=\beta$), *or* M=S* *and* $\gamma=\alpha-\beta$ (*if* $\alpha>\beta$);

(x) *If* $T=\{\bigoplus_{k=1}^{\infty} q_k^{(\alpha_k)}\} \oplus S^{(\infty)} \oplus S^{*(\infty)} \oplus V$, *then* $T \in \mathcal{U}([\bigoplus \{q_k^{(\infty)}: \alpha_k=\infty\}] \oplus S^{(\infty)} \oplus S^{*(\infty)})+\mathcal{K}$. *Furthermore, if* $\alpha_k=\infty$ *for infinitely many values of* k, *then* $T \in \mathcal{U}(\bigoplus \{q_k^{(\infty)}: \alpha_k=\infty\})+\mathcal{K}$.

Furthermore, if $T \in \mathcal{U}(L)+\mathcal{K}$, *then either* T *and* L *are compact perturbations of unitary operators and* $\sigma_e(T)=\sigma_e(L)$, *or* T *and* L *are nilpotent operators with exactly the same infinite direct summands* $q_k^{(\infty)}$, *or both* T *and* L *are the direct sum of a nilpotent and a unitary operator, the infinite direct summands* $q_k^{(\infty)}$ *are the same (for* T *and* L) *and the unitary operators have the same essential spectra, or* $\sigma_{le}(T)\cap\sigma_{re}(T)=\sigma_{le}(L)\cap\sigma_{re}(L)=\partial D\cup\{0\}$, *the nilpotent direct summand of* T *is unitarily equivalent to a compact perturbation of the nilpotent direct summand of* L *and* $\mathrm{ind}(\frac{1}{2}-T)=\mathrm{ind}(\frac{1}{2}-L)$, *or* $\sigma_{le}(T)=\sigma_{re}(T)=\sigma_{le}(L)=\sigma_{re}(L)=D^-$ *and* T *and* L *have exactly the same infinite direct summands* $q_k^{(\infty)}$.

PROOF. (ii) By Euclid's algorithm, there exist integers $s_1,s_2,\ldots,s_p$ such that $\sum_{j=1}^{p} s_jk_j=n=GCD\{k_1,k_2,\ldots k_p\}$. Let m be the remainder of the division of d by n, ie., d=kn+m for a suitably chosen $k\geq 0$.

Let $r>\max\{|s_j|:1\leq j\leq p\}$; then $r+s_j>0$ for all j and $\{\bigoplus_{j=1}^{p} q_{k_j}^{(r+s_j)}\}\oplus 0_d$ and $\{\bigoplus_{j=1}^{p} q_{k_j}^{(r)}\}\oplus q_{k_1}^{((k+1)k_1/n)}\oplus 0_m$ act on the same finite dimensional space. Hence, $T\in\mathcal{U}(\{\bigoplus_{j=1}^{p} q_{k_j}^{(\infty)}\}\oplus 0_m)+K$.

On the other hand, it follows from the analysis of the essentially n-normal operators (see, e.g.,[17] and the references given there) that if $0\leq m\leq m'<n$ and $\{\bigoplus_{j=1}^{p} q_{k_j}^{(\infty)}\}\oplus 0_{m'}\in\mathcal{U}(\{\bigoplus_{j=1}^{p} q_{k_j}^{(\infty)}\}\oplus 0_m)+K$, then $m=m'$.

Finally, observe that $m<k_1$. Thus, if $m>0$, $L=S^{(m)}\oplus 1\oplus 1\oplus\ldots\oplus 1$ and $M=S^{*(m)}\oplus 1\oplus 1\oplus\ldots\oplus 1$ with respect to the decomposition $H=\ker q_{k_1}^{(\infty)}\oplus(\ker(q_{k_1}^{(\infty)})^2\ominus\ker q_{k_1}^{(\infty)})\oplus\ldots\oplus(\ker(q_{k_1}^{(\infty)})^k\ominus\ker(q_{k_1}^{(\infty)})^{k-1})$, then $\pi(LM)=\pi(ML)=e$ and $Lq_{k_1}^{(\infty)}M\simeq q_{k_1}^{(\infty)}\oplus 0_m$, so that $t\simeq\pi(\{\bigoplus_{j=1}^{p} q_{k_j}^{(\infty)}\})$ in the Calkin algebra.

(i) is a standard consequence of the classical Weyl-von Neumann theorem [16],[18] and (iii) follows from (i) and (ii).

(iv)-(ix) follow from Proposition 4.5 and the well-known fact that $S\oplus S^*$ is a rank one perturbation of U.

(x) This will follow from Proposition 4.5 and a general argument (introduced below) to obtain upper estimates for the distances which implies, in particular, that if $L=\bigoplus_{k=1}^{\infty} q_k^{(\beta_k)}\in L(H)$ and $\beta_k<\infty$ for all k (so that $\beta_k\neq 0$ for infinitely many k's), then

$L\in U(S^{(\infty)}\oplus S^{*(\infty)})+K$ (see Corollary 4.10(4) below).

The last statement follows immediately from the previous results and the stability properties of the semi-Fredholm operators.

COROLLARY 4.7. *Let* $T=q_1^{(\alpha_1)}\oplus S^{(\alpha)}\oplus S^{*(\beta)}\oplus V$ (*V unitary*) *and* R *be two* ppi's *and let* $F=\bigoplus_{k=2}^{m} q_k^{(\alpha_k)}$, *where* $0\le d=\sum_{k=2}^{m} k\alpha_k<\infty$; *then*

(1) *If* $T=0$, *but* $R\neq 0$, *then* $\{T;R\}=1$.

(2) *If* $T\oplus F$ *and* R *are semi-Fredholm operators with different indices, then* $\{T;R\}=2$.

(3) *If* $T\oplus F$ *is semi-Fredholm, but* R *is not semi-Fredholm, then* $1\le\{T;R\}\le 2$.

(4) *If* T *is unitary, but* R *is not unitary, then* $1\le\{T;R\}\le 2$.

(5) *If* $\pi(T\oplus F)=0$, *but* $r\neq 0$, *then* $1\le\{T\oplus F;R\}\le 2$.

(6) *If* $L\in(PPI)$ *and the unitary direct summand of* L *is either equal to* U *or absent,* R *has the same property and* L *and* R *are not semi-Fredholm operators with different indices, then* $\{L;R\}\le 1$.

(7) *If* T *and* R *are not semi-Fredholm (so that* $\alpha_1=\infty$*), but* $(\frac{1}{2}-T)$ *is semi-Fredholm and* $(\frac{1}{2}-R)$ *is not a semi-Fredholm operator of the same index as* $(\frac{1}{2}-T)$, *then* $\frac{1}{2}\le\{T;R\}\le 2$.

If $L=\{\bigoplus_{k=1}^{\infty} q_k^{(\alpha_k)}\}\oplus S^{(\alpha)}\oplus S^{*(\beta)}\oplus V$ *and* $R=\{\bigoplus_{k=1}^{\infty} q_k^{(\beta_k)}\}\oplus S^{(\alpha')}\oplus$ $\oplus S^{*(\beta')}\oplus V'$ (V,V' *are unitary operators*), *then*

(8) *If* $\beta_k\neq\alpha_k$ *for some* k *and* m *is the first index such that* $\beta_m\neq\alpha_m$, *then* $\{L;R\}\ge C_m$ *for some computable constant* C_m.

(9) *If* $\alpha_m\neq 0$, $\alpha_k=0$ *for all* $k>m$ *and* $\alpha<\alpha'$ (*or* $\beta<\beta'$), *then* $\{L;R\}\ge 2^{1/m}-1$.

(10) *If* L *and* R *are non-zero nilpotent operators,* $\alpha_m\neq 0$, $\beta_n\neq 0$, *and* α_k *and* β_k *are equal to* 0 *for all* $k>m$ *and for all* $k>n$, *resp., then* $\{L;R\}\ge 1/\min\{m,n\}$.

(11) *If* L *and* R *are of the form* (10) *and* W,W' *are unitary operators, then* $\{L\oplus W;R\oplus W'\}\ge\min[1/m, 1/n,\{W,W'\}]$, *where* $\{W,W'\}$ *is defined equal to* 2 *if* $\dim H_{W'}\neq\dim H_W$.

(12) *If* L *is a nilpotent of order* m, *but* $R^m\neq 0$, *then* $\{L;R\}\ge$ $\ge 1/m$.

(13) *If* $\pi(L)$ *is a nilpotent of order* m, *but* $\pi(R)^m \neq 0$, *then* $\{L;R\} \geq 1/m$.

PROOF. (1) and (5) are trivial statements.

(2)-(4) and (7)-(11) follow from the proof of Proposition 4.5 (or minor modifications of it) and (12) and (13) follow from Lemma 4.3.

(6) If $L = S^{(\alpha)} \oplus S^{*(\beta)}$ and $R = S^{(\alpha')} \oplus S^{*(\beta')}$ and ind $L(=\beta-\alpha) =$ ind $R(=\beta'-\alpha')$, then either $\alpha=\alpha'$, $\beta=\beta'$ and $L \simeq R$ or $\gamma=\alpha-\alpha'=\beta-\beta'\neq 0$ (if α and α' are finite, but $\beta=\beta'=\infty$, we define $\beta-\beta'=\alpha-\alpha'$, etc.).

If $\gamma>0$, then $L \simeq R \oplus S^{(\gamma)} \oplus S^{*(\gamma)}$, $R \simeq_a R \oplus U^{(\gamma)}$ and it is completely apparent that $\{L;R\} = \{R \oplus S^{(\gamma)} \oplus S^{*(\gamma)}; R \oplus U^{(\gamma)}\} = \{S^{(\gamma)} \oplus S^{*(\gamma)} : U^{(\gamma)}\} = 1$. (If $\gamma<0$, interchange the roles of L and R.)

If $L = \{\bigoplus_{j=1}^{\infty} q_{k_j}\} \oplus S^{(\alpha)} \oplus S^{*(\beta)}$, $R = S^{(\alpha')} \oplus S^{*(\beta')} \oplus U^{(\gamma)}$, then $R \simeq_a R \oplus U^{(\infty)}$ (Proposition 4.5). After eliminating all common direct summands, we can directly assume that $\min\{\alpha,\alpha'\} = \min\{\beta,\beta'\} = 0$.

Assume that $\alpha'=\beta'=0$ and $\min\{\alpha,\beta\}>0$ and reorder the direct sum L as $L = (\bigoplus_{s=1}^{\alpha} S \oplus [\bigoplus_{j_s=1}^{\infty} q_{k_{j_s}}]) \oplus (\bigoplus_{t=1}^{\beta} S^* \oplus [\bigoplus_{j_t=1}^{\infty} q_{k_{j_t}}])$; then

$$\{L;R\} = \{L;U^{(\alpha+\beta)}\} \leq \max\{\sup_{1\leq s\leq\alpha} \{S \oplus [\bigoplus_{j_s=1}^{\infty} q_{k_{j_s}}];U\}, \sup_{1\leq t\leq\beta} \{S^* \oplus [\bigoplus_{j_t=1}^{\infty} q_{k_{j_t}}];U\}\} = 1.$$

To see this, write U as an $(-\infty,\infty)\times(-\infty,\infty)$ matrix with 1's in the first parallel above of the main diagonal and 0's in the remaining entries and observe that any of the operators $S \oplus [\bigoplus_{j_s=1}^{\infty} q_{k_{j_s}}]$ or $S^* \oplus [\bigoplus_{j_t=1}^{\infty} q_{k_{j_t}}]$ can be obtained from that matrix by replacing inifinitely many (suitably chosen) 1's by 0's, whence we immediately obtain $\{\ldots;U\} \leq 1$. On the other hand, $\{\ldots;U\} \geq 1$. (Use (4).)

The remaining cases can be similarly analyzed.

Lemma 4.4 gives complete information for the case when T and R are unitary operators and Corollary 4.7 provides upper and lower bounds for $\{T;R\}$. These bounds can be considered "acceptable" for the cases when $\{T;R\}$ is rather large, but the difference between these two bounds is very large in most cases. It will be shown that the right value of $\{T;R\}$ is close to the lower bound given by Corollary 4.7.

The most important ingredient to obtain upper bounds is the following lemma, which is just a mild improvement (based on the same argument) of an unpublished result of C.Apostol and D.Voiculescu (personal communication) related with a different problem of approximation of operators. A very close argument has been previously used by I.D.Berg in [4] to analyze the distance of certain operators with small self-commutator to the set of normal operators.

LEMMA 4.8. *Let* $1\leq m<n<\infty$ *and let* $m<r,s<n$ *be such that* $r+s=m+n$. *If* $\{e_i\}_{i=1}^{r}$ $(\{f_j\}_{j=1}^{s})$ *is an* ONB *of* $\mathbb{C}^r$ $(\mathbb{C}^s$*, resp.*$)$,

$$T = (\sum_{i=2}^{r} e_{i-1}\otimes e_i) + (\sum_{j=2}^{s} f_j\otimes f_{j-1})$$

and

$$L=(\sum_{i=m+2}^{r} e_{i-1}\otimes e_i) + f_1\otimes e_{m+1} + (\sum_{j=2}^{s} f_j\otimes f_{j-1})+(\sum_{i=2}^{m} e_{i-1}\otimes e_i)$$

$(T,L\in L(\mathbb{C}^r\oplus \mathbb{C}^s)$, $T\simeq q_r\oplus q_s$, $L\simeq q_n\oplus q_m)$, *then there exists a unitary operator* $V\in L(\mathbb{C}^r\oplus\mathbb{C}^s)$ *such that*

(1) $||VTV^*-L||=||T-V^*LV||=s(m)$, *where* $s(m)=2\sin\pi/(m+1)$,

(2) $Ve_i=e_i$, *for* $m+1\leq i\leq r$

and

(3) $Vf_j=f_j$, *for* $m+1\leq j\leq s$.

PROOF. Define

$$g_t=\begin{cases} e_{m+1-t}, & m+1-r\leq t\leq 0,\\ (\cos t\pi/2(m+1))e_{m-1-t}+(\sin t\pi/2(m+1))f_t, & 1\leq t\leq m,\\ f_t, & m+1\leq t\leq s,\end{cases}$$

$$k_t=(-\sin t\pi/2(m+1))e_{m+1-t}+(\cos t\pi/2(m+1))f_t, 1\leq t\leq m,$$

and

$$R = (\sum_{t=m+2-r}^{s} g_t\otimes g_{t-1}) + (\sum_{t=2}^{m} k_t\otimes k_{t-1}).$$

It is completely apparent that $(\{g_t\}_{t=m+1-r}^{s} \cup \{k_t\}_{t=1}^{m})$ is also an ONB of $\mathbb{C}^r \oplus \mathbb{C}^s$, that the pair $\{g_t, k_t\}$ generates the same two dimensional subspace as the pair $\{e_{m+1-t}, f_t\}$ for each t such that $1 \le t \le m$, and that $R \simeq q_n \oplus q_m$, so that $R \simeq L$. Now a straightforward computation shows that $L = VRV^*$, where V is the unitary operator defined by

$$Vg_t = \begin{cases} e_{m+1-t}, & m+1-r \le t \le 0 \\ f_t, & 1 \le t \le s \end{cases}$$

and

$$Vk_t = e_{m+1-t} \qquad 1 \le t \le m.$$

On the other hand,

$(T-R)g_t = 0$, for $m+1-r \le t \le -1$,

$(T-R)g_0 = (1-\cos \pi/2(m+1))e_m - (\sin \pi/2(m+1))f_1$,

$(T-R)g_t = (\cos \pi/2(m+1)-1)g_{t+1} - (\sin \pi/2(m+1))k_{t+1}$, $1 \le t \le m-1$,

$(T-R)g_m = (\sin m\,\pi/2(m+1)-1)f_{m+1}$,

$(T-R)g_t = 0$, $\quad m+1 \le t \le s$,

$(T-R)k_t = (\sin \pi/2(m+1))g_{t+1} + (\cos \pi/2(m+1)-1)k_{t+1}$, $1 \le t \le m-1$

and

$$(T-R)k_m = (\cos m\pi/2(m+1))f_{m+1}.$$

Since $\vee\{g_t, k_t\} = \vee\{e_{m+1-t}, f_t\}$ $(1 \le t \le m)$, these two-dimensional subspaces are pairwise orthogonal and $(T-R)g_t \perp (T-R)k_t$ for $1 \le t \le m-1$, we conclude that

$$\|T-R\| = \max\{[\sin^2 \pi/2(m+1) + (\cos \pi/2(m+1)-1)^2]^{\frac{1}{2}}, \max_{|a|^2+|b|^2=1} |a(\sin m\pi/2m+1)-1) + b\cos m\pi/2(m+1)|\} = [\sin^2 \pi/2(m+1) + (\cos \pi/2(m+1)-1)^2]^{\frac{1}{2}} = 2 \sin \pi/(m+1) = s(m).$$

Since $\|VTV^* - L\| = \|T - V^*LV\| = \|T-R\|$, we are done.

The above proof admits a very simple geometric description: The action of q_r can be described as

$$e_r \to e_{r-1} \to e_{r-2} \to \dots \to e_2 \to e_1 \to 0$$

or, more schematically, by an arrow of length r, and the action of $T \simeq q_r \oplus q_s$ by two arrows of lengths r and s, as follows

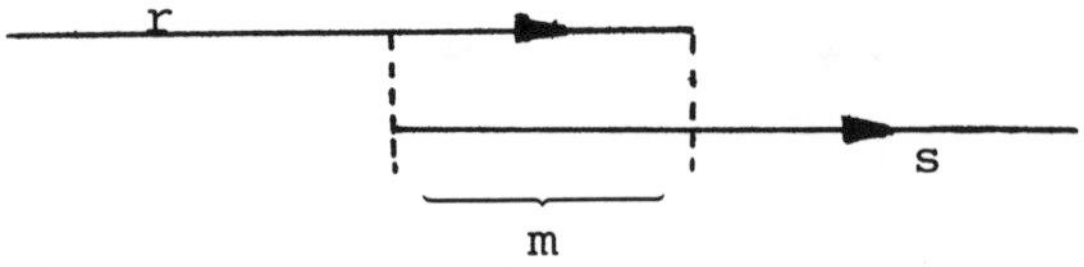

Similarly, L can be indicated as

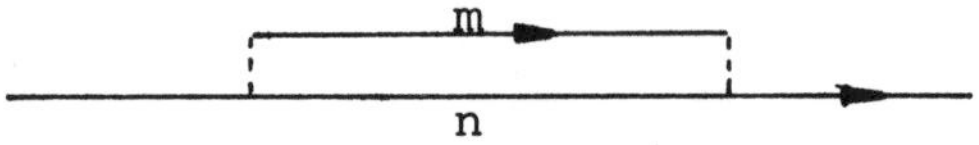

T maps e_{m+1} to e_m, $\{e_{m+1-j}, f_j\}$ onto the pair $\{e_{m-j}, f_{j+1}\}$ of "parallel" vectors ($j=1,2,\ldots,m-1$) and $\{e_1, f_m\}$ onto $\{0, f_{m+1}\}$. On the other hand, R maps e_{m+1} to $(\cos \pi/2(m+1))e_m + (\sin \pi/2(m+1))f_1$, which is equal to the result of a "slight twist" of the vector e_m in the two-dimensional space $\vee\{e_m, f_1\}$, $\{e_{m+1-j}, f_j\}$ onto a "slight twist" of the "parallel" pair $\{e_{m-j}, f_{j+1}\}$ ($j=1,2,\ldots,m-1$) and a "slight twist" (in the reverse sense) of f_m to f_{m+1}.

The accumulation of all these "slight twists" after m+1 steps will map e_m to f_{m+1} and f_1 to 0. This facts can be easily described by the following scheme

(T→R)

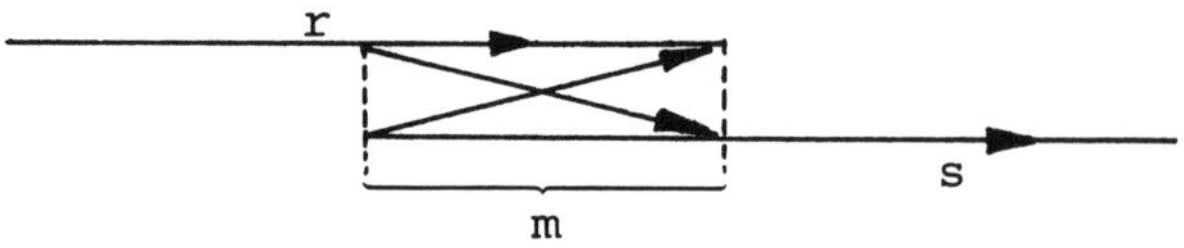

.

Conversely, if we take $(\{g_t\}_{t=m+1-r}^{s} \cup \{k_t\}_{t=1}^{m})$ as the original ONB of $\mathbb{C}^r \oplus \mathbb{C}^s$ and modify R to obtain T, then the corresponding scheme will be

(R→T)

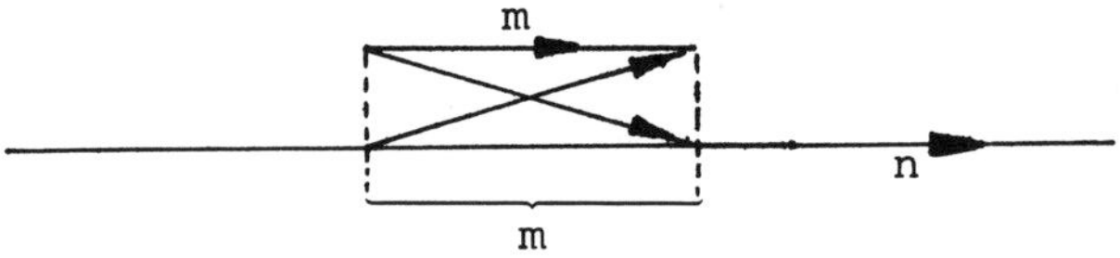

.

In this case, the twist will move g_o to k_1 to 0 and k_1 to $-g_{m+1}$.

In what follows, we shall freely use these schemes instead of analytic descriptions, in the proofs. Namely, since there are no real restrictions on the values of r,s and n, we can take them equal to ∞ and recover the above mentioned result of C.Apostol and

D.Voiculescu (in fact, a minor improvement of their estimate):

COROLLARY 4.9. *Let* $\{g_n\}_{-\infty}^{+\infty}$ *be an ONB of* H *and let* U *be the bilateral shift defined by:* $Ug_n=g_{n+1}$ *for all* $n\in\mathbf{Z}$.

Let $H_+=\vee\{g_n\}_{n\geq 0}$ $(H_-=\vee\{g_n\}_{n<0})$ *and let* $A\varepsilon L(H_+)$ $(B\varepsilon L(H_-)$*, resp.) be the forward (backward, resp.) shift defined by:* $Ag_n=g_{n+1}$ *for all* $n\geq 0$ $(Bg_{-1}=0,\ Bg_n=g_{n+1}$ *for all* $n<-1)$.

Finally, let $q_m=\sum_{t+2}^{m} k_t\otimes k_{t-1}\varepsilon L(\mathbb{C}^m)$. *Then there exists a unitary mapping* $W:H\to\mathbb{C}^m\oplus H$ *such that*

$$(1)\ \|A\oplus B-W(q_m\oplus U)W^*\|=s(m),$$

$$(2)\ Wg_0=k_1$$

and

$$(3)\ Wg_{-1}=-k_m.$$

In particular, $1/(m+1)\leq\{S\oplus S^*,q_m\oplus U\}\leq s(m)$.

PROOF. For suitably defined $A'\simeq A$ and $B'\simeq B$, we have
$(q_m\oplus U\to A'\oplus B')$

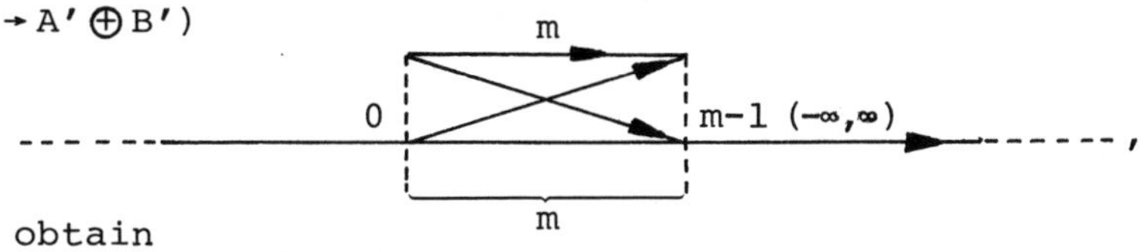

whence we obtain
$A'\oplus B'$:

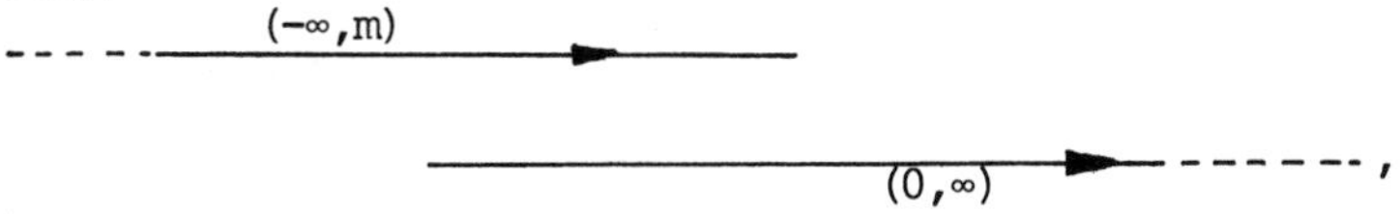

$\|(q_m\oplus U)-A'\oplus B'\|=s(m)$ and the unitary mapping W can be chosen so that $W(A'\oplus B')W^*=A\oplus B$, $Wg_0=k_1$ and $Wg_{-1}=-k_m$.

Finally, observe that nul $(q_m\oplus U)^j=m<\text{nul}(A\oplus B)^j=j$ for all $j>m$. By Lemma 4.3(1), we see that $\{A\oplus B;q_m\oplus U\}=\{S\oplus S^*;q_m\oplus U\}\geq$ $\geq 1/(m+1)$.

Similarly, we have the following

COROLLARY 4.10. (1) *If* $1\leq m<n$, *then*

$$1/(m+1)\leq\{q_n\oplus S;q_m\oplus S\}=\{q_n\oplus S^*;q_m\oplus S^*\}\leq s(m).$$

(2) *If* $p\geq 3$ *and* $1\leq r<p/2$, *then*

$$1/(r+1)\le\{q_p^{(\infty)};q_r^{(\infty)}\oplus U\}\le s(r).$$

The same estimates hold if U *is replaced by* $S^{(\alpha)}\oplus S^{*(\beta)}$ *for some* $\alpha,\beta,0<\alpha+\beta\le\infty$, *and* $\min\{\alpha,\beta\}<\infty$; $1/(p+1)\le\{q_p^{(\infty)};q_r^{(\infty)}\oplus S^{(\infty)}\oplus S^{*(\infty)}\}\le s(r)$ *and* $1/(p+1)\le\{q_p^{(\infty)};S^{(\infty)}\oplus S^{*(\infty)}\}\le 2s(r)$ (*provided* $r\ge 3$).

Moreover, the upper bounds remain true if $q_p^{(\infty)}$ *is replaced by* $q_p^{(\infty)}\oplus V$ *for an arbitrary unitary operator* V.

(3) *If* $T=\bigoplus_{k=p}^{\infty}q_k^{(\alpha_k)}$ *and* $\alpha_k\ne 0$ *for infinitely many* k's, *then*

$$\{T;S^{(\infty)}\oplus S^{*(\infty)}\}\le s(p).$$

(4) *Moreover, if* T *has the form of* (3) *and* α_k *is finite for all* k, *then given* $\varepsilon>0$ *there exists a unitary operator* $W_\varepsilon\in L(H)$ *such that*

$$K=W_\varepsilon(S^{(\infty)}\oplus S^{*(\infty)})W_\varepsilon^*-T\in K \quad \textit{and} \quad \|K\|<s(p)+\varepsilon.$$

(5) *If* $n\ge 3$, $1\le m\le[(n-1)/2]$, $p=n-m$ *and* $U_p=\sum_{j=2}^{p}e_{j-1}\otimes e_j+e_p\otimes e_1 \simeq q_p+(q_p^*)^{n-1}\in L(\mathbb{C}^p)$, *then* U_p *is unitarily equivalent to the unitary operator* V_p *defined by* $V_pe_j=(\omega_p)^j e_j$, *where* ω_p *is a primitive* p-th *root of* (-1) *and*

$$1/(m+1)\le\{q_n;q_m\oplus U_p\}\le s(m).$$

PROOF. (1) $(q_m\oplus S\rightarrow q_n\oplus S)$

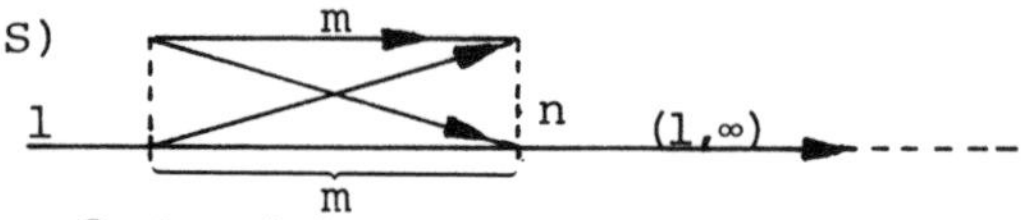

whence we obtain that $\{q_n\oplus S;q_m\oplus S\}\le s(m)$.

By taking adjoints, we have $\{q_n\oplus S^*;q_m\oplus S^*\}=\{q_n\oplus S;q_m\oplus S\}$. (Indeed, $q_k^*\simeq q_k$ for all $k\ge 1$.)

Since nul $(q_m\oplus S)^j=m<\text{nul}(q_n\oplus S)^j$ for all $j>m$, given W unitary we can always find a unitary vector $x\in\ker(q_n\oplus S)^{m+1}$ such that $\|[W(q_m\oplus S)W^*]^{m+1}x\|=\|W(q_m\oplus S)^{m+1}W^*x\|=1$. By Lemma 4.3(1), we conclude that $\{q_n\oplus S;q_m\oplus S\}\ge 1/(m+1)$.

(2) Order the infinitely many copies of q_p in correspondence with the integers; then

$(q_p^{(\infty)} \to q_r^{(\infty)} \oplus U)$

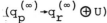

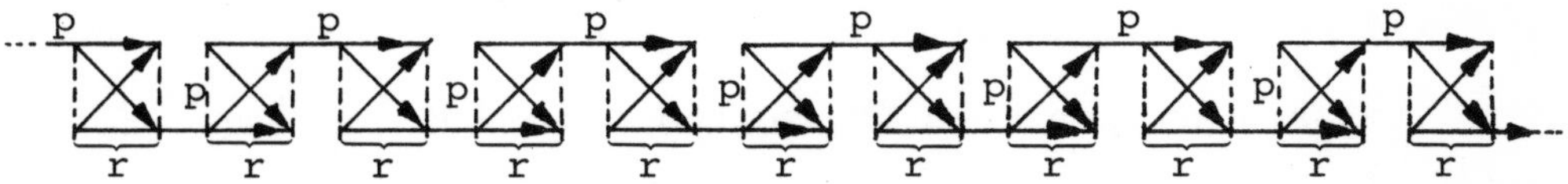

Since $p-2r\geq 1$, we always have a "gap" between any two consecutive blocks and this fact guarantees that we can consistently apply the argument of Lemma 4.8 to each step.

If U is replaced by $S^{(\alpha)} \oplus S^{*(\beta)}$ for some α,β, $0<\alpha+\beta\leq\infty$, then we write $T = [\bigoplus_{j=1}^{\alpha} \{\bigoplus_{s=1}^{\infty} q_{p(j,s)}\}] \oplus [\bigoplus_{k=1}^{\beta} \{\bigoplus_{t=-\infty}^{-1} q_{p(k,t)}\}]$, with $q_{p(j,s)} \simeq q_p \simeq q_{p(k,t)}$ for all j,s,k and t. Minor modifications of the above proof show that $\{q_p^{(\infty)}; q_r^{(\infty)} \oplus S^{(\alpha)} \oplus S^{*(\beta)}\} \leq s(r)$.

Assume that $\min\{\alpha,\beta\} = \beta<\infty$. (If $\min\{\alpha,\beta\}=\alpha<\infty$, replace $S^{(\alpha)} \oplus S^{*(\beta)}$ by its adjoint and $q_p^{(\beta)}$ by $(q_p^{(\beta)})^* \simeq q_p^{(\beta)}$.) Observe that $\ker [q_r^{(\infty)} \oplus S^{(\alpha)} \oplus S^{*(\beta)}]^r$ has codimension β in $\ker[q_r^{(\infty)} \oplus S^{(\alpha)} \oplus S^{*(\beta)}]^{r+1}$, but $\ker[q_p^{(\infty)}]^r$ has codimension $\infty (> \beta)$ in $\ker [q_p^{(\infty)}]^{r+1}$. Thus, if P_r, P_{r+1}, R_r and R_{r+1} denote the orthogonal projections of H onto $\ker [q_r^{(\infty)} \oplus S^{(\alpha)} \oplus S^{*(\beta)}]^r$, , $\ker [q_r^{(\infty)} \oplus S^{(\alpha)} \oplus S^{*(\beta)}]^{r+1}$, $\ker [q_p^{(\infty)}]^r$ and $\ker[q_p^{(\infty)}]^{r+1}$, respectively and $||P_r-R_r||<1$, then $||P_{r+1}-R_{r+1}||=1$ and therefore, given $\varepsilon>0$, we can always find a unitary vector $x\in\ker[q_p^{(\infty)}]^{r+1}$ such that $||[q_r^{(\infty)} \oplus S^{(\alpha)} \oplus S^{*(\beta)}]^{r+1}x||\geq 1-\varepsilon$. By Lemma 4.3(1) and its proof, we conclude that $||q_p^{(\infty)} - q_r^{(\infty)} \oplus S^{(\alpha)} \oplus S^{*(\beta)}|| \geq (1-\varepsilon)/(r+1)$.

On the other hand, if $||P_r-R_r||=1$, then we can find either a unitary vector $y\in\ker[q_p^{(\infty)}]^r$ such that $||[q_r^{(\infty)} \oplus S^{(\alpha)} \oplus S^{*(\beta)}]^r y|| \geq 1-\varepsilon$, or a unitary vector $z\in\ker[q_r^{(\infty)} \oplus S^{(\alpha)} \oplus S^{*(\beta)}]^r$ such that $||[q_p^{(\infty)}]^r z||\geq 1-\varepsilon$, and conclude as above that $||q_p^{(\infty)} - q_r^{(\infty)} \oplus S^{(\alpha)} \oplus S^{*(\beta)}|| \geq (1-\varepsilon)/r$.

It is completely apparent that the above inequality remain true if $q_p^{(\infty)}$ is replaced by $Wq_p^{(\infty)}W^*$, for some unitary operator W.

Since ε can be chosen arbitrarily small, we conclude that $\{q_p^{(\infty)};$ $q_r^{(\infty)} \oplus S^{(\alpha)} \oplus S^{*(\beta)}\} \geq 1/(r+1)$.

The same argument can be used to show that $\{q_p^{(\infty)}; q_r^{(\infty)} \oplus U\} \geq$ $\geq 1/(r+1)$.

Since $[q_p^{(\infty)}]^p=0$, but $[S^{(\infty)} \oplus S^{*(\infty)}]^p \neq 0$, it immediately follows from Lemma 4.3(1) that $\{q_p^{(\infty)}; L \oplus S^{(\infty)} \oplus S^{*(\infty)}\} \geq 1/(p+1)$ for every L in (PPI).

Finally, combining our first result with Corollary 4.9, we obtain

$$\{q_p^{(\infty)}; S^{(\infty)} \oplus S^{*(\infty)}\} \leq \{q_p^{(\infty)}; q_r^{(\infty)} \oplus U^{(\infty)}\} + \{q_r^{(\infty)} \oplus U^{(\infty)}; S^{(\infty)} \oplus S^{*(\infty)}\} \leq$$

$$\leq \{q_p^{(\infty)}; q_r^{(\infty)} \oplus U\} + \{q_r \oplus U; S \oplus S^*\} \leq 2s(r).$$

Replace $q_p^{(\infty)}$ by $q_p^{(\infty)} \oplus V$, where V is an arbitrary unitary operator ($0<\dim H_V=\infty$); then, by Proposition 4.5, we have

$$\{q_p^{(\infty)} \oplus V; q_r^{(\infty)} \oplus U\} = \{q_p^{(\infty)} \oplus V; q_r^{(\infty)} \oplus U \oplus V\} \leq \{q_p^{(\infty)}; q_r^{(\infty)} \oplus U\} \leq s(r).$$

(Similar inequalities hold in the other cases, by using exactly the same argument .)

(3)-(4) By Proposition 4.5 and Corollary 4.9, we have

$$\{T; S^{(\infty)} \oplus S^{*(\infty)}\} = \{T \oplus U^{(\infty)}; S^{(\infty)} \oplus S^{*(\infty)}\} = \{\bigoplus_{k=p}^{\infty} (q_k \oplus U)^{(\alpha_k)}; (S \oplus S^*)^{(\alpha_k)}\} \leq$$

$$\leq \sup_{k \geq p} s(k) = s(p).$$

If α_k is finite for all k, then $\sup_{k \geq n} \{q_k \oplus U; S \oplus S^*\} \leq s(n) \to 0$ $(n \to \infty)$ whence we immediately conclude that there exists a compact block-diagonal operator K_p such that $K_p = W(S^{(\infty)} \oplus S^{*(\infty)})W^* - T$ (for a suitably chosen unitary operator W) and $\|K_p\| = s(p)$. Now statement (4) follows from Voiculescu's theorem [18] (see Proposition 4.5, Corollary 4.6 and their proofs).

(5) It is not difficult to check that U_p is unitary and that determinant$(\lambda - U_p) = \lambda^p - (-1)^p$, whence we immediately conclude that $U_p \simeq V_p$.

Proceeding as in the proof of the main result of [4], we

"curl" our arrow of length n and modify the initial and the final segments of the curled arrow as follows

$(q_n \to q_m \oplus U_p)$

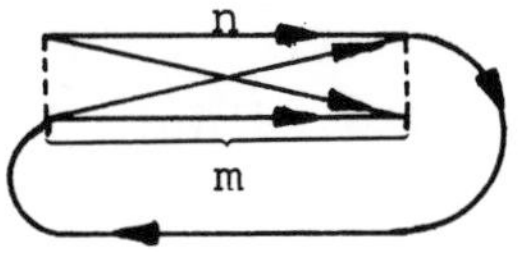

whence we conclude that $\{q_n; q_m \oplus U_p\} \le s(m)$.

PROPOSITION 4.11. *If* $T = \bigoplus_{k=1}^{n} q_k^{(\alpha_k)}$ *and* $L = \bigoplus_{k=1}^{n} q_k^{(\beta_k)}$ *are finite rank operators,* rank T^j=rank L^j *for* $j=1,2,\ldots,r+1$ *and* rank $T^{r+2} \ne$ rank L^{r+2} *for some* $r \ge 1$, *then* $1/(r+2) \le \{T;L\} \le s([r/2])$.

PROOF. Since rank T^j=rank L^j for $j=1,2,\ldots,r+1$, but rank $T^{r+2} \ne$ rank L^{r+2}, it is clear that $\alpha_j = \beta_j$ for $j=1,2,\cdots,r$ ($\alpha_1=\beta_1=\infty$), but $\alpha_{r+1} \ne \beta_{r+1}$. After eliminating all common direct summands, we can directly assume that $T = q_{r+1}^{(\alpha_{r+1})} \oplus \{\bigoplus_{k=r+2}^{n} q_k^{(\alpha_k)}\}$ and $L = \bigoplus_{k=r+2}^{n} q_k^{(\beta_k)}$ act on the same finite dimensional space $\mathbb{C}^d$ and $\alpha_k \beta_k = 0$ for all $k=r+2, \ldots, n$.

Since $r \ge 1$, T and L have exactly the same number of direct summands, which is equal to $\alpha = \sum_{k=r+1}^{n} \alpha_k$. Let $m=[r/2]$ and let $n=d-\alpha m$; then

$(T \to q_n \oplus q_m^{(\alpha)})$

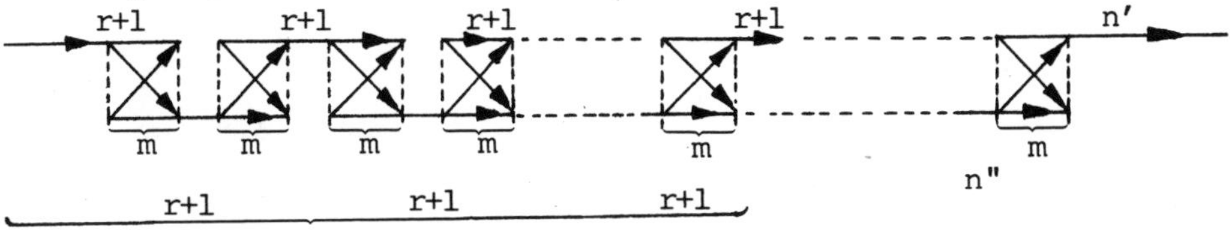

α_{r+1} blocks of length r+1

(where n′, $r+1 < n'' \le n' \le n$, is the largest block of T), whence we obtain $\{T; q_n \oplus q_m^{(\alpha)}\} \le s(m)$.

Similarly, we have $\{L; q_n \oplus q_m^{(\alpha)}\} \le s(m)$. Combining these two estimates with Lemma 4.3(1), we obtain $1/(r+2) \le \{T;L\} \le 2s(m)$.

PROPOSITION 4.12. *Let* $T = \bigoplus_{k=p}^{m} q_k^{(\alpha_k)}$ *and* R *be two* ppi's *of infinite rank such that* $R \ne_a T$ *and assume that* $\alpha_p, \alpha_m > 0$ *and* α_k *is finite for* $k=m,m-1,\ldots,m'+1$, *but* $\alpha_{m'}=\infty$ $(p \le m' \le m)$.

(ii-ii) *If* $R = \bigoplus_{k=t}^{n} q_k^{(\beta_k)}$, $\beta_t, \beta_m > 0$ *and* β_k *is finite for* $k=n, n-1, \ldots, \ldots, n'+1$, *but* $\beta_{n'} = \infty$, *then*

(1) *If* $\min\{m',n'\} \geq 3$, *then* $\{T;R\} \leq s([(m'-1)/2]) + s([(n'-1)/2] + \max\{s(p), s([(m'-1)/2])\} + \max\{s(t), s([(n'-1)/2])\}$;

(2) *If* $r = \min\{[(p-1)/2], [(t-1)/2]\} \geq 2$, *then* $\{T;R\} \leq 2s(r)$;

(3) *If* $r' = \min\{[(m'+p-1)/2], [(n'+t-1)/2]\} \geq 3$, *then* $\{T;R\} \leq s(p) + s(t) + 2s([(r'-1)/2])$;

(ii-iii to x) *Let* R *be an* (ii-ii) *and let* V *be a unitary operator acting on* H_V; *then* (1), (2) *and* (3) *of* (ii-ii) *remain true if* R *is replaced by* $R \oplus S^{(\alpha)} \oplus S^{*(\beta)} \oplus V$, $\alpha+\beta+\dim H_V > 0$, $0 \leq \alpha+\beta \leq \infty$.

Moreover,

(4) $\{T; S^{(\infty)} \oplus S^{*(\infty)}\} \leq s([(m'-1)/2]) + s(\min\{p, [(m'-1)/2]\})$, *provided* $m' \geq 3$, *and*

(5) *If* $\gamma_k \neq 0$ *for infinitely many values of* k, *then*

$$\{T; \bigoplus_{k=t}^{\infty} q_k^{(\gamma_k)}\} \leq s(t) + s([(m'-1)/2]) + s(\min\{p; [(m'-1)/2]\})$$

$(m' \geq 3)$.

PROOF. (ii-ii)(1). By Corollary 4.10(2),

$$\{T; T \oplus [q_{[(m'-1)/2]}^{(\infty)} \oplus U]^{(\infty)}\} = \{T \oplus q_{m'}^{(\infty)}; T \oplus [q_{[(m'-1)/2]}^{(\infty)} + U]^{(\infty)}\} \leq$$

$$\leq \{q_{m'}^{(\infty)}; [q_{[(m'-1)/2]}^{(\infty)} \oplus U]^{(\infty)}\} \leq s([(m'-1)/2]).$$

On the other hand, $T \oplus q_{[(m'-1)/2]}^{(\infty)} \simeq \bigoplus_{j=1}^{\infty} q_{k_j}$, where $\min\{p, [(m'-1)/2]\} \leq k_j \leq m$. Thus, applying Corollary 4.9, we see that

$$\{(T \oplus q_{[(m'-1)/2]}^{(\infty)}) \oplus U^{(\infty)}; S^{(\infty)} \oplus S^{*(\infty)}\} \leq \max\{s(p), s([(m'-1)/2])\}$$

and, a fortiori,

$$\{T; S^{(\infty)} \oplus S^{*(\infty)}\} \leq s([(m'-1)/2]) + \max\{s(p), s([(m'-1)/2])\}.$$

Similarly, we have

$$\{R; S^{(\infty)} \oplus S^{*(\infty)}\} \leq s([(n'-1)/2]) + \max\{s(t), s([(n'-1)/2])\}.$$

Since $\{T;R\} \leq \{T; S^{(\infty)} \oplus S^{*(\infty)}\} + \{R; S^{(\infty)} \oplus S^{*(\infty)}\}$ we are done.

(2) Replace the infinitely many copies of q_p by the blocks of T in the proof of Corollary 4.10(2) ($q_p^{(\infty)} \to q_{[(p-1)/2]}^{(\infty)} \oplus U$). We ob-

tain $\{T;q_r^{(\infty)}\oplus U\}\leq s(r)$.

Similarly, $\{R;q_r^{(\infty)}\oplus U\}\leq s(r)$, so that $\{T;R\}\leq\{T;q_r^{(\infty)}\oplus U\}+\{R;q_r^{(\infty)}\oplus U\}\leq 2s(r)$.

(3) Since $T\simeq\bigoplus_{j=1}^{\infty}(q_{m'}\oplus q_{k_j})$, $p\leq k_j\leq m$, it follows from Lemma 4.8 that there exists $T'\simeq\bigoplus_{k=[(m'+p)/2]}^{m} q_k^{(\alpha_k')}$ such that $\{T;T'\}\leq s(p)$. On the other hand, it follows from the proof of (5) that $\{T';q_{[(r'-1)/2]}^{(\infty)}\oplus U\}=s([(r'-1)/2])$.

Hence, $\{T;q_{[(r'-1)/2]}^{(\infty)}\oplus U\}\leq s(p)+s([(r'-1)/2])$ and, similarly, $\{R;q_{[(r'-1)/2]}^{(\infty)}\oplus U\}\leq s(t)+s([(r'-1)/2])$, whence the result follows.

(ii-iii to x)(1) Observe that (by Proposition 4.5) $S^{(\infty)}\oplus\oplus S^{*(\infty)}\simeq_a S^{(\infty)}\oplus S^{*(\infty)}\oplus S^{(\alpha)}\oplus S^{*(\beta)}\oplus V$, so that

$$\{T;R\oplus S^{(\alpha)}\oplus S^{*(\beta)}\oplus V\}\leq\{T;S^{(\infty)}\oplus S^{*(\infty)}\oplus S^{(\alpha)}\oplus S^{*(\beta)}\oplus V\}+\{R\oplus S^{(\alpha)}\oplus\oplus S^{*(\beta)}\oplus V;S^{(\infty)}\oplus S^{*(\infty)}\oplus S^{(\alpha)}\oplus S^{*(\beta)}\oplus V\}\leq\{T;S^{(\infty)}\oplus S^{*(\infty)}\}+$$

$$+\{R;S^{(\infty)}\oplus S^{*(\infty)}\}.$$

Now the result follows from the corresponding result in (ii-ii).

(2) If $\alpha=\beta=0$, proceed as in (ii-ii) (2). If $\alpha+\beta>0$, then we can assume (by Proposition 4.5) that V is absent. A minor modification of the proof of (ii-ii) (2) (see also the proof of Corollary 4.10(2)) shows that

$$\{T;R\oplus S^{(\alpha)}\oplus S^{*(\beta)}\}\leq\{T;q_r^{(\infty)}\oplus S^{(\infty)}\oplus S^{*(\infty)}\}+\{R\oplus S^{(\alpha)}\oplus S^{*(\beta)};q_r^{(\infty)}\oplus\oplus S^{(\infty)}\oplus S^{*(\infty)}\}\leq\{T;q_r^{(\infty)}\oplus S^{(\infty)}\oplus S^{*(\infty)}\}+\{R;q_r^{(\infty)}\oplus S^{(\infty)}\oplus S^{*(\infty)}\}\leq 2s(r).$$

(3), (4) and (5) follow by the same arguments.

PROPOSITION 4.13. (1) *Let* $T=F\oplus S^{(\alpha)}\oplus S^{*(\beta)}\oplus U$ *and* $R=G\oplus S^{(\alpha')}\oplus\oplus S^{*(\beta')}\oplus U$, *where* $0\leq\min\{\alpha,\beta\}<\infty$, $0\leq\min\{\alpha',\beta'\}<\infty$, $F=\bigoplus_{k=p}^{m} q_k^{(\alpha_k)}$, $G=\bigoplus_{k=t}^{n} q_k^{(\beta_t)}$, $0\leq\alpha''=\sum_{k=p}^{m}\alpha_k<\infty$, $0\leq\beta''=\sum_{k=t}^{n}\beta_k<\infty$, *be two non-invertible semi-Fredholm operators such that* ind R=ind T, *but* $R\not\simeq_a T$; *then there exists* r,

$0\le r\le \max\{m,n\}$ *such that* nul T^j=nul R^j *and* nul T^{*j}=nul R^{*j} *for* $j=1,2,\dots,r$ *but* nul $T^{r+1}\neq$nul R^{r+1} *or* nul $T^{*r+1}\neq$nul R^{*r+1}, *and* $1/(r+1)\le\{T;R\}\le s(p)+s(t)$.

(2) *If* $T=F\oplus V$ *and* $R=G\oplus V'$, *where* F *and* G *have the form of* (1) *with* α'', $\beta''>0$, V *and* V' *are unitary operators and* $F\neq G$, *then*

$$(a)\max\{1/(r+1),d_H[\sigma_e(V),\sigma_e(V')]\}\le\{T;R\}\le\{T\oplus U;R\oplus U\}+d_H[\sigma_e(V),\partial D]+$$
$$+d_H[\sigma_e(V'),\partial D];$$

(b) *On the other hand, if* $F\simeq G$, *then*

$$\max\{d_H[\sigma_e(V),\sigma_e(V')],\min[1/m,\{V;V'\}]\}\le\{T;R\}\le\{V;V'\}.$$

PROOF. (1) Since $\{T;R\}=\{T^*;R^*\}$, we can directly assume that $\beta,\beta'<\infty$ and ind $T=\beta-\alpha$ =ind $R=\beta'-\alpha'$. If $m=\max\{m,n\}$, and nul T^j=nul R^j for $j=m$ and $j=m+1$, then β=nul T^{m+1}-nul T^m=nul R^{m+1}-nul $R^m=\beta'$ and therefore $\alpha=\alpha'$, $G\simeq F$ and, a fortiori, $R\simeq T$, a contradiction.

Hence, nul T^j=nul R^j for $j=1,2,\dots,r$, but nul $T^{r+1}\neq$nul R^{r+1} for some $r\le m$. By Lemma 4.3(1), $\{T;R\}\ge 1/(r+1)$.

Assume that $\beta\le\beta'$ (if $\beta'>\beta$, then we interchange the roles of T and R); then $\gamma=\beta-\beta'$ and $\alpha''=\beta''+\gamma$. Proposition 4.5 implies that

$$T\simeq_a F\oplus U^{(\alpha'')}\oplus S^{(\alpha)}\oplus S^{*(\beta)}\oplus U \text{ and } R\simeq_a G\oplus U^{(\beta'')}\oplus S^{(\gamma)}\oplus S^{*(\gamma)}\oplus S^{(\alpha)}\oplus$$
$$\oplus S^{*(\beta)}\oplus U$$

and, by Corollary 4.8, we have

$$\{T;R\}\le\{[\bigoplus_{k=p}^{m}(q_k\oplus U)^{(\alpha_k)}]\oplus U;[\bigoplus_{k=t}^{n}(q_k\oplus U)^{(\beta_k)}]\oplus S^{(\gamma)}\oplus S^{*(\gamma)}\oplus U\}\le$$

$$\le\max[\{q_k\oplus U;S\oplus S^*\}:k\ge p]+\max[\{q_k\oplus U;S\oplus S^*\}:k\ge t]\le s(p)+s(t).$$

(2) Since $\pi(T)$ and $\pi(R)$ are unitary elements of the Calkin algebra, we immediately obtain

$$d_H[\sigma_e(V),\sigma_e(V')]\le\{T;R\}\le\{T;T\oplus U\}+\{T\oplus U;R\oplus U\}+\{R\oplus U,R\}\le\{T\oplus U;R\oplus U\}+$$
$$+\{V;U\}+\{V';U\}\le\{T\oplus U;R\oplus U\}+d_H[\sigma_e(V),\partial D]+d_H[\sigma_e(V'),\partial D].$$

Clearly, if $F\simeq G$, then $\{T;R\}\le\{V;V'\}$. The remaining inequalities follow from (1) and Proposition 4.5.

PROPOSITION 4.14. *Let* $T=\{\bigoplus_{k=p}^{m} q_k^{(\alpha_k)}\}\oplus V$, *where* V *is a unitary operator acting on* $H_V\neq\{0\}$, $\alpha_p,\alpha_m>0$ *and* α_k *is finite for* $k=m,m-1,\dots,$

$\ldots,m'+1$, *but* $\alpha_{m'}=\infty$ $(p\le m'\le m)$, *and let* R *be a* ppi *such that* $R\not\sim_a T$.

(iii-iii) *If* $R=\{\bigoplus_{k=t}^{n} q_k^{(\beta_k)}\}\oplus V'$, *where* V' *is a unitary operator acting on* $H_{V'}\neq\{0\}$, $\beta_t,\beta_n>0$ *and* β_k *is finite for* $k=n,n-1,..,n'+1$, *but* $\beta_{n'}=\infty$, *then*

(1) *If* $m'\neq n'$, *then* $\{T;R\}\ge 1/\min\{m',n'\}$;

(2) *If* $m'=n'$, *but* $\beta_k\neq\alpha_k$ *for some* $k>m'$, *then* $\{T;R\}\ge 1/\min\{k>m':\beta_k\neq\alpha_k\}$.

(3) $$\{T;R\}\le\{T\oplus q_v^{(\infty)}\oplus U;R\oplus q_v^{(\infty)}\oplus U\}+2s(v)\le 2s(v)+s(\min\{p,v\})+$$
$$+s(\min\{t,v\}),$$

where $v=\min\{[(m'-1)/2],[(n'-1)/2]\}$;

(4) $\{T;R\}\le\max[\{\bigoplus_{k=p}^{m} q_k^{(\alpha_k)};\bigoplus_{k=t}^{n} q_k^{(\beta_k)}\},\{V;V'\}]$;

(5) *If* $\dim H_{V'}=\dim H_V=\infty$, *then*

$$\{T;R\}\le\{T\oplus U;R\oplus U\}+d_H[\sigma_e(V),\partial D]+d_H[\sigma_e(V'),\partial D]\le s(p)+s(t)+$$
$$+d_H[\sigma_e(V),\partial D]+d_H[\sigma_e(V'),\partial D].$$

(iii -v to x) *If* $\alpha+\beta>0$, *then*

(1) $$\{T;\{\bigoplus_{k=t}^{n} q_k^{(\beta_k)}\}\oplus S^{(\alpha)}\oplus S^{*(\beta)}\}\le$$
$$\le\{[\bigoplus_{k=p}^{m} q_k^{(\alpha_k)}]\oplus q_{[(m'-1)/2]}^{(\infty)};\bigoplus_{k=t}^{n} q_k^{(\beta_k)}\}+s([(m'-1)/2]);$$

(2) $\{T;S^{(\infty)}\oplus S^{*(\infty)}\}\le s(p)$;

(3) *If* L *is a* ppi *such that* $\sigma_{le}(L)=\sigma_{re}(L)=D^-$, *but* $L\not\sim_a S^{(\infty)}\oplus\oplus S^{*(\infty)}$, *then* $\{T;L\}\le s(p)+s(p'')$, *where* $p''=\min\{k:q_k$ *is a direct summand of* L$\}$.

PROOF. (iii-iii)(1) and (2) follow from Lemma 4.3 (or minor modifications of its proof).

(3) By Corollary 4.9, we have

$$\{T;R\}=\{T\oplus q_{m'}^{(\infty)};R\oplus q_{n'}^{(\infty)}\}\le\{T\oplus q_{m'}^{(\infty)};T\oplus(q_v^{(\infty)}\oplus U)^{(\infty)}\}+$$
$$+\{T\oplus(q_v^{(\infty)}\oplus U)^{(\infty)};R\oplus(q_v^{(\infty)}\oplus U)^{(\infty)}\}+\{R\oplus(q_v^{(\infty)}\oplus U)^{(\infty)};R\oplus q_{n'}^{(\infty)}\}\le$$
$$\le\{q_{m'}^{(\infty)};(q_v^{(\infty)}\oplus U)^{(\infty)}\}+\{T\oplus(q_v^{(\infty)}\oplus U)^{(\infty)};R\oplus(q_v^{(\infty)}\oplus U)^{(\infty)}\}+$$

$$+\{q_{n'}^{(\infty)};(q_v^{(\infty)}\oplus U)^{(\infty)}\}\le 2s(v)+\{T\oplus(q_v^{(\infty)}\oplus U)^{(\infty)};R\oplus(q_v^{(\infty)}\oplus U)^{(\infty)}\}\le$$

$$\le 2s(v)+\{T\oplus q_v^{(\infty)}\oplus U^{(\infty)};S^{(\infty)}\oplus S^{*(\infty)}\}+\{S^{(\infty)}\oplus S^{*(\infty)};R\oplus q_v^{(\infty)}\oplus U^{(\infty)}\}\le$$

$$\le 2s(v)+s(\min\{p,v\})+s(\min\{t,v\}).$$

(4) is a trivial inequality.

(5) The proof is very close to that of (3):

$$\{T;R\}\le\{T;T\oplus U\}+\{T\oplus U;R\oplus U\}+\{R\oplus U;R\}\le\{V;U\}+\{T\oplus U;S^{(\infty)}\oplus S^{*(\infty)}\}+$$
$$+\{S^{(\infty)}\oplus S^{*(\infty)};R\oplus U\}+\{V';U\}\le d_H[\sigma_e(V),\partial D]+s(p)+s(t)+d_H[\sigma_e(V'),\partial D].$$

(iii-v to x) (1) By Proposition 4.5 and Corollary 4.10(2), we have

$$\{T;\{\bigoplus_{k=t}^{n} q_k^{(\beta_k)}\}\oplus S^{(\alpha)}\oplus S^{*(\beta)}\}=\{T\oplus q_{m'}^{(\infty)};\{\bigoplus_{k=t}^{n} q_k^{(\beta_k)}\}\oplus S^{(\alpha)}\oplus S^{*(\beta)}\}\le$$

$$\le\{T\oplus q_{m'}^{(\infty)};T\oplus q_{[(m'-1)/2]}^{(\infty)}\oplus S^{(\alpha)}\oplus S^{*(\beta)}\}+\{T\oplus q_{[(m'-1)/2]}^{(\infty)}\oplus S^{(\alpha)}\oplus S^{*(\beta)};$$
$$\{\bigoplus_{k=t}^{n} q_k^{(\beta_k)}\}\oplus S^{(\alpha)}\oplus S^{*(\beta)}\}\le\{q_{m'}^{(\infty)};q_{[(m'-1)/2]}^{(\infty)}\oplus S^{(\alpha)}\oplus S^{*(\beta)}\}+$$
$$+\{[\bigoplus_{k=p}^{m} q_k^{(\alpha_k)}]\oplus q_{[(m'-1)/2]}^{(\infty)};\bigoplus_{k=t}^{n} q_k^{(\beta_k)}\}\le s([(m'-1)/2])+$$
$$+\{[\bigoplus_{k=p}^{m} q_k^{(\alpha_k)}]\oplus q_{[(m'-1)/2]}^{(\infty)};\bigoplus_{k=t}^{n} q_k^{(\beta_k)}\}.$$

(2) follows by a similar argument and

(3) $\{T;L\}\le\{T;S^{(\infty)}\oplus S^{*(\infty)}\}+\{S^{(\infty)}\oplus S^{*(\infty)};L\}\le s(p)+s(p'')$.

It only remains to consider the cases when $\sigma(T)=\sigma(R)=D^-$ and and $0\in\sigma_e(T)\cap\sigma_e(R)$. In these cases (see Proposition 4.5) $T\simeq_a T\oplus U^{(\infty)}$ and $R\simeq_a R\oplus U^{(\infty)}$. Combining these facts with Proposition 4.5 and Corollaries 4.9 and 4.10, we obtain the following result. (The proof is similar to that of Proposition 4.14 and will be left to the reader.)

PROPOSITION 4.15. *Let* $T=\{\bigoplus_{k=p}^{\infty} q_k^{(\alpha_k)}\}\oplus S^{(\alpha)}\oplus S^{*(\beta)}\oplus U$ *and* $R=\{\bigoplus_{k=t}^{\infty} q_k^{(\beta_k)}\}\oplus S^{(\alpha')}\oplus S^{*(\beta')}\oplus U$, *where* $\alpha_p>0,\beta_t>0$ *and* $\sum_{k=p}^{\infty}\alpha_k=\sum_{k=t}^{\infty}\beta_k=\infty$; *then* $\{T;S^{(\infty)}\oplus S^{*(\infty)}\}\le s(p)$, $\{R;S^{(\infty)}\oplus S^{*(\infty)}\}\le s(t)$ *and*

$\{T;R\} \leq s(p)+s(t)$.

Finally, the topological structure of $((PPI)/\simeq_a)$ can be described as follows:

THEOREM 4.16. (i) *$\{U(V)^-: V$ is unitary$\}$ is a clopen connected subset of $((PPI)/\simeq_a)$. If V is unitary and T is a not unitary* ppi, *then* $\{V;T\} \geq 1$;

(ii) *If* $T = \bigoplus_{k=1}^{m} q_k^{(\alpha_k)}$, *then $U(T)^- = U(T)$ is an isolated point; more precisely,* $\{T;R\} \geq C_m$ *(for some computable constant $C_m > 0$ depending on* m) *for all* $R \not\simeq_a T$;

(iii) *For each* d, $1 \leq d \leq \infty$, *and each finite sequence* $\{\alpha_1, \alpha_2, \ldots, \alpha_m\}$ *such that* $d + \sum_{k=1}^{m} \alpha_k = \infty$, $\{U(\{\bigoplus_{k=1}^{m} q_k^{(\alpha_k)}\} \oplus V)^- : V$ *is unitary and* $\dim H_V = d\}$ *is a clopen arcwise connected subset of* $((PPI)/\simeq_a)$.

Moreover, if $U(R)^-$ does not belong to the component of $U(\{\bigoplus_{k=1}^{m} q_k^{(\alpha_k)}\} \oplus V)^-$, *then* $\{R; \{\bigoplus_{k=1}^{m} q_k^{(\alpha_k)}\} \oplus V\} \geq C_m$;

(iv)-(x) *If* T *belongs to any of the types* (iv) *to* (x), *with* $\alpha > 0$ *and* $\beta > 0$, *then $U(T)^-$ cannot be an isolated point of* $((PPI)/\simeq_a)$, *but the component of $U(T)^-$ consists of a single point. More precisely, if* $T = \{\bigoplus_{k=1}^{\infty} q_k^{(\alpha_k)}\} \oplus S^{(\alpha)} \oplus S^{*(\beta)}$, *where* $\alpha > 0$ *and* $\beta > 0$, *then* $\{[\bigoplus_{k=1}^{\infty} q_k^{(\alpha_k)}] \oplus q_n \oplus U \oplus S^{(\alpha-1)} \oplus S^{*(\beta-1)}; T\} \to 0$ $(n \to \infty)$ *and* $T \simeq_a T \oplus S^{(\infty)} \oplus S^{*(\infty)}$ *provided* $\alpha_k \neq 0$ *for infinitely many values of* k.

If $\min\{\alpha, \beta\} = 0$ *and* $\alpha_k = 0$ *for all* $k > m$, *then $U(T)^-$ is an isolated point and* $\{T;R\} \geq C_m$ *for all* $R \not\simeq_a T$.

5. LIMITS OF BLOCK-DIAGONAL NILPOTENTS. A PROBLEM OF L.R.WILLIAMS

In [15], the author proved that, if N is a normal operator such that $\sigma(N) = \sigma_e(N) = D^-$, then $N \oplus S^{(\alpha)} \oplus S^{*(\beta)} \in (BDN)^-$ for all $\alpha, \beta \geq 0$ and, if $T = \bigoplus_{k=1}^{\infty} c_k q_k^{(\alpha_k)}$, then $N \oplus T$ also belongs to $(BDN)^-$.

If $\alpha<\infty$ or $\beta<\infty$, then $S^{(\alpha)}\oplus S^{*(\beta)}$ is not a limit of nilpotents (indeed, either $\mathrm{ind}(S^{(\alpha)}\oplus S^{*(\beta)})=\beta-\alpha\neq 0$ or $\alpha=\beta$ and $\pi[S^{(\alpha)}\oplus S^{*(\beta)}]$ is invertible [14]) and, a fortiori, $S^{(\alpha)}\oplus S^{*(\beta)}\notin(\mathrm{BDN})^-$. For T as above, and for the case $\alpha=\beta=\infty$, we have the following improvements.

COROLLARY 5.1. (i) $S^{(\infty)}\oplus S^{*(\infty)}\in(\mathrm{BDNNor})^-$.

(ii) *If* $T=\bigoplus_{k=1}^{\infty} c_k q_k^{(\alpha_k)}$ $(0<c_k\leq C=T=\sup_n c_n<\infty)$, *then* $T\in(\mathrm{BDNNor})^-$.

PROOF. (i). Since $q_k^{(\infty)}\in(\mathrm{BDNNor})$ for all $k\geq 1$, it follows from Corollary 4.10(2) that

$$\mathrm{dist}[S^{(\infty)}\oplus S^{*(\infty)},(\mathrm{BDNNor})]=\inf_k\{S^{(\infty)}\oplus S^{*(\infty)};q_k^{(\infty)}\}\leq$$

$$\leq\lim_{k\to\infty} 2s([(k-1)/2])=0.$$

(ii) Given $\varepsilon>0$, fix N large enough so that $C/N<\varepsilon/2$ and decompose $T=\bigoplus_{j=1}^{N}[\oplus\{c_k q_k^{(\alpha_k)}:(j-1)C/N<c_k\leq jC/N\}]$.

Let $T_\varepsilon=\bigoplus_{j=1}^{N} T_{\varepsilon,j}$, where $T_{\varepsilon,j}=jC/N[\oplus\{q_k^{(\alpha_k)}:(j-1)C/N<c_k\leq$ $\leq jC/N\}]$. Clearly, $||T-T_\varepsilon||<\varepsilon$.

Let $T_\varepsilon=A\oplus B$, $A=\oplus\{T_{\varepsilon,j}:T_{\varepsilon,j}$ acts on a finite dimensional space$\}$ and $B=\oplus\{T_{\varepsilon,j}:T_{\varepsilon,j}$ acts on an infinite dimensional space$\}$.

Let $L=\bigoplus_{k=1}^{\infty} q_k^{(\beta_k)}\in L(H)$. If $\beta_k=0$ for all $k\geq n$, then $L\in(\mathrm{BDNNor})_n\subset$ $\subset(\mathrm{BDNNor})$; if $\beta_k\neq 0$ for infinitely many values of k, then it follows from Corollary 4.10(3) that $\{\bigoplus_{k=p}^{\infty} q_k^{(\beta_k)};S^{(\infty)}\oplus S^{*(\infty)}\}\leq s(p)$ for all $p\geq 3$.

According to (i), there exist operators $Q_p\simeq q_p^{(\infty)}$, $p=7,8,\ldots$, such that $||S^{(\infty)}\oplus S^{*(\infty)}-Q_p||\to 0(p\to\infty)$. A fortiori, we can also find a sequence $\{Q'_p\}_{p=7}^{\infty}$, $Q'_p\simeq Q_p$ for all $p=7,8,\ldots$, such that

$$||L-\{\bigoplus_{k=1}^{p-1} q_k^{(\beta_k)}\}\oplus Q'_p||\to 0\quad(p\to\infty),$$

so that $L\in(\mathrm{BDNNor})^-$.

It readily follows that $B\in(\mathrm{BDNNor})^-$ and, a fortiori, that $T_\varepsilon\in(\mathrm{BDNNor})^-$.

Since ε can be chosen arbitrary small, we conclude that $T\varepsilon(\text{BDNNor})^-$.

The above corollary shows, in particular, that $J = \bigoplus_{k=1}^{\infty} q_k \varepsilon$ $\varepsilon(\text{BDN})^-$, thus contradicting a conjecture of L.R.Williams [19] (see Introduction).

The following result improves Proposition 6.5(i) of [15] in two senses: 1) A better estimate, and 2) Instead of approximation by nilpotents acting on infinite dimensional spaces, now we approximate by operators in (BDNNor) and nilpotents acting on finite dimensional spaces.

COROLLARY 5.2. *Let $\mathcal{P}$ denote the set of all non-zero projections in $L(H)$; then*

$$\tfrac{1}{2}\le\delta_k=\inf\{||P-Q||:\ P\varepsilon\mathcal{P},\ Q\varepsilon(N)_k\}\le\inf\{||P-Q||:\ P\varepsilon\mathcal{P},\ Q\varepsilon(\text{BDN})_k\}\le$$

$$\le\inf\{||P-Q||:\ P\varepsilon\mathcal{P},\ Q\varepsilon(\text{BDNNor})_k\}\le\inf\{||P-Q||: P,Q\varepsilon L(\mathbb{C}^k),$$

P *is a non-zero projection and* Q *is nilpotent*$\}\le \tfrac{1}{2}+\tfrac{1}{2}s([(k-1)/2])$, *for all* $k\ge3$.

PROOF. The lower bound was obtained in [14] and the second, third and fourth inequalities are trivial.

Let $m=[(k-1)/2]$. By Corollary 4.10(5), there exists a unitary operator $W\varepsilon L(\mathbb{C}^k)$ such that $||Wq_kW^*-q_m\oplus U_{k-m}||\le s(m)$ and -1 is an eigenvalue of U_{k-m}.

Let $P\varepsilon L(\mathbb{C}^k)$ be the orthogonal projection of $\mathbb{C}^k$ onto ker $(q_m\oplus U_{k-m}+1)$; then

$$||P-(-\tfrac{1}{2})Wq_kW^*||\le||P+(\tfrac{1}{2})q_m\oplus U_{k-m}||+(\tfrac{1}{2})||Wq_kW^*-q_m\oplus U_{k-m}||\le\tfrac{1}{2}+\tfrac{1}{2}s(m),$$

whence the result follows.

Finally, as an application of I.D.Berg's results [4], we have

COROLLARY 5.3. *Let* M *be a normal operator such that* $\sigma(M)=D^-$ $(=\{\lambda:|\lambda|\le1\})$; *then* $\text{dist}[M,(\text{BDNNor})_k]= 5(\pi/k)^{\frac{1}{2}}$.

PROOF. Let $p=[\sqrt{k}/2\sqrt{\pi}]$, $\eta=p^{-1}$ and $r=[k\eta/2]$ and let $Q_k\varepsilon L(\mathbb{C}^k)$ be the operator defined by $Q_ke_j=\alpha_je_{j+1}$, $j=1,2,\ldots,k-1$, $Q_ke_k=0$, where

$$\alpha_j=\begin{cases} n\eta, & \text{for } r(n-1)<j\le rn, \quad n=1,2,\ldots,p,\\ n\eta, & \text{for } r(2p-n)<j\le r(2p-n+1), \quad n=1,2,\ldots,p,\\ 0, & \text{for } 2rp<j\le k-1.\end{cases}$$

(Roughly speaking: The weights α_j grow from η to 1 through p steps of length r and then go down from 1 to 0, through p steps of length r, so that the upper step has length 2r with weight equal to 1, i.e., $\alpha_j=1$ for $r(p-1)<j\le r(p+1)$.)

Thus, by Corollary 4.10(5), we can modify Q_k in order to obtain an operator $R_1'=T_1'\oplus U_{r+1}$, where U_{r+1} is a unitary operator acting on a subspace of dimension r+1 and there exists an orthonormal system $\{f_1^1,f_2^1,\ldots,f_{2r}^1\}$ such that $\{e_j\}_{j=1}^{r(p-1)}\cup\{f_h^1\}_{h=1}^{2r}\cup\cup\{e_j\}_{j=r(p+1)+1}^{k}$ is an ONB of $\mathbb{C}^k$, $T_1'e_j=Q_ke_j$ for all $j\notin(r(p-1), r(p+1)]$, $T_1'e_{r(p-1)}=f_1^1$, $T_1'f_h^1=f_{h+1}^1$ for $h=1,2,\ldots,r-2$, $T_1'f_{r-1}^1= =(1-\eta)e_{r(p+1)+1}$ and $U_{r+1}f_h^1=(\omega_{r+1})^h f_h^1$ for $h=r,\ldots,2r$ (ω_{r+1} is a primitive (r+1)-th root of -1); furthermore $||Q_k-R_1'||=s(r-1)$.

Let T_1 be the operator obtained from T_1' by replacing each weight equal to 1 by $1-\eta$ and $R_1=T_1\oplus U_{r+1}$; then $||Q_k-R_1||\le s(r-1)+\eta$.

Now we can apply the same argument to R_1 in order to obtain an operator $R_2=T_2\oplus(1-\eta)U_{2r}\oplus U_{r+1}$, where U_{2r} is a unitary operator acting on a subspace of dimension 2r, $T_2e_j=Q_ke_j$ for all $j\notin(r(p-2),r(p+2)]$, $T_2e_{r(p-2)}=(1-2\eta)f_1^2$, $T_2f_h^2=(1-2\eta)f_{h+1}^2$ for $h=1,2,\ldots,r$, $T_2f_{r-1}^2=(1-2\eta)e_{r(p+2)+1}$, $\{f_1^2,f_2^2,\ldots,f_{r-1}^2\}$ is an orthonormal system that spans a subspace orthogonal to the span of the vectors $(\{e_j\}_{j=1}^{r(p-2)}\cup\{e_j\}_{j=r(p+2)+1}^{k})$, $||R_1-R_2||\le(1-\eta)[s(r-1)+\eta]$ and this modification only affects the vectors in the subspace spanned by $(\{e_j\}_{j=r(p-2)+1}^{r(p+2)}\cup\{e_j\}_{j=r(p+1)+1}^{r(p+2)})$, so that $||Q-R_2||= =\max\{||Q-R_1||,||R_1-R_2||\}\le s(r-1)+\eta$, etc.

An easy inductive argument shows that after p-1 steps, we shall finally obtain an operator $L_k=U_{r+1}\oplus[\bigoplus_{j=1}^{p-1}(1-j\eta)U_{2r}]\oplus \oplus q_1^{(k+1-(2p-1)r)}$ such that $||Q_k-L_k||\le s(r-1)+\eta<2\pi/r+1/[\sqrt{k}/2\sqrt{\pi}]<$

$<5(\pi/k)^{\frac{1}{2}}$ for all $k>50$. (On the other hand, if $1\le k\le 50$, then $5(\pi/k)^{\frac{1}{2}}>1$ and our estimate is trivial.)

Let $\{r_m\}_{m=1}^{\infty}$ be an enumeration of the rational numbers in $[0,1]$ and let $N_k = \bigoplus_{m=1}^{\infty} \bigoplus_{n=1}^{\infty} r_m e^{in} Q_k$ and $M_k = \bigoplus_{m=1}^{\infty} \bigoplus_{n=1}^{\infty} r_m e^{in} L_k$. It is easily seen that $N_k \in (\mathrm{BDNNor})_k$, M_k is a normal operator such that $\sigma(M_k)=D^-$ (so that $M \simeq_a M_k$) and

$\mathrm{dist}[M,(\mathrm{BDNNor})_k]=\mathrm{dist}[M_k,(\mathrm{BDNNor})_k]\le \|M_k-N_k\|\le\|Q_k-L_k\|<5(\pi/k)^{\frac{1}{2}}$.

REFERENCES

1. Apostol, C.; Foiaş, C.; Pearcy, C.: That quasinilpotent operators are norm-limits of nilpotents operators, revisited, *Proc.Amer.Math.Soc.* 73(1979), 61-64.

2. Apostol, C.; Foiaş, C.; Voiculescu, D.: On the norm-closure of nilpotents. II, *Rev.Roumaine Math.Pures Appl.* 19(1974), 549-577.

3. Apostol, C.; Salinas, N.: Nilpotent approximation and quasinilpotent operators, *Pacific J.Math.* 61(1975),327-337.

4. Berg, I.D.: Index theory for perturbations of direct sums of normal operators and weighted shifts, *Canadian J.Math.* 30(1978), 1152-1165.

5. Brown, A.: Unitary equivalence of binormal operators, *Amer. J.Math.* 76(1954), 414-434.

6. Campbell, S.L.; Gellar, R.: On asymptotic properties of several classes of operators, *Proc.Amer.Math.Soc.* 66(1977), 79-84.

7. Foiaş, C.; Pearcy, C.; Voiculescu, D.: Biquasitriangular operators and quasisimilarity, *Linear spaces and approximation* (Proc.Conf.Oberwolfach, 1977), Birkhauser-Verlag, Basel, 1978, 47-52.

8. Hadwin, D.W.: Closure of unitary equivalent classes, *Dissertation*, Indiana University, 1975.

9. Hadwin, D.W.: An operator-valued spectrum, *Indiana Univ.Math J.* 26(1977), 329-340.

10. Halmos, P.R.: Ten problems in Hilbert space, *Bull.Amer.Math. Soc.* 76(1970), 887-933.

11. Halmos, P.R.: Limits of shifts, *Acta Sci.Math.* (Szeged) 34 (1973), 131-139.

12. Halmos, P.R.: *A Hilbert space problem book*, D.Van Nostrand, Princeton, New Jersey, 1967.

13. Halmos, P.R.; Wallen, L.J.: Powers of partial isometries,

J.Math.Mech. 19(1970), 657-663.

14. Herrero, D.A.: Normal limits of nilpotent operators, *Indiana Univ.Math.J.* 23(1974), 1097-1108.

15. Herrero, D.A.: Quasidiagonality, similarity and approximation by nilpotent operators, *Indiana Univ.Math.J.*, to appear.

16. Kato, T.: *Perturbation theory for linear operators*, Springer-Verlag, New York, 1966.

17. Pearcy, C.; Salinas, N.: Extensions of C*-algebras and the reducing essential matricial spectrum of an operator, *K-theory and operator theory*, Athens, Georgia, 1975, *Lect.Notes Math.* 575, Springer-Verlag, Berlin-Heidelberg-New York, 1977, 96-112.

18. Voiculescu, D.: A non-commutative Weyl-von Neumann theorem, *Rev.Roumaine Math.Pures Appl.*21(1976), 97-113.

19. Williams, L.R.: On quasisimilarity of operators in Hilbert space, *Dissertation*, Univ.of Michigan, 1976.

Domingo A.Herrero
I.V.I.C.,
Departamento de Matemáticas,
Apartado Postal 1827, Caracas 101,
Venezuela

Present address:
Department of Mathematics,
University of Georgia,
Athens, Georgia 30602
U.S.A.

ISOMORPHISMS OF AUTOMORPHISM GROUPS OF TYPE II FACTORS

V.F.R.Jones

1. INTRODUCTION

Let M and N be type II factors and Aut M and Aut N their automorphism groups. We shall prove the following theorem.

THEOREM 1. *Let* Φ: Aut M$\to$Aut N *be an isomorphism. Then there is a map* φ:M$\to$N, *which is either an isomorphism or an anti-isomorphism, such that*

$$\Phi(\alpha)=\varphi\ \alpha\ \varphi^{-1} \quad \textit{for any } \alpha\in\text{Aut } M.$$

The idea of the proof is to construct a projection lattice isomorphism δ_Φ from Φ using the fact that if p is a projection then Ad(2 p-1) is an involutory automorphism. Once δ_Φ is constucted we may apply Theorem 1 of Dye's paper [5] to obtain φ. Given an involutory automorphism α, we must be able to determine, by purely algebraic properties in the automorphism group, when it is of the form Ad(2p-1). Once we have done that we are faced with the problem of choosing between p and 1-p, since Ad(2p-1)= =Ad(2(p-1)-1). The trick we use is to look at the centre of the centralizer of α. If α is outer or if α=Ad(2p-1) for a projection p equivalent to 1-p, then the centre of the centraliser is finite. Otherwise it is infinite. Thus we can avoid projections equivalent to their orthogonal complements and use the trace to choose between p and 1-p. In this way we define δ_Φ on sufficiently small projections and we show that it preserves orthogonality. This means it extends uniquely to an isomorphism of the whole projection lattice.

A lot of attention has been paid recently to the group Aut M and our theorem allows us to answer one of the "classical" questions one asks about a group G: what outer automorphisms does G have? The answer in this case is that any automorphism of Aut M is given by conjugation either by an automorphism or antiautomorphism of M.

In the case of the hyperfinite II_1 factor R, we now have a large amount of information about Aut R. In [8], de la Harpe has shown that the normal subgroup Int R is simple (as is Int M for any simple factor M). Moreover Connes has shown in [3] that Out R= =Aut R/Int R is also simple so that Int R is the only non-trivial normal subgroup of Aut R. One knows all finite subgroups of Aut R ([9]) and all countable amenable subgroups (and hence all conjugacy classes [3]) of Out R ([12]). Also, there is only one involutory antiautomorphism of R ([6], [14]) and a classification of all antiautomorphisms of R should soon be established, following the methods of [6]. This wealth of information is the more remarkable when one remembers that Out R contains any separable locally compact group.

THE PROOF

If M, N and Φ:Aut M$\to$Aut N are given, we shall give a series of lemmas working towards the construction of the implementation δ_Φ on the projections of M. Lemmas 2 to 6 are announced for an arbitrary factor M. From Lemma 7 on, factors are of type II.

We remind the reader of the following facts which will be used without explicit mention: for each unitary $u\in M$, the map $Adu(x)=uxu^*$, $x\in M$ defines an automorphism of M and if $\alpha\in$Aut M then $\alpha Adu\, \alpha^{-1}=Ad\,\alpha(u)$. If p is a projection then 2p-1 is unitary and if p and q are commuting projections then Ad(2p-1)Ad(2q-1)= =Ad(2pΔq)-1) where Δ denotes the symmetric difference. The letter T will denote the circle group, identified with the unitaries in the centre of a factor.

If X is a subset of a group, let C(X) denote the centralizer of X and CC(X) the centre of C(X).

LEMMA 2. *Let* p *be a projection of* M *not equivalent to* 1-p. *Then* $\lambda\to$**Ad**(λp+1-p) *is an isomorphism from* T *to the centre of the centralizer of* Ad(2p-1) *in* Aut M.

PROOF. If $\alpha\in$C(Ad(2p-1)), then α(p)=p or 1-p. Since p is not equivalent to 1-p,α(p)=p.

Suppose $\alpha\epsilon CC(Ad(2p-1))$. Then $\alpha|_{M_p}$ and $\alpha|_{M_{(1-p)}}$ are both the identity since otherwise one could find a unitary v in M_p (or $M_{(1-p)}$) with $\alpha(v)\neq v$ so that α would not commute with $Ad(v+1-p)$ (or $Ad(p+v)$). But $Ad(v+1-p)$ (and $Ad(p+v)$) certainly commute with $Ad(2p-1)$.

Thus in particular by [2 , Prop.1.5.1], α is not outer, and since $\alpha(p)=p$, α is of the form $Ad(v+w)$ with v unitary in M_p and w unitary in $M_{(1-p)}$. By the above we know that there are numbers μ and σ in T with $v=\mu p$, $w=\sigma(1-p)$. Thus if $\lambda=\mu\bar{\sigma}$, $\alpha=Ad(\lambda p+1-p)$.

LEMMA 3. *Let* $\alpha\epsilon Aut\ M$ *be such that* $\alpha(u)=\lambda_u u(\lambda_u\epsilon T)$ *for every unitary* $u\epsilon M$. Then $\alpha=id$.

PROOF. It suffices to show that $\alpha(p)=p$ for every projection $p\epsilon M$. But $\alpha(2p-1)=\pm(2p-1)$ so that $\alpha(p)=p$ or $1-p$. If $\alpha(p)=1-p$ then p is equivalent to $1-p$. But any p is the sum of projections not equivalent to their orthogonal complements. Hence $\alpha(p)=p$ for all p.

The following lemma from Galois theory is certainly well known but does not seem to be proved explicitly anywhere.

LEMMA 4. *Let* M *be an arbitrary factor and* G *a finite group of outer automorphisms of* M. *Then if* $\alpha\epsilon Aut\ M$ *is the identity on* $M^G(=\{x\epsilon M|g(x)=x$ *for all* $g\epsilon G\})$, *then* α *coincides with some element of* G.

PROOF. Suppose M is in standard form and that G is represented by a unitary representation $g\to u_g$ ([7]). The algebra generated by M' and $\{u_g\}$ is isomorphic to the crossed product of M' by the induced action of G([1, Proposition II.3]). If $\alpha=Adu$ for some unitary u, then $u\epsilon(M^G)'=\{M'\cup\{u_g\}\}''$. Thus by [11], u is of the form xu_g for some $g\epsilon G$ and some $x\epsilon M'$. Hence $\alpha=g$.

LEMMA 5. (i) If $\alpha\epsilon Aut\ M$ *is an outer involution then* $CC(\alpha)=\{id,\alpha\}$.
(ii) If $\alpha=Ad(2p-1)$, *with p equivalent to* $1-p$, *then* $CC(\alpha)=\{id,\alpha\}$.

PROOF. (i) Note that for each $u\epsilon M^{\alpha}$, $Ad\ u\epsilon C(\alpha)$, so if $\beta\epsilon CC(\alpha)$, $\beta(u)=\lambda_u u$ for $u\epsilon M^{\alpha}$. By Lemmas 3 and 4, $\beta=$ id or α.

(ii) $C(\alpha)=\{\beta|\beta(p)=p$ or $1-p\}$. If $\beta(p)=1-p$ then β does not commute with $Ad(ip+1-p)$ so that if $\beta\in CC(\alpha)$, $\beta(p)=p$ and as in the proof of Lemma 2, we conclude that $\beta=Ad(\lambda p+1-p)$ for some $\lambda\in\mathbf{T}$. But choose x unitary with $Adx(p)=1-p$. Then $Adx\in C(\alpha)$ and β only commutes with Adx if $\lambda=\pm 1$.

LEMMA 6. *If* p *and* q *are two projections in* M *not equivalent to their orthogonal complements, then* $Ad(2p-1)$ *and* $Ad(2q-1)$ *commute iff* p *and* q *commute.*

PROOF. The "if" direction is obvious, so suppose $Ad(2p-1)$ commutes with $Ad(2q-1)$. Then $Ad(2p-1)(q)=q$ or $1-q$ and since q is not equivalent to $1-q$, q commutes with $2p-1$ and hence with p.

To show the usefulness of Lemmas 2→6, we now show that algebraic properties of Aut M allow us to decide whether M is of type II_1 or II_∞.

LEMMA 7. *Let* M *and* N *be type* II *factors and let* Φ:Aut M→Aut N *be an isomorphism. Then* M *is to type* II_1 *iff* N *is of type* II_1.

PROOF. By symmetry it suffices to prove that if M is of type II_1, then so is N. So suppose M is II_1 and choose equivalent projections p in **M** with $pq=0$ and $p+q$ equivalent to $1-p-q$. Then $Ad(2p-1)$ and $Ad(2q-1)$ are commuting conjugate elements of Aut M with infinite centralizers whose product has a finite centre of its centralizer (by Lemmas 2 and 5). The same is true of $\Phi(Ad(2p-1))$ and $\Phi(Ad(2q-1))$. But by Lemmas 2 and 5, there are finite projections p' and q' in N with $\Phi(Ad(2p-1))=Ad(2p'-1)$ and $\Phi(Ad(2q-1))=Ad(2q'-1)$. By Lemma 6, p' and q' commute so that $Ad(2p'-1)Ad(2q'-1)=Ad(2(p'\Delta q')-1)$. But $p'\Delta q'$ is finite so if N were $\mathbf{II}_\infty$, $Ad(2(p'\Delta q')-1)$ would have an infinite centre of its centralizer. Hence N is of type II_1.

We now begin to define δ_Φ. We choose sets P_M and P_N representing "half" of the projections not equivalent to their orthogonal complements. Choose a dimension function d on M normalized if M is II_1. Put $P_M=\{p\in\mathbf{M}\,|\,p$ a projection, $d(p)<\frac{1}{2}\}$ when M is II_1 and $P_M=\{p\in M\,|\,p$ a projection, $d(p)<\infty\}$ when M is II_∞. Note that P_M is globally invariant under Aut M.

Suppose we are given $p\in P_M$. Then we know by Lemmas 2 and 5 that $\Phi(Ad(2p-1))$ is of the form $Ad(2q-1)$ for some projection q in N. In fact there is only one such q in P_N so define $f:P_M \to P_N$ by $f(p)=q$. It is clear that f is a bijection between P_M and P_N. We now establish its essential properties.

LEMMA 8. *If* $\alpha \in \mathrm{Aut}\, M$ *and* $p \in P_M$ *then* $f(\alpha(p))=\Phi(\alpha)(f(p))$.

PROOF. By the definition of f, $\Phi(\mathrm{Ad}(2p-1))=\mathrm{Ad}(2f(p)-1)$, so that $\Phi(\alpha)(\mathrm{Ad}(2f(p)-1))\Phi(\alpha)^{-1}=\Phi(\alpha)\Phi(\mathrm{Ad}(2p-1))\Phi(\alpha)^{-1}=\Phi(\mathrm{Ad}(2\alpha(p)-1))=$ $=\mathrm{Ad}(2f(\alpha(p)))$.But also $\Phi(\alpha)(\mathrm{Ad}(2f(p)-1))\Phi(\alpha)^{-1}=\mathrm{Ad}(2\Phi(\alpha)(f(p))-1)$. We conclude that $\Phi(\alpha)(f(p))=f(\alpha(p))$ or $1-f(\alpha(p))$. But by the definition of f, $f(\alpha(p))\in P_N$, as does $\Phi(\alpha)(f(p))$. Hence $\Phi(\alpha)(f(p))=$ $=f(\alpha(p))$.

COROLLARY 9.*If* p *and* q *are equivalent projection in* P_M,f(p) *and* f(q) *are equivalent in* P_N.

PROOF. For projections in P_M and P_N ,equivalence is the same as the existence of an ivolutory automorphism sending one to the other. So choose $\alpha,\alpha^2=\mathrm{id}$, with $\alpha(p)=q$, and apply Lemma 5.

LEMMA 10. *The map* f *preserves commutativity of projections.*

PROOF. This follows immediately from Lemma 6.

LEMMA 11. *If* M *is of type* II_1 *then* $d(p)<\frac{1}{4}$ *implies* $d(f(p))<\frac{1}{4}$ *and* $d(p)<\frac{1}{8}$ *implies* $d(f(p))<\frac{1}{8}$.

PROOF. If $d(p)<\frac{1}{4}$, then there is no commuting conjugate α of $\mathrm{Ad}(2p-1)$ such that $CC(\mathrm{Ad}(2p-1)\alpha)$ is finite. The same is true of $\mathrm{Ad}(2f(p)-1)$and by Lemma 7, N is of type II_1. If $d(f(p))$ were larger than $\frac{1}{4}$ one could choose q, commuting with f(p), such that $d(f(p)\Delta q)=\frac{1}{2}$. But then $CC(\mathrm{Ad}(2f(p)-1)\mathrm{Ad}(2q-1))$ is finite.

The same argument (with 3 commuting conjugates) works for $d(p)<\frac{1}{8}$.

LEMMA 12. *Let* p *and* q *be commuting projections of dimension* $<\frac{1}{4}$. *Then* $f(p\Delta q)=f(p)\Delta f(q)$.

PROOF. Since $\Phi(\mathrm{Ad}(2p-1)\mathrm{Ad}(2q-1))=\mathrm{Ad}(2f(p)-1)\mathrm{Ad}(2f(q)-1)$and it also equals $\mathrm{Ad}(2f(p\Delta q)-1)$, we deduce by Lemma 10 that $f(p\Delta q)=$ $=f(p)\Delta f(q)$ or $1-f(p)\Delta f(q)$. But by Lemma 11, $f(p)\Delta f(q)\in P_N$ so $f(p\Delta q)=f(p)\Delta f(q)$.

LEMMA 13. *Let* $p\in P_M$, *then there is a (not necessarily conti-*

nuous) character $\sigma: T \to T$, *depending on* p, *such that* $\Phi(\mathrm{Ad}(\lambda p+1-p)) = \mathrm{Ad}(\sigma(\lambda) f(p)+1-f(p))$.

PROOF. Define $\mu: T \to \mathrm{Aut}\ M$ by $\mu(\lambda)=\mathrm{Ad}(\lambda p+1-p)$ and $\eta: T \to \mathrm{Aut}\ N$ by $\eta(\lambda)=\mathrm{Ad}(\lambda f(p)+1-f(p))$. By Lemma 2, μ is an isomorphism from T to $CC(\mathrm{Ad}(2p-1))$ and η is an isomorphism from T to $CC(\mathrm{Ad}(2f(p)-1))$. Thus $\sigma=\eta^{-1}\Phi\mu$ is an automorphism of T and $\Phi \circ \mu = \eta \circ \sigma$.

LEMMA 14. *Let* p *and* q *be orthogonal unitarily equivalent projections of dimension* $<\frac{1}{4}$. *Then* $f(p)f(q)=0$.

PROOF. If $r = p + q$ we have $\mathrm{Ad}(\lambda r+1-r)=\mathrm{Ad}(\lambda p+1-p)\mathrm{Ad}(\lambda q+1-q)$. Since p and q are equivalent, using Lemma 8 one sees that the characters σ associated with p and q are the same. Let σ_0 denote the character associated with r. Then we have:
$\mathrm{Ad}(\sigma_0(\lambda)f(r)+1-f(r))=\mathrm{Ad}[\sigma(\lambda)^2 f(p)f(q)+\sigma(\lambda)(f(p)\Delta f(q))+(1-f(p))\Delta(1-f(q))]$.
Now by Lemma 10, $f(p)$ commutes with $f(q)$ so that the three projections on the right are orthogonal, and there is a function $\mu: T \to T$ such that $\mu(\lambda)(\sigma_0(\lambda)f(r)+1-f(r))=\sigma(\lambda)^2 f(p)f(q)+\sigma(\lambda)f(r)+ +(1-f(p))\Delta(1-f(q))$, where we have used Lemma 12 and $p\Delta q=r$.

Now $(1-f(p))\Delta(1-f(q))$ is not zero since, if M is of type II_1, $d(f(p))$ and $d(f(q))$ are $<\frac{1}{4}$, and if M is of type II_∞, $1-f(p)$ and $1-f(q)$ are commuting projections with finite orthogonal complements. Thus multiplying by $(1-f(p))\Delta(1-f(q))$ gives $\mu(\lambda)\equiv 1$. If $f(p)f(q)$ were not zero, we would deduce $\sigma(\lambda)^2 \equiv 1$ and thus $\sigma(\lambda)\equiv 1$, a contradiction.

LEMMA 15. *Let* p *and* q *be projections of dimension* $<\frac{1}{8}$ *in* M. *Then* $pq=0$ *iff* $f(p)f(q)=0$.

PROOF. By symmetry we need only prove one implication so suppose $pq=0$. Without loss of generality suppose $d(p)<d(q)$ and that m is the smallest even number such that $md(p)\geq d(q)$. Divide q into m equivalent orthogonal parts s_i and let s be a projection orthogonal to $p+q$ of dimension $d(p)-\frac{1}{m}d(q)$. Then for each i, s_i+s is equivalent and orthogonal to p and since m is even, $q=(s_1+s)\Delta(s_2+s)\Delta\ldots\Delta(s_m+s)$. Since $d(s)<\frac{1}{8}$, we may apply Lemma 12 to deduce that $f(q)=f(s_1+s)f(s_2+s)\ldots f(s_m+s)$, and since each s_i+s is orthogonal to p, $f(q)$ is orthogonal to $f(p)$ by Lemma 14.

LEMMA 16. *There is a unique orthoisomorphism* δ_Φ *from the projection lattice of* M *to that of* N *which agrees with* f *on projections of dimension* $<\frac{1}{8}$.

PROOF. (This is properly an ortholattice result but we give a proof here for completeness.) Let p be a projection in M and write $p=\sum_i p_i$ where the p_i are orthogonal projections of dimension $<\frac{1}{8}$. Let $\delta_\Phi(p)=\sum_i f(p_i)$. This is a projection by Lemma 15. We must show that δ_Φ is well defined. To do this we shall show that if $\{q_j\}$ are orthogonal projections of dimension $<\frac{1}{8}$ such that $\sum_j q_j=1-p$, then $\delta_\Phi(p)=1-\sum_j f(q_j)$, independent of the choice of the p_i's. By Lemma 15, $\delta_\Phi(p)$ is orthogonal to $\sum_j f(q_j)$ so let $r=1-\sum_j f(q_j)-\delta_\Phi(p)$. Writing r as a sum of small orthogonal projections we may apply Lemma 15 to Φ^{-1} to deduce that r is the sum of orthogonal projections, f^{-1} of which are orthogonal to $\{q_j\}$ and $\{p_i\}$. But $\sum_j q_j+\sum_i p_i=1$ so that $r=0$ and $\delta_\Phi(p)=1-\sum_j f(q_j)$. This argument clearly shows that $1-\delta_\Phi(p)=\delta_\Phi(1-p)$. Bijectivity and uniqueness of δ_Φ are obvious, and δ_Φ clearly preserves orthogonality.

PROOF OF THEOREM 1. We may now apply Theorem 1 of [5] to deduce the existence of a $\varphi:M\to N$ which satisfies $\Phi(\alpha)=\varphi\,\alpha\,\varphi^{-1}$ (Lemma 8) on projections of dimension $<\frac{1}{8}$ and thus on all of M.

The reader should note that our argument is a modification of that of Dye in the second part of [5].

SOME CONSEQUENCES AND QUESTIONS.

COROLLARY 17. *Let* M *be a type* II *factor and* Int M *the group of inner automorphisms. Then* Int M *is a characteristic subgroup of* Aut M.

PROOF. This follows immediately from Theorem 1 and the identity $\varphi \mathrm{Ad}u\varphi^{-1}=\mathrm{Ad}\varphi(u)$.

For the hyperfinite II_1 factor R this could have been deduced from [3] and [8]. A corollary of the proof of Theorem 1 is that if M and N are type II factors and $\Phi:\mathrm{Int}\,M\to\mathrm{Int}\,N$ is an isomorphism, then there is an isomorphism or anti-isomorphism $\varphi: M \to N$ with $\Phi(\alpha) = \varphi \alpha \varphi^{-1}$. In fact the proof is even easier in this case as one does not have to worry about the possibility that $\Phi(\mathrm{Ad}(2p-1))$ is outer.

Since the centre of Aut M is trivial, conjugation determines an isomorphism from Aut M on to a normal subgroup of Aut(Aut M). There is thus an exact sequence $1 \to \mathrm{Aut}\, M \to \mathrm{Aut}(\mathrm{Aut}\, M) \to G \to 1$, where G is $\mathbb{Z}_2$ when M is anti-isomorphic to itself and {1} otherwise (one needs to check that conjugation by an antiautomorphism does not coincide with conjugation by some automorphism). It is known ([4]) that there are cases where G={1} and in [10] it is shown that, when $G = \mathbb{Z}_2$, this exact sequence is not always split.

COROLLARY 18. *There is, up to conjugacy, only one outer involutory automorphism of* Aut R.

PROOF. This follows from Theorem 1 and [6] or [14].

QUESTION 19. Is Theorem 1 true if M and N are type III factors? (It is easy to see that if M is type III then so is N. The type I case can easily be handled by our methods, but note the pathology for type I_{2n} factors in [5].)

QUESTION 20. Is every automorphism of Out R induced by an automorphism or antiautomorphism of R? (It seems unlikely that this is true for an arbitrary type II factor .)

REFERENCES

1. Aubert, P.-L.: Théorie de Galois pour une W*-algèbre, *Comment. Math.Helv.* 51(1976), 411-433.

2. Connes, A.: Une classification des facteurs de type III, *Ann.Sci.Ecole Norm.Sup.* 6(1973), 133-252.

3. Connes, A.: Outer conjugacy classes of automorphisms of factors, *Ann.Sci.Ecole Norm.Sup.* 8(1975), 383-420.

4. Connes, A.: Sur la classification des facteurs de type II, *C.R.Acad.Sci.Paris Sér.A-B* 281(1975), 13-15.

5. Dye, H.A.: On the geometry of projections in certain operator algebras, *Ann.of Math.* 61(1955), 73-89.

6. Giordano, T.; Jones, V.: Antiautomorphismes involutifs du facteur hyperfini de type II_1, *C.R.Acad.Sc.Paris Ser.A-B* 290(1980), 29-31.

7. Haagerup, U.: The standard form of von Neumann algebras, *Math. Scand.* 37(1975), 271-283.

8. Harpe, P. de la: Simplicity of the projective unitary groups defined by simple factors, *Comment.Math.Helv.* 54(1979), 334-345.

9. Jones, V.: Actions of finite groups on the hyperfinite type II_1 factor, *Memoirs of Amer.Math.Soc.*, to appear.

10. Jones, V.: A II_1 factor anti-isomorphic to itself but without involutory antiautomorphisms, *Math.Scand.*, to appear.

11. Nakamura, M.; Takeda Z.: On inner automorphisms of certain finite factors, *Proc.Japan Acad.* 37(1961), 31-32.

12. Ocneanu, A.: Actions of amenable groups on von Neumann algebras, to appear.

13. Størmer, E.: Real structure in the hyperfinite type II_1 factor, preprint.

V.R.F.Jones
Université de Genève,
Section de Mathématiques,
2-4 Rue du Lièvre,
Case Postale 124, Genève,
Suisse

A SPECTRAL RESIDUUM FOR EACH CLOSED OPERATOR

B. Nagy

1. INTRODUCTION

The theory of S-decomposable operators was first studied in the bounded case by I. Bacalu [3], and was extended to the case of a closed operator by F.-H. Vasilescu [20] (see also [18] and [19]) and the author [8]. Loosely speaking, an operator is S--decomposable if it shows a good spectral behavior (connected with decomposability in the sense of Foiaş [5]) outside a certain subset, denoted by S, of its spectrum. The main result of this paper is that for any closed operator there is a unique minimal closed subset of the spectrum, called the spectral residuum, outside which the operator shows this behavior.

The corresponding result for a bounded operator was proved by the author in [12]. The proof of the generalization here makes use of the same basic idea, originating with M.Radjabalipour [15]. However, owing partly to the fact that quotients of closed operators need not be closed (see Example 3.1), the extension is far from trivial, and requires considerable refinement upon the method. The author is indebted to E.Albrecht (Saarbrücken) for communicating the main idea of Lemma 3.2 to him.

In Section 2 we shall present the necessary terminology and notations. Section 3 will show that quotients of closed operators are closed under very mild conditions, but not in general. In Section 4 we shall show that the apparently weakest and most natural form of the good spectral behavior, i.e. having the (S,1)--decomposition property, is in fact equivalent to its strongest form (S-decomposability), and prove the main result of the paper.

2. PRELIMINARIES

Let X be a complex Banach space and let C(X) and B(X) denote the classes of the closed and the bounded linear operators in X, respectively. C and $\overline{C}$ will denote the complex plane and its compactification. For any subset H of $\overline{C}$, $\overline{H}$ denotes its closure in the topology of $\overline{C}$, further H^c means $\overline{C}\setminus H$. For any T in C(X), D(T) and R(T) are its domain and range, and $\sigma(T)$ is its extended spectrum, which is defined as its usual spectrum s(T) if $T\varepsilon B(X)$ and as $s(T)\cup\{\infty\}$ otherwise. We define $\rho(T)$ as $\sigma(T)^c$. If Y is a closed subspace of X and $T(Y\cap D(T))\subset Y$, then we write $Y\varepsilon I(T)$, and $T|Y$ or T_Y denote the restriction of T to $Y\cap D(T)$. The quotient Banach space will be denoted by X/Y or X^Y, and for any x in X the coset x+Y will also be denoted by x^Y. Define

$$D(T^Y)=\{x^Y\varepsilon X/Y;\ x^Y\cap D(T)\neq\emptyset\},$$

$$T^Y x^Y=(Tx)^Y \text{ for any } x^Y\varepsilon D(T^Y),\ x\varepsilon x^Y\cap D(T).$$

T^Y is called the quotient operator induced in X/Y by T.

Now we recall some definitions and facts of local spectral theory (cf. [18]). Let $T\varepsilon C(X)$ and $x\varepsilon X$. For any $z\varepsilon\overline{C}$ we write $z\varepsilon\delta_T(x)$ if in a neighborhood U of z there is a holomorphic function f satisfying $(u-T)f(u)=x$ for $u\varepsilon U\cap C$. Such an f is called a T-*associated function* of x (in U). There is a unique maximal open set O_T in $\overline{C}$ with the property that $f\equiv 0$ is the only T-associated function of 0 in any open subset G of O_T. Set $S_T=O_T^c$ and

$$\gamma_T(x)=\delta_T(x)^c,\ \sigma_T(x)=\gamma_T(x)\cup S_T,\ \rho_T(x)=\sigma_T(x)^c .$$

Then in $\rho_T(x)$ a unique T-associated function of x exists, which will be denoted by $\overline{x}$. If $S_T=\emptyset$, we say that T has *the single-valued extension property.*

For any $T\varepsilon C(X)$, $H\subset\overline{C}$ define

$$X_T(H)=\{x\varepsilon X;\ \sigma_T(x)\subset H\}.$$

$X_T(H)$ is a linear manifold, not necessarily closed, in X. If no misunderstanding is possible, we omit the subscript T in $\sigma_T(x)$, $X_T(H)$, etc.

Let F be a closed set in $\overline{C}$ and define

$$I(T,F)=\{Y\varepsilon I(T);\ \sigma(T_Y)\subset F\}.$$

If I(T,F) has an upper bound (with respect to the relation $\subset$), which belongs to I(T,F), then this upper bound is denoted by X(T,F). Subspaces of the form X(T,F) (with F closed in $\overline{C}$) are called *spectral maximal (sub)spaces* for T.

Let S be a closed set in $\overline{C}$. A family of n+1 (n≥1) open sets $(G_1,\ldots,G_n;G_o)$ is called an *open* (S,n)-*covering* of the closed set $H\subset\overline{C}$ if

$$\bigcup_{i=0}^{n} G_i \supset H\cup S \text{ and } \overline{G_i}\cap S=\emptyset \text{ for } i=1,\ldots,n .$$

If we do not wish to emphasize the number n, we call $(G_1,\ldots,G_n;G_o)$ simply an S-*covering*.

The operator $T\varepsilon C(X)$ is called *strongly* (S,n)-*decomposable* if for any open (S,n)-covering $(G_1,\ldots,G_n;\ G_o)$ of $\sigma(T)$

1° there are spectral maximal spaces for T, $X_i\subset D(T)$ (i=1,...,n) and $X_o\subset X$ such that

2° $\sigma(T|X_i)\subset G_i$ for i=0,1,...,n,

3° for any spectral maximal space Y for T

$$Y=\sum_{i=0}^{n}(Y\cap X_i).$$

T is called (S,n)-*decomposable* if we postulate 3° only for Y=X. If, in addition, we weaken 1° to require only that the subspaces $X_i\subset D(T)$ (i=1,...,n) and $X_o\subset X$ belong to I(T), then T is said to have the (S,n)-*decomposition property*.

T is said to be *strongly* S-*decomposable*, S-*decomposable* or to have the S-*decomposition property* if T is strongly (S,n)-decomposable, (S,n)-decomposable or has the (S,n)-decomposition property, respectively, for every positive integer n. (Strongly) ∅-decomposable operators are called *(strongly) decomposable*.

From these definitions we see that if the operator T has the (S,n)-decomposition property and $\infty\notin S$, then $T\varepsilon B(X)$. Further, $T\varepsilon C(X)$ is (S,n)-decomposable if and only if T is $(S\cap\sigma(T),n)$-decomposable. So when we consider such operators, we may and will assume that $S\subset\sigma(T)$. Finally, we note that E. Albrecht [1] has shown that not every decomposable operator is strongly decomposable.

3. ON QUOTIENTS OF CLOSED OPERATORS

Let $T\varepsilon C(X)$. We say that $z\varepsilon\overline{C}$ belongs to the set Q(T) if (i) or (ii) holds:

(i) z is finite and

$$\inf\{|(z-T)x|;\ x\varepsilon D(T),\ |x|=1\}=k(z)>0;$$

(ii) $z=\infty$ and

$$\sup\{|Tx|;\ x\varepsilon D(T),\ |x|=1\}=k(\infty)<\infty\ .$$

It is well-known that the set $Q(T)$ is open in $\overline{C}$.

It was shown in [10] that if $Y\varepsilon I(T)$ and $\sigma(T)\cup\sigma(T_Y)\neq\overline{C}$, then the quotient operator T^Y belongs to $C(X/Y)$. Now we prove by a different method

LEMMA 3.1. *If* $Y\varepsilon I(T)$, $Y\ D(T)$ *and the set* $Q(T)\cap\rho(T_Y)$ *is nonvoid, then* $T^Y\varepsilon C(X/Y)$.

PROOF. Since $Q(T)$ is open, some finite z belongs to $Q(T)\cap$ $\cap\rho(T_Y)$. Considering $z-T$ instead of T, we may and will assume that $0\varepsilon Q(T)\cap\rho(T_Y)$. Let D denote the linear manifold $D(T)$ endowed with the graph norm $|x|_T=|x|+|Tx|$. Since T is closed, D is a Banach space. The subspace Y is closed also with respect to the norm of D, thus D/Y is also a Banach space with the usual norm of the quotient space.

The linear spaces D/Y and $D(T^Y)$ are identical. They are also normed with the graph norm

(1) $$|x^Y|_{T^Y}=|x^Y|+|T^Y x^Y|.$$

Further, we have for any $x^Y\varepsilon D(T^Y)$ and any $x\varepsilon x^Y$

$$|x^Y|_{T^Y}=\inf_{y_1\varepsilon Y}|x+y_1|+\inf_{y_2\varepsilon Y}|Tx+y_2|\leq\inf_{y\varepsilon Y}(|x+y|+|Tx+Ty|)=|x^Y|_{D/Y}\ .$$

On the other hand, by assumption,

$$|x^Y|_{D/Y}=\inf_{y\varepsilon Y}(|T^{-1}(Tx+y)|+|Tx+y|)\leq(|T^{-1}|+1)|x^Y|_{T^Y}\ ,$$

where $|T^{-1}|$ denotes the norm of T^{-1} as a bounded operator from the closed subspace $R(T)$ onto $D(T)$. Thus the two norms of $D(T^Y)$ are equivalent, hence $D(T^Y)$ is a Banach space with respect to the norm (1).

Now if $|x_n^Y-x^Y|+|T^Y x_n^Y-w^Y|\to 0$ as $n\to\infty$, then $\{x_n^Y\}$ is a Cauchy sequence with respect to the norm (1). The completeness of $D(T^Y)$ implies that $T^Y x^Y=w^Y$, hence T^Y is closed.

COROLLARY. *If* $Y\varepsilon I(T)$, $Y\subset D(T)$ *and the set* $Q(T)$ *is unbounded, then* $T^Y\varepsilon C(X/Y)$.

The main idea in the proof of the following lemma is due to

E.Albrecht (oral communication).

LEMMA 3.2. *Let* $T\in C(X)$, $Y\in I(T)$, $Y\subset D(T)$ *and* $T^{Y}\in C(X/Y)$. *Assume that in a neighborhood* $N(z)$ *of* $z\in\overline{C}$ *a holomorphic function* $g:N(z)\to X/Y$ *exists such that* $(v-T^{Y})g(v)=x^{Y}\in X/Y$ *for* v *in* $N(z)\cap C$. *Then there are a neighborhood* $N'(z)\subset N(z)$ *of* z *and a function* $h:N'(z)\to X$ *such that* $h(v)^{Y}=g(v)$ *and the functions* $h(v)$ *and* $(v-T)h(v)$ *are holomorphic mappings of* $N'(z)$ *to* X.

PROOF. Since T^{Y} is closed, $D(T^{Y})$ with the graph norm (1) is a Banach space. The preceding proof shows that for any x^{Y} in $D(T^{Y})$ we have

$$|x^{Y}|_{T^{Y}}\leq|x^{Y}|_{D/Y}\;.$$

By Banach's theorem on compatible norms, the two norms are equivalent. For $v\in N(z)\cap C$ we have

$$T^{Y}g(v)=vg(v)-x^{Y}.$$

If z is finite, we may and will assume that $N(z)\subset C$. Then $T^{Y}g(v)$ is holomorphic, hence g is a holomorphic mapping of $N(z)$ to the Banach space $\{D(T^{Y}),\ |\cdot|_{T^{Y}}\}$ or, equivalently, to the Banach space D/Y. By [19, Lemma 2.1], there are a neighborhood $N'(z)\subset N(z)$ of z and a holomorphic function $h:N'(z)\to D$ such that $h(v)^{Y}=g(v)$ for $v\in N'(z)$. Since $N'(z)\subset C$, the functions $h(v)$ and $(v-T)h(v)$ are holomorphic mappings of $N'(z)$ to X.

If $z=\infty$, then g is a T^{Y}-associated function of x^{Y} in a neighborhood of ∞. The reasoning in [19, p.381] shows that the function $vg(v)$ is then also holomorphic, hence so is $T^{Y}g(v)$ in $N(z)$. Therefore g is a holomorphic mapping of $N(z)$ to D/Y. Since $g(\infty)=$ $=0$, in a neighborhood of infinity we have

$$g(v)=\sum_{k=1}^{\infty}a_k^{Y}v^{-k},$$

and this series converges in the norm of D/Y. Since $|a_k^{Y}|_{D/Y}\leq M^{k}$ $(k=1,2,\ldots)$ for some $M>0$, there are elements a_k in a_k^{Y} such that $|a_k|_{T}\leq(M+1)^{k}$ $(k=1,2,\ldots)$. Hence the series

$$h(v)=\sum_{k=1}^{\infty}a_k v^{-k}$$

converges in a neighborhood $N'(z)$ of infinity in the norm of D. Thus h is a holomorphic mapping of $N'(z)$ to D, $h(v)^{Y}=g(v)$, and the function $vh(v)$ is also holomorphic in $N'(z)$. Hence the assertions of the lemma follow.

The following example will show that the first three conditions in Lemma 3.2 do not imply the fourth.

EXAMPLE 3.1. An operator $T\varepsilon C(X)$ and a subspace $Y\varepsilon I(T)$, $Y\subset D(T)$ such that the operator T^Y is not even closable in X/Y.

Let X be the space of pairs of sequences with elements

$$x=(\beta_o,\beta_1,\beta_2,\ldots;\ \eta_1,\eta_2,\ldots)$$

and with the ℓ_1-norm

$$|x|=\sum_{k=0}^{\infty}|\beta_k|+\sum_{i=1}^{\infty}|\eta_i|.$$

Let b_k denote the element with $\beta_k=1$ and all other components 0 $(k=0,1,2,\ldots)$; similarly for y_i $(i=1,2,\ldots)$. Let

$$D(T)=\{x\varepsilon X:\ \sum_{k=1}^{\infty}k|\beta_k|+\sum_{i=1}^{\infty}|\eta_i|<\infty\} ,$$

and for x in D(T)

$$Tx=(\sum_{k=1}^{\infty}k\beta_k)b_o+\sum_{i=1}^{\infty}(\eta_i+i\beta_i)y_i .$$

Let B and Y denote the closed subspaces spanned by the vectors $b_k(k=0,1,2,\ldots)$ and y_i $(i=1,2,\ldots)$, respectively. Then T_Y is the identity on Y, thus $Y\varepsilon I(T)$ and $Y\subset D(T)$. Further, $k\to\infty$ implies

$$(k^{-1}b_k)^Y\to 0 \text{ and } T^Y(k^{-1}b_k)^Y=b_o^Y\neq 0 ,$$

hence T^Y is not closable in X/Y.

Assume now that in the norm of X

$$x^{(n)}\to x^{(0)} \text{ and } Tx^{(n)}\to w \quad (n\to\infty),$$

where

$$x^{(n)}=(\beta_o^{(n)},\beta_1^{(n)},\beta_2^{(n)},\ldots;\ \eta_1^{(n)},\eta_2^{(n)},\ldots),\qquad (n=0,1,2,\ldots),$$

$$w=(\gamma_o,\gamma_1,\gamma_2,\ldots;\ \xi_1,\xi_2,\ldots).$$

Then, for $n\to\infty$

$$\sum_{k=0}^{\infty}|\beta_k^{(n)}-\beta_k^{(o)}|+\sum_{i=1}^{\infty}|\eta_i^{(n)}-\eta_i^{(o)}|\to 0,\quad \sum_{k=1}^{\infty}k\beta_k^{(n)}\to\gamma_o ,$$

$$\sum_{i=1}^{\infty}|i\beta_i^{(n)}-\xi_i+\eta_i^{(o)}|\to 0.$$

Hence $\xi_i=i\beta_i^{(o)}+\eta_i^{(o)}$ $(i=1,2,\ldots)$, $\gamma_o=\sum_{k=1}^{\infty}k\beta_k^{(o)}$, and $\gamma_k=0$ $(k=1,2,\ldots)$.

Thus $Tx^{(o)}=w$ and $T\varepsilon C(X)$.

4. S-DECOMPOSABILITY AND THE SPECTRAL RESIDUUM

For later use we quote the following result of I.Erdelyi.

LEMMA (I.Erdelyi [6]). *Let* $T\in C(X)$ *and let* $f:D\to X$ *be holomorphic on an open connected set* $D\subset \mathbb{C}$, *be not identically* 0 *and satisfy* $(z-T)f(z)=0$ *for* $z\in D$. *If* $Y\in I(T)$ *and* $f(G)\subset Y$ *for some nonvoid open set* $G\subset D$, *then* $D\subset\sigma(T_Y)$.

LEMMA 4.1. *If* $T\in C(X)$ *has the* (S,1)*-decomposition property, then* $S_T\subset S$.

PROOF. Assume that for some open connected set $D\subset S^c$ and for some holomorphic function $f:D\to X$ we have $(z-T)f(z)=0$ for $z\in D$. We want to show that f is identically 0, therefore we may and will assume that $D\subset\sigma(T)\cap \mathbb{C}$. Let $z_0\in D$ and the positive number r be such that the sets G_1, G_0 satisfy

$$G_1=\{z;\ |z-z_0|<r\}\subset D \text{ and } G_1\neq D,$$

$$G_0=\{z;\ |z-z_0|>r/2\}\cup\{\infty\}.$$

Then (G_1,G_0) is an open (S,1)-covering of $\overline{\mathbb{C}}$ and D is not contained in G_0. By assumption, there are T-invariant subspaces $Y_1\subset D(T)$ and Y_0 such that $\sigma(T|Y_i)\subset G_i$ $(i=0,1)$ and $X=Y_1+Y_0$. Further, there is a nonvoid open set $V\subset D\setminus\overline{G}_1\subset S^c\cap G_0$ and there are functions $f_i:V\to Y_i\cap D(T)$ such that

$$f(z)=f_1(z)+f_0(z) \text{ for } z\in V.$$

By using a technique employed in the proof of [6; Theorem 4], it can be shown that $f(V)\subset Y_0$. By the Lemma above, then either $D\subset\sigma(T|Y_0)\subset G_0$, or f is identically 0 on D. Hence $S_T\subset S$.

The following result for the particular case $S=\emptyset$ (when, necessarily, T belongs to B(X)) was proved, independently and by different methods, by E.Albrecht [2], R.Lange [7] and the author [13]. We adapt the method of [13] to the proof of the general case.

THEOREM 4.1. *If* $T\in C(X)$ *has the* (S,1)*-decomposition property, then* T *is* (S,1)*-decomposable.*

PROOF. First we show that for any closed subset F of $\overline{\mathbb{C}}$ such that $F\supset S$ the spectral manifold X(F) is closed in X. Let $v\in F^c\cap \mathbb{C}$

and let 2d denote a positive number smaller than the distance between v and F. Let D(v,r) denote the open disk in C with center v and radius r, and let

$$G_o=G_o(v)=\overline{D(v,d)}^c \text{ and } G_1=G_1(v)=D(v,2d).$$

By assumption, there are subspaces $Y_i=Y_i(v)\in I(T)$ such that $\sigma(T|Y_i)\subset G_i$ $(i=1,0)$ and $X=Y_1+Y_o$. Let $x\in X(F)$ and $x=y_1+y_o$ with $y_i\in Y_i$ $(i=1,0)$.

Since $\delta_{T|Y_1}(y_1)\subset\delta_T(y_1)$, we have

$$\sigma_T(y_1)=\gamma_T(y_1)\cup S_T\subset\gamma_{T|Y_1}(y_1)\cup S\subset\sigma_{T|Y_1}(y_1)\cup F\subset\sigma(T|Y_1)\cup F\subset G_1\cup F.$$

Since $\sigma(x)\subset F$, we obtain that

$$\sigma(y_o)\subset\sigma(x)\cup\sigma(y_1)\subset G_1\cup F.$$

Hence $S_T\subset S\subset F$ implies for the local resolvents

$$\bar{x}(z)=\overline{y_1}(z)+\overline{y_o}(z) \text{ for } z\in G_1^c\cap F^c.$$

Let H be a (generally unbounded) Cauchy domain [17; p.293] such that $F\subset H$ and $\bar{H}\subset(\overline{G_1})^c$. Let B denote the positively oriented boundary of H and let $c=(2\pi i)^{-1}$.

Now we distinguish between two cases. If $\infty\notin H$, then also $\infty\notin S$. The (S,1)-decomposition property for T then implies $T\in B(X)$. Hence

$$x=c\int_{|z|=\|T\|+1}(z-T)^{-1}x\,dz=c\int_B\bar{x}(z)dz=c\int_B\overline{y_1}(z)dz+c\int_B\overline{y_o}(z)dz.$$

Further, $\sigma(T|Y_1)\subset G_1\subset(\bar{H})^c$ implies $\int_B\overline{y_1}(z)dz=\int_B(z-T|Y_1)^{-1}y_1dz=0$. Therefore

(2) $$x=c\int_B\overline{y_o}(z)dz.$$

If $\infty\in H$, then $\int_B\bar{x}(z)dz=0$, for $\bar{x}$ is holomorphic in H^c. $\sigma(T|Y_1)\subset G_1\subset C$ implies that

$$y_1=c\int_{-B}(z-T|Y_1)^{-1}y_1dz=c\int_{-B}\overline{y_1}(z)dz.$$

Hence

(3) $$y_1=c\int_B\overline{y_o}(z)dz.$$

We shall show that in either case $\overline{y_o}(z)\in Y_o$ for $z\in B$. Then the relations (2) or (3) and $x=y_1+y_o$ will imply that $x\in Y_o$.

Since T has the (S,1)-decomposition property, there are functions $g_i:B\to Y_i$ $(i=1,0)$ such that

$$\overline{y_o}(z)=g_1(z)+g_o(z) \qquad (z\in B).$$

Since $\overline{y}_o(z)$, $g_1(z)\varepsilon D(T)$, we have also $g_o(z)\varepsilon D(T)$. Hence, applying $z-T$,

$$y_o-(z-T)g_o(z)=(z-T)g_1(z)\varepsilon Y_o\cap Y_1 .$$

Since $z\varepsilon B$, z is in the principal component of the resolvent set $\rho(T|Y_1)$ of the operator $T|Y_1$, which belongs to $B(Y_1)$. By [16; Corollary 4.1], $z\varepsilon\rho(T|Y_1\cap Y_o)$. Hence the vector

$$h(z)=(z-T|Y_1\cap Y_o)^{-1}(z-T)g_1(z)$$

is in $Y_1\cap Y_o$. Since $(z-T|Y_1)$ is injective and

$$(z-T|Y_1)(h(z)-g_1(z))=0,$$

we obtain $g_1(z)=h(z)\varepsilon Y_o$. Hence $\overline{y_o}(z)\varepsilon Y_o$ for $z\varepsilon B$, thus $x\varepsilon Y_o=Y_o(v)$ for any $v\varepsilon F^c\cap C$. Therefore $X(F)$ is contained in the intersection

$$Y=\cap\{Y_o(v):v\varepsilon F^c\cap C\}.$$

Further, for any $y\varepsilon Y$ and $v\varepsilon F^c\cap C$ we have

$$\sigma_T(y)=\gamma_T(y)\cup S_T\subset\gamma_{T|Y_o(v)}(y)\cup S\subset\sigma(T|Y_o(v))\cup F\subset G_o(v).$$

Hence $\sigma_T(y)\subset\cap\{G_o(v):v\varepsilon F^c\cap C\}=F\cup\{\infty\}$. If $\infty\notin F$, then $\infty\notin S$ and $T\varepsilon B(X)$. Thus $\sigma_T(y)\subset\sigma(T)\subset C$. Therefore we always have $\sigma_T(y)\subset F$, hence $X(F)=Y$. Since $F\supset S$ and $X(F)$ is closed in X, the subspace $X(F)$ is spectral maximal for T, by [8; Lemma 2].

Assume now that M is a closed subset of $\overline{C}$ such that M is disjoint from S. Let $F=M\cup S$. Then the subspace $Z=X_T(F)=X(T,F)$ is a Banach space. Thus the operator $V=T|Z$ belongs to $C(Z)$ and $\sigma(V)\subset\subset M\cup S$. The sets $\sigma_M=\sigma(V)\cap M$ and $\sigma_S=\sigma(V)\cap S$ are disjoint spectral sets ([17; p.299]) of V. Let P_M , P_S denote the associated projections with ranges Z_M , Z_S , respectively. Then $Z=Z_M+Z_S$ and $Z_M\varepsilon I(T,M)$.

Now if $W\varepsilon I(T,M)$ then $W\subset Z$. Hence $T|W=V|W$ and $\sigma(V|W)\subset M$. Let D be a Cauchy domain (not necessarily bounded) such that $M\subset D$, $\overline{D}\subset S^c$, with positively oriented boundary $B(D)$. Then for every $w\varepsilon W$

$$P_Mw=c\int_{B(D)}(z-V)^{-1}wdz+dw=c\int_{B(D)}(z-V|W)^{-1}wdz+dw=w,$$

where $d=1$ if the domain D contains ∞ and $d=0$ otherwise. Therefore $W\subset Z_M$, hence the spectral maximal subspace $X(T,M)$ exists and equals Z_M.

Assume now that (G_1,G_o) is an open $(S,1)$-covering of $\sigma(T)$. Since T has the $(S,1)$-decomposition property, there are $X_i\varepsilon I(T)$ such that $\sigma(T|X_i)\subset G_i$ $(i=0,1)$ and $X=X_1+X_o$. By what has been proved so far, the spectral maximal spaces $Y_1=X(T,\sigma(T|X_1))$ and $Y_o=X(T,\sigma(T|X_o)\cup S)$ exist. Clearly, $X_i\subset Y_i$, $\sigma(T|Y_i)\subset G_i$ and $X=Y_1+Y_o$. Thus T is (S,1)-decomposable.

The following lemmas are crucial in proving the main results of this paper.

Let $T\varepsilon C(X)$. If K and L are closed subsets of $\bar{C}$ such that X(T,K) and X(T,L) exist and $K\subset L$, then we shall use the notations $T_{X(T,L)}=T_L$ and $(T_L)^{X(T,K)}=T_L^K$ in what follows.

LEMMA 4.2. *Let* $T\varepsilon C(X)$ *be* (S,1)*-decomposable. Let* K *be a closed subset of* $\bar{C}$ *such that* $K\subset S^c$ *and let the closed set* $L\subset\bar{C}$ *be such that* $K\subset L$, X(T,L) *exists and* $T_L^K\varepsilon C(X(T,L)/X(T,K))$. *Then*

$$\sigma(T_L^K)\subset\overline{\sigma(T)\setminus\sigma(T_K)}.$$

PROOF. Note that the spectral maximal space X(T,K) exists (see the preceding proof). According to [10; Lemma 4],

$$\sigma(T_L^K)\subset\sigma(T_L)\cup\sigma(T_K)\subset\sigma(T).$$

Assume now that for some $z\varepsilon\bar{C}$ we have

$$z\varepsilon\sigma(T_L^K)\setminus\overline{\sigma(T)\setminus\sigma(T_K)}.$$

Then

$$z\varepsilon\sigma(T)\cap(\sigma(T)^c\cup\sigma(T_K))=\sigma(T_K)\subset K\subset S^c.$$

Since $\infty\varepsilon S^c$ implies that $T\varepsilon B(X)$, hence $\infty\notin\sigma(T)$, we obtain that z is finite. There is an open S-covering $(G_1;\ G_o)$ of $\bar{C}$ such that $z\notin G_o$, $G_o\supset S\cup\overline{\sigma(T)\setminus\sigma(T_K)}$, and $G_1\cap\overline{\sigma(T)\setminus\sigma(T_K)}=\emptyset$. Since T is (S,1)-decomposable, there are spectral maximal spaces Y_i (i=1,0) with $X=Y_1+Y_o$ and $\sigma(T|Y_i)\subset G_i$. In particular, $\sigma(T|Y_1)\subset G_1\cap\sigma(T)\subset\sigma(T_K)\subset K$, hence $Y_1\subset X(T,K)$.

Let X(T,K) be denoted by Y, and assume that $(z-T_L^K)x^Y=0^Y$. It is easily seen that $Y\subset D(T)$, thus for any $x\varepsilon x^Y$ we have $(z-T_L)x=$ $=y$ with some $y\varepsilon Y$. For any decomposition

(4) $\qquad x=x_1+x_o$ with $x_i\varepsilon Y_i$ (i=1,0),

we obtain $(z-T|Y_o)x_o=y-(z-T|Y_1)x_1\varepsilon Y\cap Y_o$, for $Y_1\subset Y$. Since T is (S,1)-decomposable and $K\subset S^c$, it can be proved as in [4; Proposition 3] for the case $T\varepsilon B(X)$ or in [20; Lemma III.4.13] that $Y\cap Y_o$ is a spectral maximal space for T, and hence for $T|Y_o$ (cf. [10; Lemma 5]). Therefore $\sigma(T|Y\cap Y_o)$ is contained in $\sigma(T|Y_o)$, thus $z\notin G_o$ and $\sigma(T|Y_o)\subset G_o$ imply that

$$x_o=(z-T|Y_o)^{-1}(z-T|Y_o)x_o\varepsilon Y\cap Y_o.$$

From (4) we obtain that $x\varepsilon Y_1+Y\subset Y$, hence $x^Y=0^Y$, therefore $z-T_L^K$ is injective.

Assume now that $y\varepsilon X(T,L)$, and the element y has the decomposition

$$y=y_1+y_o \text{ with } y_i\varepsilon Y_i \quad (i=1,0).$$

Then $y_1\varepsilon Y\subset X(T,L)$, thus $y_o\varepsilon X(T,L)$. Since $z\notin\sigma(T|Y_o)$, there is an $x\varepsilon Y_o$ such that $(z-T)x=y_o$. By assumption, $z\varepsilon\sigma(T_L^K)\subset\sigma(T_L)$. Since $X(T,L)$ is a spectral maximal space for T, it is also T-absorbing (cf.[18; p.515]). Hence $y_o\varepsilon X(T,L)$ implies that $x\varepsilon X(T,L)$. Therefore $(z-T_L^K)x^Y=y_o^Y=y^Y$, thus the operator $z-T_L^K$ is also surjective. This contradicts the assumption $z\varepsilon\sigma(T_L^K)$, so the lemma is proved.

LEMMA 4.3. *Let* $T\varepsilon C(X)$ *be* (S,1)*-decomposable. Let* G *be an open set of* $\bar{C}$ *such that* $\bar{G}\subset S^c$*, and set* $Y=X(T,\bar{G})$. *Let the closed set* $L\supset\bar{G}$ *be such that* $X(T,L)$ *exists and* $T_L^Y\varepsilon C(X(T,L)/Y)$. *Then* $\sigma(T_L^Y)\subset G^c$.

PROOF. Let $z\varepsilon G\cap\sigma(T)$. There is an open set $G_o\subset\bar{C}$ such that $z\notin G_o$ and the sets $G_1=G$ and G_o form an open (S,1)-covering of $\sigma(T)$. There are spectral maximal spaces Y_i for T such that $\sigma(T|Y_i)\subset G_i$ $(i=1,0)$ and $X=Y_1+Y_o$. If $x=y_1+y_o$, where $y_i\varepsilon Y_i$, then $\gamma_T(x)\subset\gamma_T(y_1)\cup\cup\gamma_T(y_o)$ and $\gamma_T(y_i)\subset\gamma_{T|Y_i}(y_i)\subset\sigma(T|Y_i)$ $(i=1,0)$. Hence (see [18; p.513])

$$\sigma(T)=\bigcup_{x\varepsilon X}\sigma_T(x)\subset\left(\bigcup_{i=0}^{1}\sigma(T|Y_i)\right)\cup S_T.$$

Therefore, by assumption, $z\varepsilon\sigma(T|Y_1)$. Hence $z\varepsilon\sigma(T_Y)$, for Y_1 and Y are spectral maximal spaces such that $Y_1\subset Y$. Thus we have obtained that

$$\overline{G\cap\sigma(T)}\subset\sigma(T_Y).$$

Then the preceding lemma implies that

$$\sigma(T_L^Y)\subset\overline{\sigma(T)\setminus\sigma(T_Y)}\subset G^c.$$

LEMMA 4.4. *Assume that the operator* $T\varepsilon C(X)$ *is* (S,1)*-decomposable, the closed set* F *in* C *is such that* $X(T,F)$ *exists. Let* (G_1,G_o) *be an open* $S\cap F$*-covering of* F *such that* $\bar{G}_1\cap S=\emptyset$. *Let* K *denote* $\overline{G_1\cap G_o}$*, and set* $Y=X(T,K)$ *and* $H_j=F\setminus G_k$ $(j,k=0,1$ *and* $j\neq k)$. *If* $X(T,F\cup K)$ *exists and* $F\cup K\neq\bar{C}$*, then for any* x *in* $X(T,F)$ *there are* x_1,x_o,y *in* $X(T,F\cup K)$ *such that*

$$x=x_1+x_o+y \quad (y\varepsilon Y,\ \gamma_T(x_j)\subset H_j\cup K \text{ for } j=1,0).$$

PROOF. Let $x\varepsilon X(T,F)$ and $z\varepsilon F^c\cap C$, and set $L=F\cup K$. The resolvent $(z-T_F)^{-1}$ exists and, putting

$$f(z)=(z-T_F)^{-1}x \qquad \text{for } z\varepsilon F^c\cap C$$

$$f(\infty)=\lim_{z\to\infty}(z-T_F)^{-1}x=0 \qquad \text{if } \infty\varepsilon F^c,$$

the function f is holomorphic on F^c and satisfies

$$(z-T_L)f(z)=x \text{ for } z\varepsilon F^c\cap C.$$

Hence $(z-T_L^K)f(z)^Y=x^Y$ for $z\varepsilon F^c\cap C$. By assumption, $\sigma(T_L)\subset L\neq\overline{C}$, hence T_L^K belongs to $C(X(T,L)/Y)$. Thus Lemma 4.3 yields $\sigma(T_L^K)\subset(G_1\cap G_o)^c$. Define the function $\overline{f}$ by

$$\overline{f}(z)=\begin{cases} f(z)^Y & \text{for } z\varepsilon F^c \\ (z-T_L^K)^{-1}x^Y & \text{for } z\varepsilon G_1\cap G_o\cap C \end{cases}$$

$$\overline{f}(\infty)=\lim_{z\to\infty}(z-T_L^K)^{-1}x^Y=0 \qquad \text{if } \infty\varepsilon G_1\cap G_o.$$

Then $\overline{f}:F^c\cup(G_1\cap G_o)\to X(T,L)/X(T,K)$ is well-defined, holomorphic and satisfies for any finite z in its domain

$$(z-T_L^K)\overline{f}(z)=x^Y.$$

Let D be a (not necessarily bounded) Cauchy domain such that $F\cup K\subset D$, and $\infty\varepsilon D$ if and only if $\infty\varepsilon F\cup K$. Let B denote the positively oriented boundary of the domain. Then $\sigma(T_L^K)\subset\sigma(T_L)\subset F\cup K$ implies

$$(5) \qquad x^Y=dx^Y+c\int_{B(D)}(z-T_L^K)^{-1}x^Y dz=dx^Y+c\int_{B(D)}\overline{f}(z)dz,$$

where $c=(2\pi i)^{-1}$ and d=1 or 0 according as $\infty\varepsilon D$ or not. If $\infty\varepsilon D$, then either $\infty\varepsilon H_1$ or $\infty\varepsilon H_o$ or $\infty\varepsilon(H_1\cup H_o)^c=F^c\cup(G_1\cap G_o)$. In the third case we obtain that $\infty\varepsilon\overline{G}_1\subset S^c$, hence $T\varepsilon B(X)$, for T is (S,1)-decomposable. In this case we can and will modify D so that we have d=0. The sets H_1 and H_o are closed and disjoint, thus there are Cauchy domains D_j such that $H_j\subset D_j\subset D$, $\overline{D_1}\cap\overline{D_o}=\emptyset$, and $\infty\varepsilon D_j$ if and only if $\infty\varepsilon H_j$ (j=1,0). Set

$$x_j^Y=d_jx^Y+c\int_{B(D_j)}\overline{f}(z)dz \qquad (j=1,0)$$

where $d_j=1$ or 0 according as $\infty\varepsilon H_j$ or not. Then we obtain from (5)

$$x^Y=x_1^Y+x_o^Y.$$

We clearly have $x_j^Y\varepsilon X(T,L)/X(T,K)$, and shall show that $H_j^c\subset\delta_{T_L^K}(x_j^Y)$

$(j=1,0)$. For any $v_o \in H_j^c$ there is a Cauchy domain D_j' such that $H_j \subset D_j' \subset D_j$ and for some neighborhood N of v_o we have $N \cap \overline{D_j'} = \emptyset$. Then for $v \in N \cap C$

$$(v-T_L^K)\, c \int_{B(D_j')} \overline{f}(z)(v-z)^{-1} dz = c \int_{B(D_j')} \overline{f}(z)\, dz + x^Y c \int_{B(D_j')} (v-z)^{-1} dz =$$

$$= x_j^Y ,$$

since T_L^K is closed and $(z-T_L^K)\overline{f}(z) = x^Y$. The function g_j defined by $g_j(\infty)=0$ if $\infty \in N$ and by

$$g_j(v) = c \int_{B(D_j')} \overline{f}(z)(v-z)^{-1} dz \qquad (v \in N \cap C;\ j=1,0)$$

is holomorphic for $v \in N$, so we have shown that $v_o \in \delta_{T_L^K}(x_j^Y)$.

According to Lemma 3.2, in a neighborhood $N' \subset N$ of v_o there is a holomorphic function $h_j : N' \to X(T,L)$ such that $h_j(v)^Y = g_j(v)$ and the function $(v-T)h_j(v)$ is also holomorphic for $v \in N'$. Then

$$((v-T_L)h_j(v))^Y = x_j^Y \text{ for } v \in N' \cap C. \tag{6}$$

Choose an $x_j \in x_j^Y$ and for $v \in N' \cap C$ let $r_j(v) = (v-T_L)h_j(v) - x_j$. We shall assume from now on that v_o belongs to the set $H_j^c \cap K^c$. Then $v_o \in \rho(T_K)$. By (6), $r_j(v) \in Y$, hence for any v in some (possibly punched) neighborhood $N'' \subset N' \cap C$ of v_o we have

$$(v-T)(h_j(v) - (v-T_K)^{-1} r_j(v)) = x_j .$$

According to the choice of the function $h_j(v)$, the function $r_j(v)$ is also holomorphic for $v \in N'$. If $\infty = v_o \in H_j^c \cap K^c$, then $(v-T_K)^{-1}$ is holomorphic at ∞. Thus in any case $\gamma_T(x_j) \subset H_j \cup K$ and $x = x_1 + x_o + y$ for some $y \in Y$. The proof is complete.

LEMMA 4.5. *Assume that under the conditions of Lemma 4.4 the set* F *contains* S_T *, further for some* $w \in X(T, F \cup K)$ *we have* $\gamma_T(w) \subset \overline{G_1}$. *Then* $w \in X(T, \overline{G_1}) + X_T(S_T)$.

PROOF. By assumption, we have $\gamma_T(w) \subset (F \cup K) \cap \overline{G}_1$. If we set $H_1 = (F \cup K) \cap \overline{G_1}$ and $H_o = S_T$, then a reasoning closely resembling (even in notations) a part of the preceding proof yields that

$$w = dw + c \int_{B(D)} (z-T_L)^{-1} w\, dz = w_1 + w_o ,$$

where $w_j = d_j w + c \int_{B(D_j)} f(z)\, dz$ $(j=1,0)$ and $f = (H_1 \cup H_o)^c \to X$ is the uniquely determined T-associated function for w, satisfying $(z-T)f(z)=w$. Further, we have like before $\gamma_T(w_j)\subset H_j$. Hence $w_o \varepsilon X_T(S_T)$.

Let $(Q_1;Q_o)$ be an open S-covering of $\sigma(T)$ such that $Q_1 \supset H_1$ and $\overline{Q}_o \cap H_1 = \emptyset$. Since T is (S,1)-decomposable,

$$w=x_1+x_o \text{ where } x_i \varepsilon X(T,\overline{Q_i}).$$

We may assume that $B(D_1)\subset H_1^c \cap \overline{Q}_o^c$. Then in a neighborhood of $B(D_1)$ the T-associated functions $\overline{x_j}$ for x_j exist and $f(z)=\overline{x_1}(z)+\overline{x_o}(z)$. Since $\overline{x_o}$ is holomorphic for z in D_1, we have

$$d_1 x_o + c\int_{B(D_1)} \overline{x}_o(z)dz=0 .$$

Hence

$$w_1=d_1x_1+c\int_{B(D_1)} \overline{x_1}(z)dz.$$

As in the proof of Lemma 4.3, we obtain that

$$\sigma(T)=(\bigcup_{i=0}^{1} \sigma(T|X(T,\overline{Q_i})))\cup S_T .$$

Let $z\varepsilon B(D_1)$. Then $z\varepsilon \overline{Q}_o^c$, therefore

$$z\varepsilon\sigma(T|X(T,\overline{Q_1}))\cup\rho(T).$$

Since $X(T,\overline{Q_1})$ is a spectral maximal space for T, it is T-absorbing ([18; p.515]). Thus if $z\varepsilon\sigma(T|X(T,\overline{Q}_1))$, then the equality

$$(z-T)\overline{x_1}(z)=x_1$$

implies $\overline{x_1}(z)\varepsilon X(T,\overline{Q_1})$. On the other hand, if $z\varepsilon\rho(T|X(T,\overline{Q}_1))\cap\rho(T)$, then the above equality clearly yields the same conclusion.

Therefore $w_1\varepsilon X(T,\overline{Q_1})$ for any open set Q_1 such that $Q_1\supset H_1$ and $\overline{Q_1}\subset S^c$. By the results of [9], this implies that $w_1\varepsilon X(T,H_1)$. Since $X(T,H_1)\subset X(T,\overline{G_1})$, the proof is complete.

THEOREM 4.2. *Let* $T\varepsilon C(X)$ *be* (S,1)*-decomposable. Then* T *is* S*-decomposable. Further, for any closed set* F, *containing* S, *and for any open* S*-covering* $(D_1,\ldots,D_n;D_o)$ *of* F

$$X(T,F)\subset \sum_{j=0}^{n} X(T,\overline{D_j}). \tag{7}$$

PROOF. First we prove the last statement for the value n=1. If $F=\overline{C}$, then $X(T,F)=X$, thus (7) is true, for T is (S,1)-decomposable. If $F\neq\overline{C}$ and $(D_1;D_o)$ is an open S-covering of F, then there is another open S-covering $(G_1;G_o)$ of F such that $\overline{G_j}\subset D_j$ and,with the notation $K=\overline{G_1 \cap G_o}$, we have $F \cup K \neq \mathbb{C}$. Since $F \supset S$, the spectral maximal spaces $X(T,F)$ and $X(T,F\cup K)$ exist. Thus Lemmas 4.4 and 4.5 are applicable. With the notations of Lemma 4.4, for any x in $X(T,F)$ there are $x_1, x_o, y \in X(T,F\cup K)$ such that

$$x=x_1+x_o+y \quad (y \in Y,\ \gamma_T(x_j) \subset H_j \cup K \text{ for } j=1,0).$$

Here $\gamma_T(x_1) \cup \gamma_T(y) \subset \overline{G_1}$, thus Lemma 4.5 implies that $x_1+y \in X(T,\overline{G_1})+X_T(S_T)$. Further, $\gamma_T(x_o) \subset \overline{G_o}$ implies $x_o \in X_T(\overline{G_o}) \subset X(T,\overline{D_o})$, therefore $x \in X(T,\overline{D_1})+X(T,\overline{D_o})$.

Assume now that (7) is valid for n covering sets, and the covering $(D_1,\dots,D_n;D_o)$ is given. There is an open S-covering $(G_1,\dots,G_n;\ G_o)$ of F such that $\overline{G_j} \subset D_j$ for $j=0,1,\dots,n$. Since $(G_1,\dots,G_{n-1};\ G_o \cup G_n)$ is an (S,n-1)-covering of F, we have

$$X(T,F) \subset \sum_{j=1}^{n-1} X(T,\overline{G_j})+X(T,\overline{G_o \cup G_n}).$$

Since $(D_n;D_o)$ is an (S,1)-covering of $\overline{G_o \cup G_n}$, and the latter set contains S, the preceding paragraph yields

$$X(T,\overline{G_o \cup G_n}) \subset X(T,\overline{D_n})+X(T,\overline{D_o}).$$

Since $X(T,\overline{G_j}) \subset X(T,\overline{D_j})$, we obtain (7) for n+1 covering sets.

Finally, if we set in (7) $F=\sigma(T)$, we see that T is S-decomposable.

Let $T \in C(X)$ and let $S(T)$ denote the family of all closed sets S such that $S_T \subset S \subset \sigma(T)$ and T is S-decomposable. If there is $S^* \in S(T)$ such that $S^* \subset S$ for any $S \in S(T)$, then S^* is called the *spectral residuum* of T.

THEOREM 4.3. *The spectral residuum exists for each operator* T *in* C(X).

PROOF. We have $\sigma(T) \in S(T)$, hence the family S(T) is nonvoid. Since the extended spectrum $\sigma(T)$ is compact in the topology of $\overline{\mathbb{C}}$, we obtain, as in the case when $T \in B(X)$ ([12]) that any totally ordered (with respect to the relation $\subset$) subfamily of S(T) has a lower bound (its intersection) in S(T). By Zorn's lemma, there is a minimal element in S(T). To complete the proof we shall show that if $S_1, S_2 \in S(T)$, then $S=S_1 \cap S_2$ also belongs to S(T).

Let $(G;G_S)$ be an open S-covering of $\sigma(T)$. Then there are open sets G_k, G_{S_k} (k=1,2) with the following properties (cf.[11]):

$$G_k \subset G,\ \overline{G}_k \cap S_k = \emptyset,\ G_k \cup G_{S_k} \supset G,\ G_{S_k} \supset S_k \cup G_S,\ (k=1,2),\ \overline{G_{S_1}} \cap \overline{G_{S_2}} = \overline{G_S}.$$

In particular, $(G_k;G_{S_k})$ is an open S_k-covering of $\sigma(T)$. Thus there is an open set G'_{S_2} such that $\overline{G'_{S_2}} \subset G_{S_2}$ and $(G_2;G'_{S_2})$ is an S_2-covering of $\sigma(T)$. Since $S_2 \in S(T)$,

$$X = X(T,\overline{G_2}) + X_T(\overline{G'_{S_2}}).$$

Since S_1 also is in $S(T)$ and $\overline{G} \cap S = \emptyset$, a part of the proof of [11; Theorem 1] shows that the spectral maximal space $X(T,\overline{G})$ exists. Therefore

(8) $$X = X(T,\overline{G}) + X_T(\overline{G'_{S_2}}).$$

Define the sets F and G_o by

$$F = \overline{G'_{S_2}} \cap \sigma(T),\quad G_o = G_{S_1} \cap G_{S_2}.$$

By [8; Lemma 5], the subspace $X(T,F)$ exists; further we have the following relations:

$$S_1 \cap F \subset G_{S_1} \cap G_{S_2} = G_o \subset \overline{G_S},$$

$$G_1 \cup G_o \supset (G_1 \cup G_{S_1}) \cap G_{S_2} \supset \sigma(T) \cap F = F.$$

Thus $(G_1;G_o)$ is an open $S_1 \cap F$-covering of F such that $\overline{G_1} \cap S_1 = \emptyset$. We shall show that

(9) $$X(T,F) \subset X(T,\overline{G_1}) + X_T(\overline{G_o}).$$

If $F=\overline{C}$ then $X(T,F)=X$, and $(G_1;G_o)$ is an S_1-covering of $\overline{C}$. Since T is S_1-decomposable, (9) is valid. If $F \neq \overline{C}$, we may assume, replacing the sets G_1, G_o by smaller open sets if necessary (cf. the proof of Theorem 4.2), that, using the notation $K=\overline{G_1 \cap G_o}$, we have $F \cup K \neq \overline{C}$. Since $F \supset S_2$ and the operator T is S_2-decomposable, the spectral maximal space $X(T,F\cup K) = X_T(F \cup K)$ exists (cf. [8; Lemma 5]). With the notations of Lemma 4.4, for any x in $X(T,F)$

$$x = x_1 + x_o + y \qquad (y \in Y,\ \gamma_T(x_j) \subset H_j \cup K \text{ for } j=1,0).$$

Since $F \supset S_2 \supset S_T$, Lemma 4.5 is applicable and yields that $x_1 + y \in X(T,\overline{G_1}) + X_T(S_T)$. By assumption, $S_T \subset S_1 \cap S_2 \subset G_o$.

Since

$$\sigma_T(x_o) = \gamma_T(x_o) \cup S_T \subset \overline{G_o},$$

we obtain that $x \in X(T,\overline{G_1}) + X_T(\overline{G_o})$. Thus (9) is proved and yields

$$X_T(\overline{G'_{S_2}})=X(T,F)\subset X(T,\overline{G})+X_T(\overline{G_S}).$$

Taking (8) into account, we have

$$X=X(T,\overline{G})+X(T,\overline{G_S}),$$

hence T is (S,1)-decomposable. By Theorem 4.2, T is S-decomposable, which ends the proof.

REMARKS. We can deduce the assertion of [11; Theorem 1]with the help of Theorem 4.3, i.e. we can prove that there is a smallest one (called the strong spectral residuum) among the sets S for which T is strongly S-decomposable (cf. [12]). The spectral residuum $S^*(T)$ of T is, in general properly (cf.[1]), contained in the strong spectral residuum $S^{**}(T)$ of T.

$S^*(T)$ is void if and only if the operator T is decomposable (hence bounded). For an unbounded closed spectral or prespectral operator T we have $S^*(T)=S^{**}(T)=\{\infty\}$. If T is the generator operator of a strongly but not uniformly continuous, uniformly bounded group of operators, then $S^*(T)=\{\infty\}$ ([10]). For any T in C(X)

$$S^*(T)\supset S_T\cup\overline{Q(T)\cap\sigma(T)}.$$

Hence if T is a nonselfadjoint symmetric operator or a nonunitary isometry in Hilbert space, then $S^*(T)=\sigma(T)$ [14].
This may be remarkable, for selfadjoint and unitary operators have been the archetypes of spectral operators.

Finally, we note that this notion of the spectral residuum is different from that given by F.-H.Vasilescu [19] for a certain class of operators.

REFERENCES

1. Albrecht, E.: On two questions of I.Colojoară and C.Foiaş, *Manuscripta Math.* 25 (1978), 1-15.

2. Albrecht, E.: On decomposable operators, *Integral Equations and Operator Theory*, 2 (1979), 1-10.

3. Bacalu, I.: S-decomposable operators in Banach spaces, *Rev. Roumaine Math.Pures Appl.* 20 (1975), 1101-1107.

4. Bacalu, I.; Vasilescu,F.-H.: A property of (S,1)-decomposable operators (Romanian), *Stud.Cerc.Mat.* 29 (1977), 441-446.

5. Colojoară, I.; Foiaş, C.: *Theory of generalized spectral operators*, Gordon and Breach, New York, 1968.

6. Erdelyi, I.: Unbounded operators with spectral decomposition properties, *Acta Sci.Math.(Szeged)*, to appear.

7. Lange, R.: On generalization of decomposability, preprint.

8. Nagy, B.: Closed S-decomposable operators, *Ann.Univ.Sci. Budapest. Eötvös, Sect.Math.* 22-23 (1979-1980), 143-149.

9. Nagy, B.: S-spectral capacities and closed operators, *Studia Sci.Math. Hungar.*, to appear.

10. Nagy, B.: Semigroups of operators and decomposability, preprint.

11. Nagy, B.: A strong spectral residuum for every closed operator, *Illinois J.Math.* 24 (1980), 173-179.

12. Nagy, B.: On S-decomposable operators, *J.Operator Theory*, 2 (1979), 277-286.

13. Nagy, B.: Operators with the spectral decomposition property are decomposable, *Studia Sci.Math.Hungar.*, to appear.

14. Nagy, B.: Local spectral theory, *Acta Math.Sci.Hungar.*, to appear.

15. Radjabalipour, M.: Equivalence of decomposable and 2-decomposable operators, *Pacific J.Math.* 77 (1978), 243-247.

16. Scroggs, J.E.: Invariant subspaces of a normal operator, *Duke Math.J.* 26 (1959), 95-111.

17. Taylor, A.E.: *Introduction to functional analysis*, Wiley, New York, 1958.

18. Vasilescu, F.-H.: Residually decomposable operators in Banach spaces, *Tohoku Math.J.* 21 (1969), 509-522.

19. Vasilescu, F.-H.: Residual properties for closed operators on Fréchet spaces, *Illinois J.Math.* 15 (1971), 377-386.

20. Vasilescu, F.-H.: *Multidimensional analytic functional calculus* (Romanian), Editura Acad.R.S.Romania, Bucharest, 1979.

Béla Nagy
Department of Mathematics,
Faculty of Chemistry,
University of Technology,
Budapest, Stoczek u.2.H, II,
Hungary.

TWO APPLICATIONS OF HANKEL OPERATORS

N.K.Nikolskii

This report contains some new applications of Hankel operators (acting on the Hardy space H^2), namely a short proof of a special case of the Sarason-Sz.-Nagy-Foiaş lifting theorem and some results about classical exponential bases $\{e^{i\lambda_n x}\}$ in the space $L^2(0,a)$.

INTRODUCTION

A Hankel operator is (by definition) an operator from a Hilbert space to another one whose matrix (a_{ij}) with respect to some orthonormal basis has constant matrix entries on the adjoint diagonals, i.e. $a_{i,j}=c_{i+j}$ for a sequence $\{c_n\}$ $(c_n\in\mathbb{C})$.

We may think without loss of generality that this pair of Hilbert spaces is (H^2,H^2_-), H^2 being the usual Hardy class, $H^2 \overset{\text{def}}{=} \{ f\in L^2(\mathbb{T}):\hat{f}(n)=0,\ n<0\}$, $H^2_- \overset{\text{def}}{=} L^2(\mathbb{T})\ominus H^2$, where $\mathbb{T}=\{\zeta\in\mathbb{C}:|\zeta|=1\}$ is the unit circle, $L^2(\mathbb{T})=L^2(\mathbb{T},m)$, m is the normalized Lebesgue measure on $\mathbb{T}$, $\hat{f}(n)=\int_{\mathbb{T}} fz^{-n}dm$ $(n\in\mathbb{Z};\ z(\zeta)\equiv\zeta)$ are the Fourier coefficients of the function f. In this case an operator A (defined for the present only on the set $\mathcal{P}_A$ of polynomials of the complex variable z) is a Hankel operator with respect to the bases $\{z^n\}_{n\geq 0}$, $\{z^{-n}\}_{n\geq 1}$, iff

$$(1)\qquad Azp=P_-zAp,\qquad p\in\mathcal{P}_A,$$

where $P_-f \overset{\text{def}}{=} \sum_{n<0}\hat{f}(n)z^n$, $f\in L^2(\mathbb{T})$ is the orthogonal projection onto the space H^2_-.

The spectral theory of Hankel operators is based on the classical theorem of Z.Nehari (1957).

NEHARI'S THEOREM. *A Hankel operator* A *is bounded iff there exists an essentially bounded function* f $(f\in L^\infty(\mathbb{T}))$ *such that*

$$A=H_f;\quad H_f x \overset{\text{def}}{=} P_-fx,\quad x\in H^2.$$

Moreover, $\|H_f\| = \operatorname{dist}_{L^\infty(\mathbb{T})}(f, H^\infty)$, *where* $H^\infty = L^\infty(\mathbb{T}) \cap H^2$.

SKETCH OF PROOF. The equality (1) implies that

$$Az^n = P_- z^n A1 \quad (n \geq 0),$$
$$Ap = P_- pA1 \quad (p \in \mathcal{P}_A),$$
$$\|A\| = \sup\{|(Ap, \bar{q})| : p, q \in \mathcal{P}_A, \quad \|p\|_2 \leq 1, \|q\|_2 \leq 1, \hat{q}(0) = 0\} =$$
$$= \sup\left|\int_{\mathbb{T}} pqA1\,dm\right| = \inf\{\|g\|_{L^\infty} : \hat{g}(n) = (A1)^\wedge(n),\ n < 0\},$$

via the Hahn-Banach theorem and the density of the set $\{pq : p, q \in \mathcal{P}_A, \|p\|_2 \leq 1, \|q\|_2 \leq 1\}$ in the unit ball of the Hardy space

$$H^1 = \{f \in L^1(\mathbb{T}) : \hat{f}(n) = 0, \quad n < 0\}.$$

PART I. THE LIFTING THEOREM

From the simple theorem derived above and its multidimensional analogue one can deduce very easily an essential special case of the lifting theorem of D.Sarason, B.Sz.-Nagy and C.Foiaş. To do this we need to know some initial notions of the Sz.-Nagy-Foiaş model theory.

So, let E be a Hilbert space, $H^2(E)$ the corresponding Hardy class of E-valued L^2-functions on the circle $\mathbb{T}$ and θ an inner from both sides operator-valued function with the values in $L(E)$ ($\overset{\text{def}}{=}$ all linear bounded operators from E to E); that is the values $\theta(\zeta)$ are unitaries for a.e. $\zeta \in \mathbb{T}$, and θ is holomorphic in the following sense: $\theta H^2(E) \subset H^2(E)$. Then the space K_θ,

$$K_\theta \overset{\text{def}}{=} H^2(E) \ominus \theta H^2(E),$$

is called the model space and the operator T_θ,

$$T_\theta x = P_\theta zx, \quad x \in K_\theta,$$

the model operator, P_θ being the orthogonal projection on K_θ. In fact any contraction T of a Hilbert space of the "class C_{oo}" (i.e. such that $T^n \to 0$, $T^{*n} \to 0$ in the strong operator topology) is unitarily equivalent to some (essentially unique) model operator of the type T_θ.

The following theorem is the above mentioned part of the lifting theorem (the full statement deals with the model operators with not inner but arbitrary contractive characteristic functions θ).

THEOREM. *Let* θ *be an inner from both sides* $L(E)$*-valued function and let* $A\in L(K_\theta)$. *Then*

$$AT=TA \Leftrightarrow \exists F\in H^\infty(L(E)): F\theta H^2(E)\subset\theta H^2(E),$$
$$Ax=P_\theta Fx \qquad (x\in K_\theta).$$

Moreover, $||A||=\mathrm{dist}_{L^\infty}(F,\theta H^\infty(L(E)))$.

PROOF. For any operator A acting in the space K_θ introduce the operator B by the formulae

$$B=\theta^*AP_\theta, \quad B:H^2(E)\to H^2_-(E).$$

LEMMA. $AT_\theta=T_\theta A \Leftrightarrow B$ *is a Hankel operator.*

If lemma is already proved we deduce from the vector form of the Nehari theorem (the L.Page's theorem [1]; see for a simple direct proof [2], p.244-246) that there exists a function $f, f\in L^\infty(L(E))$ such that $B=P_-f|H^2(E)$. Then

$$Ax=\theta Bx=\theta P_-fx=\theta P_-\theta^*\theta fx=P_\theta Fx$$

for $x\in K_\theta$, where $F=\theta f$. The function F has the desired properties:

$$F\theta H^2(E)=\theta f\theta H^2(E)\subset\theta H^2(E), \text{ because of } P_-f\theta H^2(E)=B\theta H^2=\{0\},$$

and $FH^2(E)\subset H^2(E)$ because of

$$Fx=\theta fx=\theta P_+fx+\theta P_-fx,\ x\in H^2(E),\ (P_+ \overset{\mathrm{def}}{=\!=} I-P_-)$$

and $\theta(I-P_-)fx\in H^2(E)$ (easy), $\theta P_-fx=\theta Bx=Ax\in K_\theta\subset H^2(E)$.

The other assertions of the theorem are obvious.

PROOF THE LEMMA. "$\Rightarrow$". Let $x\in K_\theta$. Then

$$AP_\theta zx=P_\theta zAx=\theta P_-\theta^*zAx=\theta P_-z\theta^*Ax,$$
$$\theta^*AP_\theta zx=P_-z\theta^*Ax,$$
$$Bzx=P_-zBx.$$

But both operators Bz, P_-zB vanish on the space $\theta H^2(E)$. Hence B is a Hankel operator.

"$\Leftarrow$" The reverse reasoning.

PART II. EXPONENTIAL BASES

One of interesting problems of the classical harmonic analysis is to describe those sets of frequencies $\{\lambda_n\}$ for which the exponential family $\{e^{i\lambda_n x}\}$ forms a Riesz base of the space $L^2(I)$, I being an interval of the real axis $\mathbb{R}$.

A *Riesz base* of a Hilbert space H is to be understood here as a family $\{e_n\}$ of vectors of H such that

$$\text{(2)} \qquad \operatorname{span}\{e_n\}=H$$

$$c\sum_n \|a_n e_n\|^2 \le \|\Sigma a_n e_n\|^2 \le C\sum_n \|a_n e_n\|^2$$

for some constants c,C and for all finite families of complex numbers a_n. This definition is much more general and convenient than the usual one (compare for example with [3], Ch.VI). It is a well-known fact of the general Hilbert space theory that the following assertions are equivalent: (i) $\{e_n\}$ is a Riesz base, (ii) $\{e_n\}$ is an unconditional base, (iii) $\{e_n\}$ is complete (i.e. (2) holds) and $\inf \text{Angle}\{\operatorname{span}(e_n : n\in N), \operatorname{span}(e_n : n\notin N)\}>0$ where "inf" is taken over all subsets N of the set of indices and "Angle" means the angle between subspaces of a Hilbert space (see [3]).

The investigations (in the spirit of the present part of the report) were started by B.S.Pavlov; his article [4] is an important contribution to this domain and contains essential ideas and the first necessary and sufficient conditions for $\{e^{i\lambda_n x}\}$ to be a Riesz base under the assumption $\sup_{\lambda\in\Lambda}|\operatorname{Im}\lambda|<+\infty$.

HELSON-SZEGÖ THEOREM AND HANKEL OPERATORS

The principal source of the role played by Hankel operators in the problem of exponential basis is the following part of the well-known theorem of Helson and Szegö [5],[2]: *if* $w\in L^1(\mathbb{T})$, $w\ge 0$, *and* $d\mu = w\,dm$, *then*

$$\text{Angle}\{\operatorname{span}_{L^2(\mu)}(z^n : n<0), \operatorname{span}_{L^2(\mu)}(z^n : n\ge 0)\}>0 \Leftrightarrow$$

$$\Leftrightarrow \|H_{\bar h/h}\|<1,$$

h *being the outer function (in Beurling sense, see* [6],[2]) *with* $|h|^2=w$ (the requirement of the existence of h is included into the assertion of the right hand part of the last implication).

There are equivalent forms of these conditions, for example

$$||H_{\bar{h}/h}||<1 \Leftrightarrow w=e^{u+\tilde{v}};\ u,v \text{ real } L^\infty\text{-functions},$$
$$||v||_\infty<\frac{\pi}{2} \Leftrightarrow \sup_I \left(\frac{1}{|I|}\int_I w\right)\left(\frac{1}{|I|}\int_I \frac{1}{w}\right)<\infty,$$

where $\tilde{v}$ stands for the harmonic conjugation and I varies over all intervals of the real axis.

The exponential bases problem needs some estimations of angles similar to those of the Helson-Szegö theorem.

SOME REDUCTIONS

Now we begin to describe our principal results concerning exponential bases. First of all we note some isomorphisms of the $L^2(I)$-spaces preserving the exponential bases problem but changing the set $\Lambda=\{\lambda_n\}$ of frequencies or the basic interval I:

$$f(x)\to e^{i\mu x}f(x) \qquad (\Lambda\to\Lambda+\mu),\quad \mu\in\mathbb{C}$$
$$f(x)\to f(x-b) \qquad (\Lambda\to\Lambda,\ I\to I+b),\ b\in\mathbb{R}$$
$$f(x)\to f(a-x) \quad \text{if } I=(0,a) \quad (\Lambda\to-\Lambda),\ a>0.$$

Hence, any family of exponentials $\{e^{i\lambda x}\}_{\lambda\in\Lambda}$ in a space $L^2(I)$ with a set of frequencies lying in some half-plane $\{\zeta:\operatorname{Im}\zeta>\gamma\}$, $\{\zeta:\operatorname{Im}\zeta<\gamma\}$, $\gamma\in\mathbb{R}$ can be replaced by these isomorphisms with the family $\{e^{i\lambda x}\}_{\lambda\in\Lambda}$ in the space $L^2(0,a)$, $a>0$, with

$$\Lambda\subset\mathbb{C}_\delta \overset{\text{def}}{=} \{\zeta:\operatorname{Im}\zeta>\delta\},\quad \delta>0.$$

CARLESON CONDITION

The following theorem introduces into our problem the well-known Carleson condition.

THEOREM. *If $\Lambda\subset\mathbb{C}_0$ and the family of exponentials $\{e^{i\lambda x}\}_{\lambda\in\Lambda}$ forms a Riesz base in its closed linear span then Λ is a Carleson set, i.e.*

$$\text{(C)}\qquad \inf_{\lambda'\in\Lambda}\prod_{\lambda\in\Lambda\setminus\{\lambda'\}}\left|\frac{\lambda'-\lambda}{\lambda'-\bar{\lambda}}\right|>0.$$

There exist more geometrical forms of the Carleson condition (C), for example $\Lambda\in$ (C) iff 1) the discs $D(\lambda,\varepsilon\operatorname{Im}\lambda)$, $\lambda\in\Lambda$, are pairwise disjoint for some $\varepsilon>0$;

2) $\sup\{ \sum_{\substack{\lambda\in\Lambda \\ |\lambda-x|<r}} \frac{\operatorname{Im}\lambda}{r} : x\in\mathbb{R},\ r>0\}<\infty$. See for this matter [2] , for example.

The theorem above implies a simple but useful corollary.

COROLLARY. *If* $\Lambda\subset\mathbb{C}_\delta$, $\delta>0$, *then the following assertions are equivalent:* (i) *the family* $\{e^{i\lambda x}\}_{\lambda\in\Lambda}$ *forms a Riesz base in the space* $L^2(0,a)$; (ii) $\lambda\in(C)$ *and the projection map* $f\to\chi_{(0,a)}f$ *is an isomorphism from span*$_{L^2(0,\infty)}(e^{i\lambda x}:\lambda\in\Lambda)$ *onto* $L^2(0,a)$.

MAIN THEOREM

Thus the problem consists now in finding conditions for the above mentioned map to be an isomorphism. The answer is based on the following simple geometrical lemma.

LEMMA. *If* M,N *are subspaces of a Hilbert space then the restriction* $P_M|N$ *is an isomorphism of the subspace* N *onto the subspace* M *iff*

(3) $$||P_M^{\perp}P_N||<1, \qquad ||P_N P_M^{\perp}||<1.$$

For the convenience of computations we may use the inverse Fourier transform in the situation of the corollary. Because of the famous Paley-Wiener theorem the space $L^2(0,\infty)$ becomes the Hardy space $H^2(\mathbb{C}_o)$ (in the upper half-plane $\mathbb{C}_o$), the space span$_{L^2(0,\infty)}(e^{i\lambda x}:\lambda\in\Lambda)$ becomes the model space K_B (in half-plane $\mathbb{C}_o$), where $B=\prod_{\lambda\in\Lambda}\frac{z-\lambda}{z-\bar\lambda}c_\lambda$ is the Blaschke product with the zero set Λ, and the space $L^2(0,a)$ becomes the space K_{θ_a}, $\theta_a=e^{iaz}$.

Now it is clear how to compute the norms from (3) in our case $M=K_{\theta_a}$, $N=K_B$:

$$||P_{\theta_a}^{\perp}P_B||=||\theta_a P_+\bar\theta_a|K_B||=||P_+\bar\theta_a|K_B||=||\theta_a(T_B)||=||H_{\theta_a\bar B}||=\operatorname{dist}(\theta_a\bar B,H^\infty).$$

Hence a part of the next theorem follows

THEOREM. *Let* $\lambda\in\mathbb{C}_\delta$, $\delta>0$. *The following assertions are equivalent:*

1. $\{e^{i\lambda x}\}_{\lambda\in\Lambda}$ *is a Riesz base in the space* $L^2(0,a)$, $a>0$.

2. $\Lambda\in(C)$, $\|H_{\theta_a\bar{B}}\|<1$, $\|H_{\bar{B}\theta_a}\|<1$.

3. $\Lambda\in(C)$, dist $(\theta_a\bar{B},H^\infty)<1$, dist $(\bar{\theta}_a B,H^\infty)<1$.

4. $\Lambda\in(C)$, *the Toeplitz operator* $T_{\theta_a\bar{B}} \overset{\text{def}}{=} P_+\theta_a\bar{B}|H^2$ *is invertible.*

5. *There exists a function* h, $h\in L^\infty(\mathbb{R})^a$ *such that* $\|\arg\bar{\theta}_a B-\tilde{h}\|_\infty<\frac{\pi}{2}$, $\arg\bar{\theta}_a B$ *being a function satisfying* $\exp i \arg\bar{\theta}_a B=\bar{\theta}_a B$.

From this theorem one can deduce all known sufficient conditions for $\{e^{i\lambda x}\}_{\lambda\in\Lambda}$ to be a Riesz base of the space $L^2(0,a)$. See for these matters [4], [7],[8].

CONCLUDING REMARKS.

1. There exist examples of frequencies sets Λ for which the assertions of the last theorem are true and $\sup_{\lambda\in\Lambda} \operatorname{Im}\lambda=\infty$. (V.I.Vasjunin, S.A.Vinogradov; see [8]).

2. There is a least one a>0 such that the family $\{e^{i\lambda x}\}_{\lambda\in\Lambda}$, $\Lambda\subset\mathbb{C}_0$, forms a Riesz base in its span in the space $L^2(0,a)$ iff $\Lambda\in(C)$.

3. If $\Lambda\in(C)$ and $\lim_{\lambda\in\Lambda}\operatorname{Im}\lambda=+\infty$ then $\operatorname{codim}\operatorname{span}_{L^2(0,a)}(e^{i\lambda x}:\lambda\in\Lambda)=\infty$ for every a,a>0.

4. All assertions of the part II of the report can be generalized to the case of an arbitrary inner function θ (instead of θ_a) and a family of reproducing kernels $\{\frac{1-\overline{\theta(\lambda)}\theta}{\lambda-z}\}_{\lambda\in\Lambda}$ of the space K_θ (instead of $\{e^{i\lambda x}\}_{\lambda\in\Lambda}$).

5. One can find a great number of details, corollaries, special cases, connections with other parts of mathematics and so on in the papers [4],[7],[9],[2],[8].

REFERENCES

1. Page, L.B.: Applications of the Sz.-Nagy and Foiaş lifting theorem, *Indiana Univ.Math.J.* 20(1970),135-145.
2. Никольский,Н.К.: Лекции оъ операторе сдвига, М.,Наука,1980.
3. Гохберг,И.Ц; Крейн,М.Г.: Введение в теорию линейных несамосопрежённых операторов в гильбертовом пространстве, М.,Наука, 1965.

4. Павлов, Б.С.: Базисность системы экспонент и условие Макенхоупта, Докл.АН СССР 247 (1979), №.1, 37-40.

5. Helson, H.; Szegö, G.: A problem in prediction theory, *Ann. Mat.Pura Appl.* 51(1960), 107-138.

6. Hoffman, K.: *Banach spaces of analytic functions*, Englewood Cliffs, N.J., 1962.

7. Хрущёв, С.В.: Теоремы возмущения гля базисов из экспонент и условие Макенхоупта, Докл. АН СССР 247 (1979), №.1, 44-48.

8. Никольский, Н.К.; Павлов, Б.С.; Хрущёв, С.В.: Базисы Рисса из экспонент и значений воспроизводящих ядер модельных пространств, Препринт, ЛОМИ, 1980.

9. Никольский, Н.К.: Базисы из экспонент и значений воспроизводящих ядер, Дакл. АН СССР, июнь, 1980.

N.K.Nikolskii
Steklov Math.Institute,
Leningrad Branch,
Fontanka 27, 191001 Leningrad,
U.S.S.R.

A ROHLIN TYPE THEOREM FOR GROUPS ACTING ON VON NEUMANN ALGEBRAS

Adrian Ocneanu

In classical ergodic theory one considers an ergodic automorphism of a measure space; a major problem is the classification of such structures. A first step towards such a result is the Rohlin tower theorem, according to which the space may be divided into any given number of measurable subsets, cyclically permuted by the automorphism modulo some small measure sets.

A first way of generalizing this result consists of the consideration of a locally compact group G acting freely by automorphisms of a measure space. The theorem was proved for $G=\mathbb{Z}^n$ by Katznelson and Weiss [3], for discrete abelian G by Conze [2], for $G=\mathbb{R}^n$ by Lind [4], for discrete solvable G by Ornstein and Weiss [5] and for solvable or almost connected amenable locally compact G by Series [6].

A new stage of generality appears in the work of A.Connes [1], where a noncommutative Rohlin type theorem is used for the classification of the automorphisms of a finite von Neumann algebra. The theorem is stated for an aperiodic automorphism of a von Neumann algebra which leaves fixed a faithful normal trace.

In the sequel we extend the result of Connes to several commuting automorphisms of a von Neumann algebra; in fact for finite extensions of $\mathbb{Z}^n$. From the quoted paper of Connes we use the theorem of characterisation of properly outer automorphisms, but for the rest our proof is different, even for one automorphism , of the proof given there, being partly inspired by the proofs in [4], [5] for measure spaces.

Let M be a von Neumann algebra and Aut M its automorphisms. We recall ([1]) that for $g \in \mathrm{Aut}\, M$, there is a largest (central) projection $p(g)$, left fixed by g, on which g is inner; g is called *properly outer* if $p(g)=0$. A group G acting on a von Neumann algebra is said *to act freely* if $p(g)=0$ for any $g\neq 1$.

A nonvoid finite subset K of G is called *a paving set of* G if one can choose right translations of it to cover without overlappings G.

The main purposes of the paper are the following two theorems.

1. THEOREM. *Let* G *be a group, finite extension of a finitely generated abelian group. Suppose* M *is a von Neumann algebra,* τ *is a normal trace on* $M, \tau(1)=1$, *and let* G *act freely on* M *preserving* τ. *Then for any paving set* K *of* G *and any* $\delta>0$ *there is a partition of unity* $(f_k)_{k\in K}$ *in* M *such that*

$$||gf_k-f_{gk}||_1\leq\delta \text{ for all } k\in K,\ g\in G \text{ with } gk\in K$$

(*where for* $x\in M$, $||x||_1=\tau(|x|)$).

If G is a group and S is a subgrup of G, then G/S will denote the left quotient space of G modulo S.

2. THEOREM. *Let* G *be a group, finite extension of a finitely generated abelian group, and let* S *be a finite index subgroup of* G. *If* M *is a von Neumann algebra,* τ *a normal trace on* M *with* $\tau(1)=1$ *and if* G *acts freely on* M *preserving* τ, *then for any* $\delta>0$ *and for any finite subset* G_1 *of* G *there is a partition of unity* $(f_i)_{i\in G/S}$ *in* M *such that*

$$||gf_i-f_{gi}||_1\leq\delta \text{ for all } g\in G_1,\ i\in G/S.$$

3. COROLLARY. (A. Connes, [1]). *Let* M *be a finite von Neumann algebra,* τ *a faithful normal trace on* M, $\tau(1)=1$, *and* θ *an aperiodic automorphism of* M *which preserves* τ.

For any integer n *and any* $\delta>0$ *there exists a partition of unity* $(f_j)_{j\in 1,\dots,n}$ *in* M *such that*

$$||\theta(f_1)-f_2||_2\leq\delta,\dots,\ ||\theta(f_j)-f_{j+1}||_2\leq\delta,\dots,\ ||\theta(f_n)-f_1||_2\leq\delta$$

(*where* $||x||_2=\tau(x^*x)^{1/2}$, $x\in M$).

PROOF. We take $G=\mathbb{Z}$, $S=n\mathbb{Z}$, $K=\{1\}$ in Theorem 2 (where this time G is written additively) and remark that

$$||x||_2^2=||x^*x||_1\leq||x||\ ||x||_1 .$$

In the applications of Rohlin type theorems it is required that the index set of the tower (K in Theorem 1) can be chosen arbitrarily large and invariant. Lemma 6 shows that in our case such a choice is always possible.

We shall use the special form of the group in Theorem 1 only by means of one of its properties, given in the Lemma 5 below. This Lemma seems to fail for general solvable groups. We recall the following.

4. DEFINITION. Let G be a group, K a finite subset of G and $\varepsilon>0$. A finite subset G_1 of G will be called (ε,K)-*invariant* if

$$\#(G_1 \cap \bigcap_{g\varepsilon K} g^{-1}G_1) \geq (1-\varepsilon)\#G_1$$

(where # denotes the cardinality).

5. LEMMA. *Let* G *be a group, finite extension of a finitely generated abelian group. Then there exists* $a_G>0$ *such that* G *has arbitrarily large arbitrarily invariant subsets* G_1 *with*

$$\#(G_1^{-1}G_1) \leq a_G \#G_1 .$$

PROOF. For $m,n\varepsilon \mathbf{Z}$, $m\leq n$, we set $[m,n]=\{m,m+1,\dots,n\}$.

Any G as above is a finite extension of $\mathbf{Z}^N$, $N\varepsilon\mathbf{N}$. Indeed if $G'\subset G$ is a finite extension, with finitely generated abelian G', and if $G'=T \oplus \mathbf{Z}^N$, where T is the torsion part of G', then $\mathbf{Z}^N$ is completely invariant in G'. So $\mathbf{Z}^N$ is normal subgroup of G and $\mathbf{Z}^N\subset G$ is a finite extension.

If $N=0$ we can take $G_1=G$ for all K,ε and let $a_G=1$. Suppose $N>0$ and let $K\subset G$ be the image of a section of the projection $G \to G/\mathbf{Z}^N$. For $m\varepsilon\mathbf{N}$ we let $C_m=[-m,m]^N\subset\mathbf{Z}^N$. Suppose we are given an arbitrary finite subset F of G. There exists $p\varepsilon\mathbf{N}$ such that

$$F\cup K\cup K^{-1}K\cup C_1 K\subset KC_p \tag{1}$$

because $\bigcup_{p\geq 1} KC_p=K\mathbf{Z}^N=G$.

We have inductively from (1) $C_n K\subset KC_{np}$, $(n\geq 1)$ and so

$$(KC_n)(KC_m)\subset KKC_{np}C_m\subset KC_pC_{np}C_m=KC_{m+(n+1)p} .$$

Since $\#(KC_m)=(\#K)\cdot(\#C_m)=(\#K)(2m+1)^N$ we have

$$\lim_{m\to\infty}(\#(KC_{m+(n+1)p})/\#(KC_m))=1.$$

So, for each n and any $\varepsilon>0$, KC_m is (ε, KC_n)-invariant for large enough m; moreover, each finite subset of G is included in KC_n for some n. We also have

$$(KC_m)^{-1}KC_m = C_m K^{-1} KC_m \subset KC_{mp+p+1}$$

and we can take $a_G=(p+1)^N$, suitable for any $m\geq p+1$. For instance, if $G=\mathbf{Z}^2$ we can take $a_G=4$.

The following result is in fact true for all solvable groups.

6. LEMMA. *Let* G *be a group as in Theorem* 1. *Then there are arbitraryly large arbitraryly invariant paving sets* K *of* G.

PROOF. In the proof of Lemma 5 remark that KC_m are paving sets, because

$$G=K\mathbf{Z}^N=\bigcup_h KC_m h$$

where h ranges in $((2m+1)\mathbf{Z})^N$ and the sets are disjoint.

In the sequel, M will be a von Neumann algebra, P_M its lattice of projections and Aut M its group of automorphisms. We use the following fundamental result, due to A.Connes [1]:

7. THEOREM. *Let* M *be countably decomposable and* $g\in$ Aut M. *Then* g *is properly outer if and only if for any non zero* $e\in P_M$ *and any* $\varepsilon>0$, *there is a non zero* $f\in P_M$, $f\leq e$ *such that* $||f\cdot gf||\leq\varepsilon$.

This has as consequence:

8. COROLLARY. *Let* G_1 *be a finite set of properly outer automorphisms of* M, $\varepsilon>0$ *and* $0\neq e\in P_M$. *Then there is* $f\in P_M$, $0\neq f\leq e$ *with* $||f\cdot gf||\leq\varepsilon$ *for all* $g\in G_1$.

From the same paper we use the following technical result.

9. LEMMA. *If* $\varepsilon>0$, *with* $n!\varepsilon<1$ *and* $(e_j)_{j\in[1,n]}\subset P_M$ *such that* $||e_j e_k||\leq\varepsilon$ *for all* $j\neq k$, *then there is a family* $(f_j)_{j\in[1,n]}\subset P_M$ *such that* (f_j) *are mutually orthogonal*, $f_j\sim e_j$, $||e_j-f_j||\leq n!\varepsilon$ *for all* $j\in[1,n]$ *and* $\bigvee_1^n e_j=\bigvee_1^n f_j$.

In what follows, we let τ denote a normal faithful trace on M with $\tau(1)=1$. If $e_1,e_2\in P_M$ then from the parallelogram law ([7], p.94) we easily infer

$$\tau(e_1 \vee e_2)=\tau(e_1)+\tau(e_2)-\tau(e_1 \wedge e_2).$$

In the conditions of Lemma 9

$$(2) \qquad \tau(\bigvee_1^n e_j)=\sum_1^n \tau(e_j).$$

10. DEFINITION. For finite $H\subset G$ and $\delta>0$ we say that $f\in P_M$, $f\neq 0$ is (δ,H)-*invariant* if

$$\tau(f\wedge \bigwedge_{g\in H} g^{-1}f)\geq(1-\delta)\tau(f).$$

11. DEFINITION. For finite $H\subset G$ and $\varepsilon>0$ we say that $e\in P_M$ is an (ε,H)-*basis* if $e\neq 0$ and

$$||g_1e\cdot g_2e||\leq\varepsilon \quad \text{for} \quad g_1,g_2\in H,\ g_1\neq g_2 .$$

In this case we call $(ge)_{g\in H}$ the H-*tower* with basis e.

The following proposition shows, using Corollary 8, that under any sufficiently invariant projection f one can find an (ε,H)-basis e, such that the tower $(ge)_{g\in H}$ covers at least $(2a_G)^{-1}$ of f.

12. PROPOSITION. *Let* G *be a group, finite extension of a finitely generated abelian group* G, *take* a_G *as in Lemma* 5 *and suppose that* G *acts freely on* M. *Then for any finite* $K_o,K\subset G$ *and* $\delta>0$ *there is a finite* $H\subset G$ *satisfying*

$$(3) \qquad H \textit{ is } (\delta,K)\textit{-invariant and } K_o\subset H$$

such that for any $(1/2,\ H^{-1}H)$-*invariant* $f\in P_M$ *and any* $\varepsilon>0$ *there is an* (ε,H) *basis* e *such that*

$$(4) \qquad \bigvee_{g\in H} ge\leq f,$$

$$(5) \qquad \tau(\bigvee_{g\in H} ge)\geq(2a_G)^{-1}\tau(f).$$

It will be convenient to denote by $\Phi(K_o,K,\delta)$ the set of all H as above.

PROOF. The idea of the proof is the following. We take H as in Lemma 5. Suppose first f is 1, and consider a maximal (ε,H)-basis e. If e′ was orthogonal to $e_1=\bigvee_{g\in H^{-1}H} ge$, then $\bigvee_{g\in H} ge'$ would be orthogonal to $\bigvee_{g\in H} ge$, and from Corollary 8 we could find an (ε,H)-basis $e''\leq e'$. Then $e+e''$ would be an (ε,H)-basis, contradicting the maximality of e. So $e_1=1$ and from (2), e_1 is at most a_G-times larger than $\bigvee_{g\varepsilon H} ge$. In the general case, if f is sufficiently invariant, the above reasoning can be done under f.

Let us give the proof of the proposition. We choose as in Lemma 5 a finite $H\subset G$ such that

(6) H is (δ,K)-invariant, $K_o\cup\{1\}\subset H$,

(7) $(H^{-1}H)\leq a_G(\#H)$.

Let $f\varepsilon P_M$, $f\neq 0$ be a given projection such that

(8) f is $(1/2,\ H^{-1}H)$ invariant.

Let $\varepsilon>0$; we can suppose without loss of generality that

(9) $\varepsilon(\#H)!<1$.

Let $(e_i)_{i\varepsilon I}$ be a maximal family of nonzero projections such that

(10) e_i is an (ε,H)-basis, $(i\varepsilon I)$

(11) $\bigvee_{g\varepsilon H^{-1}H} ge_i\leq f$

(12) $(\bigvee_{g\varepsilon H^{-1}H} ge_i)_{i\varepsilon I}$ are mutually orthogonal.

Under these circumstances, if $I\neq\emptyset$ then $e=\sum_{i\varepsilon I} e_i$ is an (ε,H)-basis and satisfies condition (4) in the Proposition. We now proceed to prove condition (5).

Let us take $f_1=\bigwedge_{g\varepsilon H^{-1}H} g^{-1}f$, $\bar{e}=\bigvee_{g\varepsilon H^{-1}H} ge$, $f_2=f\wedge(f-\bar{e})$. We infer

(13) $$\tau(f_2)=\tau(f_1)+\tau(f-e)-\tau(f_1\vee(f-e))\geq\tau(f_1)-\tau(\bar{e})$$

As e is an (ε,H)-basis, from (9) and (2) we have

$$\tau(\bigvee_{g\varepsilon H} ge)=(\#H)\tau(e).$$

It results

$$\tau(\bar{e})\leq(\#(H^{-1}H))\tau(e)\leq a_G(\#H)\tau(e)=a_G\tau(\bigvee_{g\varepsilon H} ge)$$

and by means of (13) and (8)

$$\tau(f_2)\geq\tau(f_1)-\tau(\bar{e})\geq(1/2)\tau(f)-a_G\tau(\bigvee_{g\varepsilon H} ge).$$

If (5) was false, then $\tau(f_2)>0$ and f_2 would be nonzero. According to Corollary 8 there would be an $e'\varepsilon P_M$, $0\neq e'\leq f_2$ such that $||e'\cdot ge'||\leq\varepsilon$ for $g\varepsilon H^{-1}H\setminus\{1\}$. Then e' would be an (ε,H)-basis, e' would be orthogonal to $\bigvee_{g\varepsilon H^{-1}H} ge$ and so $\bigvee_{g\varepsilon H} ge'$ would be orthogonal to $\bigvee_{g\varepsilon H} ge$, thus contradicting the maximality of the family $(e_i)_{i\varepsilon I}$. Proposition 12 is proved.

PROOF OF THEOREM 1. For convenience the proof will be divided into three parts. The idea of the proof is to apply succesively Proposition 12, taking into account the fact, proved in part (C), that the complement of a tower $(ge)_{g\varepsilon H}$ is arbitrarily invariant if H is sufficiently invariant and if the complement is not too small. The constants are choosen for at most n times of usage of the algorithm described in part (A), but we stop earlier if the tower arrives at the desired size in less than n steps. The towers obtained this way are then, after being orthogonalized by means of Lemma 9, put together and indexed by K; then, in part (B), the desired partition of unity is obtained.

We begin the proof making some choices

(14) $\beta=1-(2a_G)^{-1}(1-\frac{\delta}{4})$, where we have supposed $\delta<1$,

(15) $n\varepsilon\mathbb{N}$ with $\beta^n<\frac{\delta}{2}$,

(16) $\delta_1=\frac{\delta}{8}$,

(17) $\gamma_1=\frac{1}{2}$,

and then for $k\varepsilon[2,n]$ we choose δ_k, $\gamma_k>0$ with

(18) $\delta_k\leq\frac{\delta}{8}$,

(19) $\gamma_{k-1}-\gamma_k>(1-\frac{\delta}{4})(1-(1-\gamma_{k-1})(1-\delta_k))$.

We put $H_o=L_o=1\varepsilon G$, and take succesively according to Proposition 12 for $k\varepsilon[1,n]$

(20) $H_k\varepsilon\Phi(L_{k-1},L_{k-1}L_{k-1}K,\delta_k)$,

(21) $L_k=L_k^{-1}=H_k^{-1}H_k$.

We choose $\varepsilon>0$ such that

(22) $\varepsilon<\frac{\delta}{16}$,

(23) $\varepsilon(\#H_k)!<1$ for all $k\varepsilon[1,n]$.

<u>Part (A)</u>. We use an algorithm, the step k of which is described below, for k=n, n-1,...,1 or until we stop in the meantime.

For k=n we take $F_k=1\varepsilon\mathcal{P}_M$. For general k we suppose inductively that we have a projection $F_k\varepsilon\mathcal{P}_M$ such that

(24) F_k is (γ_k, L_k)-invariant.

According to (20) and to the fact that $\gamma_k \le \frac{1}{2}$ we can apply Proposition 12 in order to obtain an (ε, H_k)-basis e_k with

(25) $$\bigvee_{g\varepsilon H_k} ge_k \le F_k ,$$

(26) $$(\# H_k)\tau(e_k) = \tau(\bigvee_{g\varepsilon H_k} ge_k) \ge (2a_G)^{-1}\tau(F_k).$$

We define

(27) $$G_k = \bigcap_{g\varepsilon L_{k-1}L_{k-1}} g^{-1}H_k \subset H_k .$$

From (20), as H_k is $(\delta_k, L_{k-1}L_{k-1}K)$-invariant, and making use of (23) and (2) we infer

(28) $$(\# G_k) = (1-\delta_k)(\# H_k), \quad \tau(\bigvee_{g\varepsilon G_k} ge_K) = (\# G_k)\tau(e_K).$$

If k=1 we stop. For k>1 there are two possibilites.

<u>Case 1</u>. If

(29) $$(\# H_k)\tau(e_k) = \tau(\bigvee_{g\varepsilon H_k} ge_k) \ge (1-\frac{\delta}{4})\tau(F_k)$$

then we stop. In this case, from (28) we have

(30) $$\tau(\bigvee_{g\varepsilon G_k} ge_k) = (\# G_k)\tau(e_k) \ge (1-\delta_k)(\# H_k)\tau(e_k) \ge (1-\delta_k)(1-\frac{\delta}{4})\tau(F_k) \ge (1-\frac{\delta}{2})\tau(F_k).$$

<u>Case 2</u>. If (29) does not hold, that is if

(31) $$(\# H_k)\tau(e_k) = \tau(\bigvee_{g\varepsilon H_k} ge_k) < (1-\frac{\delta}{4})\tau(F_k) ,$$

we go to the step k-1 of the algorithm taking

(32) $$F_{k-1} = F_k - \bigvee_{g\varepsilon G_k} ge_k .$$

In part (C) we shall show that F_{k-1} is (γ_{k-1}, L_{k-1})-invariant and that

(33) $$\tau(F_{k-1}) \le \beta\tau(F_k).$$

<u>Part (B)</u>. We denote by p the step at which we have stopped. From part (A) we have obtained $e_p, \ldots, e_n \varepsilon \mathcal{P}_M$ such that e_k is an (ε, G_k)-basis and the projections $\bar{e}_k = \bigvee_{g\varepsilon G_k} ge_k$ are mutually orthogonal, for $k\varepsilon[p,n]$. We have

(34) $$\tau(\sum_{k=p}^{n} \bar{e}_k) = \tau(1-F_{p-1}) \ge 1-\frac{\delta}{2} .$$

Indeed, if $p>1$, as a consequence of (31) we infer

$$\tau(F_{p-1})\leq\frac{\delta}{2}\tau(\bar{e}_p)\leq\frac{\delta}{2}$$

and if $p=1$, then (34) results from (33) for $k=n, n-1,\dots,1$ and (15).

We apply Lemma 9 under each e_k to obtain a family of mutually orthogonal projections $f_{k,g}$, $k\varepsilon[p,n]$, $g\varepsilon G_k$ with $\|f_{k,g}-ge_k\|\leq$ $\leq\varepsilon$ and $f_{k,g}\sim ge_k$ for k,g as above. They form, together with $F_{p-1}=$ $=1-\sum_{k=p}^{n}\bar{e}_k$, a partition of unity in M.

We also have

$$\|f_{k,g}-ge_k\|_1\leq\varepsilon\|f_{k,g}\vee ge_k\|_1\leq 2\varepsilon\tau(e_k). \tag{35}$$

K being a paving set of G, we can choose a partition $G=\bigcup_{h\varepsilon H}Kh$; then $G=\bigcup_{\ell\varepsilon H}H$ is a partition too. For $k\varepsilon[p,n]$, $\ell\varepsilon K$ we let

$$G_{k,\ell}=G_k\cap\ell H.$$

Then

$$gG_{k,\ell}\,\Delta\, G_{k,g\ell}\subset gG_k\,\Delta\, G_k$$

where Δ denotes the symmetric difference. As, from (20) and (27) G_k is (δ_k,K)-invariant, we infer

$$\#(gG_{k,\ell}\,\Delta\, G_{k,g\ell})\leq 2\delta_k(\# G_k)\leq\frac{\delta}{4}(\# G_k). \tag{36}$$

We take

$$f_\ell=\sum_{k=p}^{n}\sum_{g\varepsilon G_{k,\ell}}f_{k,g}\,.$$

Then for any $\ell\varepsilon K$, $g\varepsilon G$, $g\ell\varepsilon K$ we obtain

$$\|gf_\ell-f_{g\ell}\|_1\leq\sum_{k=p}^{n}\Big\|\sum_{g_1\varepsilon G_{k,\ell}}gf_{k,g_1}-\sum_{g_2\varepsilon G_{k,\ell}}f_{k,g_2}\Big\|_1\leq \tag{37}$$

$$\leq 4\varepsilon\sum_{k=p}^{n}(\# G_{k,\ell})\tau(e_k)+\sum_{k=p}^{n}\#(gG_{k,\ell}\,\Delta\, G_{k,g\ell})\tau(e_k)$$

where the first part of the inequality results remarking that for $g\varepsilon K$, $g_1\varepsilon G_{k,i}$, $g_2=gg_1\varepsilon G_{k,g_i}$ and from (29) we have

$$\|gf_{k,g_1}-f_{k,g_2}\|_1\leq\|gf_{k,g_1}-gg_1e_k\|_1+\|g_2e_k-f_{k,g_2}\|_1\leq 4\varepsilon\tau(e_k).$$

So, from (28), (37) and (36) we infer

$$\|gf_\ell-f_{g\ell}\|_1\leq\sum_{k=p}^{n}\frac{\delta}{2}(\# G_k)\tau(e_k)=\frac{\delta}{2}\sum_{k=p}^{n}\tau(\bar{e}_k)\leq\frac{\delta}{2}\,.$$

To make $(f_\ell)_{\ell\in K}$ a partition of unity, we just replace, for an arbitrary $\ell_o\in K$, f_{ℓ_o} by $f_{\ell_o}+F_{p-1}$. As from (34) $\tau(F_{p-1})\leq\frac{\delta}{2}$ the conclusion of Theorem 1 is satisfied.

Part (C). It remained to show that, in case 2 of part (A), F_{k-1} is (γ_{k-1},L_{k-1})-invariant and satisfies (33). Take

(38) $$F_k'=\bigwedge_{g\in L_{k-1}} g^{-1}F_k\leq F_k .$$

As, from (20), $L_{k-1}\subset L_k$, as a consequence of the induction hypothesis (24) we obtain

(39) $$\tau(F_k')\geq(1-\gamma_k)\tau(F_k).$$

From (27) $H_k\supset L_{k-1}L_{k-1}G_k$; so for $g_1,g_2\in L_{k-1}=L_{k-1}^{-1}$, $g\in G_k$ we get succesively from (25) and the defintion (32)

$$g_2^{-1}ge_k\leq g_1^{-1}F_k .$$

Letting g,g_1,g_2 run we infer

(40) $$\bigvee_{g\in L_{k-1}G_k} ge_k\leq \bigwedge_{g\in L_{k-1}} g^{-1}F_k=F_k' .$$

From the definition of F_{k-1} , for $g_1\in L_{k-1}$ we get

$$g_1^{-1}F_{k-1}=g_1^{-1}F_k-g_1^{-1}(\bigvee_{g\in G_k} ge_k)\geq F_k'-\bigvee_{g\in L_{k-1}G_k} ge_k .$$

Letting g_1 run we obtain

$$\bigwedge_{g\in L_{k-1}} g^{-1}F_{k-1}\geq F_k'-\bigvee_{g\in L_{k-1}G_k} ge_k$$

and from (40) the right member is a projection. We have

$$\tau(\bigwedge_{g\in L_{k-1}} g^{-1}F_{k-1})\geq\tau(F_k')-(\#(L_{k-1}G_k))\tau(e_k)\geq$$

(41) $$\geq(1-\gamma_k)\tau(F_k)-(\#H_k)\tau(e_k)\geq$$

(42) $$\geq(1-\gamma_{k-1})\tau(F_k)-(1-\gamma_{k-1})(1-\delta_k)(\#H_k)\tau(e_k)\geq$$

(43) $$\geq(1-\gamma_{k-1})\tau(F_{k-1}),$$

where (41) results from (39), (42) from (19) and (31), and (43) from (32) and (28); hence F_{k-1} is (γ_{k-1},L_{k-1})-invariant.

On the other hand

$$\tau(F_{k-1})=\tau(F_k)-(\#G_k)\tau(e_k)\leq\tau(F_k)-(1-\delta_k)(\#H_k)\tau(e_k)\leq$$
$$\leq(1-(2a_G)^{-1}(1-\delta_k))\tau(F_k)\leq\beta\tau(F_k)$$

from (26), (28) and then (14). We have proved (33) and hence the proof of Theorem 1 is done.

PROOF OF THEOREM 2. We may assume that $\delta<1$. By Lemma 6 there is a $(\frac{\delta}{4}, G_1)$-invariant paving set K of G. By means of Theorem 1 we choose a partition of unity in M, denoted by $(e_k)_{k\in K}$, such that for all $g\in G$, $k\in K$ with $gk\in K$ we have

(44) $$||ge_k-e_{gk}||_1\leq\frac{\delta}{4}(\# K)^{-1}.$$

Fix $k\in K$. Adding for all $\ell\in K$ the inequality

$$||e_k||_1=||\ell k^{-1}e_k||_1\leq||e_\ell||_1+||\ell k^{-1}e_k-e_\ell||_1\leq||e_\ell||_1+\frac{\delta}{4}(\# K)^{-1},$$

we get

(45) $$(\# K)||e_k||_1\leq 1+\frac{\delta}{4}.$$

Let $p:G\to G/S$ be the natural projection and let for $i\in G/S$ $A_i=\{k\in K|p(k)=i\}$ and $f_i=\sum_{k\in A_i} e_k$. Then for any $g\in G_1$ we infer

$$||gf_i-f_{gi}||_1\leq\sum_{k\in K_1}||ge_k||_1+\sum_{k\in K_2}||e_{gk}||_1+\sum_{k\in K_3}||ge_k-e_{gk}||_1,$$

where $K_1=\bigcup_{i\in G/S}(A_i\setminus g^{-1}A_{gi})=K\setminus g^{-1}K$

$K_2=\bigcup_{i\in G/S}(g^{-1}A_{gi}\setminus A_i)=g^{-1}K\setminus K$

$K_3=K\cap g^{-1}K$.

As K is $(\frac{\delta}{4}, G_1)$-invariant, $\#(K_1\cup K_2)\leq\frac{\delta}{2}(\# K)$, so from (44) and (45) we obtain:

$$||gf_i-f_{gi}||_1\leq\frac{\delta}{2}(1+\frac{\delta}{4})+\frac{\delta}{4}<\delta$$

and the theorem is proved.

AKNOWLEDGEMENTS. I would like to thank to Ş.Strătilă for pointing me out the subject, giving me valuable information concerning it, and for carefully reading the manuscript.

REFERENCES

1. Connes, A.: Outer conjugacy classes of automorphisms of factors, *Ann.Sci.Ec.Norm.Sup.* 8 (1975), 383-420.

2. Conze, V.P.: Entropie d'un groupe abélien de transformations, *Z.Wahr.verw.Gebiete* 25(1972), 11-30.

3. Katznelson, Y.; Weiss, B.: Commuting measure-preserving

transformations, *Israel J.Math.* 12 (1972), 161-173.

4. Lind, D.A.: Locally compact measure preserving flows, *Adv. in Math.* 15(1975), 175-193.

5. Ornstein, D.; Weiss, B.: The Kakutani-Rohlin theorem for solvable groups, preprint.

6. Series, C.: The Rohlin tower theorem and hyperfiniteness for actions of continuous groups, *Israel J.Math.* 30(1978), 99-122.

7. Strătilă, Ş.; Zsidó, L.: *Lectures on von Neumann algebras*, Turnbridge Wells, Abacus Press, 1979.

A. Ocneanu
Department of Mathematics,
INCREST,
Bdul Păcii 220, 79622 Bucharest,
Romania.

DERIVATIONS OF C*-ALGEBRAS WHICH ARE INVARIANT UNDER AN AUTOMORPHISM GROUP

C.Peligrad

1.INTRODUCTION

Let A be an algebra. By a *derivation* of A we mean a linear mapping $\delta:D(\delta)\to A$ ($D(\delta)$ being a subalgebra of A) such that $\delta(ab)=a\delta(b)+\delta(a)b$ for all $a,b\in D(\delta)$. A derivation δ of A is said to be *inner* if there exists $a_o\in A$ such that $\delta(a)=a_oa-aa_o(=ad(a_o)(a))$ for all $a\in D(\delta)$. If A is a *-algebra, a derivation $\delta:D(\delta)\to A$ is called *symmetric* if a) $D(\delta)$ is a *- subalgebra of A, and b) $\delta(a^*)=\delta(a)^*$ for all $a\in D(\delta)$.

Derivations of operator algebras were studied by several authors. We mention here only the famous theorem of Sakai [6] which asserts that if A is a simple C*- algebra with unit, then all bounded derivations (i.e. $D(\delta)=A$) of A are inner. In what follows we present a more general framework for this theorem. We also study unbounded derivations of operator algebras which commute with some group of *-automorphisms. A C*-dynamical system (or covariant system) is a triple (B,G,β) consisting of a C*-algebra B, a locally compact group G and a continuous homomorphism β of G into the group Aut(B) of *-automorphisms of B, equipped with the topology of pointwise convergence.

For the bounded derivations we shall discuss the following problem:

(*) Let (B,G,β) be a C*-dynamical system, where B is a C*-algebra with unit. Suppose the fixed point algebra $B^\beta=\{b\in B \mid \beta_g(b)=b\ (\forall)g\in G\}$ is simple. If these conditions are fulfilled, find conditions on the dynamical system such that every derivation of B which commutes with β, be implemented by an element in B^β.

Of course, in the unbounded case we give conditions such that a derivation δ be a generator of a strongly continuous one-parameter group of *-automorphisms.

2. ERGODIC GROUPS OF AUTOMORPHISMS

Let (B,G,β) be a C^*-dynamical system. Assume that B has a unit, that G is compact and acts ergodically on B. For every $b\in B$ consider the following integration:

$$\varphi(b)=\int_G \beta_g(b)\,dg$$

where dg is the normalised Haar measure on G. Then $\varphi(b)\in B^\beta=\mathbb{C}.1$ for all $b\in B$. Moreover, φ is positive, faithful and G-invariant. It is easy to see that φ is the unique G-invariant state on B.

2.1. PROPOSITION. *Let* (B,G,β) *be as above. If* $\delta:B\to B$ *is a bounded derivation which commutes with* β, *then* $\delta\equiv 0$.

PROOF. Representing B in the GNS representation defined by the G-invariant state φ we may assume $\varphi(b)=(b\xi_o,\xi_o)$ for some cyclic vector ξ_o (for B) in the Hilbert space H_φ. Furthermore, there exists a strongly continuous unitary representation $g\to u_g$ of G on H_φ such that $\beta_g(b)=u_g b u_g^{-1}$. Since φ is the unique G-invariant state on B, it follows that φ is the unique G-invariant normal state on the weak closure $\bar{B}$ of B. On the other hand, since $\beta_g(b)=u_g b u_g^{-1}$ and $g\to u_g$ is strongly continuous, $(\bar{B},G,\beta)$ is a W^*-dynamical system. Therefore we can consider the following weak *-integration in $\bar{B}$:

$$\varphi(b)=\int_G \beta_g(b)\,dg, \quad b\in\bar{B}.$$

Obviously $\bar{\varphi}(\bar{B})=\bar{B}^\beta$ and $\bar{\varphi}$ is normal. If $\bar{B}^\beta\neq\mathbb{C}.1$, then for every normal state ψ on $\bar{B}^\beta$, we have that $\psi\circ\bar{\varphi}$ is a normal G-invariant state on $\bar{B}$. Since φ is the unique normal G-invariant state on $\bar{B}$ it follows that $\bar{B}^\beta=\mathbb{C}.1$ and $\bar{\varphi}=\varphi$. Hence G acts ergodically on $\bar{B}$. Obviously, $\delta\beta_g=\beta_g\delta$ on $\bar{B}$ for all $g\in G$. We may assume that δ is a symmetric derivation. Then by [5, Corollary 8.6.6] we have $\delta\equiv 0$.

2.2. REMARK. If G is not compact, then the conclusion of Proposition 2.1 does not hold. Indeed, let $B=K(H)+\mathbb{C}.1$ where $K(H)$ is the C^*-algebra of compact operators on some Hilbert space H.

Consider an unitary $U\in\mathcal{B}(H)$ which does not commute with any compact operator. Then $\beta(b)=UbU^*$ ($b\in B$) defines an ergodic *-automorphism of B. The derivation $\delta=\mathrm{Ad}(U)$ commutes with β and is not equal to zero.

For the study of unbounded derivations we need some preliminary results.

For $f\in L^1(G)$ we denote by $\beta(f)$ the operator on B defined by:

$$\beta(f)(b)=\int_G f(g)\beta_g(b)d_g.$$

Let Π be an irreducible unitary representation of G, $\hat{\Pi}\in\hat{G}$ its unitary equivalence class and $\chi_{\hat{\Pi}}$ its normalised character $\chi_{\hat{\Pi}}=(\dim\Pi)\mathrm{Tr}(\Pi_g^{-1})$, where Tr is the usual trace on the Hilbert space of dimension $\dim\Pi$. Then $\beta(\chi_{\hat{\Pi}})$ is a bounded projection of B onto a norm-closed subspace $B(\hat{\Pi})$ of B called the *spectral subspace of* $\hat{\Pi}$ in B. We denote $\beta(\chi_{\hat{\Pi}})=\beta(\hat{\Pi})$.

2.3.LEMMA. *Let* (B,G,β) *be a* C*-*dynamical system. Assume that* B *has a unit and* G *is compact. If* $T:D(T)\to B$ ($D(T)\subset B$) *is a linear, closed, densely defined operator which commutes with* β, *then* $B(\hat{\Pi})\cap D(T)$ *is dense in* $B(\hat{\Pi})$ *for all* $\hat{\Pi}\in\hat{G}$.

PROOF. We consider the following norm on D(T):

$$|||b|||=||b||+||Tb||,\quad b\in D(T).$$

Endowed with this norm, D(T) becomes a Banach space. Since T commutes with β_g, $g\in G$ it follows that D(T) is G-invariant. On the other hand, if $g\in G$ and $b\in B$, we have:

$$|||\beta_g(b)|||=||\beta_g(b)||+||T\beta_g(b)||=||\beta_g(b)||+||\beta_g(Tb)||=|||b|||.$$

Therefore β_g, $g\in G$ are continuous on $(D(T),|||\cdot|||)$.

Also, it is obvious that for all $b\in D(T)$, the map $g\to\beta_g(b)$ is continuous from G into $(D(T),|||.|||)$. Then, we consider the following integration in $(D(T),|||.|||)$:

(1) $\tilde{\beta}(\hat{\Pi})(b)=\int_G \chi_{\hat{\Pi}}(g)\beta_g(b)dg,\quad b\in D(T).$

Obviously $\tilde{\beta}(\hat{\Pi})(b)=\beta(\hat{\Pi})(b)$, $b\in D(T)$. Since G is compact, A is generated by the spectral subspaces $B(\hat{\Pi})$, $\Pi\in\hat{G}$ [7, Theorem 2]. Therefore, since D(T) is dense in B and $\beta(\hat{\Pi})$ continuous we have that $\beta(\hat{\Pi})D(T)$ is dense in $B(\hat{\Pi})$.

2.4. LEMMA. *Let* (B,G,β) *and* T *be as in the preceding lemma. Suppose moreover that* G *acts ergodically on* B. *Then we have:*

i) $\bigcup_{\hat{\Pi}\varepsilon\hat{G}} B(\hat{\Pi})\subset D(T)$ *and* $\beta(\hat{\Pi})T\subset T\beta(\hat{\Pi})$ *for all* $\hat{\Pi}\varepsilon\hat{G}$.

ii) *If we denote by* S *the linear subspace generated by* $\bigcup_{\hat{\Pi}\varepsilon\hat{G}} B(\hat{\Pi})$ *then* S *is a dense subspace of analytic elements for* T (*see for exemple* [1, Definition 3.1.17]) *and* $TS\subset S$.

iii) S *is a core for* T (*that is the closure of* $T|_S$ *is* T).

iv) *If* T' *is a closed linear operator which commutes with* β *and* $T\subset T'$, *then* T=T'.

PROOF. (i) By [3, Proposition 2.1], $B(\hat{\Pi})$ is finite dimensional for all $\hat{\Pi}\varepsilon\hat{G}$. By Lemma 2.3. $B(\hat{\Pi})\cap D(T)$ is dense in $B(\hat{\Pi})$, $\hat{\Pi}\varepsilon\hat{G}$. Therefore, $B(\hat{\Pi})\subset D(T)$ for all $\hat{\Pi}\varepsilon\hat{G}$.

Now, let $b\varepsilon D(T)$. By (1), the integral

$$\beta(\hat{\Pi})(b)=\int_G \chi_{\hat{\Pi}}(g)\beta_g(b)dg$$

converges in $(D(T),|||.|||)$. Since T is continuous from $(D(T),|||.|||)$ into B with the original norm we have

$$T\beta(\hat{\Pi})(b)=\beta(\hat{\Pi})T(b).$$

(ii) By (i) $TS\subset S$. According to [7, Theorem 2], S is dense in B. Since $B(\hat{\Pi})$ is finite dimensional and $T(B(\hat{\Pi}))\subset B(\hat{\Pi})$, $\hat{\Pi}\varepsilon\hat{G}$, it follows that all elements of S are analytic for T.

(iii) Since β_g is a (strongly) continuous representation of G in $(D(T),|||.|||)$, by [7, Theorem 2] it follows that S is dense in $(D(T),|||.|||)$.

(iv) follows from (iii).

2.5. THEOREM. *Let* (B,G,β) *be a* C^*- *dynamical system. Suppose* B *has a unit,* G *is compact and acts ergodically on* B. *Let* δ *be a closed, densely defined symmetric derivation on* B *which commutes with* β. *Then we have:*

(i) δ *is the generator of a strongly continuous one-parameter group of* *- *automorphisms of* B, $\{\alpha_t\}_{t\varepsilon\mathbb{R}}$, *and* $\alpha_t\beta_g=\beta_g\alpha_t$ *for all* $t\varepsilon\mathbb{R}$, $g\varepsilon G$.

(ii) *If* T *is a linear, closed operator which commutes with* β *and* $\delta\subset T$ *then* $\delta=T$.

PROOF. (ii) follows from Lemma 2.4 (iv).

(i) We prove firstly that δ is a generator. In order to prove this fact, we shall verify the hypothesis of [1, Corollary 3.2.57]. Let φ be the unique G-invariant state on B (which is faithful). We show that $\varphi(\delta(D(\delta)))=\{0\}$. Obviously $\varphi(\delta(1))=0$. By Lemma 2.4 (i) and (iii) it is sufficient to prove that $\varphi(B(\hat{\Pi}))=\{0\}$ for all nontrivial $\hat{\Pi}\varepsilon\hat{G}$. Let $\hat{\Pi}\varepsilon\hat{G}$, $\hat{\Pi}$ nontrivial, and $b\varepsilon B$. Then we have:

$$\begin{aligned}\varphi(\beta(\hat{\Pi})b)&=\varphi\left(\int \chi_{\hat{\Pi}}(g)\beta_g(b)\,dg\right)=\\&=\iint \chi_{\hat{\Pi}}(g)\beta_{hg}(b)\,dg\,dh=\\&=\int dg\chi_{\hat{\Pi}}(g)\int \beta_{hg}(b)\,dh=\\&=\varphi(b)\int \chi_{\hat{\Pi}}(g)\,dg=\\&=0.\end{aligned}$$

By Lemma 2.5 (ii), δ possesses a dense set of analytic elements. By [1, Corollary 3.2.57], δ is the generator of a strongly continuous one-parameter group $\{\alpha_t\}_{t\varepsilon\mathbb{R}}$ of *-automorphisms of B. Applying the Hille-Yosida Theorem [1, Theorem 3.1.10 (2)] it follows that $\alpha_t\beta_g=\beta_g\alpha_t$ for all $t\varepsilon\mathbb{R}$, $g\varepsilon G$.

2.6. REMARK. The condition that δ be closed in Theorem 2.5 can be replaced by the following weaker one: Suppose there exist two closed operators T_1,T_2 on B such that T_1 and T_2 commute with β, T_1T_2 is densely defined and $\delta=T_1T_2$. Then it results that δ is closable and the conclusion of Theorem 2.5 holds with $\bar{\delta}$ instead of δ.

3. CROSSED PRODUCTS

Let (A,Γ,α) be a C*-dynamical system. Suppose $A\subset\mathcal{B}(H)$ for some Hilbert space H. Recall some notations and results from the theory of crossed products (see for exemple [4]). Let $C_{oo}(\Gamma,A)$ be the algebra of all continuous A-valued functions on Γ with compact support. The reduced (or regular) crossed product of A and Γ denoted $C^*_r(A,\Gamma,\alpha)$ is defined as the C*-algebra generated by the operators $\tilde{\rho}(\varphi)$ on $L^2(\Gamma,H)$:

$$\tilde{\rho}(\varphi)f(\gamma)=\int_\Gamma \alpha_{\gamma^{-1}}(\varphi(p))f(p^{-1}\gamma)\,dp\ ,$$

for $\varphi\varepsilon C_{oo}(\Gamma,A)$, $f\varepsilon L^2(\Gamma,H)$ and $\gamma\varepsilon\Gamma$.

If $\bar{\lambda}$ is the continuous representation of Γ on $L^2(\Gamma,H)$ given by:

$$(\bar{\lambda}_p f)(\gamma)=f(p^{-1}\gamma)$$

for $f\varepsilon L^2(\Gamma,H)$ and $p,\gamma\varepsilon\Gamma$ it is easy to see that

$$\overline{\lambda}_p C_r^*(A,\Gamma,\alpha) \subset C_r^*(A,\Gamma,\alpha)$$

and

$$C_r^*(A,\Gamma,\alpha)\overline{\lambda}_p \subset C_r^*(A,\Gamma,\alpha)$$

for all $p\in\Gamma$. Therefore $\overline{\lambda}_p \in M(C_r^*(A,\Gamma,\alpha))$ (the multiplier algebra of $C_r^*(A,\Gamma,\alpha)$).

We can also define a faithful *-representation of A on $L^2(\Gamma,H)$ by:

$$\tilde{\rho}(a)f(\gamma)=\alpha_{\gamma^{-1}}(a)f(\gamma),$$

$a\in A$, $f\in L^2(\Gamma,H)$, $\gamma\in\Gamma$. We will have $\tilde{\rho}(a)\in M(C_r^*(A,\Gamma,\alpha))$.

Now, we define the dual action β of α on $C_r^*(A,\Gamma,\alpha)$. Let W be the following unitary operator on $L^2(\Gamma\times\Gamma,H)$:

$$Wf(\gamma,p)=f(\gamma,\gamma p) \text{ for } f\in L^2(\Gamma\times\Gamma,H) \quad \gamma,p\in\Gamma.$$

Let also $C_r^*(\Gamma)$ denote the C*-algebra generated by the left regular representation of $C_{oo}(\Gamma)$ on $L^2(\Gamma)$. Define the map β from $M(C_r^*(A,\Gamma,\alpha))$ into $\mathcal{B}(L^2(\Gamma\times\Gamma,H))$ by:

$$\beta(a)=W^*(a\otimes 1)W.$$

We have:

$$\beta(a)=a\otimes 1 \quad \text{for } \tilde{a}\in\rho(A),$$
$$\beta(\overline{\lambda}_\gamma)=\overline{\lambda}_\gamma\otimes\lambda_\gamma \quad \text{for } \gamma\in\Gamma.$$

(Here $\lambda_\gamma\in\mathcal{B}(L^2(\Gamma))$ is defined by $(\lambda_\gamma f)(p)=f(\gamma^{-1}p)$). The following proposition is a consequence of a remarkable result of M. B.Landstad [4, Theorem 3]:

3.1. PROPOSITION. $\rho(A)$ *consists of all elements* $a\in M(C_r^*(A,\Gamma,\alpha))$ *satisfying*:

(i) $\beta(a)=a\otimes 1$,

(ii) $a\cdot\lambda(\varphi)$ *and* $\lambda(\varphi)a\in C_r^*(A,\Gamma,\alpha)$ *for all* $\varphi\in C_{oo}(\Gamma)$,

(iii) $\gamma\to\overline{\lambda}_\gamma a\overline{\lambda}_{\gamma^{-1}}$ *is norm continuous and* $\alpha_\gamma(a)=\overline{\lambda}_\gamma a\overline{\lambda}_{\gamma^{-1}}$

for all $\gamma\in\Gamma$.

The next proposition deals with norm-continuous (also called uniformly continuous) group actions on a C*-algebra. Clearly the main applications will be in the case of discrete groups.

3.2. PROPOSITION. *Let* A *be a simple* C*-*algebra with unit, and let* α *be a norm continuous action of the locally compact group*

Γ *on* A. *Then, for every derivation* $\delta: C_r^*(A,\Gamma,\alpha) \to C_r^*(A,\Gamma,\alpha)$ *which commutes with* β *in the sense that* $(\delta \otimes i)\beta = \beta\delta$, *there exists* $a_o \in \tilde{\rho}(A) \subset M(C_r^*(A,\Gamma,\alpha))$ *such that* $\delta = ad(a_o)$.

PROOF. Let $\tilde{\delta}$ and $\tilde{\beta}$ be the extensions of δ and respectively β to the weak closure of $C_r^*(A,\Gamma,\alpha)$. Obviously $(\tilde{\delta} \otimes i)\tilde{\beta} = \tilde{\beta}\tilde{\delta}$. (Since δ is inner, it follows that $\tilde{\delta} \otimes i$ has a sense). The proof of the proposition will be given in several steps:

I. (A'',Γ,α'') is a W^*-dynamical system and the W^*-crossed product $W^*(A'',\Gamma,\alpha'')$ is equal with the weak closure of $C_r^*(A,\Gamma,\alpha)$. These facts follow easily from the norm continuity of $\gamma \to \alpha_\gamma$.

II. $\tilde{\delta}(\tilde{\rho}(A)) \subset \tilde{\rho}(A)$.

Let $a \in \tilde{\rho}(A)$. We shall show that $\tilde{\delta}(a)$ satisfies Landstad's conditions (in Proposition 3.1):

(i) $\tilde{\beta}(\tilde{\delta}(a)) = (\tilde{\delta} \otimes i)\tilde{\beta}(a) = \tilde{\delta}(a) \otimes 1$.

Therefore $\tilde{\beta}(\tilde{\delta}(a)) = \tilde{\delta}(a) \otimes 1$.

(ii) Since A is unital, we have $\lambda(\varphi) \in C_r^*(A,\Gamma,\alpha)$ for all $\varphi \in C_{oo}(\Gamma)$. Since obviously $\tilde{\delta}(a) \in M(C_r^*(A,\Gamma,\alpha))$ we have that $\lambda(\varphi)a$ and $a \cdot \lambda(\varphi) \in C_r^*(A,\Gamma,\alpha)$.

(iii) From (i) and [4, Theorem 1] it follows that $\tilde{\delta}(a) \in A''$. Since α'' is uniformly continuous, it follows that $\gamma \to \bar{\lambda}_\gamma \tilde{\delta}(a) \bar{\lambda}_{\gamma^{-1}} = \alpha''_\gamma(\tilde{\delta}(a))$ is norm continuous. Therefore, by Proposition 3.1., $\tilde{\delta}(a) \in \tilde{\rho}(A)$.

III. $\tilde{\delta}(\tilde{\rho}(A)\bar{\lambda}_\gamma) \subset \tilde{\rho}(A)\bar{\lambda}_\gamma$ for all $\gamma \in \Gamma$.

Indeed let $a \in \tilde{\rho}(A)$ and $\gamma \in \Gamma$. Then as in II it can be proved that $\tilde{\delta}(a\bar{\lambda}_\gamma)\bar{\lambda}_{\gamma^{-1}} \in \tilde{\rho}(A)$. Hence $\tilde{\delta}(a\bar{\lambda}_\gamma) \in \tilde{\rho}(A)\bar{\lambda}_\gamma$.

IV. The end of the proof.

Since $\tilde{\delta}(\tilde{\rho}(A)) \subset \tilde{\rho}(A)$ and A is simple with unit, then by the Theorem of Sakai, there exists $a_o \in \tilde{\rho}(A)$ such that $\tilde{\delta}|_{\tilde{\rho}(A)} = ad(a_o)|_{\tilde{\rho}(A)}$.

Let $\delta_o = \tilde{\delta} - ad(a_o)$ on $W^*(A'',\Gamma,\alpha'')$. We shall show that $\delta_o \equiv 0$. There exists $b_o \in W^*(A'',\Gamma,\alpha'')$ such that $\delta_o = ad(b_o)$. Further, since $\delta_o(\tilde{\rho}(A)) = \{0\}$ we have $b_o \in \tilde{\rho}(A)'$. On the other hand, for $\gamma \in \Gamma$ we have

$$\delta_o(\bar{\lambda}_\gamma) = b_o\bar{\lambda}_\gamma - \bar{\lambda}_\gamma b_o = (b_o - \bar{\lambda}_\gamma b_o \bar{\lambda}_{\gamma^{-1}})\bar{\lambda}_\gamma .$$

By III, $b_o - \bar{\lambda}_\gamma b_o \bar{\lambda}_{\gamma^{-1}} \in \rho(\tilde{A})$. Obviously $\bar{\lambda}_\gamma b_o \bar{\lambda}_{\gamma^{-1}} \in \tilde{\rho}(A)'$, and therefore

$b_o - \bar{\lambda}_\gamma b_o \bar{\lambda}_{\gamma}^{-1}$ belongs to the center of $\tilde{\rho}(A)$. Since A is simple, $b_o - \bar{\lambda}_\gamma b_o \bar{\lambda}_{\gamma}^{-1} = \mu \cdot 1$ for some $\mu \in \mathbb{C}$. Hence $\delta_o(\bar{\lambda}_\gamma) = \mu \cdot \bar{\lambda}_\gamma$. From this, it results that $\delta_o(\bar{\lambda}_\gamma^n) = n\mu\bar{\lambda}_\gamma^n$ for all $n \in \mathbb{N}$. The boundedness of δ_o implies $\mu=0$. Therefore $\delta_o \equiv 0$, whence $\delta = \mathrm{ad}(a_o)$.

Now we shall study the unbounded derivations which commute with the dual action on crossed products. For this we shall assume in addition that A is separable and Γ is discrete and commutative. Let $G=\hat{\Gamma}$, $B=C^*(A,\Gamma,\alpha)$ and $\beta=\hat{\alpha}$.

3.3. LEMMA. *Let* (A,Γ,α) *be a* C^**-dynamical system. Assume that* A *is a simple* C^**-algebra with unit and* Γ *is discrete and commutative. Let* (B,G,β) *be its dual system. If* $T:D(T)\to B$ $(D(T)\subset B)$ *is a linear, closed, densely defined operator such that:*

1) $D(T)$ *is a subalgebra,*
2) $A\subset D(T)$,
3) $\beta_g T \subset T\beta_g$ $(\forall)$ $g\in G$,

then $\bigcup_{\gamma\in\Gamma} A\bar{\lambda}_\gamma \subset D(T)$ *and* $T(A\bar{\lambda}_\gamma)\subset A\bar{\lambda}_\gamma$ *for all* $\gamma\in\Gamma$.

PROOF. By Lemma 2.3, $A\bar{\lambda}_\gamma \cap D(T)$ is dense in $A\bar{\lambda}_\gamma$. Let

$$A_o^\gamma = \{a\in A \mid a\bar{\lambda}_\gamma \in D(T)\}.$$

Then, since $A\subset D(T)$ and $D(T)$ is a subalgebra it follows that A_o^γ is a two-sided ideal of A. Since $A\bar{\lambda}_\gamma \cap D(T)$ is dense in $A\bar{\lambda}_\gamma$ and A is simple, we have $A_o^\gamma = A$. Therefore $A\bar{\lambda}_\gamma \subset D(T)$. The fact that $T(A\bar{\lambda}_\gamma)\subset A\bar{\lambda}_\gamma$ may be proved similarly with the analogous fact in Lemma 2.4 (i).

3.4. LEMMA. *Let* (A,Γ,α), (B,G,β) *and* T *be as in the preceding lemma. Then* T *possesses a dense subspace* $S\subset D(T)$ *of analytic elements such that* $TS\subset S$. *Moreover* S *is a core for* T.

PROOF. The proof is an obvious adaptation of the proof of Lemma 2.4. (ii) and (iii) with $S=\mathrm{lin\ span}(\bigcup_{\gamma\in\Gamma} A\bar{\lambda}_\gamma)$.

3.5. THEOREM. *Let* (A,Γ,α) *be a* C^**-dynamical system. Assume that* A *is a separable, simple* C^**-algebra with unit and* Γ *is discrete and commutative. Denote by* (B,G,β) *its dual system. If* $\delta:D(\delta)\to B$ *is a symmetric, closed, densely defined derivation such* *that:*

1) $A \subset D(\delta)$,

2) $\beta_g \delta \subset \delta \beta_g$ $(\forall)$ $g \in G$,

then we have

(i) *There exists* $h_o \in A$, $h_o = h_o^*$ *such that* $\delta_1 = \delta - ad(h_o)$ *is the generator of a strongly continuous one parameter group of *-automorphisms of* B, $\{\tau_t\}_{t\in \mathbb{R}}$, *and* $\tau_t \beta_g = \beta_g \tau_t$ $(\forall)$ $t \in \mathbb{R}$, $g \in G$.

(ii) *If* T *is a closed, densely defined operator on* B *which commutes with* β *such that* $\delta \subset T$, *then* $\delta = T$.

PROOF. (i) By Lemma 3.3 $\delta(A) \subset A$. Since A is simple with unit, by the Theorem of Sakai there exists $h_o \in A$, $h_o = h_o^*$ such that $\delta|_A = ad(h_o)|_A$. Let $\delta_1 = \delta - ad(a_o)$ (on $D(\delta)$). We prove that δ_1 satisfies the hypothesis of [1, Corollary 3.2.57]. For $b \in B$, we consider the following integration:

$$\varepsilon_o(b) = \int_G \beta_g(b)\,dg.$$

Then $\varepsilon_o(b) \in A$ for all $b \in B$. Since A is separable there exists a faithful state ψ_o on A. Then $\varphi_o = \psi_o \circ \varepsilon_o$ is a faithful G-invariant state on B. Obviously $\varphi_o(A\bar{\lambda}_\gamma) = 0$ for all $\gamma \in \Gamma$ with $\alpha_\gamma \neq \iota$. Then $\varphi_o(\delta_1(\bigcup_{\gamma\in\Gamma} A\bar{\lambda}_\gamma)) = 0$. Since by Lemma 3.4, $S = \text{lin span} \bigcup_{\gamma\in\Gamma} A\bar{\lambda}_\gamma$ is a core for δ_1 we have $\varphi_o(\delta_1(D(\delta_1))) = 0$. (Here $D(\delta_1) = D(\delta)$.) The first condition is thus verified.

By Lemma 3.4, δ_1 possesses a dense set of analytic elements. Therefore, by [1, Corollary 3.2.57], δ_1 is a generator. The fact that $\tau_t \beta_g = \beta_g \tau_t$ ($t \in \mathbb{R}$, $g \in G$) is a consequence of the Hille-Yosida Theorem.

(ii) follows from Lemma 3.4.

REFERENCES

1. Bratteli, O.; Robinson, D.W.: *Operator algebras and quantum statistical mechanics*. I, Springer Verlag, 1979.

2. Helemskiĭ, I.; Sinai, Ja.: A description derivations in algebras of the type of local observables of spin systems (Russian), *Funkt.Analiz i pril.* 6 (1972):4, 99-100.

3. Hoegh-Krohn, R.; Landstad, M.B.; Stormer, E.: Compact ergodic groups of automorphisms, preprint, 1980.

4. Landstad, M.B.: Duality for covariant systems, *Trans.Amer. Math.Soc.* 248 (1979), 223-267.

5. Pedersen, G.K.: C^*-*algebras and their automorphism groups*, Academic Press, 1979.

6. Sakai, S.: Derivations of simple C^*-algebras, *J.Funct.Analysis* 2 (1968), 202-206.

7. Shiga, K.: Representations of a compact group on a Banach space, *J.Math.Soc.Japan* 7 (1955), 224-248.

Costel Peligrad
Department of Mathematics,
INCREST,
Bdul Păcii 220, 79622 Bucharest,
Romania.

REMARKS ON IDEALS OF THE CALKIN-ALGEBRA FOR CERTAIN SINGULAR EXTENSIONS

M.Pimsner, S.Popa and D.Voiculescu

One of the classes of extensions which are more general than those of the ideal of compact operators K(H), for which we have the Brown-Douglas-Fillmore theory ([2],[3]), are the extensions of $C_o(X) \otimes K(H)$ where X is locally compact. A class of such extensions, the homogeneous ones, for X compact have been studied in ([8],[10]) (see [7] for a more general theory). The opposite case appears to be that of the singular extensions, i.e. those for which the extension is "localised" in a certain sense at infinity in the Alexandrov compactification of X. Such extensions have been considered by Delaroche ([4]) and in connection with the C^*-algebra of the Heisenberg group, by several authors ([9], [7], [11]). The structure of such extensions appears to be rather mysterious. This is due in part to the complicated structure of the "Calkin algebra" corresponding to a singular extension problem. This "Calkin algebra" is far from being simple and the aim of the present note is to classify its closed two-sided ideals.

We begin with the notations.

Throughout, H will denote a complex separable infinite-dimensional Hilbert space and L(H), K(H) will denote the set of all bounded operators on H and respectively the ideal of compact operators on H.

Instead of a locally compact space X, it will be more convenient to consider a pointed compact space (Ω,ω), where X corresponds to $\Omega\setminus\{\omega\}$. We shall assume that Ω is metrizable and finite-dimensional. By $\mathcal{B}(\Omega,\omega,H)$ (or simply $\mathcal{B}$) we shall denote the C^*-algebra of bounded norm-continuous functions $f:\Omega\setminus\{\omega\}\to K(H)$ and by $\mathcal{I}(\Omega,\omega,H)$ (or simply $\mathcal{I}$) the C^*-algebra of norm-continuous functions $f:\Omega\to K(H)$ such that $f(\omega)=0$. Clearly, the restriction to $\Omega\setminus\{\omega\}$ gives an isometric injection of $\mathcal{I}$ into $\mathcal{B}$, which we shall use to identify $\mathcal{I}$ with a sub-algebra of $\mathcal{B}$, which is in fact a closed two-sided ideal of $\mathcal{B}$. The singular extensions will correspond to *-monomorphisms into $\mathcal{B}/_{\mathcal{I}}$, which is what might be called the "Calkin algebra" for the singular extensions of $C_0(\Omega\setminus\{\omega\})\otimes\otimes K(H)\simeq\mathcal{I}$. The problem we consider is the classification of the closed two-sided ideals of $\mathcal{B}/_{\mathcal{I}}$ or equivalently the classification of the closed two-sided ideals of $\mathcal{B}$ containing $\mathcal{I}$.

For the sake of completeness we shall record as Lemma 1 a most likely well-known consequence of the finite-dimensionality of Ω.

LEMMA 1. *Let Ω be a compact metrizable finite-dimensional space. Then there is a number* N, *depending only on the dimension of Ω such that for every open covering $\mathcal{U}=(U_j)_{j\in J}$ of $\Omega\setminus\{\omega\}$ there is a refinement $\mathcal{V}=(V_i)_{i\in I}$, which is a covering by open sets, with the following property:*

there is a partition $I=I_1\cup\ldots\cup I_N$ such that $V_p\cap V_q=\emptyset$ whenever $p\neq q$ belong to the same I_k.

For the next proposition we shall introduce some notations. By $E(\sigma;a)$ we shall denote for a positive operator $a\in L(H)$, the spectral projection corresponding to the Borel set $\sigma\subset\mathbb{R}$. Another notation we shall use, is A_+ for the positive part of a C^*-algebra A.

PROPOSITION 2. *Let $M\subset\mathcal{B}_+=\mathcal{B}_+(\Omega,\omega,H)$ and $x\in\mathcal{B}_+$. Then, the following conditions are equivalent:*

(i) x *is in the closed two-sided ideal of $\mathcal{B}$ generated by* $M\cup\mathcal{I}$.

(ii) *for every $\varepsilon>0$ there are $\delta>0$, $n\in\mathbb{N}$, $y_1,\ldots,y_n\in M$ and $V\subset\Omega$ a neighborhood of ω such that* $\operatorname{rank} E([\varepsilon,\infty);x(t))\le\sum_{j=1}^{n}\operatorname{rank} E([\delta,\infty);y_j(t))$ *for all* $t\in V\setminus\{\omega\}$.

PROOF. We shall use in the proof the following fact. Let $\tilde{\mathcal{B}}=\mathcal{B}+\mathbb{C}e$ denote the C^*-algebra obtained by adjoining a unit to $\mathcal{B}$; then (i) is equivalent with:

for every $\alpha>0$ there are $n\in\mathbb{N}$, $y_1,\dots,y_n\in M, b_1,\dots,b_n\in\mathcal{B}, d\in I_+$ such that

$$\alpha e + \sum_{j=1}^{n} b_j y_j b_j^* + d \geq x.$$

In view of the definition of I this gives that (i) is also equivalent to:

(i') *for every* $\alpha>0$ *there are* $n\in\mathbb{N}, y_1,\dots,y_n\in M, b_1,\dots,b_n\in\mathcal{B}$, *and* $V\subset\Omega$ *a neighborhood of* ω *such that*

$$\alpha I_H + \sum_{j=1}^{n} b_j(t) y_j(t) b_j^*(t) \geq x(t)$$

for all $t\in V\setminus\{\omega\}$.

With these preparations we can now pass to the proof of the proposition.

(i)$\Longrightarrow$(ii)

This will follow from (i)$\Longleftrightarrow$(i') and some remarks based on consequences of the mini-max principle.

Thus, using results in ch.II, §2 of [6] we have for $\gamma>0$ the inequality:

$$\text{rank } E([\gamma,\infty), b_j(t)y_j(t)b_j^*(t)) \leq \text{rank } E([\frac{\gamma}{\|b_j\|^2},\infty), y_j(t)).$$

Further, using Corollary 2.2 in §2 of ch.II of [6] we have:

$$\text{rank } E([\gamma,\infty), \sum_{j=1}^{n} b_j(t)y_j(t)b_j^*(t)) \leq$$
$$\leq \sum_{j=1}^{n} \text{rank } E([\frac{\gamma}{n},\infty), b_j(t)y_j(t)b_j^*(t)) \leq$$
$$\leq \sum_{j=1}^{n} \text{rank } E([\frac{\gamma}{n\|b_j\|^2},\infty), y_t(t)).$$

Assume now that

$$\alpha I_H + \sum_{j=1}^{n} b_j(t)y_j(t)b_j^*(t) \geq x(t);$$

then from the mini-max principle, it follows that for $\gamma>\alpha>0$ we have

$$\text{rank } E([\gamma-\alpha,\infty); \sum_{j=1}^{n} b_j(t)y_j(t)b_j^*(t)) \geq$$
$$\geq \text{rank } E([\gamma,\infty); x(t)).$$

This, together with our previous remarks, gives:

$$\operatorname{rank} E([\gamma,\infty);x(t)) \leq \sum_{j=1}^{n} \operatorname{rank} E([\tfrac{\gamma-\alpha}{\beta},\infty);y_t(t))$$

where $\beta = n(\max_{1\leq j\leq n} ||b_j||^2+1)$.

Thus, taking $\alpha=\varepsilon/2, \gamma=\varepsilon$ we see that (i') implies (ii) with $\delta=\varepsilon/2\beta$.

(ii) $\Longrightarrow$ (i)

Let (i") denote condition (i') with M replaced by the closed two-sided ideal generated by M. It will be clearly sufficient to prove that (ii)$\Longrightarrow$(i"). Thus, assume (ii) holds. Then for every $t \in V\setminus\{\omega\}$ we can find $b_t^{(h)} \in \mathcal{B}$ $(1\leq h\leq n)$ such that

$$\sum_{h=1}^{n} b_t^{(h)}(t)y_h(t)b_t^{(h)*}(t)+\varepsilon I_H \geq x(t),$$

$$||b_t^{(h)}|| \leq \left(\frac{||x||}{\delta}\right)^{\frac{1}{2}}.$$

But then, for every $t\in V\setminus\{\omega\}$ there is an open set $U_t \subset \Omega\setminus\{\omega\}$, $t \in U_t$ such that

$$\sum_{h=1}^{n} b_t^{(h)}(s)y_h(s)b_t^{(h)*}(s)+2\varepsilon I_H \geq x(s)$$

for all $s\in U_t$.

Assuming V is compact (which is no loss of generality) we can apply Lemma 1 and find a covering $(V_j)_{j\in J_1} \cup \ldots \cup (V_j)_{j\in J_N}$ by open subsets of $V\setminus\{\omega\}$ (in the relative topology of $V\setminus\{\omega\}$) such that $V_j \subset U_{t(j)}$ and $V_p \cap V_q = \emptyset$ whenever $p\neq q$ belong to the same set J_k. Let further $(g_j)_{j\in J_1\cup\ldots\cup J_k}$ be a partition of unity subordined to this covering of $V\setminus\{\omega\}$. Then we may define bounded continuous K(H)-valued functions $c_k^{(h)}$ on $V\setminus\{\omega\}$ $(1\leq k\leq N, 1\leq h\leq n)$ by

$$c_k^{(h)}(s) = \sum_{j\in J_k} \sqrt{g_j(s)}\, b_{t(j)}^{(h)}(s).$$

We have

$$\sum_{h=1}^{n} \left(\sum_{k=1}^{N} c_k^{(h)}(s)y_h(s)c_k^{(h)*}(s)\right)+2\varepsilon I_H =$$

$$= \sum_{h=1}^{n} \sum_{k=1}^{N} \left(\sum_{j\in J_k} g_j(s)b_{t(j)}^{(h)}(s)y_h(s)b_{t(j)}^{(h)*}(s)\right)+2\varepsilon I_H =$$

$$= \sum_{k=1}^{n} \sum_{j\in J_k} g_j(s)\left(\sum_{h=1}^{n} b_{t(j)}^{(h)}(s)y_h(s)b_{t(j)}^{(h)*}(s)+2\varepsilon I_H\right)\geq$$

$$\geq \sum_{k=1} \sum_{j\in J_k} g_j(s)x(s)=x(s).$$

Remarking that the K(H)-valued functions $c_k^{(h)}$ can be prolonged from $V\setminus\{\omega\}$ to all of $\Omega\setminus\{\omega\}$ we see that we have proved that (ii)$\Longrightarrow$(i").

We turn now to the classification of the closed two-sided ideals of $\mathcal{B}$ which contain $\mathcal{I}$. This will be achieved by exibiting a bijection between these ideals and the class of cones $\mathcal{C}$ of positive continuous functions on $\Omega\setminus\{\omega\}$, satisfying the following "completeness" property:

(*) *If* $f:\Omega\setminus\{\omega\}\to[0,\infty)$ *is a continuous function such that for every* $\varepsilon>0$ *there exists a neighborhood* V_ε *of* ω *and a function* $g_\varepsilon \in \mathcal{C}$ *such that*

$$f(t)\leq g_\varepsilon(t)+\varepsilon \textit{ for all } t\in V_\varepsilon$$

then f *belongs to* $\mathcal{C}$.

We pass now to the construction of the correspondence between ideals and cones.

By $\mathcal{F}$ we shall denote the set of continuous functions $\phi:[0,\infty)\to[0,\infty)$ such that supp $\phi\subset(0,\infty)$. Let further, for $\varepsilon>0,\psi_\varepsilon$ stand for the following particular function in $\mathcal{F}$ $\psi_\varepsilon(t)=\max(t-\varepsilon,0)$.

For $x\in\mathcal{B}_+$ and $\phi\in\mathcal{F}$ we get a continuous function $T_\phi x$ on $\Omega\setminus\{\omega\}$ defined by $T_\phi x(t)=\mathrm{Trace}\ \phi(x(t))$.

Let us note the following properties of the functions $T_\phi x$:

1) $T_\phi x(t)\leq||\phi(x(t))||\cdot\mathrm{rank}\ E([\delta,\infty);x(t))$

where $\delta>0$ is the greatest lower bound of supp ϕ.

2) $\varepsilon\cdot\mathrm{rank}\ E([2\varepsilon,\infty);x(t))\leq T_{\psi_\varepsilon}x(t)$.

3) Assume $\phi\in\mathcal{F}$ is an increasing function, then for $x,y\in\mathcal{B}_+$, $x\leq y$ we have $T_\phi x(t)\leq T_\phi y(t)$ for all $t\in\Omega\setminus\{\omega\}$.

The last property is a consequence of the mini-max principle, which shows that the n-th eigenvalue of y(t) is greater than the n-th eigenvalue of x(t) (eigenvalues being listed in decreasing order, multiple eigenvalues repeated), so that the same is true for the n-th eigenvalues of $\phi(y(t))$ and $\phi(x(t))$.

For a closed two-sided ideal J containing I we shall denote by $C(J)$ the smallest cone of continuous positive functions satisfying property (*) containing all the functions $T_\phi x$, where x runs over J_+ and ϕ runs over F.

Conversely, for a cone C satisfying (*), let $J_+(C)$ be the set of all positive elements $x\in B_+$ such that $T_\phi(x)\in C$ for all $\phi\in F$. $J(C)$ will be the set of all elements $x\in B$ such that $|x|=(x^*,x)^{\frac{1}{2}}\in J_+(C)$.

LEMMA 3. *$J(C)$ is a closed two-sided ideal of B, which contains I. Moreover $(J(C))_+=J_+(C)$.*

PROOF. Remark first that $x\in B_+$ is in $J_+(C)$ if $T_{\psi_\varepsilon}x\in C$ for all $\varepsilon>0$. This follows from the fact that every $\phi\in F$ is dominated by a function of the form $\alpha\psi_\varepsilon$ on the spectrum of x and from property (*).

Also, if $f:[0,\infty)\to[0,\infty)$ is a continuous function such that $f(0)=0$, then $\phi_0 f\in F$ for every $\phi\in F$. Hence, if $x\in J_+(C)$ then also $f(x)\in J_+(C)$.

In particular, for $x\in B_+$ we have that $x\in J_+(C)$ if and only if $x^2\in J_+(C)$.

We will first show that $J_+(C)$ is a closed convex hereditary cone in B. To this end we apply the remarks preceding the Lemma and Corollary 2.2 in §2 of ch.II of [6], to get:

$$T_{\psi_\varepsilon}(x+y)(t)\le||x+y||\cdot\text{rank } E([\varepsilon,\infty);x(t)+y(t))\le$$

$$\le||x+y||(\text{rank } E([\tfrac{\varepsilon}{2},\infty);x(t))+\text{rank } E([\tfrac{\varepsilon}{2},\infty);y(t)))\le$$

$$\le\frac{4}{\varepsilon}||x+y||(T_{\psi_{\varepsilon/4}}y(t)),\ x,y\in B_+,$$

$$T_{\psi_\varepsilon}\lambda x=\lambda T_{\psi_{\varepsilon/\lambda}}x,\ x\in B_+,\ \lambda>0.$$

Also, if $0\le x\le y$ and $y\in J_+(C)$ then $T_{\psi_\varepsilon}x\le T_{\psi_\varepsilon}y$ since ψ_ε is increasing. This together with the preceding remarks yield that $J_+(C)$ is a convex hereditary cone.

To see that $J_+(C)$ is also closed, let x be in the closure of $J_+(C)$. Then for anx $\varepsilon>0$ we can find $y\in J_+(C)$ such that:

$$x\le y+\frac{\varepsilon}{2}e$$

where e is the unit of $\tilde{\mathcal{B}}$. It follows that

$$T_{\psi_\varepsilon} x \le T_{\psi_\varepsilon}(y + \frac{\varepsilon}{2} e) = T_{\psi_{\varepsilon/2}} y$$

and the remark at the beginning of the proof yields the desired conclusion.

Also by one of the remarks at the beginning of the proof we have that

$$\mathcal{J}(\mathcal{C}) = \{x \in \mathcal{B} \mid x^* x \in \mathcal{J}_+(\mathcal{C})\}.$$

A standard argument shows now that $\mathcal{J}(\mathcal{C})$ is a closed left ideal of $\mathcal{B}$, such that $(\mathcal{J}(\mathcal{C}))_+ = \mathcal{J}_+(\mathcal{C})$. Moreover since $T_\varphi x^* x = T_\varphi x x^*$ it follows that $\mathcal{J}(\mathcal{C})$ is self-adjoint and hence a two-sided ideal.

Since for $x \in \mathcal{I}_+$ and $\varphi \in \mathcal{F}$, $\varphi(x)$ is zero on some neighborhood of ω, property (*) implies that $\mathcal{I}_+ \subset \mathcal{J}_+(\mathcal{C})$ and hence $\mathcal{I} \subset \mathcal{J}(\mathcal{C})$.

THEOREM 4. *The correspondence*

$$\mathcal{C} \to \mathcal{J}(\mathcal{C})$$

is a bijection between cones satisfying property (*) *and closed two-sided ideals of* $\mathcal{B}$ *containing* $\mathcal{I}$. *The inverse of this bijection is*

$$\mathcal{J} \to \mathcal{C}(\mathcal{J}).$$

PROOF. It will be sufficient to prove that

$$\mathcal{J} \supset \mathcal{J}(\mathcal{C}(\mathcal{J}))$$
$$\mathcal{C} \supset \mathcal{C}(\mathcal{J}(\mathcal{C}))$$

the opposite inclusions being obvious.

To prove the first inclusion, let $x \in \mathcal{J}_+(\mathcal{C}(\mathcal{J}))$ and $\varepsilon > 0$ be fixed. Since $T_{\psi_\varepsilon} x$ is in $\mathcal{C}(\mathcal{J})$ we can find a neighborhood V_ε of ω, functions $\varphi_1, \ldots, \varphi_n \in \mathcal{F}$ and $y_1, \ldots, y_n$ elements of $\mathcal{J}_+$ such that

$$T_{\psi_\varepsilon} x(t) \le \sum_{i=1}^{n} T_{\phi_i} y_i(t) + \varepsilon/4 \quad \text{for all} \quad t \in V_\varepsilon.$$

The remarks preceding Lemma 3 imply that

$$(\varepsilon/2) \operatorname{rank} E([\varepsilon,\infty); x(t)) \le c \sum_{i=1}^{n} \operatorname{rank} E([\delta,\infty); y_i(t)) + \varepsilon/4$$

for all $t \in V_\varepsilon$ and where $c = \max_{1 \le i \le n} (\sup_{t \in V_\varepsilon} \|\varphi(y_i(t))\|)$ and $\delta = \inf(\bigcup_{1 \le i \le n} \operatorname{supp} \phi_i)$.

Repeating the y_i's several times if necessary, we may assume that

$2c<\varepsilon$ so that

$$\text{rank } E([\varepsilon,\infty); x(t)) \le \sum_{i=1}^{n} \text{rank } E([\delta,\infty); y_i(t)) + \tfrac{1}{2}$$

and since the rank of a projection is an integer, this gives:

$$\text{rank } E([\varepsilon,\infty); x(t)) \le \sum_{i=1}^{n} \text{rank } E([\delta,\infty); y_i(t)) \text{ for } t\in V_\varepsilon .$$

Using Proposition 2, we conclude that $x\in J$. Using Lemma 3, we have

$$(J(C(J)))_+ = J_+(C(J)) \subset J$$

and hence the desired conclusion.

To prove that $C\subset C(J(C))$ fix $f\in C$. Consider further $e_1, e_2, \ldots$, an orthonormal basis of H and let E_i denote the orthogonal projection onto $\mathbb{C}e_i$. For $\varepsilon>0$ let $f_{n,\varepsilon}:\Omega\setminus\{\omega\}\to[0,\infty)$ be the functions defined recurrently by $f_{0,\varepsilon}=0$, $f_{n+1,\varepsilon}=\min(f-\sum_{k=0}^{n} f_{n,\varepsilon}, \varepsilon)$. Define now $x_\varepsilon\in B$ to be the element

$$x_\varepsilon(t) = \sum_{n\ge 1} f_{n,\varepsilon}(t) E_n \quad \text{for} \quad t\in\Omega\setminus\{\omega\}$$

and note that Trace $(x_\varepsilon(t)) = f(t)$.

Our assertion will follow from property (*) once we have shown that $x_\varepsilon \in J(C)$ and that there is $\phi\in F$ such that $f\le 2T_\varphi x_\varepsilon+\varepsilon$. Clearly $x_\varepsilon\in B_+$ and $||x_\varepsilon||\le\varepsilon$.

The inequality

$$T_{\psi_\varepsilon} x_\varepsilon(t) \le \text{Trace } x_\varepsilon(t) = f(t) \quad \text{for every} \quad \delta>0,$$

together with one of the remarks at the beginning of the proof of Lemma 3 shows that $x_\varepsilon\in J_+(C)$.

For the remaining assertion, note that

$$\varepsilon + 2T_{\psi_{\varepsilon/2}} x_\varepsilon(t) \ge f(t)$$

for all $t\in\Omega$.

REMARK 5. *Let* $M\subset B_+$, *and let* J *be the closed two-sided ideal of* B *generated by* $M\cup J$. *Then* $C(J)$ *is the smallest cone with property* (*) *containing* $\{T_{\psi_\varepsilon} y \mid \varepsilon>0,\ y\in M\}$.

Indeed, the smallest cone with property (*) containing the above set is clearly contained in $C(J)$ and on the other hand the ideal corresponding to this cone contains M and hence J, so that this cone must coincide with $C(J)$.

REFERENCES

1. Brown, L.G.: Extensions and the structure of C*-algebras, *Symposia Math.* XX(1976), 539-566, Academic Press.

2. Brown, L.G.; Douglas, R.G.; Fillmore, P.A.: Unitary equivalence modulo the compact operators and extensions of C*-algebras, *Springer Lecture Notes in Math.*, 345(1973), 58-128.

3. Brown, L.G.; Douglas, R.G.; Fillmore, P.A.: Extensions of C*-algebras and K-homology, *Ann. of Math.* 105(1977), 265-324.

4. Delaroche, C.: Extensions des C*-algèbres, *Bull. Soc. Math. France*, Mémoire 29(1972).

5. Effros, E.G.: Aspects of non-commutative geometry, *Marseille*, 1977.

6. Gohberg, I.; Krein, M.G.: *Introduction to the theory of linear nonselfadjoint operators.* (*Russian*), Nauka, Moscow, 1965.

7. Kasparov, G.G.: K-functor in the extension theory of C*-algebras, preprint.

8. Pimsner, M.; Popa S.; Voiculescu, D.: Homogeneous C*-extentions of $C(X) \otimes K(H)$. Part I, *J. Operator Theory* (1979), 55-109; Part II, *J. Operator Theory* 4(1980).

9. Ru-Ying Lee: Full algebras of operator fields trivial except at one point, *Indiana Univ. Math. J.* 26(1977), 351-372.

10. Schochet, C.: Homogeneous extensions of C*-algebras and K-theory, preprint.

11. Voiculescu, D.: Remarks on the singular extension of the C*-algebra of the Heisenberg group, INCREST preprint no.36/ /1979.

M.Pimsner, S.Popa and D.Voiculescu
Department of Mathematics,
INCREST
Bdul Păcii 220, 79622 Bucharest,
Romania.

MODELLING BY L^2-BOUNDED ANALYTIC FUNCTIONS

Ioan Suciu

1. MOTIVATIONS

Let E, F be two separable Hilbert spaces. We shall denote as in [5] by $\{E,F,\Theta(\lambda)\}$ an analytic function defined in the open unit disk $\mathbb{D}$ of the complex plane with values bounded operators from E into F. We say that $\{E,F,\Theta(\lambda)\}$ is *inner* if there exists, a.e. with respect to Lebesgue measure on the unit circle $\mathbb{T}$, the strong limit

$$\Theta(e^{it})=\lim_{r\to 1}\Theta(re^{it})$$

and $\Theta(e^{it})$ is an isometry for almost all $t\in[0,2\pi]$.

Let $\{E,F,\Theta(\lambda)\}$ be either inner or the null function. Then the pointwise multiplication by $\Theta(\lambda)$ on $H^2(F)$ defines an isometry Θ from $H^2(E)$ into $H^2(F)$ and the closed subspace $\Theta H^2(E)$ of $H^2(F)$ is invariant to the shift operator S_F on $H^2(F)$. It results that the subspace $H=H^2(F)\ominus\Theta H^2(E)$ of $H^2(F)$ is invariant to S_F^*. Let T^* be the restriction of S_F^* to H. Then between the contraction T and the function $\{E,F,\Theta(\lambda)\}$ there exists an intimate connection, intrinsically described by the B.Sz.-Nagy-C.Foiaş model for T based on the characteristic function theory.

Let us consider the function $\{H,F,\Omega(\lambda)\}$ defined on $\mathbb{D}$, with values bounded operators from H into F, by

(1.1) $$\Omega(\lambda)h=h(\lambda), \qquad \lambda\in\mathbb{D},\ h\in H.$$

Clearly this function is analytic in $\mathbb{D}$ and the operator V_Ω from H into $H^2(F)$ defined by

(1.2) $$(V_\Omega h)(\lambda)=\Omega(\lambda)h, \qquad \lambda\in\mathbb{D},\ h\in H$$

is an isometry. The subspace $V_\Omega H$ of $H^2(F)$ is semi-invariant to the shift S_F and the compression of S_F to $V_\Omega H$ gives to the abstract operator T the concrete functional model we start with.

The following questions naturally arise: Does there exist a canonical intrinsic connection between the contraction T and the analytic function $\{H,F,\Omega(\lambda)\}$? What kind of analytic functions $\{H,F,\Omega(\lambda)\}$ furnish, along this line, models for contractions on H?

Let us firstly remark that the function $\{H,F,\Omega(\lambda)\}$ is not necessarily bounded. Indeed, if we take $E=F=\mathbb{C}$ - the complex field- - and $\{E,F,\Theta(\lambda)\}$ the null function, then H is the Hardy scalar space H^2. In this case

$$||\Omega(\lambda)||=(1-|\lambda|^2)^{-1/2} \qquad \lambda\in\mathbb{D} ,$$

hence $\{E,F,\Omega(\lambda)\}$ is not bounded. This example also shows that it can happen that $\Omega(\lambda)$ has no radial limit in strong sense. Indeed, if for some $t_o\in[0,2\pi]$ there exists (in strong sense) $\lim_{r\to 1}\Omega(re^{it_o})$ it results that for any $h\in H^2$ there exists $\lim_{r\to 1} h(re^{it_o})$ which is impossible.

These two remarks point out that the problem of modelling by such a function $\Omega(\lambda)$ presents some difficulties which can not be overcome by the methods used in the Sz.-Nagy-Foiaş theory based on bounded analytic functions.

2. L^2-BOUNDED ANALYTIC FUNCTIONS

We shall deal with the class of analytic functions $\{H,F,\Omega(\lambda)\}$ for which the operator V_Ω from H into $H^2(F)$ defined by

$$(V_\Omega h)(\lambda)=\Omega(\lambda)h, \qquad \lambda\in\mathbb{D},\ h\in H \tag{2.1}$$

is bounded. This means that there exists a constant M such that for any $h\in H$ we have

$$\sup_{0<r<1} \frac{1}{2\pi}\int_0^{2\pi}||\Theta(re^{it})||^2dt\le M^2||h||^2. \tag{2.2}$$

If $\Omega(\lambda)=\Sigma\Omega_k\lambda^k$ is the Taylor expansion of Ω then (2.2) is equivalent to

$$\Sigma||\Omega_k h||^2\le M^2||h||^2 , \qquad (h\in H). \tag{2.3}$$

Such a function will be called L^2-*bounded analytic function*. The function $\{H,F,\Omega(\lambda)\}$ is called *inner* if it is bounded and its radial limits are a.e. isometries. The L^2-bounded analytic function $\{H,F,\Omega(\lambda)\}$ is called *outer* if the subspace $V_\Omega H$ is a cyclic subspace for the shift operator on $H^2(F)$.

Let E_F be the spectral measure of the unitary operator given by the multiplication by e^{it} on $L^2(F)$. Setting for any Borel subset σ of the unit cicle $\mathbb{T}$

$$F_\Omega(\sigma)=V_\Omega^* E_F(\sigma)V_\Omega \ , \tag{2.4}$$

we obtain an $L(H)$-valued semi-spectral measure on $\mathbb{T}$. This semi-spectral measure will supply, in a certain sense, the lack of the boundary function of $\Omega(\lambda)$. In case $\Omega(\lambda)$ has boundary limit, i.e. there exists a measurable function $\Omega(e^{it})$ defined on $\mathbb{T}$ with values operators from H into F such that $\Theta(re^{it})$ tends a.e. to $\Theta(e^{it})$ in the strong sense, when $r\to 1$, then we have

$$dF_\Omega(e^{it})=\frac{1}{2\pi}\Omega(e^{it})^*\Omega(e^{it})dt \ . \tag{2.5}$$

Working with F_Ω instead $\Omega(e^{it})^*\Omega(e^{it})dt$ we can reproduce in this context the main factorization theorem proved in [5] in the bounded case.

THEOREM 1. (Lowdenslager, Sz.-Nagy-Foiaş factorization theorem). *Let* F *be an* $L(H)$*-valued semi-spectral measure on* $\mathbb{T}$. *Then there exists a unique* L^2*-bounded outer function* $\{H,F,\Omega(\lambda)\}$ *such that*

(i) $F_\Omega\le F$;

(ii) *If* $\{H,F',\Omega'(\lambda)\}$ *is* L^2*-bounded analytic function such that* $F_{\Omega'}\le F$ *then* $F_{\Omega'}\le F_\Omega$.

The proof of this theorem was given in [3]. Let us outline only the construction of $\Omega(\lambda)$. The semi-spectral measure F admits by Naimark dilation theorem a dilation $\{K,V,E\}$, i.e. there exist a Hilbert space K, a bounded operator V from H into K and an $L(K)$-valued spectral measure E on $\mathbb{T}$ such that for any Borel subset σ of $\mathbb{T}$ we have

$$F(\sigma)=V^*E(\sigma)V \ . \tag{2.6}$$

Let U be the unitary operator corresponding to E. We suppose that the spectral dilation $\{K,V,E\}$ of F was chosen minimal, i.e.

$$K=\bigvee_{-\infty}^{\infty} U^n VH. \tag{2.7}$$

Denote

(2.8) $$\mathcal{K}_+=\bigvee_0^{\infty} U^n VH$$

and $U_+=U|\mathcal{K}_+$. Then U_+ is an isometry on $\mathcal{K}_+$ and using Wold decomposition for U_+, we can write

(2.9) $$\mathcal{K}_+=M_+(\mathcal{F}) \oplus \mathcal{R},$$

were $\mathcal{F}=\mathcal{K}_+ \ominus U_+ \mathcal{K}_+$ is a wandering subspace for U, $M_+(\mathcal{F})=\bigoplus_0^{\infty} U^n\mathcal{F}$ and $\mathcal{R}$ reduces U_+ to a unitary operator. From the minimality condition (2.7) it follows

(2.10) $$\mathcal{K}=M(\mathcal{F}) \oplus \mathcal{R}$$

where $M(\mathcal{F})=\bigoplus_{-\infty}^{\infty} U^n\mathcal{F}$. Let $P^{\mathcal{F}}$ be the orthogonal projection from $\mathcal{K}$ onto $M(\mathcal{F})$ and $\Phi^{\mathcal{F}}$ be the Fourier representation of $M(\mathcal{F})$ on $L^2(\mathcal{F})$. Then $P^{\mathcal{F}}\mathcal{K}_+\subset M_+(\mathcal{F})$ and $\Phi^{\mathcal{F}}M_+(\mathcal{F})=H^2(\mathcal{F})$.

The function $\{H,\mathcal{F},\Omega(\lambda)\}$ defined by

(2.11) $$\Omega(\lambda)h=(\Phi^{\mathcal{F}}P^{\mathcal{F}}Vh)(\lambda), \quad \lambda\in\mathbb{D},\ h\in H$$

is the unique L^2-bounded outer function verifying the conditions (i) and (ii) of Theorem 1.

We shall call the function $\{H,\mathcal{F},\Omega(\lambda)\}$ uniquelly attached to F by Theorem 1 *the maximal outer function of* F and we shall denote it by Ω_F.

Let now T be a contraction on H. Denote by F_T the semi-spectral measure of T, i.e. the $\mathcal{L}(H)$-valued semi-spectral measure on $\mathbb{T}$ obtained by the compression to H of the spectral measure of the minimal unitary dilation of T. Let Ω_T be the maximal outer function of F_T. Using Sz.-Nagy-Foiaş geometry of the space $\mathcal{K}$ of the minimal unitary dilation U of T it is easy to show that Ω_T coincides with the function $\{H,L_*,\Omega_T(\lambda)\}$ defined by

(2.12) $$\Omega_T(\lambda)=(I-UT^*)(I-\lambda T^*)^{-1}$$

where $L_*=\overline{(I-UT_*)H}$. Identifying L_* with the defect subspace $\mathcal{D}_{T^*}=\overline{D_{T^*}H}$ of T, $D_{T^*}^2=I-TT^*$, Ω_T can be identified also to the function $\{H,\mathcal{D}_{T^*},\Omega_T(\lambda)\}$ given by

(2.13) $$\Omega_T(\lambda)=D_{T^*}(I-\lambda T^*)^{-1}.$$

In [6], I.Valuşescu established other interesting connections between Ω_T and the Sz.-Nagy-Foiaş functional model based on the characteristic function Θ_T of T.

Let now $\{E,F,\Theta(\lambda)\}$, H, $\{H,F,\Omega(\lambda)\}$ and T be as in Section 1. Then it is known that Θ coincides to the characteristic function Θ_T of T and it is easy to see that Ω coincides to the maximal outer function Ω_T of T. In this case we have also the exact factorization $F_\Omega=F_T$. Therefore between T and Ω there exists the intimate intrinsic connection given by Theorem 1. We can formulate now the second part of our problem in the following general and precise form:

Let $\{H,F,\Omega(\lambda)\}$ *be an* L^2*-contractive outer function. Find conditions on* Ω *in order to exist a contraction* T *on* H *such that the maximal outer function* Ω_T *of* T *coincides to* Ω.

We say that the contraction T on H *extrapolates* the L^2-contractive outer function $\{H,F,\Omega(\lambda)\}$ provided Ω_T coincides to Ω.

We can also consider the problem of *uniqueness of* T *which extrapolates* Ω *or, more generally, the problem of labelling by a system of free manevrable parameters of the set of all contractions* T *on* H *which extrapolate* Ω.

We can consider also the following weaker extrapolation problem: *Given an* L^2*-contractive outer function* $\{H,F,\Omega(\lambda)\}$ *does there exist an* $L(H)$*-valued semi-spectral measure on* $\mathbb{T}$ *such that* $F(\mathbb{T})=I_H$ *and* $\Omega_F=\Omega$?

In [1] T.Constantinescu showed that this problem always has a solution.

But the extrapolation by contraction is not always possible. Indeed, if $\{\mathbb{C},\mathbb{C},\Omega(\lambda)\}$ is a scalar outer function from H^2 with $\|\Omega\|\leq 1$, such that Ω can be extrapolated to a contraction on $\mathbb{C}$ then Ω has necessarily the form

$$\Omega(\lambda)=\alpha(1-|c|^2)^{1/2}(1-c\lambda)^{-1}, \qquad (\lambda\in\mathbb{D}) \tag{2.14}$$

with the constants α and c verifying $|\alpha|=1$, $|c|\leq 1$. Let us remark that these functions (excluding the case $\Omega(\lambda)\equiv 0$) are the normalized eigenvectors for the adjoint of the shift operator S on H^2.

Similar restrictive conditions are also necessary in the general case: if the L^2-contractive outer function $\{H,F,\Omega(\lambda)\}$ can be extrapolated to the contraction T on H then it is an *operator eigenvector* for the adjoint of the shift S_F on $H^2(F)$ in the sense that

(2.15) $$S_F^*(V_\Omega h)=V_\Omega T^*h \ , \qquad (h\in H).$$

This condition is equivalent to the following relations between the coefficient Ω_k of Ω and the contraction T:

(2.16) $$|\Omega_o|=D_{T^*} \ , \ \Omega_k=\Omega_o T^{*k}, \qquad k=0,1,\ldots \ .$$

In general it is difficult to express these conditions only in terms of Ω and, even if we do this, it is not a simple task to obtain T from (2.16).

The problem of labelling the set of all solutions, in the both cases of extrapolation by semi-spectral measures of total mass 1 and by contractions, presents also several difficulties.

However, the solution of such problems will offer large possibilities to construct lucrative models of semi-spectral measures or contractions having prescribed behaviour for its analytic part.

3. LABELLING BY THE SYSTEMS OF POSITIONS

In this section we propose a way to handle the problem of extrapolation by contractions which may be a first step for a recursive construction of the solution.

Let $\{H,F,\Omega(\lambda)\}$ be an L^2-contractive outer function with the Taylor expansion

$$\Omega(\lambda)=\sum_{k=0}^{\infty}\Omega_k\lambda^k \ , \qquad \lambda\in\mathbb{D} \ .$$

For a Hilbert space G let us consider the direct sum

(3.1) $$K=\ldots\oplus F_{-2}\oplus F_{-1}\oplus H\oplus G_o\oplus G_1\oplus\ldots$$

where for $k=1,2,\ldots$, $F_{-k}=F$ and for $k=0,1,\ldots$, $G_k=G$. For $f\in F$ we shall denote by $f^{(-k)}$ the element of K which has only one nonzero component, namely that from F_{-k}, which is f. Similar notation $g^{(k)}$ for $g\in G$.

Let H_n, H_{-n}, $n\geq 1$ be the subspaces in K defined as

(3.2) $$H_n=H\oplus G_o\oplus G_1\oplus\ldots\oplus G_{n-1} \ ,$$
$$H_{-n}=F_{-n}\oplus\ldots\oplus F_{-2}\oplus F_{-1}\oplus H \ .$$

We shall say that a pair of sequences $\{X_n\}_0^\infty$, $\{Y_{-n}\}_1^\infty$ defines an Ω-*good position for G* provided:

$1)_o$ $X_o: F\to H_1$ is an isometry and

$X_o F \cap G_o = \{0\}$.

For $n\geq 1$,

$1)_n$ $X_n: F\to H_{n+1}$

$Y_{-n}: G\to H_{-n}$

are isometries;

$2)_n$ $X_n F \subset H_{n+1} \ominus [\bigoplus_{k=0}^{n-1} X_k F]$

$Y_{-n} F \subset H_{-n} \ominus [\bigoplus_{k=1}^{n-1} Y_{-k} G]$;

$3)_n$ For $1\leq k\leq n$, $1\leq m\leq n$ and $f\in F$, $g\in G$ we have

$(X_k f, g^{(n)}) = (X_{k-1} f, g^{(m-1)})$

$(f^{(-m)}, Y_{-k} g) = (f^{(-m+1)}, Y_{(-k+1)} g)$, $m,k\neq 1$

$(f^{(-1)}, Y_{-1} g) = (X_o f, g^{(0)})$

$(X_k f, Y_{-m} g) = (X_{k-1} f, Y_{-m-1} g)$, $m\neq n$

$(X_k f, Y_{-n} g) = (X_{k+1} f, Y_{-n+1} g)$, $k\neq n$;

$4)_n$ $||h-\sum_{k=0}^{n} X_k \Omega_k h||^2 = ||h||^2 - \sum_{k=0}^{n} ||\Omega_k h||^2$;

$5)_n$ $(h-\sum_{k=0}^{n} X_k \Omega_k h, X_m f) = 0$ for $m\leq n$, $h\in H$, $f\in F$;

6) setting for $n\geq 0$ $F_n = X_n f$ and for $n\geq 1$ $G_{-n} = Y_{-n} G$ we have

$$K = \bigoplus_{-\infty}^{\infty} F_n \bigvee \bigoplus_{-\infty}^{\infty} G_n .$$

Let T be a completely non unitary contraction on H and U acting on K be its minimal unitary dilation. From [5] it is known that

(3.3) $K = \dots \oplus U^{*2} L_* \oplus U^* L_* \oplus H \oplus L \oplus UL \oplus \dots$,

where $L = \overline{[U-T]H}$, $L_* = \overline{[I-UT^*]H}$. Let $\{H, L_*, \Omega(\lambda)\}$ be the maximal outer function of T identified as in (2.12). Then the coefficient Ω_k of $\Omega_T(\lambda)$ are given by

(3.4) $$\Omega_k h=[I-UT^*]T^{*k}h , \quad k=0,1,\ldots, h\in H.$$

Identifying K in the obvious way with the direct sum

(3.5) $$K=\ldots \oplus L_{*-2} \oplus L_{*-1} \oplus H \oplus L_o \oplus L_1 \oplus \ldots$$

and setting $X_n=U^n|L_*$, $n=0,1,\ldots$ and $Y_{-n}=U^{*n}|L$, $n=1,2,\ldots$, then the pair $\{X_n\}_0^\infty$, $\{Y_n\}_1^\infty$ is an Ω_T-good position for L. Indeed, the conditions $1)_n$, $2)_n$, $3)_n$ and 6) result from the known properties of the geometry of the minimal unitary dilation of completely nonunitary contractions (cf. [5]). The conditions $4)_n$, $5)_n$ also result by a simple computation using the form (3.4) of the coefficients of $\Omega_T(\lambda)$.

More important is the following:

THEOREM 2. *Let* $\{H,F,\Omega(\lambda)\}$ *be an* L^2*-contractive outer function. To any* Ω*-good position of a Hilbert space* G *it corresponds a completely nonunitary contraction* T *on* H *such that* Ω_T *coincides with* Ω.

PROOF. Let K be given by (3.1). We shall define the unitary operator U on K in the following manner: let $k_1\in\bigoplus_{-\infty}^{\infty} F_k$ and $k_2\in \bigoplus_{-\infty}^{\infty} G_k$ be of the form

$$k_1=\sum_{-\infty}^{\infty} f_k^{(k)} , \qquad f_k\in F ,$$

$$k_2=\sum_{-\infty}^{\infty} g_k^{(k)} \qquad g_k\in G.$$

Define

(3.6) $$U(k_1+k_2)=\sum_{-\infty}^{\infty} f_k^{(k+1)}+\sum_{-\infty}^{\infty} g_k^{(k+1)} .$$

Using $3)_n$ for any n we can prove that $||U(k_1+k_2)||=||k_1+k_2||$ and from 6) it results that U can be extended to a unitary operator on K.

Denote

(3.7) $$K_+=H \oplus G_o \oplus G_1 \oplus \ldots .$$

Since clearly

$$K \ominus K_+=\ldots \oplus F_{-2} \oplus F_{-1} ,$$

it results $K \ominus K_+$ is invariant to U^*, therefore K_+ is invariant to U. Denote $U_+=U|K_+$.

We shall show that

(3.8) $$K_+=\bigvee_0^\infty U^n H.$$

First, let us remark that if $k\in K_+$ is of the form $k=g^{(0)}$, $g\in G$ then

$$U_+^* K=P_{K_+} U^* g^{(0)}=P_{K_+} Y_{-1} g=P_H Y_{-1} g \ ,$$

i.e.

(3.9) $$U_+^* k\in H \ , \ k=g^{(0)}, \quad g\in G \ .$$

Let now $k\in K_+$ be orthogonal to $\bigvee_0^\infty U^n H$. It results $U_+^{*n} k\in K_+ \ominus H$ for each $n\geq 0$. Write

(3.10) $$U_+^{*n} k=\sum_{j=0}^\infty g_{n,j}^{(j)}$$

with $g_{n,j}\in G$, $n,j=0,1,\ldots$.

Then, for $n\geq 1$ we have

$$\sum_{j=0}^\infty g_{n,j}^{(j)}=U_+^{*n}k=U_+^*U_+^{*n-1}k=U_+^*\sum_{j=0}^\infty g_{n-1,j}^{(j)}=U_+^* g_{n-1,0}^{(0)}+\sum_{j=0}^\infty g_{n-1,j+1}^{(j)} .$$

Using (3.9) we obtain

(3.11) $$U_+^* g_{n-1,0}^{(0)}=0 \text{ and } g_{n,j}=g_{n-1,j+1} \ , \ n\geq 1, \ j=0,1,\ldots \ .$$

It results

(3.12) $$g_{n,0}=g_{n-1,1}=\ldots=g_{0,n} \ , \qquad n\geq 1.$$

Since from (3.11) we obtain

$$(P_H Y_{-1} g_{n,0}, h)=(P_H U^* g_{n,0}^{(0)}, h)=(U_+^* g_{n,0}^{(0)}, h)=0$$

for any $n\geq 0$, it results

(3.13) $$Y_{-1} g_{n,0}\in F_{-1} \ , \quad \text{for} \quad n\geq 0 \ .$$

Let $f_n^{(-1)}=Y_{-1} g_{n,0}$. Then

(3.14) $$X_o f_n=U f_n^{(-1)}=UU^* g_{n,0}^{(0)}=g_{n,0}^{(0)} \ .$$

From (3.14) it results $g_{n,0}^{(0)}\in X_o F\cap G_o$ and from $1)_0$ we obtain $g_{n,0}=0$ for $n\geq 0$. Using now (3.12) we conclude $g_{0,n}=0$ for any n i.e. $k=0$.

It results that H is semi-invariant to U and if we denote by T the compression of U to H then T is a contraction on H and U acting on K is the minimal unitary dilation of T.

Let now $R \subset K_+$ such that

(3.15) $$K_+ = \bigoplus_0^{\infty} F_n \oplus R.$$

It results

$$K = \bigoplus_{-\infty}^{\infty} F_n \oplus R.$$

Clearly then R reduces U and consequentely U_+ and $U_+|R$ is unitary.

It results that (3.15) is the Wold decomposition of the minimal isometric dilation U_+ of T. Then from the known geometry of the minimal isometric dilation (cf. [5], Ch.II) it results

(3.16) $$F_o = K_+ \ominus U_+ K_+ = \overline{[I-UT^*]H} = L_*$$

$$G_o = [K_+ \ominus H] \ominus U[K_+ \ominus H] = \overline{[U-T]H} = L.$$

Using (3.16) and 6) we have

$$M(L_*) \vee M(L) = \bigoplus_{-\infty}^{\infty} U^n L_* \bigvee \bigoplus_{-\infty}^{\infty} U^n L = \bigoplus_{-\infty}^{\infty} F_n \bigvee \bigoplus_{-\infty}^{\infty} G_n = K ,$$

which implies that T is completely nonunitary.

Define now for any $n \geq 0$

(3.17) $$Q_n h = h - \sum_{j=0}^{n} X_j \Omega_j h, \qquad h \in H.$$

From $4)_n$ it results that Q_n is a contraction from H into K_+. Since for any $h \in H$ we have

$$\sum_{j=0}^{\infty} ||X_j \Omega_j h||^2 = \sum_{j=0}^{\infty} ||\Omega_j h||^2 = ||V_\Omega h||^2 \leq ||h||^2$$

it results that $\sum_{j=0}^{n} X_j \Omega_j h$ tends in $\bigoplus_{j=0}^{\infty} F_j$ to $\sum_{j=0}^{\infty} X_j \Omega_j h$. Therefore there exists the strong limit

(3.18) $$Q = \text{s-lim}\, Q_n$$

and for any $h \in H$

(3.19) $$h = \sum_{j=0}^{\infty} X_j \Omega_j h + Qh .$$

From $5)_n$ it results that for any $n \geq 0$ and $h \in H$, $Q_n h$ is orthogonal to $\bigoplus_{j=0}^{n} F_n$. It results $Qh \in R$ and from (3.19) we obtain

$$(3.20)\qquad \begin{cases} Qh=P_R h \\ \Sigma X_j \Omega_j h = P^{L_*}h\ , \qquad h\in H\ , \end{cases}$$

which proves that the function $\{H,F,\Omega(\lambda)\}$ coincides to the maximal outer function $\{H,L_*,\Omega_T(\lambda)\}$ of T.

The proof of the Theorem is complete.

For an Ω-good position $\sigma=\{\{X_n\}_0^\infty,\ \{Y_{-n}\}_1^\infty, G\}$ let us denote by K_σ the Hilbert space attached by (3.1) to σ. We say that two Ω-good positions $\sigma=\{\{X_n\}_0^\infty,\{Y_{-n}\}_{-1}^\infty,G\}$ and $\sigma'=\{\{X'_n\}_0^\infty,\{Y'_{-n}\}_{-1}^\infty,G'\}$ *coincide* iff there exists a unitary operator Z from K_σ onto $K_{\sigma'}$ such that $Z|H=I_H$ and $ZX_n=X'_n$, $n\geq 0$, $ZY_{-n}=Y'_{-n}$, $n\geq 1$.

Summing up the above results we obtain the following labelling of the set of all completely nonunitary contractions which extrapolate a given L^2-contractive outer function $\{H,F,\Omega(\lambda)\}$:

THEOREM 3. *There exists a one-to-one correspondence between the set of all Ω-good positions $\sigma=\{\{X_n\}_0^\infty\ ,\{Y_{-n}\}_1^\infty\ ,G\}$ and the set of all completely nonunitary contractions T on H which extrapolate Ω.*

4. EXTRAPOLATION BY NORMAL CONTRACTIONS

If we look for a normal contraction T which extrapolates the L^2-bounded outer function $\{H,F,\Omega(\lambda)\}$ then the necessary and sufficient conditions on $\Omega(\lambda)$ are easier to describe.

Indeed, suppose that there exists a normal contraction T such that $\Omega_T(\lambda)$ coincides $\Omega(\lambda)$. Then using the form (2.13) of Ω_T and taking into account that $D_T=D_{T^*}$ we obtain

$$|\Omega_k|^2=T^kD_T^2T^{*k}=D_T^2(T^*T)^k=|\Omega_o|^2(I-|\Omega_o|^2)^k\ .$$

Let $T^*=Z|T|$ and $\Omega_k=Z_k|\Omega_k|$ be the polar decomposition of T^* and Ω_k. Then

$$\Omega_k=\Omega_oT^{*k}=Z_o|\Omega_o|Z^k|T|^k=Z_oZ^k|\Omega_o|(I-|\Omega_o|^2)^{k/2}=Z_oZ^k|\Omega_k|\ .$$

It results that Z_k coincides with Z_oZ^k on $\overline{|\Omega_k|H}$. In fact we have the following:

THEOREM 4. *Let $\{H,F,\Omega(\lambda)\}$ be an L^2-contractive outer function on $\mathbb{D}$ with Taylor expansion $\Omega(\lambda)=\Sigma\Omega_k\lambda^k$. Let $\Omega_k=Z_k|\Omega_k|$ be the polar* *decomposition of* Ω_k. *Then* $\{H,F,\Omega(\lambda)\}$ *can be extrapolated to a normal contraction on* H *if and only if*:

i) $|\Omega_k|^2=|\Omega_o|^2(I-|\Omega_o|^2)^k$

ii) *There exists a unitary operator* Z *on* $(I-|\Omega_o|^2)H$ *such that* $Z_k=Z_oZ^k$ *on* $\overline{|\Omega_k|H}$.

In case $\{H,F,\Omega(\lambda)\}$ satisfies i) and ii) then we can also describe the system of the free parameters which produce the normal extrapolators T. Set $D_k=\overline{|\Omega_k|H}$. From i) it results that $D_k\subset D_{k+1}$. Let $G_{k+1}=D_k\ominus D_{k+1}$ and $G_\infty=\bigcap_o^\infty D_k$. Then to each system $\{U_k\}$ where for $k=0,1,\ldots,\infty$, U_k is a unitary operator on D_k, it corresponds a normal contraction T which extrapolates $\Omega(\lambda)$.

For the proof we shall take $G=\overline{|\Omega_o|H}$ and using the sequence $\{U_n\}_o^\infty$ we shall produce recursively the sequences $\{X_n\}_o^\infty$, $\{Y_{-n}\}_1^\infty$ which form an Ω-good position for G. The complete proofs and other facts related to normal extrapolators will be given in [2].

5. MOTIVATIONS FROM PREDICTION THEORY

In the classical prediction theory for the stationary proceses (cf. [7]) the factorization of the spectral distribution (as in Theorem 1) plays a crucial role in the construction of the linear filter for prediction and in the evaluation of the prediction error.

In [4], working with the notion of complete correlated action as the time domain, a prediction theory for the infinite variate stationary processes was developed including the construction of the linear fileter for prediction, in case the spectral distribution satisfies certain boundedness conditions.

Recall that to any complete correlated action we can attach its operatorial model as follows:if H is the Hilbert space of parameters then there exists the Hilbert space K (the measuring space) such that the states can be described by operators from H into K. If V_1, $V_2\in L(H,K)$ then the correlation is given by

(5.1) $$\Gamma[V_1,V_2]=V_1^*V_2 .$$

A *stationary process* is a sequence $\{V_n\}_{-\infty}^\infty$ of states such that the autocorrelation function $\Gamma[k]=\Gamma[V_n , V_{n+k}]$ is well defined ($\Gamma[V_n ,V_{n+k}]$ depends only on k). Then $k\to\Gamma[k]$ is a positive definite function on the group of integers with values operators on H. The spectral distribution of the process is the unique $L(H)$-valued semi-spectral measure F on $\mathbb{T}$ wich represents Γ, i.e.

(5.2) $$\Gamma[k]=\int e^{-ikt}dF(t) , \qquad k\in\mathbb{Z}.$$

We suppose that $K=\bigvee_{-\infty}^{\infty} V_nH$. Then there exists a unique unitary operator U on K such that $UV_nh=V_{n-1}h$, $n\in\mathbb{Z}$, $h\in H$ the so-called backward shift of the process. If we denote $V=V_o$ then the process can be written as

(5.3) $$V_n=U^{*n}V$$

and $\{K,V,U\}$ is the minimal unitary dilation of the semi-spectral measure F.

The prediction problems for the process $\{V_n\}_{-\infty}^{\infty}$ were formulated in [4] as follows:

(i) Does there exists the state $\hat{V}_o$ in $L(E,K)$ such that

(5.4) $$\Gamma[V_o-\hat{V}_o,V_o-\hat{V}_o]=\inf_Z \Gamma[V_o-Z,V_o-Z]$$

where the infimum in (5.4) is taken (in the partially ordered set of positive operators on H) from the set of all operators Z on H of the form $Z=\sum_{j=1}^{n} A_jV_{-j}$, n arbitrary integer and $\{A_1\ldots A_n\}$ an arbitrary system of operators on H (the so called past and present of the processes)?

(ii) Does there exists the sequence $\{A_n\}_o^{\infty}$ of operators on H (of actions) such that the *predictible* part $\hat{V}_o$ of V_o can be obtained as the response of the Wiener filter with coefficients A_n , i.e.

(5.5) $$\hat{V}_o=\sum_{n=0}^{\infty} A_nV_{-(n+1)}$$

where the series in (5.5) is supposed to be convergent in the strong sense in $L(H,K)$?

For the convenience we denoted by AV, $A\in L(H)$, $V\in L(H,K)$ the right action of $L(H)$ on $L(H,K)$.

The positive operator $G=\Gamma[V_o-\hat{V}_o,V_o-\hat{V}_o]$ on H is the square of the *prediction error operator*.

In [4] it was proved that $\hat{V}_o$ always exists and is given by

(5.6) $$\hat{V}_o h = P_{UK_+} V_o h \quad , \qquad h \in H$$

where $K_+ = \bigvee_0^{\infty} U^n H$.

Let $\{H, F, \Omega(\lambda)\}$ be the maximal outer function of F. Then $G = \Omega(0)^* \Omega(0)$. In case F satisfies the boundedness condition

(5.7) $$c\, dt \le F \le 1/c\, dt$$

with $0<c<1$ and dt the normalized Lebesgue measure on $\mathbb{T}$, then the maximal outer function of F has the form $\{H, H, \Omega(\lambda)\}$, is bounded and invertible, its inverse $\{H, H, \Omega'(\lambda)\}$ being also a bounded analytic function. In this case the Wiener filter for prediction has the coefficients given by

$$A_n = \sum_{p=0}^{j} \Omega_{n+1} \Omega'_{n-p}$$

where Ω_k , Ω'_k are the coefficients of Ω and Ω', respectively.

Suppose now that there exists a contraction T on H such that $F = F_T$. Then $V_o = V$ is an isometry, the usual embedding of H in the space K of minimal unitary dilation. In this identification (5.6) gives:

$$\hat{V}_o h = P_{UK_+} h = h - P_{L_*} h = UT^* h$$

or in the time domain

(5.8) $$\hat{V}_o = T^* V_{-1} \ .$$

Therefore in this case the Wiener filter has the form $A_o = T^*$ and $A_n = 0$ for $n \neq 0$. The prediction error operator is D_{T^*}.

Suppose now that $F(\mathbb{T}) = I_H$ and that there exists a contraction T on H which extrapolates the maximal outer function of F. Then the prediction error operator is again D_{T^*} and taking $\hat{\hat{V}}_o = T^* V_{-1}$ we obtain

$$D^2_{T^*} \le \Gamma[V_o - \hat{\hat{V}}_o,\ V_o - \hat{\hat{V}}_o] = [V_o - UV_o T^*]^*[V_o - UV_o T^*] =$$

$$= D^2_{T^*} + [2TT^* - V_o^* U V_o T^* - T V_o^* U^* V_o] = D^2_{T^*} + 2[TT^* - \mathrm{Re}\Gamma(-1) T^*].$$

Hence $\hat{\hat{V}}_o$ is an estimator for V_o with an error which can be controlled making a careful choice of the extrapolator T.

REFERENCES

1. Constantinescu, T.: Thesys, Math.Fac.Univ.Bucharest, 1980.

2. Constantinescu, T.; Suciu, I.: Extrapolation by normal contractions, to appear.

3. Suciu, I.; Valuşescu, I.: Factorization of semispectral measures, *Rev.Roumaine Math.Pures Appl.* 21 (1976), 773-793.

4. Suciu, I.; Valuşescu, I.: Factorization theorems and prediction theory, *Rev.Roumaine Math.Pures Appl.* 23 (1978), 1393--1423.

5. Sz.-Nagy, B.; Foiaş, C.: *Harmonic analysis of operators on Hilberts space*, Acad.Kiadô, Budapest and North-Holland, Amsterdam/London.

6. Valuşescu, I.: The maximal function of a contraction, *Acta Sci.Math.(Szeged)* 42 (1980), 183-188.

7. Wiener, N.: *The extrapolation, interpolation and smoothing of stationary time series*, New-York, 1950.

Ioan Suciu
Department of Mathematics,
INCREST,
Bdul Păcii 220, 79622 Bucharest,
Romania.

THE MAXIMAL FUNCTION OF DOUBLY COMMUTING CONTRACTIONS

N.Suciu and I.Valuşescu

1. Let $\mathbb{D}$ be the open unit disc and $\mathbb{T}$ be the unit torus in the complex plane $\mathbb{C}$. Denote by m the normalized Lebesgue measure on $\mathbb{T}$ and by $m_2=m \otimes m$ the normalized Lebesgue measure on the bidimensional torus $\mathbb{T}^2$. For a complex separable Hilbert space H, let $L^2(\mathbb{T}^2;H)$ be the Hilbert space of the measurable functions from $\mathbb{T}^2$ to H, with the scalar product

$$(1.1) \qquad (u,v)_{L^2(\mathbb{T}^2;H)} = \int_{\mathbb{T}^2} (u(w),v(w))_H dm_2(w).$$

As in the unidimensional case, we also have (see [3]) a Poisson formula in the bidisc. Namely, if $z=(r_1e^{it_1},r_2e^{it_2})$, and $w=(e^{is_1},e^{is_2})$, where $0\leq r_j<1$ and $0\leq t_j,s_j\leq 2\pi$, $j=1,2$, then for any $u\in L^2(\mathbb{T}^2;H)$ we have

$$(1.2) \qquad P[u](z)=\int_{\mathbb{T}^2} P(z,w)u(w)dm_2(w)= \sum_{n,j=-\infty}^{\infty} r_1^{|n|}r_2^{|j|}e^{i(nt_1+jt_2)}\hat{u}(n,j)$$

where $P(z,w)$ is the bidimensional Poisson kernel

$$(1.3) \qquad P(z,w)=\frac{(1-r_1)^2(1-r_2^2)}{(1-2r_1\cos(t_1-s_1)+r_1^2)(1-2r_2\cos(t_2-s_2)+r_2^2)}$$

and $\hat{u}(n,j)$ are the Fourier coefficients of the function u:

$$(1.4) \qquad \hat{u}(n,j)=\int_{\mathbb{T}^2} \bar{w}_1^n\bar{w}_2^j u(w_1,w_2)dm_2(w_1,w_2) .$$

Let $L_+^2(\mathbb{T}^2,H)$ be the subspace of the functions $u\in L^2(\mathbb{T}^2;H)$ with the property that $P[u]$ are analytic functions on $\mathbb{D}^2$. As in the scalar case [3] we have $u\in L_+^2(\mathbb{T}^2;H)$ if and only if its Fourier coefficients $\hat{u}(n,j)=0$ for $n<0$ or $j<0$. Moreover, if $u\in L^2(\mathbb{T}^2;H)$, $f=P[u]$, and for $w_1,w_2\in\mathbb{T}$, $0\leq r<1$ we put $f_r(w_1,w_2)=f(rw_1,rw_2)$ then we have

(1.5) $$||u||_{L^2(\mathbb{T}^2;H)} = \sup_{0\le r<1} \int_{\mathbb{T}^2} ||f_r(w_1,w_2)||^2 dm_2(w_1,w_2) = \sum_{n,j=0}^{\infty} ||\hat{u}(n,j)||^2.$$

If (T_1,T_2) are doubly commuting contractions on the Hilbert space H, then [5] there exists a minimal unitary dilation (U_1,U_2) on a Hilbert space $K\supset H$ which is called the *natural unitary dilation* of (T_1,T_2). Let us sketch the construction of this dilation. First take the minimal unitary dilation S_2 of T_2 on the space $K_o=\bigvee_{n=-\infty}^{+\infty} S_2^n H$. Then take the $*$-extension S_1 on K_o of T_1 such that $S_2S_1=S_1S_2$, $||S_1||=||T_1||$, and consider the minimal unitary dilation U_1 of S_1 on the space $K=\bigvee_{-\infty}^{\infty} U_1^n K_o$. Finally, take the $*$-extension U_2 on K of S_2 such that $U_1U_2=U_2U_1$. For more details see [5].

If we consider the space

(1.6) $$K^+=\bigvee_{n,j=0}^{\infty} U_1^n U_2^j H$$

and $V_i=U_i|K^+$, $(i=1,2)$, then V_1 and V_2 are doubly commuting isometries on K^+ and (V_1,V_2) is a minimal isometric dilation of (T_1,T_2). The Wold decomposition of (V_1,V_2) is given by

(1.7) $$K^+=\bigoplus_{n,j=0}^{\infty} U_1^n U_2^j L \oplus (R_1(H)\vee R_2(H)),$$

where

(1.8) $$L=U_1U_2\overline{(U_1^*U_2^*+T_1^*T_2^*-U_1^*T_2^*-U_2^*T_1^*)H},$$

and for $i=1,2$,

(1.9) $$R_i(H)=\bigcap_{n=0}^{\infty} V_i^n K^+,$$

the subspaces of K^+ which reduce V_i to the unitary parts in the corresponding Wold decomposition of V_i.

2. Let H_1, H_2 be two separable Hilbert spaces. The triplet $\{H_1,H_2,\Theta(z_1,z_2)\}$ is called an *analytic function* on $\mathbb{D}^2$ if

(2.1) $$\Theta(z_1,z_2)=\sum_{n,j=0}^{\infty} z_1^n z_2^j \Theta_{nj} \qquad (z_1,z_2\in\mathbb{D}),$$

where $\{\Theta_{nj}\}$ $(n,j\ge 0)$ is a system of bounded linear operators from H_1 to H_2 and the series (2.1) is convergent (weakly, strongly or in norm, which is the same for power series) in $\mathbb{D}^2$.

The analytic function $\{H_1, H_2, \Theta(z_1, z_2)\}$ is L^2-*bounded* if there exists a positive constant M such that for any $h \in H_1$

$$\sup_{0\leq r<1} \int_{\mathbb{T}^2} \|\Theta(rw_1, rw_2)h\|^2 dm_2(w_1, w_2) \leq M^2 \|h\|^2. \tag{2.2}$$

The analytic function $\{H_1, H_2, \Theta(z_1, z_2)\}$ is *bounded* if

$$\|\Theta(z_1, z_2)\| \leq M \qquad (z_1, z_2 \in \mathbb{D}). \tag{2.3}$$

Let us remark that (2.2) is equivalent with

$$\sum_{n,j=0}^{\infty} \|\Theta_{nj} h\|^2 \leq M^2 \|h\|^2, \quad (h \in H_1). \tag{2.4}$$

Also, we remark that if $\{\Theta_{nj}\}$ $(n, j \geq 0)$ is a sequence of bounded linear operators form H_1 to H_2 with the property (2.4), then (2.1) defines an L^2-bounded analytic function on $\mathbb{D}^2$. Indeed, for any $h \in H_1$ we have

$$\sum_{n,j=0}^{\infty} \|z_1^n z_2^j \Theta_{nj} h\| = \sum_{n=0}^{\infty} |z_1^n| \sum_{j=0}^{\infty} |z_2^j| \|\Theta_{nj} h\| \leq$$

$$\leq \sqrt{\left(\sum_{n=0}^{\infty} |z_1^{2n}|\right)\left(\sum_{j=0}^{\infty} |z_2^{2j}|\right)\left(\sum_{n,j=0}^{\infty} \|\Theta_{nj} h\|^2\right)}$$

and the series (2.1) is convergent.

As in the unidimensional case, we can define the $L(H)$-valued *semi-spectral measure* on $\mathbb{T}^2$ to be a map F from the family $B(\mathbb{T}^2)$ of the Borel sets of $\mathbb{T}^2$ into $L(H)$ such that for any $h \in H$, $\sigma \to (F(\sigma)h, h)$ is a positive Borel measure. A semi-spectral measure E is *spectral* if for any $\sigma_1, \sigma_2 \in B(\mathbb{T}^2)$ one have $E(\sigma_1 \cap \sigma_2) = E(\sigma_1)E(\sigma_2)$ and $E(\mathbb{T}^2) = I_H$. Of a particular interest are the spectral measures $E_H^{\times}$ on $\mathbb{T}^2$ corresponding to the unitary operators $U_j^{\times}$ of multiplication by the coordinate functions on $L^2(\mathbb{T}^2; H)$

$$(U_j^{\times} f)(w_1, w_2) = w_j f(w_1, w_2) \qquad (f \in L^2(\mathbb{T}^2; H);\ j=1,2). \tag{2.5}$$

By a *spectral dilation* of an $L(H)$-valued semi-spectral measure F on $\mathbb{T}^2$ we mean a triplet $[K, V, E]$, where K is a Hilbert space, V is a bounded operator from H into K and E is an $L(K)$-valued spectral measure on $\mathbb{T}^2$ such that for any $\sigma \in B(\mathbb{T}^2)$ we have

$$F(\sigma) = V^* E(\sigma) V. \tag{2.6}$$

The Naimark dilation theorem assures that any semi-spectral

measure has a spectral dilation.

As in [7] one can show that the L^2-bounded analytic functions on $\mathbb{D}^2$ correspond to a class of semi-spectral measures on $\mathbb{T}^2$, so called semi-spectral measures of *analytic type*, i.e. the $L(H_1)$-valued semi-spectral measures which admit a spectral dilation of the form $[L^2(\mathbb{T}^2;H_2),V,E^{\times}_{H_2}]$ such that $VH_1\subset L^2_+(\mathbb{T}^2;H_2)$.

THEOREM 1. *If* $\{H_1,H_2,\Theta(z_1,z_2)\}$ *is an* L^2*-bounded analytic function, then there exists an* $L(H_1)$*-valued semi-spectral measure* F_Θ *of analytic type on* $\mathbb{T}^2$ *such that for any* $h\varepsilon H_1$

$$\Theta(z_1,z_2)h=P[V_\Theta h](z_1,z_2), \qquad ((z_1,z_2)\varepsilon\mathbb{D}^2). \tag{2.7}$$

Conversely, if F *is an* $L(H_1)$*-valued semi-spectral measure of analytic type on* $\mathbb{T}^2$ *and* $[L^2(\mathbb{T}^2;H_2),V,E^{\times}_{H_2}]$ *is its spectral dilation then*

$$\Theta(z_1,z_2)h=P[Vh](z_1,z_2), \qquad (z_1,z_2\varepsilon\mathbb{D};h\varepsilon H_1) \tag{2.8}$$

defines an L^2*-bounded analytic function* $\{H_1,H_2,\Theta(z_1,z_2)\}$ *on* $\mathbb{D}^2$ *such that* $V_\Theta=V$, $F_\Theta=F$.

PROOF. Let $\{H_1,H_2,\Theta(z_1,z_2)\}$ be an L^2-bounded analytic function. From (2.1) and (2.4) we can define for any $h\varepsilon H_1$ the function $u_h\varepsilon L^2_+(\mathbb{T}^2;H_2)$ by

$$u_h(w_1,w_2)=\sum_{n,j=0}^{\infty} w_1^n w_2^j \Theta_{nj}h \tag{2.9}$$

and $V_\Theta:H_1\to L^2(\mathbb{T}^2;H_2)$ by $V_\Theta h=u_h$. The operator V_Θ is bounded, since for any $h\varepsilon H_1$ we have

$$||V_\Theta h||^2_{L^2(\mathbb{T}^2;H_2)}=||u_h||^2_{L^2(\mathbb{T}^2;H_2)}=\sum_{n,j=0}^{\infty}||\Theta_{nj}h||^2\le M^2||h||^2.$$

From (2.9) it follows that $V_\Theta H_1\subset L^2_+(\mathbb{T}^2;H_2)$ and for any $z_1,z_2\varepsilon\mathbb{D}$ and $h\varepsilon H_1$ we have $P[V_\Theta h](z_1,z_2)=\Theta(z_1,z_2)h$. If we consider

$$F_\Theta(\sigma)=V^*_\Theta E^{\times}_{H_2}(\sigma)V_\Theta, \qquad (\sigma\varepsilon B(\mathbb{T}^2)), \tag{2.10}$$

then we obtain an $L(H_1)$-valued semi-spectral measure F_Θ on $\mathbb{T}^2$ of analytic type which satisfies (2.7).

Conversely, if F is an $L(H_1)$-valued semi-spectral measure of analytic type on $\mathbb{T}^2$ and $[L^2(\mathbb{T}^2;H_2),V,E^{\times}_{H_2}]$ is its spectral dilation, then by (1.5) we have

$$(2.11)\qquad \sum_{n,j=0}^{\infty} ||\hat{Vh}(n,j)||^2 = ||Vh||^2_{L^2(\mathbb{T}^2;H_2)} \leq ||V||^2||h||^2, \qquad (h\in H_1).$$

Therefore, if we take $\Theta_{nj}h=\hat{Vh}(n,j)$, $(h\in H_1,\ n,j\geq 0)$ then $\{\Theta_{nj}\}_{n,j\geq 0}$ is a sequence of bounded linear operators from H_1 to H_2 which verifies (2.4), and

$$\Theta(z_1,z_2)h=\sum_{n,j=0}^{\infty} z_1^n z_2^j \Theta_{nj}h=P[Vh](z_1,z_2), \qquad ((z_1,z_2)\in\mathbb{D}^2)$$

defines an L^2-bounded analytic function $\{H_1,H_2,\Theta(z_1,z_2)\}$ on $\mathbb{D}^2$. Moreover, we have $V_\Theta=V$ and $F_\Theta=F$, and the proof is finished.

Let us remark that if $\{H_1,H_2,\Theta(z_1,z_2)\}$ is a bounded analytic function and $N_i\subset H_i$ with card $N_i=\aleph_0$, $\bar{N}_i=H_i$ (i=1,2) and we consider the operator $V_\Theta:H_1\to L^2_+(\mathbb{T}^2;H_2)$ associated to $\{H_1,H_2,\Theta(z_1,z_2)\}$ in the preceding theorem, then (see [3], Theorem 2.3.1) there exists $\sigma\in\mathcal{B}(\mathbb{T}^2)$, $m_2(\sigma)=0$, such that for any $(w_1,w_2)\in\mathbb{T}^2\setminus\sigma$ and any $h\in N_1$, $k\in N_2$ we have

$$((V_\Theta h)(w_1,w_2),k)=\lim_{r\to 1}(\Theta(rw_1,rw_2)h,k).$$

It follows that for any $(w_1,w_2)\notin\sigma$ and $h\in N_1$

$$||(V_\Theta h)(w_1,w_2)||\leq \sup_{(z_1,z_2)\in\mathbb{D}^2}||\Theta(z_1,z_2)||\,||h||.$$

Now we can assert a boundedness condition for an L^2-bounded analytic function as follows.

PROPOSITION 2. *An L^2-bounded analytic function $\{H_1,H_2,\Theta(z_1,z_2)\}$ is bounded if and only if its semi-spectral measure F_Θ is bounded dominated by the Lebesque measure m_2 on $\mathbb{T}^2$.*

PROOF. If $\{H_1,H_2,\Theta(z_1,z_2)\}$ is a bounded analytic function, then by the preceding theorem and the above remark there exists a positive constant M such that for any positive trigonometric polynomial p on $\mathbb{T}^2$ and $h\in N_1$ we have

$$\int_{\mathbb{T}^2} p(w_1,w_2)\,d(F_\Theta(w_1,w_2)h,h)=\int_{\mathbb{T}^2} p(w_1,w_2)\,d(E^{\times}_{H_2}(w_1,w_2)V_\Theta h,V_\Theta h)=$$

$$=(p(U_1^{\times},U_2^{\times})V_\Theta h,V_\Theta h)_{L^2(\mathbb{T}^2;H_2)}=\int_{\mathbb{T}^2}((p(U_1^{\times},U_2^{\times})V_\Theta h)(w_1,w_2)\,dm_2(w_1,w_2)=$$

$$=\int_{\mathbb{T}^2} p(w_1,w_2)\|(V_\Theta h)(w_1,w_2)\|^2 dm_2(w_1,w_2) \le M^2 \int_{\mathbb{T}^2} p\|h\|^2 dm_2 .$$

It follows that

$$(2.12) \qquad (F_\Theta(\sigma)h,h) \le M^2 m_2(\sigma)\|h\|^2, \qquad (\sigma\in\mathcal{B}(\mathbb{T}^2),\ h\in H_1),$$

i.e. the semi-spectral measure F_Θ is bounded dominated by m_2 on $\mathbb{T}^2$.

Conversely, if F_Θ is bounded dominated by the Lebesgue measure m_2 on $\mathbb{T}^2$, then for any positive trigonometric polynomial p on $\mathbb{T}^2$ and any $h\in H_1$, we have

$$\int_{\mathbb{T}^2} p(w_1,w_2)\|(V_\Theta h)(w_1,w_2)\|^2 dm_2(w_1,w_2) \le M^2 \int_{\mathbb{T}^2} p\|h\|^2 dm_2 ,$$

whence

$$(2.13) \qquad \|(V_\Theta h)(w_1,w_2)\| \le M\|h\| \quad \text{a.e. .}$$

Using (1.2), Theorem 1 and (2.13), it follows that

$$\|\Theta(z_1,z_2)h\| = \|P[V_\Theta h](z_1,z_2)\| \le \int_{\mathbb{T}^2} P(z,w)\|(V_\Theta h)(w)\| dm_2(w) \le$$

$$\le M\|h\| \int_{\mathbb{T}^2} P(z,w)\, dm_2(w) = M\|h\|,$$

i.e. the analytic function $\{H_1,H_2,\Theta(z_1,z_2)\}$ is a bounded one, and the proof is finished.

Let us remark that if H is a Hilbert space and $U_1^\times, U_2^\times$ are the multiplication operators defined by (2.5), then if we put $V_i^\times = U_i^\times | L_+^2(\mathbb{T}^2;H)$, $i=1,2$, then $V_1^\times$ and $V_2^\times$ are doubly commuting isometries on $L_+^2(\mathbb{T}^2;H)$. Like in the scalar case [1] one can prove the following

PROPOSITION 3. $V_1^\times$ *and* $V_2^\times$ *are completely non-unitary operators on* $L_+^2(\mathbb{T}^2;H)$.

PROOF. Let us suppose that $M \subset L_+^2(\mathbb{T}^2;H)$ is a closed doubly invariant subspace for $V_1^\times$ and $V_1^\times|_M$ is a unitary operator on M. Then for $u\in M$, $u\neq 0$ and any integer n we have

$$(2.14) \qquad \bar{w}_1^n u \in M \subset L_+^2(\mathbb{T}^2;H).$$

On the other hand, since $u\neq 0$, there exist integers n_o, j_o such that $\hat{u}(n_o,j_o)\neq 0$, i.e.

$$(2.15)\qquad \int \bar{w}_1^{-1}\bar{w}_2^{j_0}(\bar{w}_1^{n_0+1}u(w_1,w_2))\,dm_2(w_1,w_2)\neq 0.$$

It follows that $\bar{w}_1^{n_0+1}u\notin L_+^2(\mathbb{T}^2;H)$ which contradicts (2.14). Therefore there exists no non-null space $M\subset L_+^2(\mathbb{T}^2;H)$ which reduces $V_1^{\times}$ to a unitary operator, i.e. V_1^* is a completely non-unitary operator.

The proof of the fact that $V_2^{\times}$ is a completely non-unitary operator is similar and the proposition is proved.

It is known that the associated semi-spectral measure of a contraction is unique by the uniqueness of its minimal unitary dilation. In the case of a pair of commuting contractions this is no longer valid. In what follows we will consider the semi-spectral measure attached to a pair of doubly commuting contractions by its natural unitary dilation.

Let us prove now the Lowdenslager-Sz.-Nagy-Foiaş factorization theorem ([9], [7]) extended to the case of a pair of doubly commuting contractions.

THEOREM 4. *Let* (T_1,T_2) *be a pair of doubly commuting contractions on* H, *and* F *be the* $L(H)$*-valued semi-spectral measure on* $\mathbb{T}^2$ *attached to* (T_1,T_2) *via the natural unitary dilation* (U_1,U_2). *Then there exists an* L^2*-bounded analytic function* $\{H,L,\Theta(z_1,z_2)\}$ *on* $\mathbb{D}^2$ *with the properties:*

(i) $\bigvee_{n,j=0}^{\infty} V_1^{\times n}V_2^{\times j}V_\Theta H=L_+^2(\mathbb{T}^2;L)$.

(ii) $F_\Theta\le F$. *The equality* $F_\Theta=F$ *holds if and only if* $R_i(H)=\{0\}$, $i=1,2$.

(iii) *For any* L^2*-bounded analytic function* $\{H,H',\Theta'(z_1,z_2)\}$ *with the property* $F_{\Theta'}\le F$ *we have also* $F_{\Theta'}\le F_\Theta$.

Proof. Let $R_i(H)$ and L be the spaces defined by (1.9) and (1.8), respectively. Denote by P^L the orthogonal projection from K^+ on $M_+(L)=\bigoplus_{n,j=0}^{\infty} U_1^nU_2^jL$, and by Φ^L the Fourier representation of $M_+(L)$ on $L_+^2(\mathbb{T}^2;L)$ given by

$$(2.16)\qquad \Phi^L\Big(\sum_{n,j=0}^{\infty} U_1^nU_2^jx_{nj}\Big)(w_1,w_2)=\sum_{n,j=0}^{\infty} w_1w_2x_{nj}\ ,$$

where $x_{nj}\in L$ and $(w_1,w_2)\in\mathbb{T}^2$.

If we define $V:H\to L^2(\mathbb{T}^2;L)$ by $V=\Phi^LP^L|_H$ and the $L(H)$-valued semi-spectral measure F_o on $\mathbb{T}^2$ by

(2.17) $$F_o(\sigma)=V^*E_L^{\times}(\sigma)V, \qquad (\sigma\in\mathcal{B}(\mathbb{T}^2)),$$

then, by Theorem 1, there exists an L^2-bounded analytic function $\{H,L,\Theta(z_1,z_2)\}$ such that $V_\Theta=V$ and $F_\Theta=F_o$.

The orthogonal projection P^L commutes with the isometries $V_i=U_i|K^+$, $i=1,2$. Indeed, if $k=k_1+k_2\in K^+$ with $k_1\in M_+(L)$ and $k_2\in R_1(H)\vee R_2(H)$, then for any $k'\in M_+(L)$ we have

$$(V_iP^Lk,k')=(V_ik_1,k')=(V_i(k_1+k_2),k')=(V_ik,k')=(P^LV_ik,k'),$$

whence it follows that $V_iP^Lk=P^LV_ik$ for any $k\in K^+$, hence $V_iP^L=P^LV_i$ $i=1,2$.

If there exists $u\in L_+^2(\mathbb{T}^2;L)$ orthogonal on $V_1^{\times n}V_2^{\times j}V_\Theta h$ for any $n,j\geq 0$ and $h\in H$, then putting $u=\Phi^Lk_u$, $P^Lh=k_h$, where k_u and k_h are given by

$$k_u=\sum_{n,j=0}^{\infty}U_1^nU_2^jx_{nj},\quad k_h=\sum_{n,j=0}^{\infty}U_1^nU_2^jy_{nj},\qquad (x_{nj},y_{nj}\in L),$$

$$0=(u,V_1^{\times n}V_2^{\times j}V_\Theta h)_{L^2(\mathbb{T}^2;L)}=(\Phi^Lk_u,V_1^{\times n}V_2^{\times j}\Phi^Lk_h)=(k_u,U_1^nU_2^jk_h)_{K^+}=$$
$$=(k_u,U_1^nU_2^jP^Lh)=(k_u,U_1^nU_2^jh)_{K^+}.$$

Therefore $k_u\perp K^+$ and $u=\Phi^Lk_u\perp L_+^2(\mathbb{T}^2;L)$. Since $u\in L_+^2(\mathbb{T}^2;L)$ it results that $u=0$ and (i) is proved.

Let F be the $L(H)$-valued semi-spectral measure on $\mathbb{T}^2$ attached to the pair (T_1,T_2), via the natural unitary dilation (U_1,U_2), i.e.

(2.18) $$F(\sigma)=P_HE(\sigma)|_H \qquad (\sigma\in\mathcal{B}(\mathbb{T}^2)),$$

where E is the spectral measure of the pair of unitary operators (U_1,U_2). For any analytic polynomial $p\in A(\mathbb{D}^2)$ and $h\in H$ we have

$$\int_{\mathbb{T}^2}|p(w_1,w_2)|^2d(F_\Theta(w_1,w_2)h,h)=\|p(U_1^{\times},U_2^{\times})V_\Theta h\|^2_{L^2(\mathbb{T}^2;L)}=\|pV_\Theta h\|^2=$$
$$=\|p\Phi^LP^Lh\|^2=\|\Phi^Lp(U_1^{\times},U_2^{\times})P^Lh\|^2=\|p(U_1,U_2)P^Lh\|^2_{K^+}=\|P^Lp(U_1,U_2)h\|^2_{K^+}\leq$$
$$\leq\|p(U_1,U_2)h\|^2_{K^+}=\int_{\mathbb{T}^2}|p(w_1,w_2)|^2d(F(w_1,w_2)h,h).$$

Since any positive continuous function on $\mathbb{T}^2$ is uniformly approximable by the modulus of functions in the bidisc algebra $A(\mathbb{D}^2)$ (see [2]), it follows that $F_\Theta\leq F$. Moreover, we have $F_\Theta=F$ if and only if $P^{L}=I_{K^+}$ or equivalent $K^+=M_+(L)$, i.e. $R_1(H)\vee R_2(H)=\{0\}$, and the assertion (ii) is proved.

Let $\{H,H',\Theta'(z_1,z_2)\}$ be an L^2-bounded analytic function such that $F_{\Theta'}\leq F$. For any analytic polynomial $p\in A(\mathbb{D}^2)$ and $h\in H$ we have

$$\|pV_{\Theta'}h\|^2_{L^2(\mathbb{T}^2;H')}=(pV_{\Theta'}h,pV_{\Theta'}h)=\int_{\mathbb{T}^2}|p(w_1,w_2)|^2\|(V_{\Theta'}h)(w_1,w_2)\|^2dm_2=$$

$$=\int_{\mathbb{T}^2}|p(w_1,w_2)|^2d(F_{\Theta'}(w_1,w_2)h,h)\leq\int_{\mathbb{T}^2}|p(w_1,w_2)|^2d(F(w_1,w_2)h,h)=$$

$$=\|p(U_1,U_2)h\|^2 .$$

It follows that

$$Yp(U_1,U_2)h=pV_{\Theta'}h \tag{2.19}$$

defines a contraction $Y:K^+\to L^2_+(\mathbb{T}^2;H')$. From (2.19) it is obvious that $YU_i=V^{\times}_iY$ and it results that

$$YR_1(H)\;R_2(H)\subset\bigcap_{n=0}^{\infty}YU_1^nK^+\vee\bigcap_{n=0}^{\infty}YU_2^nK^+=\bigcap_{n=0}^{\infty}V_1^{\times n}YK^+\vee\bigcap_{n=0}^{\infty}V_2^{\times n}YK^+\subset$$

$$\subset\bigcap_{n=0}^{\infty}V_1^{\times n}L^2_+(\mathbb{T}^2;H')\vee\bigcap_{n=0}^{\infty}V_2^{\times n}L^2_+(\mathbb{T}^2;H')=\{0\},$$

since by Proposition 3 we have

$$\bigcap_{n=0}^{\infty}V_i^{\times n}L^2_+(\mathbb{T}^2;H')=\{0\} \qquad (i=1,2).$$

Therefore, for any $k\in K^+$ we have $Yk=Y(P^Lk+(I-P^L)k)=YP^Lk$, i.e. $Y=YP^L$, and for any analytic polynomial $p\in A(\mathbb{D}^2)$ and $h\in H$ we have

$$\int_{\mathbb{T}^2}|p(w_1,w_2)|^2d(F_{\Theta'}(w_1,w_2)h,h)=\|pV_{\Theta'}h\|^2_{L^2(\mathbb{T}^2;H')}=$$

$$=\|Yp(U_1,U_2)h\|^2=\|YP^Lp(U_1,U_2)h\|^2\leq\|P^Lp(U_1,U_2)h\|^2_{K^+}=$$

$$=\|p(U_1,U_2)P^Lh\|^2=\|\Phi^Lp(U_1,U_2)P^Lh\|^2_{L^2(\mathbb{T}^2;L)}=\|pV_{\Theta}h\|^2=$$

$$=\int_{\mathbb{T}^2}|p(w_1,w_2)|^2d(F_{\Theta}(w_1,w_2)h,h) .$$

The proof of the theorem is finished.

The L^2-bounded analytic function $\{H,L,\Theta(z_1,z_2)\}$ on $\mathbb{D}^2$ attached to a pair of doubly commuting contractions (T_1,T_2) on H as in

Theorem 4 is called *the maximal function* of (T_1,T_2).

3. If $\alpha\varepsilon\{+,-\}$ and T a contraction on a Hilbert space H, then we put $T^\alpha=T$ for $\alpha=+$ and $T^\alpha=T^*$ for $\alpha=-$. The *defect operators* associated to a contraction are defined by

$$D_{T^\alpha}=(I-T^{-\alpha}T^\alpha)^{1/2}, \qquad \alpha\varepsilon\{+,-\}. \tag{3.1}$$

For a pair of doubly commuting contractions (T_1,T_2) on H let us denote by $D_i^\alpha=D_{T_i^\alpha}$, i=1,2. Then the *defect operators of the pair* (T_1,T_2) are defined by

$$D_\alpha^\beta=D_1^\alpha D_2^\beta, \qquad \alpha,\beta\varepsilon\{+,-\}. \tag{3.2}$$

Corresponding to the defect operators, we can associated the *defect spaces* by

$$\mathcal{D}_i^\alpha=\overline{D_i^\alpha H} \quad \text{and} \quad \mathcal{D}_\alpha^\beta=\overline{D_\alpha^\beta H}. \tag{3.3}$$

Also, for $\alpha,\beta\varepsilon\{+,-\}$ we define the operator

$$L_\beta^\alpha=(U_1^\alpha U_2^\beta+T_1^\alpha T_2^\beta-U_1^\alpha T_2^\beta-U_2^\beta T_1^\alpha)|_H, \tag{3.4}$$

and the spaces

$$\mathcal{L}_\alpha^\beta=\overline{L_\alpha^\beta H}, \tag{3.5}$$

where (U_1,U_2) is the natural unitary dilation of the pair of doubly commuting contractions (T_1,T_2).

LEMMA 5. *The spaces $\mathcal{L}_\alpha^\beta$ and $\mathcal{D}_\alpha^\beta$ have the same dimension.*

PROOF. Taking into account the construction of the natural unitary dilation (U_1,U_2) of the doubly commuting contractions (T_1,T_2), we have

$$||L_\alpha^\beta h||^2=||(U_1^\alpha U_2^\beta+T_1^\alpha T_2^\beta-U_1^\alpha T_2^\beta-U_2^\beta T_1^\alpha)h||^2=$$
$$=((U_1^\alpha U_2^\beta+T_1^\alpha T_2^\beta-U_1^\alpha T_2^\beta-U_2^\beta T_1^\alpha)h,(U_1^\alpha U_2^\beta+T_1^\alpha T_2^\beta-U_1^\alpha T_2^\beta-U_2^\beta T_1^\alpha)h)=$$
$$=||h||^2+(U_1^\alpha U_2^\beta h,T_1^\alpha T_2^\beta h)-(U_2^\beta h,T_2^\beta h)-(U_1^\alpha h,T_1^\alpha h)+(T_1^\alpha T_2^\beta h,U_1^\alpha U_2^\beta h)+$$
$$+||T_1T_2h||^2-(T_1^\alpha T_2^\beta h,U_1^\alpha T_2^\beta h)-(T_1^\alpha T_2^\beta h,U_2^\beta T_1^\alpha h)-(T_2^\beta h,U_2^\beta h)-$$
$$-(U_1^\alpha T_2^\beta h,T_1^\alpha T_2^\beta h)+||T_2^\beta h||^2+(U_1^\alpha T_2^\beta h,U_2^\beta T_1^\alpha h)-(T_1^\alpha h,U_1^\alpha h)-$$
$$-(U_2^\beta T_1^\alpha h,T_1^\alpha T_2^\beta h)+(U_2^\beta T_1^\alpha h,U_1^\alpha T_2^\beta h)+||T_1^\alpha h||^2=||h||^2-||T_1^\alpha h||^2-$$

$$-||T_2^\beta h||^2+||T_1^\alpha T_2^\beta h||^2=((I-T_1^{-\alpha}T_1^\alpha-T_2^{-\beta}T_2^\beta+T_1^{-\alpha}T_1^\alpha T_2^{-\beta}T_2^\beta)h,h)=$$
$$=((I-T_1^{-\alpha}T_1^\alpha)(I-T_2^{-\beta}T_2^\beta)h,h)=||D_\alpha^\beta h||^2.$$

Hence, if we put

(3.6) $$\omega_\alpha^\beta(L_\alpha^\beta h)=D_\alpha^\beta h\ ,$$

then (3.6) defines an unitary operator $\omega_\alpha^\beta : L_\alpha^\beta \to \mathcal{D}_\alpha^\beta$, and the proof is finished.

The next proposition will give an explicit form of the maximal function of a pair of doubly commuting contractions. One says that two analytic functions $\{E,F,\Theta(z_1,z_2)\}$, $\{E',F',\Theta'(z_1,z_2)\}$ *coincide* [9] if there exist unitary operators $X:E\to E'$ and $Y:F\to F'$ such that $Y\Theta(z_1,z_2)=\Theta'(z_1,z_2)X$.

PROPOSITION 6. *The maximal function* $\{H,L,\Theta(z_1,z_2)\}$ *of the doubly commuting pair of contractions* (T_1,T_2) *coincides with* $\{H,\mathcal{D}_-^-,\tilde{\Theta}(z_1,z_2)\}$ *where*

(3.7) $$\tilde{\Theta}(z_1,z_2)=D_-^-(I-z_1T_1^*)^{-1}(I-z_2T_1^*)^{-1} \qquad (z_1,z_2\in\mathbb{D}^2).$$

PROOF. Let (U_1,U_2) be the natural unitary dilation of (T_1,T_2). First let us remark that

(3.8) $$L=U_1U_2L_-^-$$

and the operator $\omega : L\to\mathcal{D}_-^-$ defined by

(3.9) $$\omega=\omega_-^-U_1^*U_2^*|_L$$

is unitary. We shall show that

(3.10) $$\tilde{\Theta}(z_1,z_2)=\omega\Theta(z_1,z_2) \qquad (z_1,z_2\in\mathbb{D}^2).$$

If $\Theta_{nj}:H\to L$ $(n,j\geq 0)$ are the Taylor coefficients of the maximal function $\{H,L,\Theta(z_1,z_2)\}$, and P_L is the orthogonal projection of K on L, then for any $h\in H$ and $k\in L$ we have

$$(\Theta_{nj}h,k)_L=(\widehat{Vh}(n,j),k)_L=\int_{\mathbb{T}^2}\bar{w}_1^n\bar{w}_2^j((Vh)(w_1,w_2),k)dm_2(w_1,w_2)=$$
$$=\int_{\mathbb{T}^2}((Vh)(w_1,w_2),w_1^nw_2^jk)_L dm_2(w_1,w_2)=\int_{\mathbb{T}^2}((Vh)(w_1,w_2),$$
$$,\Phi^L(U_1^nU_2^jk)(w_1,w_2))dm_2=(Vh,\Phi^LU_1^nU_2^jk)_{L^2(\mathbb{T}^2;L)}=$$
$$=(\Phi^LP^Lh,\Phi^LU_1^nU_2^jk)_{L^2(\mathbb{T}^2;L)}=(P^Lh,U_1^nU_2^jk)_K=(h,P^LU_1^nU_2^jk)=$$

$$=(h,U_1^nU_2^jk)=(U_1^{*n}U_2^{*j}h,k)=(P_L U_1^{*n}U_2^{*j}h,k)_L .$$

Hence

(3.11) $$\Theta_{nj}=P_L U_1^{*n}U_2^{*j}|_H \qquad (n,j\geq 0) .$$

Therefore, to prove (3.10) it is enough to verify that

(3.12) $$\Theta_{nj}=U_1U_2L_-^-T_1^{*n}T_2^{*j} \qquad (n,j\geq 0) ,$$

or, by (3.11), to verify that

(3.13) $$U_1U_2L_-^-T_1^{*n}T_2^{*j} \perp L.$$

To this end, let K_o be the space of the minimal unitary dilation of T_2. Using the fact that in the natural unitary dilation (U_1,U_2) of (T_1,T_2), U_1 is minimal unitary dilation of the $*$-extension of the minimal unitary dilation of T_2, for any $h_1,h_2\varepsilon H$ and $n,j\geq 0$ we have

$$(U_1^{*n}U_2^{*j}h_1-U_1U_2L_-^-T_1^{*n}T_2^{*j}h_1,U_1U_2L_-^-h_2)=$$
$$=2(T_1T_2T_1^{*(n+1)}T_2^{*(j+1)}h_1,h_2)-(U_1T_1^{*(n+1)}T_2^{*j}h_1,U_2T_2^*h_2)-$$
$$-(U_2T_1^{*n}T_2^{*(j+1)}h_1,U_1T_1^*h_2)=2(T_1T_2T_1^{*(n+1)}T_2^{*(j+1)}h_1,h_2)-$$
$$-(P_{K_o}U_1T_1^{*(n+1)}T_2^{*j}h_1,U_2T_2^*h_2)-(U_2T_1^{*n}T_2^{*(j+1)}h_1,P_{K_o}U_1T_1^*h_2)=$$
$$=2(T_1T_2T_1^{*(n+1)}T_2^{*(j+1)}h_1,h_2)-(T_1T_1^{*(n+1)}T_2^{*j}h_1,T_2T_2^*h_2)-$$
$$-(T_2T_1^{*n}T_2^{*(j+1)}h_1,T_1T_1^*h_2)=0.$$

The proof is finished.

If $T_i^{*n}\to 0$ (strongly) for $i=1,2$, then [5] we have $K^+=M_+(L)=$ $=\bigoplus_{n,j\geq 0} U_1^nU_2^jL$ and consequently, $P^L=I_{K^+}$. Therefore, if $\tilde{\Phi}^L$ is the Fourier representation of K^+ on $H^2(\mathbb{D}^2;L)$ then for any $h\varepsilon H$ we have

$$(\tilde{\Phi}^Lh)(z_1,z_2)=P[V_\Theta h](z_1,z_2)=\Theta(z_1,z_2)h,$$

where $\{H,L,\Theta(z_1,z_2)\}$ is the minimal function of (T_1,T_2). Since $\tilde{\Phi}^Lh$ is the image of h in the space of the functional model (see [5]) of the pair (T_1,T_2) we have

PROPOSITION 7. *Let* T_1,T_2 *be doubly commuting contractions on* H *such that* $T_i^{*n}\to 0$, $(i=1,2)$ *and* $\{H,L,\Theta(z_1,z_2)\}$ *be the maximal function of* (T_1,T_2). *The image of an element* $h\varepsilon H$ *in the space of the functional model of the pair* (T_1,T_2) *is the function*

$u_h \in H^2(\mathbb{D}^2;L)$ *given by*

$$u_h(z_1,z_2)=\Theta(z_1,z_2)h, \qquad (z_1,z_2\in\mathbb{D}^2). \tag{3.14}$$

In the sequel we need the following:

LEMMA 8. *Let* (T_1,T_2) *be a doubly commuting pair of contractions with the spectral radii* $\rho(T_i)<1$, $i=1,2$. *Then the semi-spectral measure of* (T_1,T_2) *is boundedly dominated by the Lebesgue measure on* $\mathbb{T}^2$.

PROOF. Let (U_1,U_2) be the natural minimal unitary dilation of (T_1,T_2) on the Hilbert space K. Then, by construction, U_1 is the minimal unitary dilation of a *-extension S_1 of T_1 and $\|S_1\|=\|T_1\|$. It results that $\|S_1^n\|=\|T_1^n\|$, $n=0,1,2,\ldots$ and it follows that $\rho(S_1)=\rho(T_1)<1$. Then the series

$$\sum_{n=-\infty}^{+\infty} \bar{w}^n S_1^{(n)} \qquad (w\in\mathbb{T}), \tag{3.15}$$

where $S_1^{(n)}=\begin{cases} S_1^n, & n\geq 0 \\ S_1^{*|n|}, & n<0\end{cases}$, defines (see[4]) a positive function $S:\mathbb{T}\to\mathcal{B}(K_o)$, continuous in the norm,which verifies

$$\int_{\mathbb{T}} w^n S(w)\,dm(w)=S_1^{(n)} \qquad (n\in\mathbb{Z}). \tag{3.16}$$

Moreover, since for any $n\in\mathbb{Z}$, $S_1^{(n)}$ commutes with $S_2^{(n)}$, the operators $S(w)$, $(w\in\mathbb{T})$ commute with the values $E(\sigma)$, $\sigma\in\mathcal{B}(\mathbb{T})$, of the spectral measure E corresponding to S_2. Let F be the compression of the spectral measure of (U_1,U_2) on the Hilbert space H. Then for any integers n,j and any $h\in H$ we have

$$\begin{aligned}\int_{\mathbb{T}^2} w_1^n w_2^j d(F(w_1,w_2)h,h) &= (U_1^n U_2^j h,h)=(P_{K_o}U_1^n U_2^j h,h)=\\ &=(S_1^{(n)}U_2^j h,h)=\int_{\mathbb{T}} w_1^n (S(w_1)U_2^j h,h)\,dm(w_1)=\\ &=\int_{\mathbb{T}} w_1^n\Big(\int_{\mathbb{T}} w_2^j d(E(w_2)h,S(w_1)h)\Big)dm(w_1).\end{aligned}$$

Using the weak density of the trigonometric polynomials in $L^\infty(m_2)$ it follows that

$$(F(\sigma_1\otimes\sigma_2)h,h)=\int_{\sigma_1}(S(w)E(\sigma_2)h,h)\,dm(w) \qquad (\sigma_1,\sigma_2\in\mathcal{B}(\mathbb{T})). \tag{3.17}$$

Since $\rho(T_2)<1$, there exists a constant $c>0$ such that

(3.18) $$(E(\sigma_2)h,h)\le cm(\sigma_2)\|h\|^2 ,$$

and by (3.17) it follows that for any $\sigma_1,\sigma_2\in\mathcal{B}(\mathbb{T})$ and any $h\in H$ we have

$$(F(\sigma_1\otimes\sigma_2)h,h)\le c \sup_{|w|=1}\|S(w)\|m_2(\sigma_1\otimes\sigma_2)\|h\|^2 ,$$

i.e. F is boundedly dominated by m_2 on $\mathbb{T}^2$, and the proof is finished.

PROPOSITION 9. *If* T_1,T_2 *are doubly commuting contractions and* $\rho(T_i)<1$, $i=1,2$, *then the maximal function of* (T_1,T_2) *is bounded.*

PROOF. Let F be the semi-spectral measure of (T_1,T_2) and $\{K,L,\Theta(z_1,z_2)\}$ be its maximal function. Since $F_\Theta\le F$, using Lemma 8 and Proposition 2, it follows that the maximal function of (T_1,T_2) is bounded, and the proof is finished.

PROPOSITION 10. *The semi-spectral measure* F *of a doubly commuting pair of contractions* (T_1,T_2) *is of analytic type and the corresponding maximal function is bounded if and only if* $\rho(T_i)<1$, *and* $R_i(H)=\{0\}$, $(i=1,2)$.

PROOF. Let F be the semi-spectral measure of (T_1,T_2) of analytic type and the corresponding maximal function $\{K,L,\Theta(z_1,z_2)\}$ be bounded. Then, by Proposition 2, $F_\Theta=F$ is bounded dominated by the Lebesgue measure m_2 on $\mathbb{T}^2$ and (see [8], Theorem 1) it follows that $\rho(T_i)<1$, $i=1,2$. Since $F_\Theta=F$, by Theorem 4, (2.15) and (1.1) it results that $R_i(H)=\{0\}$, $i=1,2$.

By Theorem 4 (ii) and Proposition 9 the converse follows.

REFERENCES

1. Briem, E.; Davie, A.M.; Oksendal, B.K.: A functional calculus for pairs of commuting contractions, *J. London Math. Soc.* (2) 7 (1973), 709-718.

2. Glicksberg, I.: Measures orthogonal to algebras and sets of antisymmetry, *Trans. Amer. Math. Soc.* 105 (1962), 415-435.

3. Rudin, W.: *Function Theory on Polydiscs*, Benjamin, 1969.

4. Schreiber, M.: Absolutely continuous operators, *Duke Math. J.* 29 (1962), 175-190.

5. Slocinski, M.: Isometric dilation of doubly commuting con-

tractions and related models, *Bull.Acad.Polon.Sci.Sér.Sci. Math.Astr.Phys.* XXV, 12 (1977), 1233-1242.

6. Suciu, I.: Analytic relations between functional models for contractions, *Acta Sci.Math. (Szeged)* 34 (1973), 359-365.

7. Suciu, I.; Valuşescu, I.: Factorization of semi-spectral measures, *Rev.Roumaine Math.Pures Appl.* 21 (1976), 773-793.

8. Suciu, N.: Absolutely continuous semispectral measures for pairs of commuting contractions, *Rev.Roumaine Math.Pures Appl.*, to appear.

9. Sz.-Nagy, B.; Foiaş, C.: *Harmonic Analysis of Operators on Hilbert Space*, Akad.Kiado Budapest-North Holland Company, Amsterdam-London, 1970.

10. Valuşescu, I.: The maximal function of a contraction *Acta Sci.Math.(Szeged)*, 42 (1980), 183-188.

N.Suciu
Faculty of Natural Sciences,
University of Timişoara,
Bdul V.Pârvan 4, 1900 Timişoara,
Romania.

I.Valuşescu
Department of Mathematics,
INCREST,
Bdul Păcii 220, 79622 Bucharest,
Romania.

REMARKS ON HILBERT-SCHMIDT PERTURBATIONS OF ALMOST - - NORMAL OPERATORS

Dan Voiculescu

We have shown in a recent note [15], that quasi-triangularity relative to the Hilbert-Schmidt class can be used to give a new proof and an extension of the Berger-Shaw inequality [3]. This suggests that a study of almost normal operators modulo Hilbert-Schmidt perturbations may be interesting. When at least one of two almost normal operators, which differ by a Hilbert-Schmidt operator, has finite multicyclicity, we prove below that their Helton-Howe measures [8], or equivalently their Pincus-G-functions [5], are equal. On the other hand we have also other invariants: those of quasitriangularity and quasidiagonality relative to the Hilbert-Schmidt class. This leads to a question asked by R.G.Douglas in connection with [15], namely, whether the two kinds of invariants are related.

The present paper contains a few remarks in this direction. We show that the quasitriangularity of an almost-normal operator, relative to the Hilbert-Schmidt class is in a simple relation with that of its adjoint and with the quasidiagonality.

We prove that if an almost normal operator is quasi-triangular with respect to the Hilbert-Schmidt class then its Helton-Howe measure is ≤ 0.

For certain subnormal operators we obtain complete results: their adjoint is quasitriangular relative to the Hilbert-Schmidt class and we get exact formulas for the quasitriangularity and quasidiagonality invariants.

We conclude the paper with some questions which seem natural in connection with Hilbert-Schmidt perturbations of almost normal operators.

Throughout H will denote a complex separable infinite-dimensional Hilbert space. By $\mathcal{L}(H)$, $\mathcal{C}_p(H)$, $\mathcal{R}_1^+(H)$, $\mathcal{P}(H)$ (or simply $\mathcal{L}$, $\mathcal{C}_p$, $\mathcal{R}_1^+$, $\mathcal{P}$) we shall denote the bounded operators on H, the Schatten-von Neumann p-class, the finite rank positive contractions on H and respectively the finite rank orthogonal projections.

The norms on $\mathcal{L}(H)$ and $\mathcal{C}_p(H)$ will be denoted by $\|\ \|$ and respectively $|\ |_p$.

The class of almost-normal operators on H, i.e. the class of operators $T\in\mathcal{L}(H)$ such that $[T^*,T]\in\mathcal{C}_1$, will be denoted by $\mathcal{AN}(H)$ (or simply $\mathcal{AN}$). For $T\in\mathcal{AN}(H)$ we shall denote its Helton-Howe measure by P_T and its Pincus G-function by G_T ([8], [5], [6]). We recall, that it has been shown by J.D. Pincus that P_T is equal $\frac{1}{2\pi}G_T d\lambda$, where $d\lambda$ is Lebesgue measure on $\mathbb{R}^2$.

Quasitriangular operators and quasidiagonal operators have been introduced by P.R. Halmos [9] and the corresponding notions relative to other norm-ideals than the compacts have been considered in [12].

The analogs of Apostol's moduli of quasitriangularity and quasidiagonality, relative to a Schatten-von Neumann class ([1], [12]) are:

$$q_p(T)=\liminf_{P\in\mathcal{P}}|(I-P)TP|_p$$

$$qd_p(T)=\liminf_{P\in\mathcal{P}}|[P,T]|_p$$

where the liminfs are with respect to the natural order on $\mathcal{P}$. We shall also consider the number

$$k_p(T)=\liminf_{A\in\mathcal{R}_1^+}|[A,T]|_p$$

from [13], where again the liminf is with respect to the natural order on $\mathcal{R}_1^+$. All these numbers are invariant with respect to $\mathcal{C}_p$--perturbations, i.e. $q_p(T+X)=q_p(T)$, $qd_p(T+X)=qd_p(T)$, $k_p(T+X)=$ $=k_p(T)$ for $X\in\mathcal{C}_p$.

Concerning q_p we recall the following inequality from [15]

$$q_p(T)\le(m_T)^{1/p}\|T\|$$

where m_T denotes the multicyclicity of T.

For the class $\mathcal{AN}$ it seems that the class of perturbations which gives interesting results is $\mathcal{C}_2$. Many of the results will be derived in fact from the following easily checked relation, which was implicit in [15]

$$(*)\qquad |(I-P)TP|_2^2=\mathrm{Tr}(P[T^*,T]P)+|(I-P)T^*P|_2^2$$

where $T\varepsilon L$, $P\varepsilon P$.

PROPOSITION 1. *Let* $T\varepsilon AN$. *Then the following equalities hold:*

$$(q_2(T))^2=(q_2(T^*))^2+\mathrm{Tr}[T^*,T]$$

$$(q_2(T))^2+(q_2(T^*))^2=(qd_2(T))^2$$

PROOF. Let $P_n\uparrow I, P_n\varepsilon P$ be such that

$$\lim_{n\to\infty}|(I-P_n)TP_n|_2=q_2(T)$$

By Proposition 1.1 of [12], we have $\liminf_{n\to\infty}|(I-P_n)T^*P_n|\geq$ $\geq q_2(T^*)$ and hence using relation (*) and the fact that $[T^*,T]\varepsilon C_1$ we infer:

$$(q_2(T))^2\geq \mathrm{Tr}[T^*,T]+(q_2(T^*))^2.$$

Comparing this inequality with the inequality which is obtained by replacing T with T^* we get

$$(q_2(T))^2=\mathrm{Tr}[T^*,T]+(q_2(T^*))^2.$$

This implies also that $\lim_{n\to\infty}|(I-P_n)T^*P_n|_2=q_2(T^*)$. But this gives then:

$$(qd_2(T))^2\leq\liminf_{n\to\infty}|[P_n,T]|_2^2=$$

$$=\liminf_{n\to\infty}(|(I-P_n)TP_n|_2^2+|(I-P_n)TP_n)|_2^2)=(q_2(T))^2+(q_2(T^*))^2$$

where we used the easily checked relation $|[P,T]|_2^2=|(I-P)TP|_2^2+$ $+|(I-P)T^*P|_2^2$ for $P\varepsilon P$, $T\varepsilon L$. For the reverse inequality, let $Q_n\uparrow I$, $Q_n\varepsilon P$ be such that $\lim_{n\to\infty}|[Q_n,T]|_2=qd_2(T)$. Then we have:

$$(qd_2(T))^2=\lim_{n\to\infty}(|(I-Q_n)TQ_n|_2^2+|(I-Q_n)T^*Q_n|_2^2)\geq$$

$$\geq\liminf_{n\to\infty}|(I-Q_n)TQ_n|_2^2+\liminf_{n\to\infty}|(I-Q_n)T^*Q_n|_2^2\geq(q_2(T))^2+(q_2(T^*))^2.$$

COROLLARY 2. *Let* $T\varepsilon AN$ *be such that* $q_2(T)<\infty$. *Then* $k_2(T)=0$. *In particular if* $m_T<\infty$ *then* $k_2(T)=0$.

PROOF. If $q_2(T)<\infty$, then $(qd_2(T))^2=2(q_2(T))^2+\mathrm{Tr}[T^*,T]<\infty$ and hence $k_2(T)\leq qd_2(T)<\infty$. This implies $k_2(T)=0$, since we have shown in [14] that k_p for $1<p<\infty$ can take only the values 0 or ∞.

If $m_T<\infty$, then $q_2(T)\leq(m_T)^{1/2}||T||$.

Since in the next proposition we shall use the hypothesis $q_2(T)<\infty$ for $T\in AN$, let us underline that, as in the proof of the preceding corollary, it is a consequence of Proposition 1, that $q_2(T)<\infty \Leftrightarrow q_2(T^*)<\infty \Leftrightarrow qd_2(T)<\infty$ and $m_T<\infty \Rightarrow q_2(T)<\infty$.

PROPOSITION 3. *Let* $S\in AN(H)$, $T\in AN(H)$ *be such that* $q_2(S)<\infty$ *and* $S-T\in C_2$. *Then we have* $P_S=P_T$.

PROOF. In view of the definition of the Helton-Howe measure it is easily seen that all we have to prove is that for any *--polynomial $F(X,X^*)$ the traces of the self-commutators of $F(S,S^*)$ and $F(T,T^*)$ are equal. Since $F(S,S^*)$, $F(T,T^*)\in AN$, $F(S,S^*)-F(T,T^*)\in C_2$ and $q_2(S)<\infty \Rightarrow qd_2(S)<\infty \Rightarrow qd_2(F(S,S^*))<\infty$ we see that the proof of this fact is the same as the proof of the equality $\mathrm{Tr}[T^*,T]=\mathrm{Tr}[S^*,S]$.

Since $qd_2(S)<\infty$ there is a sequence $(P_n)_{n=1}^{\infty}\subset P$ $P_n\uparrow I$ such that $|(I-P_n)SP_n|_2\le C$, $|(I-P_n)S^*P_n|_2\le C$ for some constant C independent of n.

Using relation (*) and the fact that $S,T\in AN$, we have

$$\begin{aligned}|\mathrm{Tr}[T^*,T]-\mathrm{Tr}[S^*,S]| &= \lim_{n\to\infty}\Big| |(I-P_n)TP_n|_2^2-|(I-P_n)SP_n|_2^2- \\ &-|(I-P_n)T^*P_n|_2^2+|(I-P_n)S^*P_n|_2^2\Big| \le \limsup_{n\to\infty}\Big| |(I-P_n)TP_n|_2^2- \\ &-|(I-P_n)SP_n|_2^2\Big|+\limsup_{n\to\infty}\Big| |(I-P_n)T^*P_n|_2^2-|(I-P_n)S^*P_n|_2^2\Big| \le \\ &\le 2C(\limsup_{n\to\infty}|(I-P_n)(S-T)P_n|_2+\limsup_{n\to\infty}|(I-P_n)(S-T)^*P_n|_2)=0\end{aligned}$$

where the last equality follows from $S-T\in C_2$ and $P_n\uparrow I$.

PROPOSITION 4. *Let* $T\in AN(H)$ *be such that* $q_2(T)=0$. *Then* $P_T\le 0$.

PROOF. Since $q_2(T)=0$, there is a sequence $(P_n)_1^{\infty}\subset P$, $P_n\uparrow I$, such that $\lim_{n\to\infty}|(I-P_n)TP_n|_2=0$. Consider $T_n=(I-P_n)T(I-P_n)$, $X_n=(I-P_n)TP_n$, $Y_n=P_nT(I-P_n)$. We have

$$[T_n^*,T_n]=(I-P_n)[T^*,T](I-P_n)+X_nX_n^*-Y_n^*Y_n\ .$$

Thus for $A_n=(I-P_n)[T^*,T](I-P_n)+X_nX_n^*$ and $B_n=Y_n^*Y_n$ we have $A_n\in C_1$, $B_n\in C_1$, $B_n\ge 0$, $\lim_{n\to\infty}|A_n|_1=0$, $[T_n^*,T_n]=A_n-B_n$.

The remaining part of the proof will be similar to an argument used in the proof of a theorem of C.A.Berger (see [6], page 112).

Let r, s be real-valued polynomials on $\mathbb{R}$.

Denoting by C_n and D_n the hermitian and respectively the antihermitian part of T_n, consider:

$$F_n=r(s(C_n)D_n s(C_n))C_n r(s(C_n)D_n s(C_n))+is(C_n)D_n s(C_n).$$

Then we have:

$$[F_n^*,F_n]=R_nS_n[T_n^*,T_n]S_nR_n$$

where

$$S_n=s(C_n),\ R_n=r(s(C_n)D_n s(C_n)).$$

Since $T-T_n\in C_1$, we have $P_{T_n}=P_T$ and using the definition of the Helton-Howe-measure, we have:

$$\mathrm{Tr}[F_n^*,F_n]=2\iint_{\mathbb{R}^2} r^2(s^2(x)y)s^2(x)dP_T .$$

On the other hand

$$\lim_{n\to\infty}\mathrm{Tr}[F_n^*,F_n]=\lim_{n\to\infty}(\mathrm{Tr}(R_nS_nA_nS_nR_n)-\mathrm{Tr}(R_nS_nB_nS_nR_n))\le$$

$$\le\lim_{n\to\infty}(||R_nS_n||^2|A_n|_1)=0.$$

Hence we have proved that

$$\iint_{\mathbb{R}^2} r^2(s^2(x)y)s^2(x)dP_T\le 0.$$

Since r,s are arbitrary real polynomials, this gives $P_T\le 0$.

PROPOSITION 5. *Let* $T\in AN$ *be subnormal and assume the spectrum of its minimal normal dilation is contained in the right essential spectrum of* T. *Then we have:*

$$q_2(T^*)=0$$
$$(q_2(T))^2=(qd_2(T))^2=\mathrm{Tr}[T^*,T].$$

PROOF. In view of Proposition 1, it will be sufficient to prove that $q_2(T^*)=0$. Let

$$N=\begin{bmatrix} T & X \\ 0 & S \end{bmatrix}\in L(H\oplus H')$$

be the minimal normal dilation of T. Since $T\in AN$ we have $X\in C_2$. Because of the assumption $\sigma(N^*)\subset\sigma_{le}(T^*)$ we can apply Proposition 3.3 of [12], which gives:

$$q_2(T^*)\le q_2(T^*\oplus N^*\oplus N^*\oplus\ldots)\le q_2(T^*)+q_2(N^*\oplus N^*\oplus\ldots).$$

In view of the fact that normal operators can be diagonalized modulo the Hilbert-Schmidt class [13], we have $q_2(T^*) = q_2(T^* \oplus N^* \oplus N^* \oplus \dots)$.

For $T^* \oplus N^* \oplus \dots$ acting on $\mathcal{H} \oplus (\mathcal{H} \oplus \mathcal{H}') \oplus (\mathcal{H} \oplus \mathcal{H}') \oplus \dots$ the subspaces

$$K_n = \mathcal{H} \oplus \underbrace{(\mathcal{H} \oplus \mathcal{H}') \oplus \dots \oplus (\mathcal{H} \oplus \mathcal{H}')}_{n\text{-times}} \oplus (0 \oplus \mathcal{H}') \oplus (0 \oplus 0) \oplus \dots$$

are invariant subspaces. By Proposition 2.4 of [12] we have

$$q_2(T^* \oplus N^* \oplus N^* \oplus \dots) \le \liminf_{n \to \infty} q_2((T^* \oplus N^* \oplus N^* \oplus \dots) | K_n) =$$

$$= \liminf_{n \to \infty} q_2(T^* \oplus S^* \oplus \underbrace{N^* \oplus \dots \oplus N^*}_{n\text{-times}}) = \liminf_{n \to \infty} q_2(\underbrace{N^* \oplus \dots \oplus N^*}_{(n+1)\text{-times}}) = 0$$

where we did use the fact that $T^* \oplus S^* - N^* \varepsilon C_2$.

PROPOSITION 6. *Let*

$$N = \begin{bmatrix} T & X \\ Y & S \end{bmatrix} \varepsilon L(\mathcal{H} \oplus \mathcal{H}')$$

be normal, and assume $X, Y \varepsilon C_2$. *Then* $T \varepsilon AN$ *and we have*

$$q_2(T \oplus N \oplus N \oplus \dots) \le |X|_2.$$

PROOF. That $[T^*, T] \varepsilon C_1$ follows immediately from $[T^*, T] = XX^* - Y^*Y$.

Let $K_n = \mathcal{H} \oplus \overbrace{(\mathcal{H} \oplus \mathcal{H}') \oplus \dots \oplus (\mathcal{H} \oplus \mathcal{H}')}^{n\text{-times}} \oplus (0 \oplus \mathcal{H}') \oplus (0 \oplus 0) \oplus \dots$. Then by an easy generalization of Proposition 2.4 of [12], we have

$$q_2(T \oplus N \oplus N \oplus \dots) \le \liminf_{n \to \infty} (q_2(P_{K_n}(T \oplus N \oplus \dots) | K_n) +$$

$$+ |(I - P_{K_n})(T \oplus N \oplus \dots) P_{K_n}|_2) = \liminf_{n \to \infty} (q_2(T \oplus S \oplus \underbrace{N \oplus \dots \oplus N}_{n\text{-times}}) +$$

$$+ |X|_2) = \liminf_{n \to \infty} (q_2(\underbrace{N \oplus \dots \oplus N}_{(n+1)\text{-times}}) + |X|_2) = |X|_2.$$

We think it is natural to conclude this paper by asking: to what extent do the Brown-Douglas-Fillmore theorem on essentially normal operators [4] and the Apostol-Foiaş-Voiculescu theorem on quasitriangular operators ([2], see also [7]) admit analogs for almost normal operators, relative to the Hilbert-Schmidt class? The question concerning quasitriangularity is another way of stating R.G.Douglas' question mentioned in the introduction. Both theorems mentioned above have many particular cases, the analogs of which would be of interest, but which to state all would make a rather long list, so we think it may be useful to state the most far-fetched guesses about analogs of these theorems, with the hope that some small part may turn out to be true.

GUESS A. *Let* $T_1 \varepsilon AN(H)$, $T_2 \varepsilon AN(H)$ *be such that* $P_{T_1} = P_{T_2}$. *Then there is a normal operator* $N \varepsilon L(H)$ *and a unitary operator* $U \varepsilon L(H \oplus H)$ *such that*

$$U(T_1 \oplus N)U^* - T_2 \oplus N \varepsilon C_2$$

Among the particular cases we mention:

A1) *If* $T \varepsilon AN(H)$ *is such that* $P_T = 0$ *then there is a normal operator* N *such that:*

$$T \oplus N = \text{normal} + \text{Hilbert-Schmidt}.$$

A2) *If* $T \varepsilon AN(H)$ *then there is* $S \varepsilon AN(H)$ *such that*

$$T \oplus S = \text{normal} + \text{Hilbert-Schmidt}.$$

GUESS B. *For* $T \varepsilon AN$ *we have*

$$(q_2(T))^2 = 2\iint_{\mathbb{R}^2} dP_T^+$$

where P_T^+ *is the positive part of* P_T.

Among the particular cases we mention:

B1) T *hyponormal*, $T \varepsilon AN \Longrightarrow q_2(T^*) = 0$.

B2) $P_T \leq 0 \Longrightarrow q_2(T) = 0$.

REFERENCES

1. Apostol, C.: Quasitriangularity in Hilbert space, *Indiana Univ.Math.J.* 22(1973), 817-825.

2. Apostol, C.; Foiaş, C.; Voiculescu, D.: Some results on non-quasitriangular operators. VI., *Rev.Roumaine Math.Pures Appl.* 18 (1973), 1473-1494.

3. Berger, C.A.; Shaw, B.I.: Self-commutators of multicyclic hyponormal operators are always trace class, *Bull.Amer.Math. Soc.* 79 (1973), 1193-1199.

4. Brown, L.G.; Douglas, R.G.; Fillmore, P.A.: Unitary equivalence modulo the compact operators and extensions of C*-algebras, *Springer Lecture Notes in Math.* 345 (1973), 58-128.

5. Carey, R.W.; Pincus, J.D.: Commutators, symbols and determining functions, *J.Functional Analysis* 19 (1975), 50-80.

6. Clancey, K.: *Seminormal operators*, Springer Lecture Notes in Math. 742 (1979).

7. Douglas, R.G.; Pearcy, C.: Invariant subspaces of non-quasi-triangular operators, *Springer Lecture Notes in Math.* 345 (1973), 13-57.

8. Helton, J.W.; Howe, R.: Integral operators, commutator traces, index and homology, *Springer Lecture Notes in Math.* 345 (1973), 141-209.

9. Halmos, P.R.: Quasitriangular operators, *Acta Sci.Math. (Szeged)* 29 (1968), 283-293.

10. Pearcy, C.: *Some recent developments in operator theory*, C.B.M.S. Regional Conference Series in Mathematics, no.36, Amer.Math.Soc., Providence, 1978.

11. Pincus, J.D.: Commutators and systems of integral equations. I., *Acta Math.* 121 (1968), 219-249.

12. Voiculescu, D.: Some extensions of quasitriangularity, *Rev. Roumaine Math.Pures Appl.* 18 (1973),1303-1320.

13. Voiculescu, D.: Some results on norm-ideal perturbations of Hilbert space operators, *J.Operator Theory* 2 (1979), 3-37.

14. Voiculescu, D.: Some results on norm-ideal perturbations of Hilbert space operators II, *J.Operator Theory* 5 (1981).

15. Voiculescu, D.: A note on quasitriangularity and trace-class self-commutators, *Acta Sci.Math.(Szeged)* 42 (1980), 195-199.

Dan Voiculescu
Department of Mathematics,
INCREST,
Bdul Păcii 220,
79622 Bucharest,
Romania.

DERIVATION RANGES: OPEN PROBLEMS

J.P.Williams[1)]

1. INTRODUCTION

For A in the algebra $\mathcal{B}(\mathcal{H})$ of bounded linear operators on a separable complex Hilbert space $\mathcal{H}$ the corresponding inner derivation δ_A on $\mathcal{B}(\mathcal{H})$ is given by $\delta_A(X)=AX-XA$. If $\dim \mathcal{H}<\infty$ then

(*) $\mathcal{B}(\mathcal{H})=\mathcal{R}(\delta_A)\oplus\{A^*\}'$

is the orthogonal direct sum of the range of δ_A and the commutant of A^* with respect to the inner product $(X,Y)=\text{trace }(XY^*)$. This simple formula suggests that $\mathcal{R}(\delta_A)$ is just as natural a subspace of $\mathcal{B}(\mathcal{H})$ as its orthogonal complement $\{A^*\}'$ and hence is worthy of its own investigation.

Our purpose in this paper is not to provide a comprehensive survey of the literature but rather to mention several questions that remain unresolved despite some ten years work on derivation ranges. The paper is an expanded version of a lecture given at the Vth Annual Conference in Operator Theory, Timişoara, Romania, 1980.

2. ALGEBRAS

The decomposition (*) immediately implies that the *inclusion algebra* $\mathcal{I}(A)=\{B\in\mathcal{B}(\mathcal{H}):\mathcal{R}(\delta_B)\subseteq\mathcal{R}(\delta_A)\}$ coincides with the bicommutant $\{A\}''$ of A, that is, with the algebra of polynomials in A. The *multiplier algebra* $\mathcal{M}(A)=\{X\in\mathcal{B}(\mathcal{H}):X\mathcal{R}(\delta_A)+\mathcal{R}(\delta_A)X\subseteq\mathcal{R}(\delta_A)\}$ is also readily identified as the commutant of A, and the *commutator algebra* $\mathcal{C}(A)=\{Z\in\mathcal{B}(\mathcal{H}):Z\mathcal{B}(\mathcal{H})+\mathcal{B}(\mathcal{H})Z\subseteq\mathcal{R}(\delta_A)\}$ reduces to {0} by a sim-

1) Research supported in part by a grant from the National Science Foundation

ple trace argument. (The terminology is justified by the results mentioned in §6 below.)

These algebras are much harder to identify when H is infinite-dimensional, of course, and $I(A)$ is really understood only for A normal. (See [11].) One knows in general that $I(A)$ neither contains [17] nor is contained in [10] the bicommutant of A. But the identities

$\delta_B(A')X=\delta_B(A'X)-A'\delta_B(X), X\delta_B(A')=\delta_B(XA')-\delta_B(X)A'$

imply that $I(A)\subseteq\{A\}''$ if it is also known that $R(\delta_A)$ has the curious property that this linear subspace contains no left (or right) ideals of $B(H)$. In fact the relation $I(A)\subseteq\{A\}''$ is equivalent to the condition that $R(\delta_A)$ does not contain *both* a left and a right ideal [10]. So one is naturally led to the problem of finding all left (right) ideals of $B(H)$ contained in a given derivation range. (There are no bilateral ideals contained in any derivation range [15].) We shall discuss a special case of this problem in §5 below.

3. DECOMPOSITION OF $B(H)$

The formula (*) is known to be not valid if dim $H=\infty$. For example if A is normal with infinite spectrum then $R(\delta_A)+\{A\}'$ is not even norm dense in $B(H)$ [3]. And again, for A normal, the sum is closed only in the trivial case in which $\sigma(A)$ is finite [3]. As there is a norm one projection from $B(H)$ onto the commutant that annihilates the derivation range (see [22] for example), the theorem just mentioned describes which normal operators have closed derivation range. Another proof was given in [11], and the result was extended to hyponormal operators in [16]. C. Apostol [5], using the powerful theorem of Voiculescu, finally obtained the general result: $R(\delta_A)$ is norm closed if and only if A is similar to an operator that generates a finite-dimensional C^*-algebra, or equivalently, A is algebraic and $p(A)$ has closed range for each polynomial $p(z)$.

It is suprising that the following is still open:

PROBLEM 1. Must $\mathcal{R}(\delta_A)\cap\{A^*\}'=0$ for any operator A?

The answer is affirmative for any unilateral weighted shift with nonzero weights [10].

One might argue that in passing to the general case one ought to replace the range of the derivation by its norm closure. But that problem is settled negatively either by reference to Stampfli's example [15] of a compact weighted unilateral shift K with $\mathcal{R}(\delta_K)^-$ equal to the full ideal of all compact operators on $\mathcal{H}$, or by reference to Anderson's example [2] of an operator A with $1\in\mathcal{R}(\delta_A)^-$. (Such operators are not norm dense in $\mathcal{B}(\mathcal{H})$ [10].)

PROBLEM 2. For which A is $\mathcal{R}(\delta_A)^-\cap\{A^*\}'=0$?

This class of operators includes any A that is normal [11], isometric [22], or subnormal with a cyclic vector [10]. But does it include any A with $A^3=0$?

Ho [9] has obtained sufficient conditions that $A^*\notin\mathcal{R}(\delta_A)^-$ among these being that A has norm equal to its spectral radius, that $A^3=0$, or that A is a unilateral weighted shift with weights w_n such that $\underline{\lim}_n |w_n|\neq 0$.

4. IDEALS IN THE COMMUTANT

For any A the set $J(A)=\mathcal{R}(\delta_A)\cap\{A\}'$ is a bilateral ideal in $\{A\}'$ and a theorem of Kleinecke [13] and Shirokov [14] asserts that each element of J(A) is a quasinilpotent operator. What about the converse? More generally,

PROBLEM 3. Describe the set $\mathcal{J}=\bigcup\{J(A):A\in\mathcal{B}(\mathcal{H})\}$.

In finite dimensions $\mathcal{J}$ is exactly the set of nilpotent operators [18].

The set $\bar{J}(A)=R(\delta_A)^- \cap \{A\}'$ is a closed bilateral ideal in the commutant. (Despite the notation this is *not* the closure of the ideal mentioned above; in fact [9] one can have $J(A)=0$, $\bar{J}(A)\neq 0$.) The result of Anderson mentioned earlier shows that $\bar{J}(A)$ need not be a *proper* ideal of $\{A\}'$ so that the Kleinecke-Shirokov theorem certainly fails for $\bar{J}(A)$. But it is true that any *compact* operator in $\bar{J}(A)$ must be quasinilpotent. In fact the same assertion is true if in the definition of $\bar{J}(A)$ we replace $R(\delta_A)^-$ by its closure in the weak operator topology [12,18].

Yang Ho [9] showed that if A has norm equal to its spectral radius then $\bar{J}(A)$ contains no isometry or co-isometry. As a consequence the simple unilateral shift does not belong to $\bar{J}=\bigcup\{\bar{J}(A):A\in B(H)\}$. Does the shift of infinite multiplicity belong to $\bar{J}$? Which normal operators belong to $\bar{J}$? Can $\bar{J}$ contain an operator of the form 1 + compact (Herrero [8])?

The earliest theorem in the subject is that of Wielandt [19] and Wintner [23] that 1 cannot belong to the range of a derivation. The complete solution to the problem of determining precisely which other operators have this property, however, was not obtained until 1965 by Brown and Pearcy: exactly those of the form $\lambda+K$ with λ a nonzero scalar and K compact. But it is still unknown which cannot belong to the *closure* of a derivation range:

PROBLEM 4. Must $\bigcup\{R(\delta_A)^-:A\in B(H)\}=B(H)$?

Note here that the set on the left certainly includes all commutators XY-YX and is therefore dense in $B(H)$ [6].

Several remarks are relevant to this last problem; namely, every operator is the *sum* of two commutators [6], or better [17], if U and V are nonunitary isometries with ranges that are orthogonal complements then $B(H)=R(\delta_U)+R(\delta_V)$. (This is not a direct sum, however, as any two nonzero derivation ranges have nonzero intersection [21].) Also, there are [20] operators A such that 0 belongs to the essential numerical range of each operator $T\in R(\delta_A)^-=[C^*(A),B(H)]$ and hence [1] each of these is a commutator with one factor Hermitian. Such is the case if, say, A has essential norm equal to its essential numerical radius. So the *closure* of a nonclosed derivation range may consist entirely of commutators. Finally, although it is easy for a derivation range to be dense in $\mathcal{B}(H)$ for the weak or ultraweak operator topologies [21] none can be norm dense [15].

5. ANALYTIC FUNCTIONS

For the unilateral shift S on the Hardy space H^2 with orthonormal basis $e_n(e^{i\theta})=e^{in\theta}$ one knows [22] that $\mathcal{R}(\delta_S)$ contains no right ideals but lots of left ideals of $\mathcal{B}(H^2)$ as the following result shows (recall that for vectors f and g the operator $f\otimes g$ is defined by $(f\otimes g)(h)=(h,g)f$):

THEOREM 1. *These are equivalent for* $f\in H^2$:

(a) $\mathcal{B}(H^2)(f\otimes f)\subseteq\mathcal{R}(\delta_S)$,

(b) $\sup\{\|(1-zS^*)^{-1}f\|_2 : z\in\mathbf{D}\}=K<\infty$.

(c) $\sup\{\int\left|\dfrac{f(e^{i\theta})-f(z)}{e^{i\theta}-z}\right|^2 d\theta : z\in\mathbf{D}\}=K<\infty$.

(d) $He_n=S^{*n}f$ $(n\geq 0)$ *defines a bounded (Hankel) operator such that* $\|Hg\|_\infty\leq K\|g\|_2$ $(g\in H^2)$.

(e) $\sum_{n\geq 0}|(S^{*n}f)(z)|^2\leq K^2$ $(z\in\mathbf{D})$.

THEOREM 2. *Let L be the subset of* H^2 *defined by the conditions of Theorem 1. Then*

(a) *L is a subalgebra of* H^∞.

(b) *If* $f\in L$ *then* $|f'(z)|\leq K(1-|z|)^{-\frac{1}{2}}$; *equivalently,* f *extends to be continuous on* $\bar{\mathbf{D}}$ *and*
$|f(e^{i\alpha})-f(e^{i\beta})|\leq K|\alpha-\beta|^{\frac{1}{2}}$ $(\alpha,\beta\in\mathbf{R})$.

(c) *If* $f\in L$ *then* $f\circ\phi\in L$ *for any automorphism* $\phi(z)=(z+\alpha)(1+\bar{\alpha}z)^{-1}$ of $\mathbf{D}$.

(d) *If* $f(z)=\sum a_n z^n\in L$ *then* $\sum(n+1)|a_n|^2<\infty$.

Hence an inner function belongs to L if and only if it is a finite Blaschke product.

(e) *If* $f\in L$ *then the outer factor of* f *belongs to L.*

More generally, $P_{H^2}(\bar{\phi}f)\varepsilon L$ *for any* $\phi\varepsilon H^\infty$.

(f) *If* f *is analytic on* $\bar{\mathbb{D}}$ *or, more generally, if* $f\varepsilon H^2$ *and* $f'\varepsilon H^\infty$, *then* $|f(e^{i\alpha})-f(e^{i\beta})|\leq C|\alpha-\beta|$, *hence* $f\varepsilon L$.

PROOF OF THEOREM 1: The equivalence of (a), (b), and (c) is proved in [21].

If $\xi_\lambda=(1-\bar{\lambda}S)^{-1}e_0$ then $g(\lambda)=(g,(1-\bar{\lambda}S)^{-1}e_0)=(g,\xi_\lambda)=\sum_0^\infty(g,e_n)\lambda^n$ is the usual extension of a function $g\varepsilon H^2(\partial\mathbb{D})$ to a function that is analytic on $\mathbb{D}$. If (b) holds then

$$H(\sum_0^n\alpha_je_j)(\lambda)=(\Sigma\alpha_jS^{*j}f)(\lambda)=\Sigma\alpha_j(S^{*j}f,\xi_\lambda)=$$
$$=\Sigma\alpha_j(S^{*j}f,(1-\bar{\lambda}S)^{-1}e_0)=\Sigma\alpha_j((1-\lambda S^*)^{-1}f,e_j)$$

so that $||Hg||_\infty\leq K||g||_2$ for any polynomial $g\varepsilon H^2$. It follows that H extends to a bounded operator on H^2 and that (d) holds. The same argument also shows that (d) implies (b).

As $||(1-zS^*)^{-1}f||^2=\Sigma|((1-zS^*)^{-1}f,e_n)|^2=\Sigma|(S^{*n}f,(1-\bar{z}S)^{-1}e_0)|^2=\Sigma|(S^{*n}f)(z)|^2$ for $z\varepsilon\mathbb{D}$ the equivalence of (b) and (e) is clear.

PROOF OF THEOREM 2: If $f\varepsilon L$ then Theorem 1 (b) shows that $f(z)=(f,\xi_z)=((1-zS^*)^{-1}f,e_0)$ is bounded on $\mathbb{D}$. Assertion (a) follows as L is closed with respect to multiplication by Theorem 1 (c).

If $f\varepsilon L$ then $f(\lambda)-f(z)=((1-\lambda S^*)^{-1}f,e_0)-((1-zS^*)^{-1}f,e_0)=(\lambda-z)((1-zS^*)^{-1}(1-\lambda S^*)^{-1}S^*f,e_0)$, so that $|(f(\lambda)-f(z))(\lambda-z)^{-1}|\leq K||(1-\bar{\lambda}S)^{-1}e_0||\leq K(1-|\lambda|)^{-\frac{1}{2}}$. The first part of assertion (b) follows by letting $\lambda\to z$. The second part of (b) on the equivalence of the growth condition on f′ with the Lipschitz condition on the boundary function is a theorem of Hardy and Littlewood [7: p.74]. The same theorem gives (f).

Theorem 1 (e) implies that the Hankel operator H is Hilbert-Schmidt so that $\Sigma(n+1)|a_n|^2=\sum_{j,k}|(He_j,e_k)|^2\leq K^2$ which gives (d).

Assertion (e) is an immediate consequence of the observation that $R(\delta_S)$ is invariant under multiplication on the right by the operator $\phi(S)\varepsilon\{S\}'$.

It remains to prove (c). For this let $S_\alpha=(S-\alpha)(1-\bar{\alpha}S)^{-1}$. Then $R(\delta_{S_\alpha})=R(\delta_S)$ and $U_\alpha(e_j)=(1-|\alpha|^2)^{\frac{1}{2}}S_\alpha^j\xi_\alpha$ is a unitary operator on H^2 such that $S_\alpha U_\alpha = U_\alpha S$. If $f \varepsilon L$ then $U_\alpha^* g \otimes U_\alpha^* f = U_\alpha^* (g \otimes f) U_\alpha \varepsilon R(\delta_S)$ for all $g \varepsilon H^2$ so that $U_\alpha^* f \varepsilon L$. As $(U_\alpha^* f)(z) = (1-|\alpha|^2)^{\frac{1}{2}} (1+\bar{\alpha} z)^{-1} f((z+\alpha)(1+\bar{\alpha} z)^{-1})$ and L contains all polynomials assertion (c) follows.

PROBLEM 5. Give a more illuminating description of the functions in L. The curious condition on the associated Hankel operator in (d) in particular seems to demand further study. Does L coincide with some known class of analytic functions?

In [11]it was shown that an operator B belongs to the inclusion algebra $I(N)$ of a given normal operator N if and only if $B=f(N)$ where f is a continuous function on the spectrum $\sigma(N)$ of N with the following property: for any sequence $\{\lambda_i\}$ of points of $\sigma(N)$ the matrix with entries

$$\lambda_{ij} = \begin{cases} \dfrac{f(\lambda_i)-f(\lambda_j)}{\lambda_i - \lambda_j} & \text{if } \lambda_i \neq \lambda_j \\ 0 & \text{otherwise} \end{cases}$$

is a Schur multiplier of $B(\ell^2)$; that is, $(\lambda_{ij}\, x_{ij})$ is the matrix of a bounded operator for any bounded operator (x_{ij}) on ℓ^2. Stated another way, $f(N) \varepsilon I(N)$ if and only if $f(M) \varepsilon I(M)$ for all normal operators M with $\sigma(M) \subseteq \sigma(N)$.

This multiplier condition on f implies a generalized Lipschitz condition:

$$||f(N_1)X - Xf(N_2)|| \le K||N_1 X - X N_2|| \qquad (X \varepsilon B(H))$$

for any two normals with $\sigma(N_i) \subseteq \sigma(N)$, K being a fixed constant depending only on f. It also implies [11] that f is differentiable relative to $\sigma(N)$ at each accumulation point of $\sigma(N)$. In particular if $\sigma(N)$ is the closed unit disk $\mathbb{D}$ then f and f′ belong to H^∞, f has absolutely convergent Taylor series, and

$$|f(e^{i\alpha}) - f(e^{i\beta})| \le K|\alpha - \beta| \quad \text{for } \alpha, \beta \text{ real.}$$

PROBLEM 6. Suppose that $\sigma(N) = \bar{\mathbb{D}}$. Must f′ be continuous?

Does the class of analytic functions defined by the above Schur multiplier condition reduce to some known class of functions?

There is, of course, no *a priori* reason why this problem ought to have an affirmative solution, but if one replaces $\bar{\mathbb{D}}$ by an interval of real numbers then the multiplier condition is satisfied by any $f \in C^{(3)}(\mathbb{R})$[11].

6. C*- ALGEBRAS

It is an interesting and not obvious fact that the norm closure of the range of a normal derivation is a self-adjoint subspace. The same is true for any isometry, any essentially normal operator whose commutant contains no nonzero trace class operator, and lots of other operators. These so called *d-symmetric operators* were studied in [4] but many questions remain open.

These operators are of interest mainly because if one defines the algebras $\bar{I}(A), \bar{M}(A), \bar{C}(A)$ as in §2 with the exception that $R(\delta_A)$ is replaced by its norm closure then each is a C^*-algebra, $\bar{C}(A)$ is the commutator ideal of $\bar{I}(A)$, and the C^*-algebra $\bar{M}(A)/\bar{C}(A)$ has center $\bar{I}(A)/\bar{C}(A)$ which is isomorphic to the C^*- algebra $C^*(A)$ generated by A and 1 modulo *its* commutator ideal. The ideal $\bar{C}(A)$ is the linear span of the positive operators in $R(\delta_A)^-$, is a hereditary subspace of $B(H)$, and is a nonseparable superspace of the compact operators if A has no reducing eigenvalues and is not essentially normal with countable spectrum.

One has $I(A)=C^*(A)+\bar{C}(A)$, the intersection of these two subspaces being the commutator ideal of $C^*(A)$, and so the sum is direct exactly when A is normal. $\bar{C}(A)=0$ for a d-symmetric operator A only if A is normal with a spanning set of eigenvectors, or equivalently, if and only if $\bar{M}(A)=\{A\}'$. Finally, if A is d-symmetric then so is $\pi(A)$ for any irreducible representation of $C^*(A)$.

Thus although one may claim to understand $\bar{I}(A)$ modulo the ideal $\bar{C}(A)$ the above facts suggest that this ideal is quite mysterious. $\bar{I}(A)$ itself is a novel C^*- algebra even in the only case for which it has been able to be computed — when A is a diagonal operator.

PROBLEM 7. Determine the above three C^*- algebra when A is the simple unilateral shift, or when A is multiplication by the independent variable in $L^2(\mu)$.

REFERENCES

1. Anderson, J.H.: Derivations, commutators, and the essential numerical range, Ph.D.thesis, Indiana University, 1971.
2. Anderson, J.H.: Derivation ranges and the identity, *Bull. Amer. Math.Soc.* 79(1973), 705-708.
3. Anderson, J.H.; Foiaş, C.: Properties which normal operators share with normal derivations and related operators, *Pacific J.Math.* 61(1975), 313-325.
4. Anderson, J.H.; Bunce, J.W.; Deddens, J.A.; Williams, J.P.: C^*-algebras and derivation ranges: d-symmetric operators, *Acta Sci. Math.* (Szeged) 40(1978),211-227.
5. Apostol, C.: Inner derivations with closed range, *Rev. Roumaine Math.Pures et Appl.* 21(1976), 249-265.
6. Brown, A.; Pearcy, C.: Structure of commutators of operators, *Ann. Math.*82(1965), 112-127.
7. Duren, P.L.: *Theory of* H^p *Spaces*, Academic Press, New York, 1970.
8. Herrero, D.A.: Intersections of commutants with closures of derivation ranges, *Proc.Amer.Math.Soc.* 74(1979),29-34.
9. Yang Ho: Derivations on $B(H)$, Ph.D. thesis, Indiana University, 1973.
10. Yang Ho : Commutants and derivation ranges, *Tôhoku Math.J.* 27(1975), 509-514.
11. Johnson, B.E.; Williams J.P.: The range of a normal derivation, *Pacific J.Math.* 58(1975), 105-122.
12. Kim, H.W.: On compact operators in the weak closure of the range of a derivation, *Proc.Amer.Math.Soc.* 40(1973), 482-486.
13. Kleinecke,D.C.: On operator commutators, *Proc.Amer.Math. Soc.*8(1975), 535-536.
14. Shirokov, F.V.: Proof of a conjecture of Kaplansky, *Uspekhi Mat.Nauk.* 11(1956), 167-168.
15. Stampfli, J.G.: Derivations on $B(H)$: The range, *Ill. J.Math.* 17(1973), 518-524.
16. Stampfli, J.G.: On the range of a hyponormal derivation, *Proc.Amer.Math.Soc.* 52(1975), 117-120.

17. Weber, R.E.: Analytic functions, ideals, and derivation ranges, *Proc.Amer.Math.Soc.* 40(1973), 492-497.

18. Weber, R.E.: Derivations and the trace class operators, *Proc.Amer.Math.Soc.* 73(1979),79-82.

19. Wielandt, H.: Über die Unbeschränktheit de Operatoren des Quantenmechanik, *Math.Ann.*121(1949), 21.

20. Williams,J.P.: Finite operators, *Proc.Amer.Math.Soc.*26(1970), 129-136.

21. Williams,J.P.: On the range of a derivation, *Pacific J.Math.* 38(1971), 273-279.

22. Williams, J.P.: On the range of a derivation.II, *Proc.Roy. Irish Acad. Sect.A* 74(1974), 299-310.

23. Wintner, A.: The unboundedness of quantum-mechanical matrices, *Phys. Rev.* 71(1947), 738-739.

J.P.Williams
Department of Mathematics
Indiana University
Bloomington, Indiana 47405
USA

PROBLEM LIST

This is a list of unsolved problems in operator theory from the participants at the conference. Some of the problems are new and some are not new, but all are yet unsolved as far as we know and have been discussed among participants.

I. E.ALBRECHT, Ș.FRUNZĂ, F.-H.VASILESCU: SOME PROBLEMS IN THE THEORY OF DECOMPOSABLE OPERATORS

(1) An n-tuple $T=(T_1,\ldots,T_n)$ of commuting bounded linear operators on a Banach space X is said to have the m-*spectral decomposition property* $(m\geq 2)$ if for every open covering $\{U_1,\ldots,U_m\}$ of $\mathbb{C}^n$ there are closed subspaces $Y_1,\ldots,Y_n$ of X such that

(i) $Y_1,\ldots,Y_n$ are invariant for $T_1,\ldots,T_n$ and $\sigma(T,Y_j)\subset U_j$ for $j=\overline{1,m}$, where $\sigma(T,Y_j)$ denotes the Taylor spectrum of T with respect to Y_j,

(ii) $X=\sum_{j=1}^{m} Y_j$

QUESTION. *Is every* n-*tuple with the* m-*spectral decomposition property* $(m\geq 2)$ m-*decomposable or even decomposable?*

For n=1 the answer is positive. Different proofs of this fact have been given by E.Albrecht, R.Lange and B.Nagy; see E. Albrecht: On decomposable operators, *Integral Equations and Operator Theory* 2 (1979), 1-10.

(2) QUESTION. *Is every* 2-*decomposable* n-*tuple decomposable?*

For n=1 the answer is positive, see M.Radjabalipour: Equivalence of decomposable and 2-decomposable operators, *Pacific J. Math.* 77 (1978), 243-247. For arbitrary n a partial answer is given in E.Albrecht and F.-H.Vasilescu: On spectral capacities, *Revue Roumaine Math.Pures Appl.* 19 (1974), 701-705.

(3) QUESTION. *Let* $T_1,\ldots,T_n$, $S_1,\ldots,S_m$ *be commuting bounded*

linear operators on a Banach space X, *such that* $T=(T_1,\dots,T_n)$ *and* $S=(S_1,\dots,S_m)$ *are decomposable. Is then* $(T,S)=(T_1,\dots,T_n, S_1,\dots,S_m)$ *decomposable?*

If not try it for strongly decomposable tuples.

(4) QUESTION. *Are the sum and the product of two commuting (strongly) decomposable operators of the same type?*

A positive answer to Question (3) would imply a positive answer to Question (4).

(5) QUESTION. *Let* $T=(T_1,\dots,T_n)$ *be a decomposable* n-*tuple of operators on a complex Banach space* X. *Is the dual* n-*tuple* $T'=(T_1',\dots,T_n')$ *also decomposable on* X'?

The answer is yes if n=1, see Ş.Frunză: A new result of duality for spectral decompositions, *Indiana Univ.Math.J.* 26 (1977), 473-482.

Does the decomposability of T' *imply the decomposability of* T?

As it was proved by Ş.Frunză the answer is again yes for a single operator.

For the definition and some results concerning decomposable n-tuples of operators, see Ş.Frunză: The Taylor spectrum and spectral decompositions, *J.Functional Analysis* 19 (1975), 390-421.

II. J.A. ANDERSON: QUESTIONS.

1. Fix an orthonormal basis $\{e_n\}_{n\in\mathbb{N}}$ for a Hilbert space H and define a projection P of $B(H)$ onto $\mathcal{D}$, the diagonal operator in $\{e_n\}$, by $P(T)=\Sigma(Te_n,e_n)e_n\otimes e_n$. If h is a complex homomorphism on $\mathcal{D}$, then is $h\circ P$ the unique state extension of h to $B(H)$?

2. Question 1 is equivalent to the following: Given an operator T with $P(T)=0$ and $\varepsilon>0$ do then exist projections $\{P_1,\dots,P_n\}\subset\mathcal{D}$ with $P_iP_j=0$ $i\neq j$, $P_1+\dots+P_n=1$ such that $\|P_iTP_i\|<\varepsilon$, $1\le i\le n$?

3. Do Toeplitz operators with zero diagonal have the property given in 2?

4. If f is a pure state on $B(H)$, does it have the form $h\circ P$ when h and P are as above?

III. T.ANDO: CONJECTURE

Let S,T be bounded linear operators on a Hilbert space. If S commutes with T, then

$$w(ST)\le w(S)\,||T||,$$

where w(S) is the numerical radius defined by

$$w(S)=\sup_{||x||\le 1}|(Sx,x)|.$$

IV. E.DURSZT: UNSOLVED PROBLEMS

1. Lebow has proved that the "Foguel-Halmos counterexample" is not polynomially bounded. Give an *elementary* proof of this theorem.

2. It is known (Holbrook, *Acta Sci.Math.*) that $\bigcup_{\rho>0} C_\rho$ is dense in the set of power-bounded operators, and (Durszt, *Acta Sci.Math.* 1975) that an operator belongs to C_ρ if and only if there exists a contraction C such that $T=\rho(\rho+(\rho-2)C^*C)^{-1/2}(I-C^*C)^{1/2}C$. From these facts, does any factorization theorem (structure theorem) for power-bounded operators follow in general? (See also Okubo-Ando, *Manuscripta Math.*)

V. L.FIALKOW

1. Let S and T be quasisimilar Hilbert space operators. If T is quasinilpotent, does there exists a (possibly trivial) "basic sequence" of S-invariant subspaces $\{M_n\}$ such that each restriction $S|M_n$ is quasinilpotent ? (If S is decomposable, then S must be quasinilpotent; the answer is also affirmative for weighted shifts.)

2. For any bounded Hilbert space operator T, $\mathrm{diam}(w(T))\le$ $\le\inf_{\lambda\in\mathbb{C}}||T-\lambda||$, where w(T) is the numerical range. Equality can be attained for certain subnormal operators. Does there exist a non-zero quasinilpotent operator for which equality is attained?

VI. P.FILLMORE

Does the Calkin algebra have outer automorphism? Is there

an outer automorphism that reverses index? Is every automorphism α "locally inner", i.e. given a separable subalgebra A, is there a unitary element u with $\alpha = \mathrm{ad}\,u$ on A?

VII. D.A. HERRERO: PROBLEMS

1. (Due to L.R.Williams) Assume that T is a quasidiagonal (QD) operator acting on a complex separable Hilbert space H and that T is a norm-limit of nilpotent operators. Is T the norm-limit of a sequence $\{Q_n\}_{n=1}^{\infty}$ of block-diagonal nilpotents (BDN)?

2. In particular, is every quasidiagonal quasinilpotent a norm-limit of block-diagonal nilpotents?

3. Let $T \in (QD)$ and let $t = \pi(T)$ be its image in the Calkin algebra. Does $C^*(t)$ (the C^*-algebra generated by t and $\pi(1)$) always admit a unital (*not necessarily faithful*) *-representation ρ in $L(H_\rho)$ $(0 < \dim H_\rho \leq \infty)$ such that either $\dim H_\rho < \infty$ or $\rho(t) \in (QD)$?

An affirmative answer would also provide an affirmative answer to Question 2.

4. It is well-known (S.Campbell and R.Gellar: *On asymptotic properties of several classes of operators*, Proc.Amer.Math.Soc. 66 (1977), 79-84) that there exist functions $\varphi_k(\varepsilon)$ such that: $T \in L(\mathbb{C}^n)$ (for some $n, 1 \leq n < \infty$), $\|T\| \leq 1$ and $\|T^k\| \leq \varepsilon^k$ imply that dist[T, Nilpotents of order k $(\mathbb{C}^n)] < \varphi_k(\varepsilon)$ $(\varphi_k(\varepsilon) \to 0$, as $\varepsilon \to 0)$.

Does there exist a function $\varphi(\varepsilon)$ $(\varphi_\varepsilon \to 0$, as $\varepsilon \to 0)$ such that

$$\text{dist}[T, \text{Nilpotents of order } k(\mathbb{C}^n)] < \varphi(\varepsilon),$$

whenever T satisfies the above conditions? (I.e., is it possible to show that $\varphi_k(\varepsilon)$ does not depend on k?)

A weaker form: Does there exists $\varphi(\varepsilon)$ $(\varphi(\varepsilon) \to 0$, as $\varepsilon \to 0)$ and $\psi(k)$ $(\psi(k) \to \infty$, $k \to \infty)$ such that $T \in L(\mathbb{C}^n)$, $\|T\| \leq 1$ and $\|T^k\| \leq \varepsilon^k$ imply that dist [T, Nilpotents of order $\psi(k)$ $(\mathbb{C}^n)] < \varphi(\varepsilon)$? Once again, an affirmative answer would also provide an affirmative answer to Question 2.

5. Assume that $\sigma(T) \subset \sigma(N) = \sigma_e(N)$, where N is a *normal* operator and that $\sigma(N)$ is a *spectral set* for T. Does $N \oplus T \in (QD)$?

6. Does there exist a function $\omega(\varepsilon)$ $(\omega(\varepsilon) \to 0$, as $\varepsilon \to 0)$ such

that $T\in L(\mathbb{C}^n)$, $\|T\|\le 1$ and $\|T^*T-TT^*\|\le\varepsilon$ imply that dist [T, Normal operators]$\le\omega(\varepsilon)$ (for all n=1,2,...)?

VIII. N.K.NIKOLSKII: SOME UNSOLVED PROBLEMS

1. Let $H^2(\mathbb{C}^m)$ the Hardy space of $\mathbb{C}^m$-valued holomorphic functions in the unit disk $\mathbb{D}=\{\zeta\in\mathbb{C}^1:|\zeta|<1\}$ with usual norm $\|f\|_2^2=$
$= \sup\limits_{0\le r\le 1}\int_{\partial\mathbb{D}}\|f(r\zeta)\|^2_{\mathbb{C}^m}dm(\zeta)$; m is normalized Lebesgue measure on $\partial\mathbb{D}$.
Let $e_k\in\mathbb{C}^m$, $\lambda_k\in\mathbb{D}$ (k=1,2,...) and let $X=\{x_k\}_{k\ge 1}$, $x_k=$
$=e_k(1-|\lambda_k|^2)^{1/2}(1-\bar\lambda_k z)^{-1}$, $\|e_k\|=1$. For the case m=1 the following properties are equivalent*): i) X is uniformly minimal sequence ($\equiv\inf\limits_k \operatorname{dist}_{H^2(\mathbb{C}^m)}(x_k,$ span $(x_s:s\neq k))>0$); ii) X is a Riesz bases (unconditional bases) in the space span$X$. Is it equivalent for m=2 also (in general for m>1)?

For details and motivations see [1], and N.K.Nikolskii, B.S.Pavlov, V.I.Vasjunin in the book [2].

2. Let Θ_1, Θ_2 two inner functions (in the Beurling sense) in the unit disk $\mathbb{D}$ and let

$$\left(\prod_k \frac{\lambda_k-z}{1-\bar\lambda_k z}\cdot\frac{|\lambda_k|}{\lambda_k}\right)\exp\left(-\int_{\partial\mathbb{D}}\frac{\zeta+z}{\zeta-z}d\mu(\zeta)\right),$$

$\lambda_k=\lambda_k(\Theta_i)$, $\mu=\mu(\Theta_i)$, i=1,2,being their canonical forms. Then $\Theta\overset{\mathrm{def}}{=}$ $\Theta_1(\Theta_2(z))$ is also inner function. What are his representing measure $\mu=\mu(\Theta)$ and his zeros $\lambda_u=\lambda_u(\Theta)$? (Find them in terms of $\lambda_k(\Theta_i)$, $\mu(\Theta_i)$, i=1,2).

The spacial case $\Theta_1=\exp\frac{z+1}{z-1}$ is of great interest because of his value for the exponential bases theory in the space $L^2(a,b)$ See for details and motivations [1], [3].

3. Let X a Banach space of holomorphic functions in the unit disk $\mathbb{D}$, and let the following properties be fulfilled:

a) $f\to f(\lambda)$ is continuous functional on X ($\forall\ \lambda\in\mathbb{D}$),

b) $(1-\lambda z)^{-1}\in X$ ($\forall\ \lambda\in\mathbb{D}$) and X=span$((1-\lambda z)^{-1}:\lambda\in\mathbb{D})$,

c) $\lambda\to(1-\lambda z)^{-1}$ is holomorphic X-valued function on $\mathbb{D}$,

---

*) This is a simple consequence of the Carleson-Shapiro-Shields theorem about rational bases and interpolation, see [1].

d) $z^*X\subset X$, where $z^*f \overset{\text{def}}{=} \frac{f-f(0)}{z}$.

Let also k an divisor on $\mathbb{D}$ ($\equiv \mathbb{Z}_+$-valued function on $\mathbb{D}$) and

$$X_k \overset{\text{def}}{=} \{f\in X: k_f \geq k\},$$

where k_f is the divisor of zeros multiplicity of function f.

It is clear that $z^*X_k\subset X_k$ $(\forall k)$.

Conjecture 1. There exists a (closed) z^*-invariant subspace E of the space X such that $E\neq X_k$ $(\forall k)$.

Conjecture 2. For every z^*-invariant subspace E, $E\subset X$, there exists a sequence of divisors $\{k_n\}_{n\geq 1}$ such that $\dim X_{k_n} < +\infty$ $(\forall\, n)$ and $E = \underline{\lim}_n X_{k_n} \overset{\text{def}}{=} \{x\in X: \lim_n \text{dist}\,(x, X_{k_n}) = 0\}$. About these problems (conjectures) see also [1], [2].

REFERENCES

1. Nikolskii , N.K.: *Lectures on the shift operator* (Russian), Moscow, 1980.

2. 99 *unsolved problems in linear analysis and function theory*, v. 81 of "Zapiski of LOMI seminars in mathematics" (ed. V. P.Havin, S.V.Hruščev, N.K.Nikolskii, Leningrad, 1978).

3. Hruščev, S.V.; Nikolskii, N.K.; Pavlov, B.S.: *Riesz bases of exponentials and reproducing kernels*, LOMI-preprint, Summer, 1980.

IX. R.F.OLIN: QUESTIONS

1. If S is a pure subnormal operator then does S^* have a cyclic vector? *Weaker question*: does S^* have a rationally n multi-cyclic vector in the sense of Berger and Shaw?

2. Let μ be a regular Borel measure with compact support in the plane. Let $H^2(\mu)$ denote the closure of the polynomials in $L^2(\mu)$. If every bounded real-valued function in $H^2(\mu)$ is constant then does there exist a nonzero weak-star continuous multiplicative linear functional on $H^2(\mu)\cap L^\infty(\mu)$?

3. Let A be a norm closed algebra $\subset B(H)$ such that

(*) $T\in A$ and $T^{-1}\in B(H)$ $T^{-1}\in A$.

Let A_1 and A_2 denote the weak-star and w.o.t. closure of A, respectively. When is property (*) valid for A_1 or A_2?

X. K.SCHMÜDGEN

Let A and B be selfadjoint operators in a separable Hilbert space $\mathcal{H}$. Suppose that A and B are unbounded. A is called related to B (notations: A~B) if there exist a unitary operator U in $\mathcal{H}$ and a dense linear subspace $\mathcal{D}$ of the domain D(A) such that $A\mathcal{D}\subset\mathcal{D}$ and $A\Phi=U^{-1}BU\Phi$ for all $\Phi\in\mathcal{D}$. Further, let S_A resp. S_B be the intersection of the unit sphere of $\mathcal{H}$ with the domain D(A) resp. D(B).

<u>Problem</u>: Suppose that $\sup_{\Phi\in S_A} \langle A\Phi,\Phi\rangle = \sup_{\Phi\in S_B} \langle B\Phi,\Phi\rangle = +\infty$ or $\inf_{\Phi\in S_A} \langle A\Phi,\Phi\rangle = \inf_{\Phi\in S_B} \langle B\Phi,\Phi\rangle = -\infty$. Does it follow that A~B?

Remarks:

1. The converse implication is obviously true.
2. For operators with complete system of eigenvectors and some other classes of operators the answer is affirmative. A positive answer in the general case would imply that two arbitrary unbounded selfadjoint operators A and B in a separable Hilbert space are always related after two steps, i.e. there exist a unbounded selfadjoint operator C so that A~C and C~B.

Operator Theory: Advances and Applications

Published volumes

OT 1:
H. Bart, I. Gohberg, and M. A. Kaashoek
Minimal Factorization of Matrix and
Operator Functions
1979. 236 pages. Paperback
ISBN 3–7643–1139–8

OT 2:
Topics in Modern Operator Theory
5th International Conference on
Operator Theory, Timişoara and
Herculane (Romania), June 2–12, 1980
Edited by C. Apostol, R. G. Douglas,
B. Sz.-Nagy, D. Voiculescu
Managing Editor: Gr. Arsene
1981. 336 pages. Hardcover
ISBN 3–7643–1244–0

In preparation

C. Foias
Applications of the
Commutant Lifting Theorem
1981. Approx. 250 pages. Hardcover

H. G. Kaper, C. G. Lekkerkerker, J. Hejtmanek
Spectral Methods in
Linear Transport Theory
1981. Approx. 380 pages. Hardcover